Ferenc Hörcher is Director of the Hungarian Academy of Sciences and Professor at Pázmány Péter Catholic University in Hungary. He is on the editorial board of *Politeja* (Krakow) and *Hungarian Review* (Budapest). Along with book publications in the history of political and aesthetic thought, he has published chapters and articles on Hungarian constitutionalism, including *Is the Historical Constitution of Hungary Still a Living Tradition?: A Proposal for Reinterpretation* (2017) and *Communal Values in the New Hungarian Fundamental Law: The Habermas-Ratzinger Debate and the Use of the Humanities in Constitutional Interpretation* (2014).

Thomas Lorman teaches Central European History at the School of Slavonic and East European Studies (SSEES), University College London (UCL). He is the author of *Counter-Revolutionary Hungary 1920–1925* (2006) and *The Making of the Slovak People's Party* (Bloomsbury, forthcoming). He has also published extensively in peer-reviewed journals and is an editor of the journal *Central Europe*.

A HISTORY OF THE HUNGARIAN CONSTITUTION

Law, Government and Political Culture in Central Europe

EDITED BY
FERENC HÖRCHER AND THOMAS LORMAN

BLOOMSBURY ACADEMIC
LONDON • NEW YORK • OXFORD • NEW DELHI • SYDNEY

BLOOMSBURY ACADEMIC
Bloomsbury Publishing Plc
50 Bedford Square, London, WC1B 3DP, UK
1385 Broadway, New York, NY 10018, USA

BLOOMSBURY, BLOOMSBURY ACADEMIC and the Diana
logo are trademarks of Bloomsbury Publishing Plc

First published in Great Britain 2019
Paperback edition first published 2020

Copyright © Ferenc Hörcher and Thomas Lorman and contributors, 2019

Ferenc Hörcher and Thomas Lorman have asserted their right under the Copyright,
Designs and Patents Act, 1988, to be identified as Editors of this work.

For legal purposes the Acknowledgements on p. xvii
constitute an extension of this copyright page.

Cover design: Ian Parfitt

All rights reserved. No part of this publication may be reproduced or
transmitted in any form or by any means, electronic or mechanical,
including photocopying, recording, or any information storage or
retrieval system, without prior permission in writing from the publishers.

Bloomsbury Publishing Plc does not have any control over, or responsibility for,
any third-party websites referred to or in this book. All internet addresses given
in this book were correct at the time of going to press. The author and publisher
regret any inconvenience caused if addresses have changed or sites have
ceased to exist, but can accept no responsibility for any such changes.

A catalogue record for this book is available from the British Library.

A catalogue record for this book is available from the Library of Congress

ISBN: HB: 978-1-7883-1263-9
PB: 978-1-3501-7018-6
ePDF: 978-1-7867-3530-0
eBook: 978-1-7867-2530-1

Series: International Library of Historical Studies

Typeset in Garamond Three by OKS Prepress Services, Chennai, India

To find out more about our authors and books visit
www.bloomsbury.com and sign up for our newsletters.

For László Péter (1929–2008), in Memoriam

CONTENTS

List of Illustrations xiii
List of Contributors xiv
Acknowledgments xvii

1. **Introduction** 1
   Philip Barker and Thomas Lorman

   A New/Old Constitution 1
   Scope and Structure 5
   A Historical Overview – The Medieval Kingdom 6
   The Habsburg Era 10
   Reform, Revolution and Reorganization 15
   From Dictatorship to Dictatorship 19
   A New Era of Constitutionalism 23

2. **Law and the Ancient Constitution in Medieval and Early Modern Hungary** 29
   Martyn Rady

   Introduction 29
   The Royal Succession 30
   Diets and Statutes 35
   Liberties, the Golden Bull and the Right of Resistance 40
   Conclusion 42

3. **The Birth of the Constitution in Eighteenth-Century Hungarian Political Thought**   46
   István M. Szijártó

   Taxes and Compromises   50
   The Constitution and the Common Good   53
   Nation and Confrontation   56

4. **Resurrecting the Past, Reshaping the Future: The Rise of the 'Ancient Constitution' at the Diet of 1790/1**   63
   Philip Barker

   The Ancient Constitution versus Josephinian Absolutism   68
   The Ancient Constitution of the Middle Nobility   71
   Ürményi's Speech on the Ancient Constitution   75
   Draft Constitutions for the Diet   77
   Religion   80
   Conclusions   82

5. **Reforming or Replacing the Historical Constitution? Lajos Kossuth and the April Laws of 1848**   92
   Ferenc Hörcher

   The Historiographical Issue and Eyewitness Accounts of Early 1848   95
   Hungary and Europe in 1848: Parallels and Differences   100
   The Last Days of the Process that Led to the April Laws   103
   Conclusions Drawn from the Slow-Motion Historical Narrative   107
   Continuity or Break? 1848 and the Constitutional Tradition in Hungary   109
   Once More on Péter's Views and The Enduring Relevance of 1848   112

6. Reform Fever and Disillusionment: Constitutional
   Codification Fiascos of the Hungarian Liberals after
   the Settlement of 1867   122
   András Cieger

   A Constitutional Moment in 1867   123
   The Years of Change   127
   Penal Code   129
   Police Act   131
   Two Models of State: Aristocracy or Democracy?   133

7. The Use and Abuse of Flexibility: Hungary's
   Historical Constitution, 1867–1919   141
   Thomas Lorman

   The Benefits of Autonomy   142
   Reasons for Dissatisfaction   143
   The Post-1867 Constitution Framework   144
   Exploiting Ambiguities   147
   The Growing Power of the State   150
   Delegitimization and Destruction, 1918–19   153

8. Law I of 1920 and the Historical Constitution   160
   István Szabó

   Prologue   160
   The Concepts of a Continuity of Form and of Substance   163
   The Debate over the Future Form of Government
       in Hungary   166
   The Points of Separation with the Arrangement of the
       State between 1867 and 1918   172
   Conclusion   177

9. Law I of 1946 and Law XX of 1949: Continuity
   or Discontinuity in Traditional Hungarian
   Constitutionalism?   184
   Balázs Fekete

   Thesis and Overview   185
   A Constitutional Moment? The Years 1945 and 1946   186
   Law I of 1946: An Overview   187

Codification of Human Rights and Fundamental Constitutional Principles	188
The Status of the President of the Republic	189
General Assessment	190
Law I of 1946 in the Light of Former Constitutional Traditions	191
Towards a More 'Empathic and Realistic' Reading of Law I of 1946	195
The Emergence of the Hungarian Workers' Party as a Political Power Centre	196
Law XX of 1949: An Overview	197
General Assessment	201
The Afterlife of Law XX of 1949	203
Conclusion	204

10. **Is a Revival Possible?: Theoretical Reflections on the Historical Constitution** — 211
Kálmán Pócza

Introduction	211
The Historical Constitution in the New Fundamental Law	213
Reasons for Rejecting the Idea of the Historical Constitution	215
What is a Constitution?	219
What was the Historical Constitution?	222
Is there a *Differentia Specifica*?	223
The Constitution: An Interplay between Written Norms, Judicial Interpretations and Unwritten Norms	223
Empirical Counter-Arguments	227
Conclusion	230

11. **Epilogue: On the Future(s) of the Historical Constitution** — 237
Ferenc Hörcher and Kálmán Pócza

Preliminary Considerations	237
The Utility of the Revival	238
The Desirability of the Revival	239
Final Considerations	244

Contents

Primary Sources on Hungarian Constitutional History	
Appendix I: The Golden Bull of 1222	247
Appendix II: The Rákos Declaration (1505)	252
Appendix III: Extracts from Stephen Werbőczy's *Tripartitum* (1517)	256
Part One, Chapter 3	256
Part One, Chapter 9	256
Appendix IV: The Laws of 1687	259
Law I [The Coronation Oath]	259
Law II	259
Appendix V: The Laws of 1790/1	261
The Royal Oath Sworn by Leopold II upon his Coronation	263
Article X of 1790/1	263
Article XII of 1790/1	264
Article XVI of 1790/91	264
Appendix VI: Robert Townson's Translation of Law XXVI of 1790/1	266
Appendix VII: The 'April Laws' of 1848	273
Law III of 1848	274
Law IV of 1848	278
Law V of 1848	280
Law VIII of 1848	281
Law XVIII of 1848	281
Law XX of 1848	281
Appendix VIII: Law XII of 1867	283
Appendix IX: The Declaration of the First Hungarian Republic (November 1918)	302
Appendix X: The Preamble to the Constitution of the Hungarian Socialist Federal Republic of Councils (1919)	304

Appendix XI: The Preamble to Law I of 1920   307

Appendix XII: The Preamble to Law I of 1946:
On the form of Government of Hungary   309

Appendix XIII: The Constitution of the Hungarian People's Republic (1949): Constitution of the Hungarian People's Republic   312

    Section One   313
    Section Two   313
    Section Three   315
    Section Four   319
    Section Five   321
    Section Six   324
    Section Seven   325
    Section Eight   326
    Section Nine   329
    Section Ten   330
    Section Eleven   330

Appendix XIV: Excerpts from the Constitution of the Republic of Hungary: (As Amended by Act No. XXXI. of 1989)   332

    Chapter I   332
    Chapter XII   335

Appendix XV: The Fundamental Law of Hungary   341

    National Avowal   341

Bibliography   344
Index   356

LIST OF ILLUSTRATIONS

Figure 4.1   A contemporary depiction of the arrival of the
Holy Crown in Buda on 21 February, 1790.   70

Figure 4.2   A Hungarian peasant and nobleman in their
'national' dresses.   85

Figure 4.3   Hussar-style noble-national costumes from 1790.   86

Figure 6.1   The opening of the Parliament by Francis Joseph
in the Buda Castle Palace on 11 December 1865.   122

LIST OF CONTRIBUTORS

PHILIP BARKER, who served as assistant editor of this volume, graduated from UCL-SSEES, London, in 2002, where he read East European Languages, Literature and Regional Studies. After subsequently relocating to Hungary, he taught translation studies at Pázmány Péter Catholic University (2003–13) and Corvinus University (2007–13), and worked as a freelance translator and interpreter across a wide range of fields, including academia, business, drama, literature and film. In 2013/14 he obtained an MA in Sociocultural Linguistics from Goldsmiths, London, with a thesis entitled 'The Creed of Illiberal Constitutionalism', which focused on the language of the preamble to Hungary's 2010 constitution. In 2014 he returned to UCL-SSEES to pursue a doctoral degree in the development of Hungarian political vocabulary during the late eighteenth century.

ANDRÁS CIEGER is currently Senior Research Fellow at the Research Centre for the Humanities, Institute of History, Hungarian Academy of Sciences. His main areas of research are the political and social history of Hungary, the history of Hungarian parliamentarism, and the development of civil rights in the nineteenth century. His works also include a biography of Prime Minister Count Menyhért Lónyay, and a book on the history of political corruption in Hungary (1867–1918). His relevant publication on the subject of the present volume is 'National identity and constitutional patriotism in the context of modern Hungarian history: An overview' (*The Hungarian Historical Review* v/1 (2016), pp. 123–50).

List of Contributors

BALÁZS FEKETE has an LLM degree (*magna cum laude*, 2007) from the Katholieke Universiteit Leuven, and completed his PhD at the Faculty of Law and Political Sciences of Pázmány Péter Catholic University (*summa cum laude*, 2011). He is Senior Lecturer in Law at Eötvös Loránd University, and Fellow of the Centre for Social Sciences of the Hungarian Academy of Sciences. He has published in the *Review of Central and East European Law*, *Maastricht Journal of European and Comparative Law* and *Jahrbuch für Ostrecht*, and he has also contributed chapters to volumes published by Hart, Springer, and Peter Lang.

FERENC HÖRCHER is Director of the Institute of Philosophy at the Hungarian Academy of Sciences and Professor at Pázmány Péter Catholic University in Hungary. He is on the editorial board of *Politeja* (Krakow) and *Hungarian Review* (Budapest). Along with book publications in the history of political and aesthetic thought, he has published chapters and articles on Hungarian constitutionalism, including *Is the Historical Constitution of Hungary Still a Living Tradition?: A Proposal for Reinterpretation* (2017) and *Communal Values in the New Hungarian Fundamental Law: The Habermas-Ratzinger Debate and the Use of the Humanities in Constitutional Interpretation* (2014).

THOMAS LORMAN is a teaching fellow at the School of Slavonic and East European Studies (SSEES), University College London (UCL). He is the author of *Counter-Revolutionary Hungary 1920–1925* (2006) and *The Making of the Slovak People's Party* (Bloomsbury, forthcoming). He has also published extensively in peer-reviewed journals and is an editor of the journal *Central Europe*.

MARTYN RADY is Masaryk Professor of Central European History at University College London, and General Editor of the *Slavonic and East European Review*. His main research fields include medieval and early modern Hungary, and he has also published on Romanian, as well as German, Croatian, Austrian and British history. His most recent books include *Customary Law in Hungary: Courts, Texts, and the Tripartitum* (Oxford, 2015) and *The Habsburg Empire: A Very Short Introduction* (Oxford, 2017).

ISTVÁN SZABÓ is Professor of History at the Department of Legal History, Pázmány Péter Catholic University. His main research areas include post-1848 constitutional developments in Hungary, Germany and Austria, focusing on the Hungarian state in the interwar period, with a particular focus on the historical constitution. His most important work of recent years is his book entitled *An der Grenze von Demokratie und autoritärem Regime: Charakteristische Merkmale der ungarischen Staatsorganisation in der Zwischenkriegszeit*, published by Nomos (Baden-Baden, 2014).

ISTVÁN M. SZIJÁRTÓ is Associate Professor of History at Eötvös Loránd University, Budapest. His main field of research is the institutional, social and cultural history of Hungarian politics in the eighteenth century. His publications include *A diéta. A magyar rendek és az országgyűlés, 1708–1792* (Budapest, 2005, 2nd edition: 2010); *Nemesi társadalom és politika. Tanulmányok a 18. századi magyar rendiségről* (Budapest, 2006); and *A 18. századi Magyarország rendi országgyűlése* (Budapest, 2016).

ACKNOWLEDGMENTS

The publication of this volume was made possible with the support of Pázmány Péter Catholic University, through funding allocated by Központi Alapok Programme kap17-61019-1.8, and additional support from the School of Slavonic and East European Studies, University College London.

The authors would also like to extend their thanks to Katalin Balogné Bérces, Simon Dixon, Rebecca Haynes, László Kontler and Xavier Gil Pujol of the European society for the history of political thought, as well as Thomas Stottor, Arub Ahmed, Trevor Thomas, the editors of *Közjogi Szemle*, and the archivists and librarians who helped make this book possible.

CHAPTER 1

INTRODUCTION

Philip Barker and Thomas Lorman

A New/Old Constitution

New constitutions always provoke controversy. Their language cannot be entirely cleansed of ambiguity; their norms, presented as established facts, are invariably contested, and their authority depends not only on the merits of their claims, but also on the circumstances of their enactment, not to mention the transitory power and fluctuating reputations of their authors. Their implementation is a political act, and politics is never free from disagreement. New constitutions, therefore, are potential sources of socio-political division, as well as cohesion, among professional elites and the broader populace. By way of illustration, when a new constitutional framework was inaugurated in Hungary on 1 January 2012, it was greeted with jubilation by some Hungarians and vitriol by a substantial swathe of their fellow citizens. On that day, the new Fundamental Law (*Alaptörvény*, a calque of German *Grundgesetz*) came into force. It had been passed by the Hungarian parliament on 18 April 2011 with 262 votes in favour, 44 against, one abstention, and two opposition parties boycotting proceedings. According to the prime minister, Viktor Orbán, whose ruling Fidesz party had won elections with an absolute majority in 2010, the new law 'renewed the community that we call the Hungarian nation'. In contrast, left-wing and liberal opposition parties, as well as an assortment of civic organizations, denounced the Fundamental Law as a 'comedy' (*komédia*) which had 'removed Hungary from the family of liberal democracies'.[1]

Although exaggerated rhetoric is perhaps a predictable by-product of everyday parliamentary wrangling, members of the opposition further denounced their lack of involvement in the constitution-making process, and also voiced serious concerns over many of the text's provisions. In particular, controversy arose over the Fundamental Law's claim to restore continuity with what was described as Hungary's 'historical constitution' (*történeti alkotmány*), the 'achievements' of which, it was asserted, embodied 'the constitutional continuity of Hungary's statehood and the unity of the nation'.[2]

This was not, however, the first attempt to 'restore' what was claimed to be Hungary's 'historical constitution', also referred to as the 'ancient constitution' (*ősi alkotmány*). In the nineteenth century, the 1848 revolution, a failed war of independence, and the imposition of direct rule by the Habsburg emperor, broke with traditional arrangements for almost two decades until the pre-existing constitutional framework was 'restored' in 1867. The end of World War I caused another rupture. Hungary was briefly transformed from a kingdom into a republic, and then into a short-lived 'Hungarian Socialist Federal Republic of Councils' (*Magyarországi Szocialista Szövetséges Tanácsköztársaság*) which, in June 1919, imposed the first written constitution on what was left of the country. This brutal dictatorship and its constitution was, however, almost immediately invalidated, first by government decree on 1 August 1919, and then by a new legislative body that, with Law I of 1920, restored the pretence of continuity with earlier legal models.[3] The occupation of the country by Nazi Germany on 19 March 1944 marked another clear rupture with constitutional governance as parliament was dissolved, legal norms were eviscerated, many of Hungary's Jews were deported to Nazi-run death camps, and a fascist regime led by Ferenc Szálasi was then imposed upon the country on 15 October 1944. The subsequent occupation of the country by the Red Army in 1945 helped turn Hungary into a satellite state of the Soviet Union. The new Stalinist ideology demanded a new legal framework and, in 1949, a written constitution was once again imposed on the country by the Communist regime that had consolidated its hold on power in the previous year. That constitution remained in force for the next 63 years, albeit with substantial amendments. In particular, as communism fell, the 'Round Table' negotiations of 1989 substantially rewrote the constitution in conformity with various contemporary Western European practices, albeit with the understanding that a new constitution would subsequently be enacted. This stopgap solution was not, however, annulled until the Fundamental Law was enacted in 2012, with its sweeping declaration that 'we do not recognize the communist constitution of 1949 since it was the basis of a tyrannical rule; therefore we proclaim it to be invalid.'[4]

Simultaneously, the new Fundamental Law of 2012 also claimed to have restored continuity with the historical constitution that was thought to have operated until 1944. As the Fundamental Law declared, 'we do not recognize the suspension of our historical constitution due to foreign occupations.'[5] Prime Minister Orbán later explained that the term constitution 'means more from a Hungarian perspective (*fölfogás*) than a value-neutral legal catalogue'. He proceeded to elaborate that

> the traditional perspective was that the historical constitution consists of all those written and unwritten regulations which made Hungarian society function from the moment of the foundation of the state [...] We have adopted this perspective. It is our conviction that the historical constitution exists and always will exist as long as the Hungarian state remains.[6]

A broad swathe of academic opinion is, however, convinced that the attempt to restore the constitutional framework that existed before 1944 is completely impractical or evidence of a 'backsliding' from democratic norms. The European Commission for Democracy through Law (Venice Commission), for example, stated in its 'Opinion 621/2011 issued on 17–18 June 2011 on the New Constitution of Hungary' that 'the concept of the "historical constitution" [...] brings with it a certain vagueness into constitutional interpretation. There is no clear definition what the "achievements of the historical constitution" referred to [...] are' and 'the reference to the "historical constitution" is quite unclear, since there have been different stages in the development of different historical situations in Hungary and therefore there is no clear and no consensual understanding of the term "historical constitution".'[7]

The Fundamental Law's recommitment to the values of the pre-World War II constitution has also been condemned as a dangerous idealization of the semi-democratic and elitist values which are associated with that period of Hungarian history. Prominent legal scholars have asserted that 'references to the historic[al] constitution invite (among other things) revisiting the 1920 Treaty of Trianon' which had endorsed Hungary's loss of much of its territory at the end of World War I.[8] János Kis, philosopher and earlier president of the Alliance of Free Democrats (SZDSZ), went even further with his claim that although the current Hungarian government had 'correctly insisted on the necessity of a moral break with the communist regime [...] condemning the communist regime [...] involved rehabilitating the pre-war authoritarian one. In its rhetoric, anti-communism went hand in hand with coded antisemitism and not so-coded anti-liberalism.'[9] Concerns were also raised by an amendment to the constitution in 2013 which removed the statute of limitations on crimes committed under communism, which was seen as a veiled attack on the Hungarian Socialist Party (MSZP), the successor of the Communist Party and Fidesz's main political rival. Further critiques were even levelled at certain passages of the Fundamental Law that appeared to entail the state's intrusion into the private sphere with regard to sexual identities. For example, the Fundamental Law's valorization of the past and the virtues of 'fidelity, faith and love' was attacked as an implicit return to traditional heteronormative values, fuelling concerns over the potential restriction of women's access to abortions. In addition, the alleged marginalization of non-heteronormative relationships, on the grounds that they do not conform to the traditional values espoused in the Fundamental Law, was seen to implicitly suggest that members of sexual minority groups were second-rate citizens, who were not afforded the full protection of the law.[10]

The ongoing debate concerning the merits of the restoration of the pre-World War II constitution has been, however, marred not only by rhetorical ambiguity, party-political disputes and ingrained suspicions in a deeply divided cultural elite, but also by the paucity of academic scholarship devoted to what had traditionally been viewed as an arcane topic. Following the Communist takeover in 1948, studies of Hungary's constitutional development were considered by professionals to be devoid of practical relevance to the future of the country, or only useful

INTRODUCTION 5

for exposing the injustices of the pre-Communist era. It was not until the 1980s that, for example, a new effort was launched 'to bring into print the laws of Central and Eastern Europe, both historical and contemporary'. Five volumes of medieval laws have subsequently been published in English within the scope of this project since 1989, but this effort remains a long way from completion.[11] That this is the first book in the English language to explicitly take as its remit the history of Hungary's constitution demonstrates how little overarching work has been published on the topic, either in Hungary or abroad.[12]

Scope and Structure

As this book seeks to demonstrate, the evolution of Hungary's constitution cannot be separated from the broader development of the country. Rupture, restoration and contestation have always been hallmarks of Hungary's constitutional development, shaping not only its governmental institutions and laws, but also the language and practices of its political culture. Chapters 2–9 of this book are arranged chronologically to explore precisely how the idea of a historical constitution came to evolve and transform Hungary's politics over a span of seven centuries, from the early medieval period to the middle of the twentieth century, when the imposition of Communist rule, and the enaction of a new codified constitution in 1949, signified a complete break with what were conceived of as constitutional traditions. The final two chapters (10 and 11) examine the debate over whether this historical constitution could, or should, be restored. Bolstered by the inclusion of contributions from both British and Hungarian experts, this book thus seeks to explore Hungarian and wider Central European history from a fresh perspective, and acquaint readers with some of the key debates over the Hungarian historical constitution, many of which continue to animate both scholarly and public discourse within the country. To the latter end, this book also includes, in the Appendix, a selection of cardinal laws and declarations which mark key points in the history of the Hungarian constitution, ranging from the Golden Bull of 1222 (erroneously compared to England's Magna Carta), to the controversial National Avowal that served as the preamble to the Fundamental Law of 2011. As many of these texts have never before been translated into English, their inclusion here permits readers to familiarize themselves with both the ideas and the language that shaped the history of the Hungarian constitution.

Having thus noted the book's ambitious scope, however, caveats remain. Because no single volume can ever provide an exhaustive account of Hungarian constitutional history over the centuries, the authors readily acknowledge that restrictions of space have resulted in limited attention to important topics, such as the question of women's suffrage, and the constitutional regulation of other gender-sensitive issues. Other underrepresented periods of transition and development (such as 1944–5, 1956 and 1989) have already received much attention in domestic and international scholarship. Recognizing these limitations, the authors have nevertheless attempted to select topics that explore vital but often underrepresented facets of Hungary's constitutional development.

A Historical Overview – The Medieval Kingdom

A good starting point for any reassessment of Hungary's historical constitution is the fairly concise description of its contents provided by C.A. Macartney, who wrote that it was 'an agglutination of laws, privileges and concessions, which [had] grown up around an ancient core as a result of bargainings, concessions, and unilateral acts on the part of the monarch or the nation'.[13] While Macartney's definition implies that the parts of this historical constitution amounted to a welded, unified, whole, and thus imposes a sense of coherence and consensus upon a series of often chaotic contestations, it nevertheless indicates a commonly held view that Hungary's legal development was organic and inseparable from both the broader history of the country, and the Habsburg Empire into which it was incorporated between 1526 and 1918. A brief overview of this history, with a particular emphasis on the development of public law and governance, will, therefore, now be provided.

The Magyars (or Hungarians) as they came to be known were a loose alliance of tribes that had migrated from the Eurasian Steppe and settled, by the end of the ninth century, in the Carpathian Basin. Medieval accounts of the arrival of the Hungarians into Europe, which were accorded new attention from the eighteenth century onwards, claimed that they had conquered the basin through force of arms, and that they already exhibited the hallmarks of a recognizable system of governance replete with a hereditary leadership, loyalty reinforced by oath-taking, a system of land donation, and extensive autonomy for each of the seven (supposedly) conquering tribes, that broke down almost immediately into subgroups. They even allegedly possessed a rudimentary form of legislature in which all warriors were required to participate and which, according to Macartney, 'had a voice in decisions of peace and war'.[14]

More plausibly, the beginnings of recognizable governance and the rule of law in Hungary (also frequently referred to as the 'foundation of the state') can be dated back to the conversion of the Hungarians to Christianity in the eleventh century. This conversion was symbolized by the 'Holy Crown' (*Szent Korona*), which was reputedly sent by Pope Sylvester II to King (later St) Stephen (*István*) as a reward for his conversion to the Catholic faith in the year 1000. Stephen, and his successors, realized that an alliance with the Church would allow them to extend their personal authority over the entirety of the kingdom, which encompassed the earlier Romanian and Slavonic settlements. This process was completed by the end of the eleventh century, although the south-eastern part of the kingdom (known as Transylvania) retained some autonomy, and various localities (particularly the towns, as in other parts of contemporary Europe) were granted specific rights in order to attract and retain migrants who could contribute to the economic growth and security of the kingdom.[15]

Emboldened royal power secured the acquisition of much of present-day Croatia (the kingdoms of Croatia and Dalmatia), which was added to the 'Lands of the Holy Crown' around AD 1100, although the precise demarcation of the kingdom's southern borders fluctuated according to the fortunes of war and the rise and fall of the Balkan medieval kingdoms.[16] After the first ruling dynasty, the House of Árpád, died out in 1301, a succession of kings followed, some of whom also ruled other territories including Bohemia, Poland and the Holy Roman Empire. While the kingdom was afflicted by factional infighting, it remained, however, an independent and unitary political entity, with its own distinct laws and its own distinct customs.[17]

Royal power was further reinforced by the adoption of other Western European norms of governance and social organization. Hereditary kingship went hand in hand with the emergence of a hereditary land-owning nobility, which occupied a lasting position at the top of a social hierarchy, and which was demarcated by the sixteenth century into different 'estates' and 'orders' (Latin *status et ordines*, Hungarian *státusok és rendek*), status groups that represented the most important sociopolitical subdivisions of the pre-modern state. As in other countries, and most famously in England, but owing to different political circumstances, the nobility obtained from the king an important codification of their rights through the Golden Bull of 1222. Even so, this did not prevent the nobility from dividing into a mass of lesser nobles and a small group of magnates (barons) who often enjoyed a greater share of political power all the way down to 1848. Nevertheless, the entirety of the nobility, as well as the prelates and a surprisingly large part of the urban population, were regarded as members of the *natio hungarica*, that is the Hungarian nation or political community, the conceptualization of which was devoid of ethnic or linguistic connotations until the end of the eighteenth century.[18] The official language of the nobility was, in fact, Latin, and most Hungarians, just like most of the non-Hungarian inhabitants of the kingdom, constituted the *misera contribuens plebs*, ignobles who were excluded from political influence, but who were still expected to pay taxes.

Medieval Hungary also witnessed the emergence of other long-lasting institutions. The position of Palatine (*Nádor*) emerged as the chief officer of the royal court and first minister of the administration. A royal chancellery served as the administrative organ of the Crown, while significantly, local governance was overseen by the patchwork of counties that spread across the kingdom, and gave local elites instruments to express their political will. Each of these was overseen by a sheriff (*ispán*, later *főispán*), who was appointed directly by the Crown, but constrained by the body of nobles participating in the operations of the counties. Along with the royal court, located in the royal palace, each county also possessed its own court that interpreted, exercised and formulated the law.

The growth of the law was also fuelled by the arrival of a literate clergy who could compile formal records, although the transformation 'from memory to written record' took centuries.[19] The *Corpus Juris Hungarici*, a later compilation of Hungary's entire corpus of codified law, recorded the first incidence of Hungarian law as a 'first book of decrees' (*decretorum liber primus*) issued prior to 1038, but legislation in the present sense of the term (which was understood to comprise general statements of universal application) only began to be issued during the thirteenth century.[20] Gradually, however, the law became not only a guarantor of social distinctions and a vital means of arbitrating disputes, but also the mechanism by which the increasingly complicated structures of government were regulated. Eventually it even became an instrument by which the nobility and the country's expanding bureaucracy could influence the governance of the country.

Assemblies of nobles (*gyűlések*) initially summoned to oversee each royal succession and to approve or disapprove increased taxation gradually developed into a Diet which occasionally served as a check and balance on the power of the Crown and was an integral part of the governmental system by the end of the thirteenth century. As Martyn Rady argues in Chapter 2, the growing power of the Diet encouraged a more formal process of law-making to emerge. The Diet, rather than ad hoc councils, came by the middle of the fifteenth century to oversee the often thorny question of the royal succession, and legislation began to be passed 'in the manner of a treaty' in which propositions presented by the Crown were 'debated, modified and added to' by the Diet, while complaints of the Diet were sent to the Crown for redress.[21]

In reality, however, the law that was followed in the many courts of the kingdom was, for the most part, not legislative in origin, as its provisions 'were not defined or written down in normative instruments'.[22] As elsewhere in Europe, medieval Hungarian law, and thus the basis of the country's constitution, continued, as László Péter has emphasized, to be 'generated by custom'.[23] Gradually, however, as Rady has argued, 'lawyerly interpretation made the customary law lawyerly, imposing an order upon it and stiffening it with a vocabulary that [...] was also formed by interaction with the learned law and the written word'; even so, abrupt changes in political circumstances meant that 'shifts, contradictions and instabilities' were characteristic of the development of Hungarian law, and by extension the constitution, in the medieval and early-modern eras.[24]

It was Stephen Werbőczy's monumental compendium of customary law, the *Tripartitum*, published in 1517, which gave Hungarian customary law the capacity to endure and flourish up until the nineteenth century. In contrast to other parts of Europe, including neighbouring Austria, customary law was not comprehensively superseded by statute and codification in Hungary. It was thus appropriate that the *Tripartitum*, which came to be regarded as the cornerstone of Hungary's legal tradition all the way down to 1848, never received the seal of royal approval.

It was also Werbőczy who inspired the transformation of the Holy Crown into a symbol of the power of the state, the territorial unity of the kingdom, and the mystical bond that united the Crown and the noble nation (*ország*), with his claim that 'neither can exist without the other'. From this relationship, as Rady has argued, the politically active Werbőczy 'deduced two propositions that had little basis in customary law [...] the elective nature of Hungarian kingship and the nobility's right to resist the monarch'. After the lost battle of Mohács, which resulted in the occupation of a major part of the country by a Turkish invasion, a mere 12 years after Werbőczy published his *Tripartitum*, these constitutional innovations began to be put into practice.[25]

The Habsburg Era

The expansion of the Ottoman Empire, which had conquered the medieval kingdom of Serbia in 1389 and eliminated Byzantium with its conquest of Constantinople in 1453, eventually destroyed the medieval Hungarian kingdom. At the battle of Mohács in 1526, King Louis II was killed and his army was annihilated by the immensity of the Ottoman army. According to one reading of the hereditary principle, the Crown then passed to the House of Habsburg, although, in practical terms, only the northern and western parts of the old kingdom were actually incorporated into the expanding Habsburg Empire. Much of the rest of the kingdom was, for the next 150 years, under direct Ottoman rule, while Transylvania was transformed into a separate principality and accorded a degree of autonomy by the Sultan.

For that section of the political elite which survived this catastrophe, the law provided a means by which they could preserve some measure of self-government, even under alien Habsburg rule. That need was made more evident by the fact that large numbers of Hungarians converted to various forms of the Protestant faith, while the Habsburgs remained wedded to Catholicism, and were generally enthusiastic about advancing the cause of the Counter-Reformation. While the separate Croatian Diet had immediately recognized the House of Habsburg, the Hungarian nobility clung to Werbőczy's claim that they possessed the customary right to elect their own 'national king', and a rival candidate, János

Szapolyai, claimed the throne from 1526 to 1540. It was not until 1687 that the Hungarian Diet definitively accepted the Habsburg Succession in the male line, and not until 1723 that it also accepted succession in the female line through the Pragmatic Sanction.

To assuage antagonism, the Habsburgs took care to recognize the distinct identity of Hungary which continued to be referred to as the 'lands of the Hungarian Crown'.[26] Skilful politicking also played a role in securing the loyalties of the Hungarian nobility, as demonstrated by Maria Theresa at the coronation Diet of 1741, when she appealed both to Hungarian patriotism and the nobility's sense of masculinity to ensure their support when her legitimacy as the first female Habsburg monarch was hanging in the balance. Swayed by her flattery and fragility, the nobility subsequently pledged *vitam nostram et sanguinem* ('our life and our blood') for the security of the empire. In return, successive emperors accepted the principle, endorsed by Leopold II in Law X of 1790/1, that Hungary was an independent country that possessed its own 'constitution', and that it could only be governed in accordance with its own laws and customs, unlike other provinces of the Habsburg Empire.[27] They also generally submitted to a separate coronation to become lawful kings of Hungary, and swore an oath prior to coronation, the exact content of which was negotiated with representatives of the nation, usually the Diet, in the form of an 'inaugural diploma'. This usually included, as Macartney summarizes, a promise to 'respect, and ensure the respect by others, of the rights, constitution, independence, liberty and territorial integrity of the Lands of the Holy Crown and of all liberties, privileges, recognized usages and laws sanctioned by previous kings or to be in the future enacted by parliament and sanctioned by the king excepting only that clause of the Golden Bull which allowed the right of resistance (*ius resistendi*)'.[28] The process of negotiation, oath-taking and solemn coronation in Hungary was carried out by every Habsburg monarch with the exception of Joseph II, whereas in Bohemia coronations were infrequent. The coronation, which took place amidst great pomp and ceremony, was designed to affirm the sovereignty and autonomous nature of the Hungarian kingdom. It affirmed that the authority of Habsburg monarchs in Hungary derived not from their position as emperors of Austria, but solely from their coronation as king (or queen) of Hungary, whereby all the rights and responsibilities that were ascribed to the Holy Crown were conferred on them. As István

Szijártó argues in Chapter 3, each coronation was a clear expression of the power of Hungary's nobility, who had, for example, retained authority over the institutions of local government, and regained control of taxation.

The chaos provoked by Ottoman rule allowed what remained of the Hungarian nobility to flex its muscles and insist that it still possessed the medieval prerogatives it enjoyed when Hungary was an independent kingdom, including the right to participate in government. By the eighteenth century, the dictates of custom ruled that the 50 or so counties that existed in Hungary all possessed a legal personality distinct from that of the kingdom, and that they exercised autonomous corporate rights. Increasingly, these counties did not merely function as the kingdom's basic administrative units, but could also become bastions of opposition to Habsburg rule. They possessed their own assemblies (*közgyűlések*) which passed local legislation and established local legal norms (*statutum*), and also sent their delegates to the Lower House of the Diet. While formally the counties could not refuse to carry out royal decrees that conformed to the law of the land, in reality the interpretation of the law permitted a measure of discretion, and their authority thus remained considerable.[29]

It needs, nevertheless, to be emphasized that except for the enlightened effort of Joseph II in the 1780s, the Habsburgs' desire to impose their own centralized rule on what remained of Hungary has been exaggerated. Their varied dominions had always been permitted a substantial degree of autonomy, and the Habsburgs themselves were often distracted by the risks and rewards that they derived from their substantial territorial holdings in Western and Central Europe. From the Habsburg perspective, Hungary was an inheritance by accident rather than design, and an often uncomfortable addition to their long list of dominions. It was not until the 1680s that, alarmed by another attempt by the Ottomans to lay siege to the capital of Vienna, the Habsburgs finally resolved to impose their authority upon the entirety of the medieval kingdom of Hungary, and with the assistance of the Polish–Lithuanian Commonwealth in particular, they drove back the Ottoman Empire. Even then, as the reconquest of Hungary gathered pace, a detailed plan drawn up by the imperial chancellery in 1688 to crush the rebellious spirit that supposedly animated much of Hungary's nobility was scrapped. Large numbers of settlers from other parts of Central

Europe, the so-called *Donauschwaben*, were, however, invited in the eighteenth century to colonize those areas that had been depopulated by the Ottoman occupation, adding further to the kingdom's thriving multi-ethnic population.[30] But while the Habsburgs ruled by virtue of their right of succession, most of Hungary's reconquered territories were directed in agreement with the demands of the Hungarian nobility. The lands of the Crown were governed according to Hungarian law and custom, and administered through the autonomous county system, which remained obedient to an increasingly confident Hungarian Diet.

Although Hungary essentially retained both its autonomous status and the power of the estates, Habsburg monarchs still possessed considerable prerogatives which were vested in their office. They could, for example, either initiate or veto legislation, and convoke, prorogue or dissolve the Diet.[31] Nevertheless, as Szijártó explains in his account of Hungarian legal development in the eighteenth century, the Habsburgs' primary objective was to raise funds, and on occasion troops, from an often truculent nobility, in order to preserve the great-power status of their empire. This practical ambition gave the Diet many opportunities to extract concessions and preserve the nobility's historical liberties in exchange for cooperation. Indeed, it was this institutional 'bipolarity', as László Péter termed it, with both Crown and Diet compelled to participate in a recurring bargaining process (*tractatus*), that remained the defining feature of Hungary's constitutional framework until the Habsburg Empire was abolished in 1918.[32]

The danger of disregarding this bargaining process was illustrated during the short rule of Joseph II (r. 1780–90) who sought to centralize the monarchy and embark upon a programme of enlightened reform. As even some contemporary Hungarians recognized, Joseph II 'wished to bestow upon Hungary the benefits of a providential state caring for the welfare of all of its subjects equally', but the means by which he set about this task were offensive even to those who favoured reform.[33] Driven by the Enlightenment zeal for efficiency, he dismissed the Hungarian obsession with its historic liberties as a medieval hangover and an obstacle to good governance. A believer in absolutism, Joseph II refused to convene the Diet, confiscated the Holy Crown, and promoted the use of German as an administrative language, a move that was seen to constitute an attempt to 'Germanize' Hungary. He was also convinced that social reforms, such as granting peasants the freedom to move if they wished and hereditary tenures if they stayed, would ensure him the same level of support in Hungary as he had cultivated in some other parts of the empire. These plans were, however, sabotaged by the endless distractions of running a vast empire, and a personal crisis of confidence. By the time of his untimely death he had provoked growing resentment among the Hungarian political elite, who began to plot an insurrection. It took the masterful skills of the new emperor Leopold II to avert a crisis and regain the obedience of the Hungarian nobility.

As Philip Barker explains in Chapter 4, the reign of Joseph II not only saw controversial and far-reaching attempts at reform, but also the reshuffling of existing political vocabularies as the ideas of the Enlightenment, including those related to the idea of a 'constitution', were debated on an unprecedented scale across the country. In the run-up to the Diet of 1790/1 the Hungarian term *alkotmány* 'constitution, creation' was first used to describe a 'body' of laws, as opposed to individual decrees and edicts. But how was this constitution conceived? On the one hand, Joseph II's attempts at state centralization had emboldened a new sense of Hungarian nationalism that manifested itself in opposition to the Crown's absolutist aspirations, and on the other in an enthusiasm for outward signs of 'national' identity, such as language, clothing and law (indeed, in 1791 legislation was passed to ensure that the records of the Diet were written not only in Latin, but also in Hungarian). Even Hungarian noblewomen began to demonstrate an interest in legislative politics, and sought attendance, if not participation, at the Diet.[34] But outward displays of patriotism should not be mistaken for consensus over what shape and form the 'constitution' of the 'nation' should take. While a small group of radical reformers sought to emulate the new fashion in Europe and the Americas for a written constitution as a means of reforming the 'nation' (often according to the egalitarian ideals of 'French' constitutionalism), traditionalists rather spoke of an 'ancient constitution' (*ősi alkotmány*), and instead lauded the supposedly organic development of Hungarian customary law. But even this conception of a 'historical' constitution was contested, as different political groupings crafted usable histories to support their own polemical and ideological ends. Eventually, the death of Leopold II (a genuine believer in constitutional rule), and enmity between the Habsburgs and Revolutionary France during the reactionary reign of Francis II ensured that proponents of a written constitution modelled on emancipatory ideals would eventually be hounded by the authorities and condemned by many of their fellow nobles. The execution on 20 May 1795 of the Hungarian 'Jacobins', led by Ignác Martinovics (who remarkably conceived of a written constitution based upon federalist principles), stifled any demands for radical constitutional reform for a generation.

In the aftermath of Napoleon's defeat the Diet was rarely summoned, censorship was harsh and the Crown appeared inflexible. At the same time, however, political ideas continued to percolate throughout the country as a period of cultural rejuvenation ensued.[35] This involved a variety of attempts to remould the identity of the 'nation' through programmes of linguistic reform, literary endeavour and the establishment of cultural institutions. Claims of Hungarian cultural supremacy, which drew inspiration from the rise of German nationalism, were met, however, by the simultaneous development of competing nationalisms among the other peoples of what remained a multi-ethnic kingdom.[36] The decision by the Diet in 1839 that its proceedings would be conducted solely in Hungarian (which also became the language of the administration), and the resistance this engendered, not least in Croatia, underscored Macartney's point that 'to the old pair of protagonists in Hungary's secular struggle – the nation and the Crown – was added a third: the nationalities', with the result that 'the whole history of Hungary from 1840 to 1918 consists essentially of a triangular contest between these three factors.'[37]

Reform, Revolution and Reorganization

The rise of ethnic nationalism had its own remorseless logic that was unleashed by the news in 1848 that revolutions had once again broken out across Europe, but it was also fuelled, in Hungary, by a conviction that the law was on the side of the revolutionaries. As Lajos Kossuth, the leading force in the Hungarian Diet, put it in a speech on 3 March 1848 addressed to the Crown, 'since your Majesty's imperial government is not constitutional, it cannot therefore be in harmony with our own separate government or our constitutional life.'[38] Ferenc Hörcher, endorsing the influential work by István Deák on the 1848 revolution, also argues in Chapter 5 that the events of the spring of 1848 should be interpreted as a 'lawful revolution', because it was the Diet, operating according to custom, and approved by the Crown, which remade the country. He stresses the leadership skills of Kossuth, whose reform bills known as the 'April Laws' embodied a vision of liberal nationalism that swept away the old feudal system and gave Hungary its own government that was responsible not only to the ruler but also to the Hungarian parliament.

The possibility that the Crown and the noble-led nation would now proceed to govern in harmony required genuine restraint and a strict deference to both the letter and the spirit of the law from both the royal court, pressed hard by simultaneous revolutions in other parts of the empire, and the new government of Hungary. That restraint, however, evaporated by the end of 1848. Not only did some Croats, Serbs, Slovaks and Romanians make a violent bid for self-governance; the Hungarian government increasingly behaved like the leaders of an independent country while Kossuth, gathering extra power by holding the position of governor, resolved to achieve complete independence for Hungary from 'the pestilential air that breathes on us from the charnel-house of Vienna'.[39]

In response, the new Habsburg emperor, Francis Joseph, appointed specifically to restore order, dispatched the imperial army into Hungary. With Russian military assistance, Hungarian resistance was finally crushed by the overwhelming preponderance of the great powers at the battle of Világos in August 1849, and Kossuth and many of his allies fled into exile. Thirteen generals and Hungary's first prime minister were executed, and harsh centralized rule was imposed on the turbulent kingdom to snuff out any remaining spark of revolutionary fervour. The Diet, which had been transformed in 1848 into a parliament elected on a relatively liberal franchise, was disbanded after the takeover; Austrian law was imported wholesale without either debate or modification, and officials directly appointed by the Crown (mainly military men) imposed a stern and entirely unrepresentative governance on the kingdom.

The Crown had, however, overplayed its hand. Popular opinion manifested itself in a lasting 'cult of Kossuth' that became evident in poetry, song and widespread attempts to emulate his sizeable beard. His impassioned appeals to the peasantry to support the cause of Hungarian independence had fused together the ideal of national freedom from the Habsburg Empire and personal freedom from oppression, an ideal that would continue to resonate down through the generations. But conservative-minded nobles were also appalled by the Crown's disregard for legal traditions. Their representatives insisted that only the restoration of the historical constitution could ensure good governance in Hungary and even throughout the empire.[40]

Habsburg weakness, demonstrated by defeat at the hands of France in 1859 and Prussia in 1866, persuaded Francis Joseph to change course. The Hungarian parliament was briefly restored in 1861, and negotiations began to find a way out of the impasse. The result, guided by Ferenc Deák from the Hungarian side, and an emperor who had grown more astute in the nearly two decades since he had ascended to the throne, produced a settlement in 1867 which reunited Transylvania with Hungary for the first time since 1526 and granted the lands of the Holy Crown home rule and constitutional equality with Cisleithania (from 1917 Austria). With the help of a legal fiction that annulled both the revolutionary legislation passed by the Hungarian government in late 1848/early 1849 and subsequent legislation passed during the period of direct rule by Vienna, both sides could claim that legal continuity had been restored and constitutional rule had resumed following the coronation of Francis Joseph in Buda in 1867. Even though the April Laws were back in force, Kossuth railed at the settlement from exile, and opponents of the settlement, known as '48-ers', blustered from the opposition benches of the newly elected parliament that the ideals of 1848 had been betrayed.

The series of governments from 1867 to 1905, formed by the so-called '67-ers' who supported the settlement, were particularly keen to glorify the restoration of what they considered to be the 'ancient constitution' as it legitimized their authority; at the same time, they set about reconstructing the kingdom to justify their claims to greatness. As András Cieger argues in Chapter 6, their optimism rapidly gave way, however, to an instrumental approach to the law that was increasingly understood as a means of upholding the authority of the government rather than empowering the wider population. Certainly, a mass of new legislation was issued each year by the rejuvenated parliament as the pressures of creating a modern country created an inexhaustible need for reform. Landmark reforms concerning marriage, divorce, and the status of religious minorities became the crowning achievement of a liberal elite intent on reconstructing the law with the same confidence that drove their reconstruction of the country. Nevertheless, some of this legislation was hastily and sloppily drafted, large gaps remained, and the government increasingly relied on ministerial decrees to clarify the law and, if necessary, provide substitutes in the absence of relevant legislation. These ministerial decrees, as custom dictated, only remained in force until they were superseded by the will of parliament. That, however, rarely happened. Furthermore, even when parliament had passed legislation, it could be disregarded by the government. Such was the case, for example, with the Nationalities Law of 1868, which had granted various concessions to the disgruntled nationalities, but was regarded by later governments as excessively generous.

Indeed, as Thomas Lorman argues in Chapter 7, the government was happy to use and abuse the 'flexibility' provided by a legal framework that generally empowered rather than constrained its activities. Such shenanigans could, however, be excused while the economy enjoyed long periods of economic growth, and while rapid development engendered a sense of national confidence that was epitomized by the grandiose millennial anniversary of 1896, which celebrated the reputed conquest of the Carpathian Basin by the Hungarian tribes. However, Hungary continued to be overseen by the Crown, which not only retained direct control over foreign policy and the imperial army, but also made the final appointment of all government ministers. The common ambition of the entire Hungarian political class to centralize power and secure further concessions from Vienna had therefore to be achieved within the limits of the 1867 settlement, but there was no one who could replicate the successes of Ferenc Deák, the original architect of this arrangement. While cantankerous discussions produced the occasional concession from the Crown, they also gave rise to considerable ill-feeling between the Austrian and Hungarian halves of the empire. A sense of begrudging unease meant that promises of electoral reform were not enacted until 1917 for fear that they would empower either the opposition, the nationalities, or the vast swathes of the population (impoverished, ill-educated or simply women) whose passions were feared to lead to uncontrolled and destructive social movements. In spite of all these shortcomings, this period was later idealized as an unrivalled Golden Age in Hungarian public consciousness as far as industrial output, urbanization, infrastructural development and cultural innovation was concerned.

From Dictatorship to Dictatorship

It was World War I that put an end to this era of peaceful, if uneven and often unjust, development. Launched by Francis Joseph to crush the threat posed by aggressive South Slav nationalism, the empire was unable to cope either militarily or economically with the pressure of war on a number of different fronts. German military assistance temporarily helped stave off collapse, but by October 1918 the new emperor Charles I of Austria, who also reigned as King Charles IV of Hungary, concluded that an armistice was unavoidable. However, his admission of defeat stripped him of his authority even before his formal abdication on 13 November 1918. By the end of October, 'national councils' had emerged in the various parts of the empire, all determined to achieve their conflicting ambitions for independence. The Hungarian government, which had been privately sceptical about the merits of the conflict, but publicly resolute, was equally discredited. The parliament, which unlike its Austrian equivalent had remained in session throughout the war, also finally began in October 1918 to reflect the switch in public sentiment from initial enthusiasm to increasing bitterness about the conduct and cost of the war.

The final push came, however, from those nationalist and socialist politicians most of whom had never even managed to secure parliamentary representation. Led somewhat improbably by one of Hungary's richest men, Count Mihály Károlyi, who was inspired by both nationalist and socialist ideals, the Hungarian National Council (*Magyar nemzeti tanács*) seized power on 31 October 1918 and proceeded to dethrone the House of Habsburg with the promise of radical social reform. This council proclaimed the creation of a new Hungarian 'People's Republic', dissolved parliament and governed by so-called 'people's decrees' (*néphatározatok*). But promises of a new era of governance in the interests of all the people of the country proved to be too little, too late. By January 1919, approximately 70 per cent of the former kingdom of Hungary had been annexed by Serbia, Romania and the new Czechoslovak Republic. This territorial dismemberment was subsequently ratified on 4 June 1920, with slight amendments (mostly in Hungary's favour) by the Paris Peace Conference, referred to as the Treaty of Trianon as it was signed in the Grand Trianon Palace.

At the same time, the economy collapsed, a wave of refugees poured into what was left of the country, and the Károlyi government proved to be ineffectual at leading the country. By March 1919, those ministers who had not already resigned agreed to hand over power to the Bolsheviks led by Béla Kun. The short-lived Republic of Councils, which survived until the end of July, proved itself to be energetic, ruthless and intolerable. A military campaign to reclaim Hungary's lost territories ran out of steam, the attempt to copy Leninist methods devastated what remained of the economy and infuriated many segments of the population, while the Bolshevik penchant for brutality against 'class enemies' provoked further resistance. The new government did manage to enact by decree a provisional 'Constitution of the Republic of Councils' (*Tanácsköztarsaság Alkotmánya*) on 2 April 1919, but the full constitution enacted at the end of June 1919, a tedious document primarily concerned with the minutiae of governance rather than general principles, remained in force for barely more than a month. The occupation of Budapest by the Romanian army, encouraged to invade by Britain and France, forced the surviving Bolsheviks to flee into exile.[41]

The series of counter-revolutionary governments that then took power rapidly restored order with the help of a new national army, led by the former commander of the Habsburg navy, Miklós Horthy. The army carried out what became known as the 'white terror' against Bolsheviks and those suspected of collaboration. At the same time, nationalist fury at the dismemberment of the country was infused with militant Christian rhetoric and a search for scapegoats that turned the Jews in particular into an obvious target.[42] Residual anti-Habsburg sentiment also ensured that Charles IV was declared dethroned for a second time following a botched attempt to reclaim his throne by force in 1921. As István Szabó, however, argues in Chapter 8, the debate over the restoration of the House of Habsburg was bound up in a broader debate about how to restore the 'legal continuity' that had been disrupted by the revolutionary changes that had taken place since the end of World War I. The result, he shows, was another carefully constructed settlement, embodied by Law I of 1920, which failed to restore genuine formally enacted legal continuity, but restored 'substantive' or *de facto* continuity with the historical constitution that had endured until 1918. The institutional bipolarity between Crown and country that had existed before 1918 was, however, less evident in the interwar period. Horthy, who was appointed Regent because the new parliament could not agree on who should ascend to the throne which Charles IV had temporarily vacated, was granted the powers that had previously been exercised by the Crown, generally distanced himself from day-to-day politics and deferred to his prime ministers, even when he found their policies distasteful.[43]

The obsession with legal continuity, which also manifested itself in the Horthy regime's annulment of almost all legislation passed since November 1918, did not entirely preclude legal change. The middle classes, including privileged women, were granted the vote, although universal suffrage was not permanently entrenched until after World War II.[44] The Upper House was reformed, and even the hated Treaty of Trianon was grudgingly placed on the statute books.[45] Furthermore, the supposed restoration of the constitution did not prevent the temporary enactment of the *numerus clausus* in the 1920s, which limited the number of Jews in higher education, and the wave of antisemitic legislation passed from 1938 onwards that systematically stripped the Jews of their rights. As parliamentary government endured until March 1944, one of Hungary's sharpest legal minds, Ferenc Eckhart, could still insist at the beginning of that year that German-style 'dictatorship is alien to the Hungarian people'.[46]

There was, however, a price that had to be paid for Nazi Germany's assistance in reclaiming a part of Hungary's former territory, including a large swathe of southern Slovakia, Trans-Carpathian Ruthenia and almost half of Transylvania. In 1941, Hungary agreed to join the German invasion of Yugoslavia in order to reclaim further territory, and then joined the assault on the Soviet Union. By March 1944 Germany had decided to take complete military control of the entire country, dissolving parliament and imposing martial law. There was minimal resistance, in part because it was hoped that the German occupation would halt the advance of the Soviet Union's Red Army. Many of Hungary's Jews and a part of her Roma minority were then dispatched to their deaths in German concentration camps in a joint operation by German SS officials and the Hungarian authorities. When, on 15 October 1944, Horthy finally attempted to break with Nazi Germany and proclaim Hungary's neutrality he was arrested and replaced by the Hungarian fascist leader Ferenc Szálasi, who, in spite of taking his oath of office in front of the Holy Crown, presided over a German-backed government whose brutality was unconstrained by legal norms and constitutional traditions.[47]

The parties of the Left that took power after the Red Army's arrival in Hungary were confronted by an impoverished and traumatized country that was once again returned to its post-World War I borders. Optimism was, however, engendered by the coalition government led by the Smallholders' Party, that resulted from the relatively free elections of 1946 and in which the Communist Party occupied only a junior position. The government was convinced that the reconstruction of the country required a new legal framework. This was provided by Law I of 1946 which proclaimed that Hungary was now a republic which would uphold the rights of all of its citizens. Balázs Fekete argues in Chapter 9, however, that this law, with its emphasis on creating a balance of power between the president and the legislature, was in fact inspired by the traditional balance of power between the Crown and the legislature, in the very spirit of the 'historical constitution'. Moreover, the robust historical justification of the Act, as elaborated by the Prime Minister in the explanatory notes attached to the Act, also demonstrated its strong connection with the well-known narratives of historical constitutionalism.

As Fekete also makes clear, however, the Communist Party was already manipulating politics and disregarding legal norms by 1946, and following its seizure of power in 1948 it imposed a ruthless dictatorship on the country. Its new constitution, which was enacted in 1949, was based upon principles that often differed from those of the historical constitution, as it was modelled on, and even copied from, the Communist Soviet Union's own 1936 constitution. Moreover, the politicians and the judges who were guided by the contents of this constitution also aspired to erase all traces of the laws and customs that had shaped the country prior to the Communists' seizure of power. Even so, fragments of the old legal framework remained in force. A new civil code was not, for example, drawn up until 1959, but even then its authors retained some elements of the previous code, such as 'traditional methods of inheritance [...] even though they sat uneasily with socialist principles'.[48] Ultimately, however, the constitution was a sham. The Communist regime's totalitarian aspirations could tolerate no real checks on the power of the party-state. Elections were rigged, courts invariably deferred to the requirements of the ruling party, and the formal rights and liberties of the populace were ignored whenever the authorities found this to be expedient.

A New Era of Constitutionalism

The collapse of communism across Central Europe in 1989–90 saw attempts to construct fledgling democratic states based upon 'Western' constitutional norms in the hope of securing genuine civil liberties. Continuity, rather than rupture, underpinned the legal changes that took place in Hungary in 1989. As one of the more liberal of the Warsaw Pact countries after 1956, Hungary allowed opposition associations to form in the late 1980s, and subsequent changes to Hungary's constitution were not triggered by a revolutionary break with the previous regime, or by mass strikes or clashes to the extent they were in certain other Eastern-bloc countries. Rather, scholars have characterized the situation as a 'resolution' with, or 'extrication' from, the Communist regime:[49] following peaceful demonstrations in the late 1980s representatives of the governing Hungarian Socialist Workers' Party (MSzMP) eventually bowed to both domestic and international calls for economic and political reform, and invited the 'Opposition Roundtable', a coalition of opposition parties, to a series of formal roundtable talks that began on 13 June 1989. While these talks frequently broke down, parliament eventually approved a radical overhaul of the old constitution by a vote of 333–5 on 18 October 1989. The amended constitution entered into force on 23 October 1989, the anniversary of the outbreak of the 1956 uprising. This revised constitution, as its preamble stated, was an interim solution, as an entirely new constitution had not yet been drafted.

In subsequent years, four referenda were held by opposition parties with a view to modifying key provisions, and several additional alterations were made to the already heavily revised text. But a further attempt in 1994–5 to draft a completely new constitution failed. For many, the amendments enacted in 1989 had been substantial enough to successfully facilitate the transition to a multi-party democracy and market economy: only one sentence from the old constitution had been left untouched – that the capital of Hungary is Budapest. The text proclaimed that Hungary was a republic (as opposed to a socialist state), introduced multi-party elections, restored the legal status of the president, established parliamentary democracy and a new constitutional court, and introduced the idea of judicial review, a practice unknown in the earlier Hungarian constitutional system. However, because these changes had been implemented on the basis of legal continuity – meaning that changes to the constitution were enacted in full compliance with the laws of the previous system that governed the power to legislate – others claimed that no full break had been made with either the chief constitutional document of the Communist era, or indeed with the Communist nomenklatura, who had been included in the negotiations.[50]

In the following decades public trust in democratic institutions both waxed and waned in response to a variety of fundamental changes to Hungary's political standing, including the benefits, crises and inequalities of economic transformation, membership in NATO, accession to the European Union, and frequent allegations of corruption and scandal at both ends of the political spectrum. During these years, however, the first symbolic steps were also taken to restore some of the 'national' traditions that had been overturned in the aftermath of World War II. The pre-war coat of arms, for example, surmounted by the symbol of the Holy Crown, was restored; soldiers' uniforms and forms of address were modelled upon those used during the interwar period, and public celebrations that existed prior to 1945 were also restored (such as St Stephen's Day on 20 August, formerly known as 'Constitution Day').[51] The new judges of the constitutional court were, required to take their oath of obedience to the constitution in front of a copy of the medieval Golden Bull, a document popularly conceived as being Hungary's 'Magna Carta', and in 2000 the Holy Crown itself was moved with great pomp and ceremony from the National Museum to the parliament, a politically sensitive act as it represented the community of all Hungarians and the integrity of all the territories which had formally been part of the kingdom of Hungary prior to 1918.[52] Then, in 2012, following a self-styled 'revolution in the polling booths', the new Fundamental Law formally restored continuity with what it described as the pre-1944 'historical constitution', as discussed above. The merits and criticisms of this restoration are discussed in the contribution to this book by Kálmán Pócza, in Chapter 10.

The claim that historical continuity had been restored did not, however, lead to the restoration of either the monarchy, or the Regent, or the Upper House of parliament, or the pre-war franchise, or the system of county administration, or any of the other institutions, laws and customs that had been in place prior to World War II. Rather, in keeping with the agreements of the roundtable negotiations, the wishes of the first freely elected government after 1990 and the rulings of the new constitutional court, all legislation which had been placed on the statute books since 1949 remained in force, unless it had been specifically overturned by subsequent legislation. Furthermore, neither the constitutional court nor any other court in Hungary appears, hitherto, to have based any of its judgements on the legal framework that existed up until 1944. These considerations do not, of course, exclude a more substantial attempt to restore the historical constitution in the future. But what might the significance of any such endeavour be? Is this merely a politically motivated venture to find a 'usable past' to support ideological commitments? Or are there valuable lessons that may be learned from the development of historical 'constitutional' laws? Any attempt to answer these and similar questions underscores the need for a fuller understanding of Hungary's legal history, and a clearer assessment of the arguments both for and against such a restoration, to which it is hoped this book will contribute.

The reasons why the 'historical constitution' has again become such a hot political topic can, therefore, only be properly understood if the historical and regional context is taken into account. As this book illustrates, Hungary's legal history was, from 1526 until 1918, dependent on broader developments within the Habsburg Empire, the contours of which were roughly coterminous with the region now frequently referred to as Central Europe.[53] Thus, although the Hungarian political elite repeatedly asserted the distinctive nature of their kingdom and their constitution, the nature of the relationship between law and government in Hungary was always influenced by the broader regional context. Likewise, efforts to impose a new constitutional framework on the country in 1918–19, and again after 1945, mirrored similar constitutional experimentation that occurred throughout Central Europe after World Wars I and II.[54] It is, therefore, unsurprising that the claim by the current Hungarian government that it has restored the historical constitution has occurred in tandem with the broader effort by Central European states to re-evaluate their histories, an initiative that has gathered pace since the collapse of communism in 1989. At the very least, the renewed interest in Hungary's historical constitution suggests that, even within the confines of the European Union, the precise relationship between law and government in Central Europe remains both contingent and contested.

Notes

1. János Kis, 'Introduction', in G.A. Tóth (ed.), *Constitution for a Disunited Nation: On Hungary's Fundamental Law* (Budapest and New York, 2012), p. 2. See also *Népszabadság*, 1 and 2 January, 2012. English translation provided in Toth, *Constitution*, appendix I, pp. 381–2.
2. Ibid. For further discussion see Zoltán Szente, 'Az Alaptörvény és az alkotmányos változások szakmai és tudományos reflexiói 2010 után', *Fundamentum* ix/2–3 (2015), pp. 62–70.
3. See *Népszava*, 2 August 1919, and Law I in *Corpus Juris Hungarici*. English translation provided in Toth, *Constitution*, appendix I, pp. 381–2.
4. Ibid.
5. Ibid.
6. See: www.kormany.hu/hu/a-miniszterelnok/beszedek-publikaciok-interjuk/ tortenelmi-feladat-volt-az-alaptorveny-megalkotasa (accessed 3 March 2018).
7. Toth, *Constitution*, appendix I, pp. 499–501.
8. Miklós Bánkuti, Gábor Halmai and Kim Lane Scheppele, 'Disabling the constitution', *Journal of Democracy* xxiii/3 (2012), pp. 138–46.
9. Kis, 'Introduction', p. 18.
10. Andrew Arato et al. (eds), *Opinion on the Fundamental Law of Hungary* (Budapest, 2011), p. 17; Tamas Boros, *Constitutional Amendments in Hungary: The Government's Struggle against the Constitutional Court* (Budapest, 2013), p. 2; László Tóth, 'A magyarországi LMBT-mozgalmi színtér politikai aktivitásának alakulása, különös tekintettel a 2010-től kezdődő időszakra', *Replika* 84 (2013), pp. 98–101.
11. János Bak, 'Introduction', in M. Rady (ed.), *Custom and Law in Central Europe* (Cambridge, 2003), pp. 1–4.
12. See, however, the magisterial study of Hungary's constitutional development in the Habsburg Empire by László Péter in 'Die Verfassungsentwicklung in Ungarn', in *Die Habsburgermonarchie 1848–1918, Vol. VII* (Vienna, 2000).
13. C.A. Macartney, *Hungary* (London, 1934), p. 126.
14. Ibid., p. 40.
15. On the multi-ethnic and multi-religious character of Hungary in this period see Nora Berend, *At the Gate of Christendom: Jews, Muslims and 'Pagans' in Medieval Hungary* (Cambridge, 2010).
16. Martyn Rady, *Customary Law in Hungary. Courts Texts and the Tripartitum* (Oxford, 2015), p. 2.
17. Pál Engel has described the period after 1301 as the apogee of the modernization of the medieval kingdom. See Pál Engel, *The Kingdom of Hungary, 896–1526* (Budapest, 2006).
18. The precise composition of the *natio hungarica* was, however, only codified with Law I of 1608; see Béla Király, 'Napoleon's proclamation of 1809 and its Hungarian echo', in Stanley Winters and Joseph Held (eds), *Intellectual and Social Developments in the Habsburg Empire from Maria Theresa to World War One* (New York and London, 1975), p. 50.

INTRODUCTION

19. Rady, *Customary Law in Hungary*, pp. 3–4.
20. Bak, 'Introduction', p. 2. See also *Corpus Juris Hungarici, 1000–1526*, pp. 2–3.
21. Rady, *Customary Law in Hungary*, p. 7.
22. Ibid.
23. László Péter, 'The principle of consuetudo', in M. Rady (ed.), *Custom and Law in Central Europe* (Cambridge, 2003), p. 101.
24. Rady, *Customary Law in Hungary*, pp. 8–9.
25. Ibid., p. 68.
26. C.A. Macartney, *The Habsburg Empire 1790–1918* (London, 1968), pp. 8–9.
27. A discussion of this law is provided in Chapter 4 of this volume. A translation of the law can also be found in the Appendix.
28. Macartney, *Hungary*, pp. 129–30.
29. Macartney, *The Habsburg Empire*, p. 24.
30. Martyn Rady, *The Habsburg Empire: A Very Short Introduction* (Oxford, 2017), pp. 54–6.
31. Macartney, *Hungary*, pp. 131–2.
32. See, in particular, Péter, 'Die Verfassungsentwicklung in Ungarn', pp. 253–8.
33. Quoted approvingly in Sándor Radnóti, 'A sacred symbol in a secular country', in Toth, *Constitution for a Disunited Nation*, p. 93; see also the brief but balanced account in Denis Sinor, *History of Hungary* (Woking and London, 1959), pp. 242–5, and the monumental study by Derek Beales, *Joseph II against the World, 1780–1790* (Cambridge, 2009).
34. See, for example, *A magyar anyáknak az országgyűlésére egybegyült ország nagyjai s magyar atyák elejébe terjesztett alázatos kérések* (Pest, 1790), penned by Péter Bárány (1763–1829), but published anonymously.
35. For an analysis of continuity and discontinuity, see Ferenc Hörcher, 'Enlightened reform or national reform? The continuity debate about the Hungarian reform era and the example of the two Széchenyis (1790–1848)', *Hungarian Historical Review* v/1 (2016), pp. 22–45.
36. For an excellent overview of the rising Hungarian nationalism in this period see János Gyurgyák, *Ezzé lett Magyar hazátok* (Budapest, 2013), pp. 27–90; see also George Barany, *Stephen Széchenyi and the Awakening of Hungarian Nationalism, 1791–1841* (Princeton, NJ, 1968).
37. Macartney, *Hungary*, p. 94; see also, for example, Keith Hitchens, 'The sacred cult of nationality: Rumanian intellectuals and the church in Transylvania', in S. Winters and J. Held (eds), *Intellectual and Social Developments in the Habsburg Empire from Maria Theresa to World War One* (New York and London, 1975).
38. Quoted in R.J.W. Evans, *Austria, Hungary and the Habsburgs* (Oxford, 2006), p. 252.
39. Quoted in Amy Oakes, *Divisionary War: Domestic Unrest and International Conflict* (Stanford, CA, 2012).
40. On post-1848 nostalgia for the Hungarian constitution see Evans, *Austria, Hungary and the Habsburgs*, p. 258.

41. Mária Ormos, 'World war and revolutions', in M. Ormos and B. Király (eds), *Hungary: Government and Politics 1848–2000* (New York, 2001). See also András Siklós, *Magyarország 1918/1919* (Budapest, 1978), pp. 267–75.
42. See Paul Hanebrink, *In Defense of Christian Hungary: Religion, Nationalism and Antisemitism, 1890–1944* (Ithaca, NY, 2009).
43. For a balanced account of Horthy's career, see Thomas Sakmyster, *Hungary's Admiral on Horseback: Miklós Horthy, 1918–1944* (New York, 1994).
44. Judit Acsády, 'The debate on parliamentary reforms in women's suffrage in Hungary', in *Suffrage, Gender and Citizenship* (Cambridge, 2009), pp. 242–59.
45. Rady, *Customary Law in Hungary*, p. 227.
46. Ferenc Eckhart, 'A magyar alkotmány', in *Magyar Szemle* 1944/3, pp. 119–21.
47. See Rudolf Paksa, *Magyar Nemzeti-Szocialisták* (Budapest, 2013), pp. 268–324.
48. Rady, *Customary Law in Hungary*, p. 241.
49. See Gábor Halmai, 'The reform of constitutional law in Hungary after the transition', *Legal Studies* xviii/2 (1998), p. 189, and András Bozóki, 'The roundtable talks of 1989: Participants, political visions, and historical references', *Hungarian Studies* xiv/2 (2001), p. 242.
50. For more detailed accounts of the constitutional debates of this era see, for example, András Bozóki (ed.), *The Roundtable Talks of 1989* (Budapest, 2002); István Kukorelli and Károly Tóth, *A rendszerváltozás államszervezeti kompromisszumai* (Lakitelek, 2016); László Sólyom, 'The role of constitutional courts in the transition to democracy, with special reference to Hungary', *International Sociology* xviii/1 (2003), pp. 137–65, and Sólyom, László and Georg Brunner, *Constitutional Judiciary in a New Democracy. The Hungarian Constitutional Court* (Ann Arbor, MI, 2000).
51. Ignác Romsics, 'The first four years', in M. Ormos and B. Király (eds), *Hungary: Government and Politics 1848–2000* (New York, 2001).
52. For a discussion of the Holy Crown's role in Hungarian law after 1989 see Dániel István Hegedüs, 'A történeti Magyar közjog jelenkori hagyatéka: A történeti alkotmány és a Szent Korona', *Studia Iuvenum Iurisperitorum* viii (2016), pp. 161–78.
53. For a critical assessment of the meaning of the term 'Central Europe', see R.J.W. Evans, 'Central Europe, past and present', *Central Europe* i/2 (2003). See also Steven Beller, 'Including the middle: A response to R.J.W. Evans', *Central Europe* i/2 (2003).
54. For example, the Republic of Austria enacted its first constitution in 1920 which was reinstated in 1945; the Czechoslovak Republic enacted its first constitution in 1920 and, following its reconstruction, enacted a second constitution in 1948; Poland enacted new constitutions in 1919 (expanded in 1921 and revised in 1935) and in 1952.

CHAPTER 2

LAW AND THE ANCIENT CONSTITUTION IN MEDIEVAL AND EARLY MODERN HUNGARY

Martyn Rady

Introduction

It was only at the end of the eighteenth century that Hungarians realized that the bundle of miscellaneous provisions affecting the relationship of the ruler to the political nation might amount to a constitution. Until then, the legal relationship between the sovereign and the noble community, which made up the bulk of the political nation, was understood as being composed of private rights. Stephen Werbőczy's compilation of Hungarian law, published in 1517 and known as the *Tripartitum*, thus moved effortlessly from a discussion of the rights and duties of the monarch to the system of land donation and to aspects of the law as they affected the administration of noble properties. Indeed, Werbőczy's Romanist division of the law into persons, things and actions left no room for the separate discussion of what might be considered today to be public and constitutional law. For Werbőczy, and for the lawyers who for several centuries adhered to his prescriptions, all branches of the law were subsumed within the broad category of rights or *iura*, which were themselves determined according to customary law.[1]

Hungarian law was customary in the sense that it rested either upon observance or upon what observance was said to be.[2] Statute was subordinate to custom insofar as its provisions depended for their efficacy upon being accepted in legal practice. Statutes that were not routinely observed thus had no force. This meant that the courts played an important role in determining what the law was and in deciding upon the degree to which measures were applicable, redundant or to be enforced. No concept, however, of precedent or *stare decisis* prevailed, and previous judgements were seldom referred back to in litigation. Instead, courts frequently judged according to what their members felt was right, expedient or equitable, rather than lawyerly or principled, on account of which their appeals to customary practice were often only rhetorical.[3]

In Hungary, therefore, the customary law did not develop in the direction of an integrated body of law, but instead as a medley of often discordant practices. As in much of medieval Europe, what was said to be *Gewohnheitsrecht* or the customary law comprised in fact separate and often contradictory *Rechtsgewohnheiten* or legal customs.[4] But whereas elsewhere in Europe the Roman Law Reception of the sixteenth century urged the articulation of formal, binding rules, Hungary remained largely isolated from Romanizing trends. Attempts to stabilize the law through the production of codes or summaries of judgements were accordingly ineffective there, for the components of what was said to be the customary law were malleable, being constantly redefined according to circumstance and the composition and will of the courts.

What might be called the public law was even less rooted in substantive principles than the private law, and was even more fluctuating in its content. In what follows, the shifts, contradictions and instabilities will be demonstrated that existed in respect of medieval and early-modern Hungary's most important institutions: the royal succession, the Diet, the right of resistance and the so-called liberties of the nobility. One would expect the elapsing of over half a millennium to have brought about changes. The critical point, however, is that there was seldom any contemporary agreement as to what rights obtained concerning these institutions and the nature of their relations. Indeed, even the basic elements of their relations were contested.

The Royal Succession

The most important aspect of public law was the appointment of the sovereign. From an early stage in its history, the coronation ceremony was broadly fixed and in its essential elements unswerving. The king should be crowned with the holy diadem by the archbishop of Esztergom at Székesfehérvár (later at Pozsony, which is now Bratislava). It took Charles Robert at the beginning of the fourteenth century at least three attempts to bring these elements together in such a way as to be acknowledged as Hungary's indubitable king. Yet the process of establishing who was worthy of coronation and the substantive law of succession was less clear. Hereditary descent, the measure of genetic proximity, the approval of the previous king and the recognition of the political community were all considered important, but the weight given respectively to each depended upon political circumstance and expediency.

A fourteenth-century example shows the interplays at work. On 16 July 1342, the powerful Angevin king of Hungary, Charles Robert (Charles I), died. Five days later, his eldest son, the teenage Louis, was crowned in the coronation church in Székesfehérvár. The event was subsequently described in the leading royal chronicle as having taken place 'with the consent and unanimous will of all the barons and of the entire nobility of the entire realm of Hungary, and with the Holy Crown'. Plainly, the chronicler considered it worth reporting that Louis's succession depended not only upon primogeniture but also upon the appropriate diadem having been used and upon the unanimous consent of all. The chronicler did not grade these elements in any order – all were equal marks of kingship and authority, and of the right to succeed.[5]

There is nothing unusual about this conflation. We may note the same in regard to late medieval France and even, in literature, to the circumstances attending King Arthur's promotion to the throne: pulling the sword out of the stone was not enough, for, as Merlin pointed out, Arthur's legitimacy also rested on his royal descent.[6] In Hungary, however, the elective principle became enlarged. This development had its origin in the misfortune that for almost two centuries from the death of Charles Robert in 1342, no Hungarian ruler left an indubitable male heir: Louis I (1342–82), Sigismund (1387–1437), Wladislas I (1440–4), Ladislas V (1445–57) and Matthias Corvinus (1458–90) all died without surviving sons. Albert (1437–9), Sigismund's son-in-law and successor, did eventually produce a male heir, Ladislas (V), but only after he had died and in defiance of the widowed queen's midwives and seers, who had confidently predicted a girl. So, by the time he was born, the kingdom had passed into the possession of Wladislas I; a faction managed, however, to have him properly crowned. Each royal death prompted in its turn a political emergency, which was resolved to begin with by the royal council. After 1444 and the death of Wladislas I at the battle of Varna, however, the Diet moved into the foreground, for in the ensuing chaos the various baronial factions were keen to build a consensus. From this point onwards, when there was no obvious heir, the Diet decided.

So, when Ladislas V died in 1457, it was the Diet that recognized Matthias Corvinus as the rightful heir, following the coup organized by his mother and uncle. Matthias had not a drop of royal blood in him and his reputation largely hung on the inherited charisma of his father, John Hunyadi, who had been governor of Hungary during Ladislas V's minority. On Matthias's death in 1490, the Diet rejected the claims put forward by his illegitimate son, John Corvin, and opted instead for the Bohemian king, Wladislas II. In so doing, they rejected the idea of descent by genetic proximity, for both Frederick III of Habsburg and his son, Maximilian, stood closer biologically to Matthias's predecessor, Ladislas, than did the Polish Jagiello ruler of Bohemia, Wladislas. Moreover, the Diet chose on this occasion to ignore the succession pacts agreed between Frederick III and Matthias, according to which the one would succeed to the other's lands in the event that he died without an heir. The Diet did not see itself as bound by such private arrangements.

The test came with the reign of Wladislas II. Wladislas was already in his forties when he succeeded to the Hungarian throne, and in poor health. After two marriages without issue, he took the 18-year-old Anne de Foix-Candale as his wife. In 1506, she produced a male heir – the new-born baby was so weak that he had to be put in an incubator made of the carcasses of freshly slain pigs, but the treatment worked.[7] The boy, Louis, was an indubitable heir and his father's rightful successor. Nevertheless, Wladislas still thought it expedient to have Louis crowned in his own lifetime and to obtain the consent of the Diet to this unusual arrangement. The coronation was accompanied by a ceremony in which the assembled nobility were expressly asked by the Palatine whether they accepted Louis as king – the first occasion upon which this so-called 'old custom' was in fact invoked.[8] Louis entered upon his inheritance following his father's death in 1516. There was no second coronation.

Even, therefore, when the biological line of succession was unimpeded, the approval of the Diet was considered an aspect of king-making. Suitability, as determined by the Diet, and biology were thus the ingredients determining the succession, but their measure and sufficiency were not quantified, depending instead upon circumstance. Nevertheless, Stephen Werbőczy wrote otherwise. Back in 1505, Werbőczy had been a party to the so-called Rákos Declaration (he may indeed have written it), by which the Diet affirmed that in the case of Wladislas's death it should elect a 'national king'.[9] But, at this point, Wladislas was still lacking a male heir and the danger was that, should he die, a Habsburg would succeed. The text of the Declaration was, however, specific on the point that biology trumped election, the consent of the Diet only being required in the event that 'there be no male heirs who by the law and custom of this kingdom are entitled to succeed'. But in his *Tripartitum*, written just a decade later, Werbőczy stated the complete opposite. Having adumbrated the interrelationship of the monarch and the nobility, he wrote: 'these two, by virtue of some reciprocal transfer and mutual bond between them, depend upon each other so closely that neither can exist without the other. For *the prince is elected by the nobles* [emphasis mine], and nobles are created and adorned with the dignity of nobility only by the prince.'[10]

Werbőczy's elegant description lacked nuance and was, to that extent, misleading, but it provided the underpinning for elective monarchy. Following the death in 1526 of Louis II at the battle of Mohács, the Hungarian Diet split, for Louis had left no son. One faction favoured the succession of Ferdinand (I) of Habsburg, who was married to the dead king's sister, Anne, and whose own sister, Mary, was in turn the dead king's widow. Ferdinand based his claim on heredity, as the closest relative to Louis, albeit through marriage. The other faction looked to John Zápolya, the voivode of Transylvania, and to the terms of the Rákos Declaration. By this measure, since there was no successor to Louis, a 'national king' might be elected. Two diets accordingly met and elected two kings, both of whom were crowned with the sacred diadem in Székesfehérvár by the same bishop of Eger (the Archbishop of Esztergom having perished in the recent battle). There was, however, a difference. For the pro-Zápolya side, which included Stephen Werbőczy, election was the decisive mark of legitimacy, but for the pro-Habsburg group it was an act not of constitution but of recognition.

These opposing strands would be teased out in the century following. The Zápolya monarchy was transformed first into an 'East Hungarian Kingdom' (the rest having been occupied by the Habsburgs and Ottomans) and then, in 1570, into the Principality of Transylvania, the ruler of which was elected by the Transylvanian Diet. Until the principality's collapse at the end of the seventeenth century, there would be at least 20 princes – the precise number depends on how one counts rivals and pretenders. On average, therefore, the government changed hands about every five years as princes were elected, deposed or murdered. Transylvania was the home of noble republicanism at its most raw.[11] By contrast, the crown in Habsburg Hungary proceeded from father to son, and in the absence of direct heirs even to collaterals. Elections were held, but usually these were organized in the previous king's lifetime so that the reigning monarch might put pressure on the representatives attending the Diet. So embedded was the tradition of Habsburg inheritance that in 1618 the Diet approved the succession of King Matthias II's cousin, Ferdinand of Styria, even though Ferdinand's religious policy threatened the fragile confessional status quo in the kingdom.[12] (Matthias II was also Emperor Matthias I, and Ferdinand of Styria became in turn Emperor Ferdinand II.)

Ferdinand I obtained in 1547 the Diet's agreement to the permanent succession of his heirs. Exactly 140 years later, in 1687, Leopold obliged the Diet to give its renewed consent to the Hungarian Crown remaining hereditary in the House of Habsburg.[13] Nevertheless, in a customary regime, the authority of statute is legally incomplete unless confirmed and approved by popular observation and consensus. The difficulties involved in measuring the degree and temporal extent of this approbation meant that every law might in principle be contested. Ferenc Rákóczi's *Recrudescunt* manifesto of 1703, which launched his rebellion against Leopold I, thus repudiated the idea of a hereditary monarchy, affirming instead the right of election, 'which custom was maintained for centuries unimpaired'.[14] Two years later, the Diet appointed Rákóczi 'ruling prince', and shortly afterwards deposed Leopold's successor, Joseph I. At the end of the century, it was similarly argued that the Habsburgs had by their usurpations broken the thread of dynastic succession, on which account the kingdom had reverted to the customary status of an elective monarchy.[15] The deposition of Francis Joseph and of the House of Habsburg in 1849 was likewise made on the grounds that the dynasty had forfeited its right to rule, on which account the hereditary monarch was replaced by an elected head of state. The contest between hereditary and elective principles – between so-called Legitimists and Free Electors – would sharpen almost to the point of civil war after World War I.[16]

Diets and Statutes

Several types of representative assembly operated in Hungary up to the fourteenth century. One was an extended meeting of the royal council and another was an open session of the royal court, convened to deal with specific political emergencies. Sigismund's need for cash and troops, both to repel the Ottomans and, later, to make good his claim to the Bohemian throne, obliged him to convoke diets to which the nobility sent elected and empowered deputies. In the decades that followed Sigismund's death, diets met with increasing regularity, comprising at first noble deputies chosen by the counties. Increasingly, however, they became mass events, at which many thousands of nobles attended. Part of the reason for this was political expediency and the need to form a consensus that embraced as many noblemen as possible. Another reason lay in the structure of noble landholding. Since noble land in Hungary was not subinfeudated, nobles held their land directly of the monarch. They were thus his immediate vassals, as much entitled to give him aid and counsel as any of the kingdom's great lords. As Werbőczy himself put it, in an enduring tag, great lords and nobles were equal to the extent that they enjoyed 'one and the same liberty' (*una eademque libertas*).[17]

The first mass assemblies of the nobility took place in Hungary during the succession crises of the 1440s and 1450s, and Matthias Corvinus continued to summon them at key political moments. During the reigns of Wladislas II and Louis II, however, the momentum for mass diets became almost unstoppable, with individual diets mandating that their next assembly or assemblies be attended by all nobles on pain of fine (or worse). Since there was no limit to the business of the realm in which the opinion of the kingdom's nobles might be sought, their meetings became increasingly frequent. During the reign of Matthias Corvinus (1458–90), the Diet met about 25 times, less than once a year. But under his successors, it convened on at least 43 occasions in 36 years, often meeting twice or even three times in some years. On most occasions, the press of noblemen in attendance meant that the Diet had to be convened in the open, on the Field of Rákos beside Pest.[18]

Since diets might also act as military musters, the nobles often attended armed and accompanied by their retinues. Mass diets could be shambolic and violent events – 'tumultuous' is the term used by some historians – but this was not always the case. Two fairly detailed accounts survive of the Hatvan Diet of 1525, and these provide almost all that we know of how Hungarian diets operated in practice in the Middle Ages.[19] It would appear that matters were actually quite orderly, although this may have been due to the Hatvan Diet being held at a distance from the provocations of the capital and its shops. Accordingly, the vicinity was not raided for supplies, but instead the provision of some sort of market made foodstuffs plentiful – so much so that geese and hens, we are told, wandered freely about the encampment. The Diet itself assembled in some sort of fenced compound that was patrolled by armed horsemen, with only two gateways providing access. Within the enclosure, Gypsies – who traditionally fulfilled the role of executioners – maintained a conspicuous presence. Here, a wooden stage was set up, 'in the form of a theatre', on which the king and members of the royal council gathered. These were then berated by the assembled noblemen.

As the Hatvan example suggests, the Diet was at the start of the sixteenth century organizationally immature, remaining more an event than an institution. Although it appointed a speaker (*orator*) to articulate its demands, the Diet had no structure of committees, nor any mechanism to ensure the fulfilment of its will between sessions. It could not be summoned except by the royal command, and its right to be able to convoke itself was never acknowledged. The Diet's order of business seems, moreover, to have been decided by the royal council, which not only drew up in advance a list of the royal propositions for debate but also occasionally drafted proposals of its own for royal approval. Petitions arising from the floor of the Diet, possibly conveyed through the speaker, were then added to the agenda and, if approved, incorporated within the statute issued after the Diet's close.

Nevertheless, the way the Diet met and the manner in which it conducted its affairs indicates the 'double polarity' (*Doppelpoligkeit*) or structural dualism which underpinned the political order. The king physically confronted the political community – *rex* versus *regnum*, and executive versus the noble nation. Transactions between the two similarly emphasized the duality of their relations, with both exchanging proposals for legislation until agreement – or rupture – occurred. In the working-out of legislation, *rex* and *regnum* each comprised separate subjects of right. Their authority was autarkically derived and self-generating. It did not rest on the conferral of rights from one to the other, for the prerogatives of each were complete in and of themselves. Although the aim of their negotiation was to arrive at a common position, summarized in a statute or *decretum*, the outcome was not so much a body of legislation as a treaty. For this reason, we may say that the ensuing provisions were not made, as in England, by the king *in* parliament, but by the king *and* parliament.

Following the Habsburg takeover, meetings of the Diet became fewer, the numbers of those attending more controlled, and the venue more comfortable, now consisting of whatever large buildings were available. The council, which had at its core the leading royal officeholders, was in 1608 transformed officially into an Upper House, but it had been operating more or less in this capacity for at least the previous century. The Lower House consisted of representatives drawn from the noble counties, to which were added deputies of the principal cities and religious houses. The dualist structure that had developed in the Middle Ages continued to determine relations between Crown and community. The king advanced his *propositiones*. The two houses submitted in turn their counter-proposals (known as *gravamina* or 'grievances'), often with groups sending in their recommendations separately, after which *rex* and *regnum* bargained in a process that could last for several years. The idea that only the Crown should initiate legislation was qualified in the 1790s, with the appointment of commissions of the Diet for the drafting of legislation (but, even then, they failed to push through their work).[20]

During the later seventeenth century, the work of the diets became more streamlined through the use of committees and through formalized arrangements for the exchange of information and opinions between the two houses. Nevertheless, procedures were never firmly established, but continued to be regulated by custom and by what, depending on the occasion, custom was said to be. First, it was uncertain what the Diet might discuss. Matters of foreign policy and defence as well as the broad ambit of executive authority were considered *reservata*, as belonging to the monarch alone. Justice and administration were, by contrast, shared powers or *communicata*, while the determination of taxes and military recruitment depended almost entirely upon the Diet's consent. Yet the distinctions between the spheres were in practice blurred. Precise definition suited no one, for it imposed limitations.

Secondly, there was no established voting system. Sometimes, the Lower House voted by blocks, according either to status group or to geography (city deputies, clergy, Trans-Danubian deputies, and so on). On other occasions, each deputy voted individually. This was not, however, a numerically driven process. Voting was public and often took the form of a speech. In the expression of the time, however, votes were not counted, but 'weighed' (*vota non numerantur sed ponderantur*), with greater influence given to the opinions of the 'wise and powerful'. On occasions, noise alone was sufficient. The appointment in 1741 of Francis of Lorraine as Maria Theresa's co-ruler was thus achieved against the wishes of the majority by a claque of the queen's supporters, who at the appropriate moment cried out 'Long live the co-regent!'[21] In the Upper House, to the extent that it voted at all, decisions were mostly reached by reference to the volume of shouts.[22]

At the end of the Diet, a statute or *decretum* was composed, which brought together the resolutions agreed in readiness for the royal seal. The chancellery composed this, and in the seventeenth century abused its position by editing the final document according to the royal interest. Most notoriously, in 1604 the agreed articles were rewritten so as to ban Protestant worship and prevent any future diet discussing matters of religion. By the eighteenth century, however, it was usual for the drafting to be undertaken by a mixed commission of the Diet and the chancellery. In the event that there was such disagreement between ruler and Diet that no statute could be agreed upon, the monarch might bypass the Diet completely and enforce the royal will by decree. The text of the statute of 1526, which permitted the monarch to use his 'power and authority' to do all that was necessary for 'the defence, liberty and other needs of the realm', might thus be invoked to permit legislation by decree.[23] So when in 1765 the Diet refused the Queen's proposals for a reform of conditions on the land, she forced the changes she wanted by decree. The extent to which the ruler might make law by his or her own volition (*proprio motu*) was contested and, as an expedient, dangerous. The Hungarian counties might in extreme circumstances simply refuse to implement the terms of the decree, declaring it to be legally invalid. In this case, the only recourse was either to resume negotiations or for the ruler to impose commissioners, backed up by troops.

Rulers published hundreds of decrees every decade, mostly of an administrative nature – on, for instance, temporary quarantine restrictions, the use of post horns, fire regulations, and so on. These were read out in county assemblies, filed away (or lost) and sometimes implemented. There was no corpus of decrees to which the obedient official might turn. The earliest compilation was made only in the early nineteenth century as a private work and it just contained epitomes.[24] The content of most decrees was accordingly forgotten, unless absorbed into practice. In this respect, the authority of royal decrees rested over time upon customary use. Incredibly too, the statutes agreed by ruler and Diet were not retained in an official archive or on a parliamentary roll. Their texts were distributed and sold (often in abbreviated form), and it was up to the purchasers to keep the copies safe. Collections of statutes were until the sixteenth century made by hand and thereafter printed privately. By this time, most of the medieval statutes had been lost or garbled in their transmission. After 1600, statutes were routinely published in printed form. Even so, they were subsequently reprinted in compendia with errors and omissions. If they had space to spare, editors often added in at the end of a compilation some extraneous material, which by its inclusion acquired a measure of unmerited legal authority.

The privately printed *Corpus Juris Hungarici*, published in successive and updated editions from the late sixteenth century, was therefore a deficient resource. For instance, the version of the statute of 1492 given in the 1779 edition of the *Corpus Juris* contained 600 errors; the text of the *Tripartitum*, as published in the same collection, had about 2,000, including even the length of the bar that supposedly determined the kingdom's scheme of measurement. It was later estimated that the entire body of the *Corpus Juris* contained over 13,000 errors.[25] On top of this, most of the provisions included in the *Corpus Juris* were no longer relevant, while others were contradictory. Courts borrowed haphazardly from whatever portions seemed to offer the best justification for their determinations. Attempts to reorder the *Corpus Juris* into a manageable whole (of which there were many) proved stillborn. The authority of successive editions had been sanctified by use and thus the *Corpus Juris* could not be set aside. Likewise, so it was maintained, the errors that had crept into its text had been adopted in practice and so carried a greater authority than the pristine version.[26]

Liberties, the Golden Bull and the Right of Resistance

Despite the indeterminacy about the actual content of the kingdom's statutes, Hungarians were convinced that there were a few provisions that were clear, known and true. These they called their 'liberties' or 'freedoms'. The charter to which they most frequently appealed in this context was the Golden Bull of 1222.[27] The Golden Bull had been issued by King Andrew II at a time of chaos and of institutional flux, and contains at its heart a petition presented to the King by some of his subjects. The vocabulary of the Golden Bull is archaic: noblemen are called *servientes*, only the greater lords are referred to as nobles, and the royal office-holders and retainers are described as *iobagiones*, which is a debased Turkic word. Many of the Golden Bull's provisions related to practices that disappeared in the century or so following its issue: the annual debasement of the coinage, the management of the royal finances by Muslims and Jews, the free disposition of property in the event of death without a male heir, and the assignment of semi-free warriors to earthwork castles. The Golden Bull also included a provision which permitted nobles to resist the ruler should he breach its terms, which probably at the time of its publication meant only that they might counsel the king without fear of retribution. The 'right of resistance' was not included in the Golden Bull's reissue in 1231, but replaced with what was understood at the time to be the more powerful sanction of excommunication.

The provisions of the Golden Bull, but not including the resistance clause, were amplified over the succeeding decades in four further 'charters of liberty' (in 1231, 1267, 1290 and 1298). These charters were, however, soon lost, misplaced or forgotten. So, when in 1351 King Louis I sought to codify the rights and obligations of the nobility, the Golden Bull provided the sole starting point. Louis accordingly confirmed its contents verbatim (he did, however, modify arrangements in respect of the right of succession to landed estate). From this point onwards, the Golden Bull was regarded as emblematic of noble liberty and frequently reissued, often on the occasion of a new king's inauguration. In 1440, the Golden Bull was included in a *libellus*, which was confirmed by Wladislas I several days after his coronation. Matthias Corvinus, on the occasion of the coronation Diet held in 1464, also expressly agreed to uphold the terms of the Golden Bull. Matthias's successor, Wladislas II, similarly committed himself after being crowned in 1490 to maintain the terms of the Golden Bull. On the occasion of his wife's coronation in 1521, Louis II likewise promised to uphold the Golden Bull's contents. From the sixteenth century onwards, the text of the Golden Bull was included in successive editions of the kingdom's laws, as the only surviving piece of thirteenth-century legislation.

In the *Tripartitum* of 1517, Stephen Werbőczy rehearsed the liberties of the nobility: their freedom from arrest, their subordination to the king's justice alone, their exemption from taxation and other imposts, and their right to extract revenue, and thus servile labour, from their landed estates. To these, however, he attached the right of resistance as declared in the Golden Bull.[28] Despite the inventiveness of their explanations for rebellion, Hungarians had never before justified their actions by reference to the Golden Bull. Now, however, it was written into the most popular legal text in pre-modern Hungary and provided part of the ideological baggage by which the Hungarian nobility justified armed insurrection against the Habsburg ruler.

In 1687, the Diet agreed to Leopold I's demand that the right of resistance included in the Golden Bull be abolished along with the right to elect the ruler.[29] Nevertheless, the right of resistance was by this time considered so embedded in customary observance as to make it impervious to statute. It was thus invoked as justification for Rákóczi's rebellion, formed part of the intellectual arsenal deployed against the government of Joseph II in the late 1780s and provided a little of the rhetorical underpinning behind the deposition of the House of Habsburg in 1849. The right of resistance was also assumed by Hungary's county governments, expressing itself in the nineteenth century in the *vis inertiae* (the 'respectfully putting aside' of royal instructions), in breaking the seats of commissioners appointed over them and in the sealing-up of committee rooms. Like the right to elect the ruler, the right of resistance was deemed a privilege that was so rooted in history as to be impossible to efface.[30]

In an unusual twist, however, the coronation oath altered in 1687 on the occasion of Joseph I's succession to the throne in the lifetime of his father.[31] (Joseph was nine years old at the time.) Hitherto, the terms of the coronation oath had been generalized, including such promises as the maintenance of justice and the Church, and the preservation of the kingdom's territory and of its liberties. To these was now attached specific reference to the resistance clause in the Golden Bull which was declared void. Recollection of the Golden Bull and of the resistance clause thus entered into the coronation ceremony, albeit in an oblique and roundabout way, and remained there indeed until the collapse of the historic kingdom in 1918.

If the resistance clause in the Golden Bull was now declared abolished, presumably the rest of the charter retained weight. Yet this was plainly not the case, for most of its clauses had lapsed. Nor, indeed, did the formulation which Werbőczy gave in the *Tripartitum* of the nobility's rights provide any guarantee that these rights would be maintained. For instance, the nobleman's freedom to extract whatever revenues he chose from his estates was frequently thwarted by the intervention of royal officials and finally laid aside by Maria Theresa in 1765, when she imposed an upper limit on servile obligations. The liberties of the political nation remained imprecise, depending on who had the political upper hand. Indeed, the prevailing regime of uncertainty was acknowledged in the so-called *Revisionsklausel*, which after 1687 was included in either the royal oath or the inaugural diploma published on the occasion of the coronation, or sometimes in both. In this clause, the king promised to uphold the rights of the kingdom's nobility 'as the king and the assembled estates shall agree on the interpretation and application thereof' (*prout super eorum intellectu, et usu, regio ac communi statuum consensu diaetaliter conventum fuerit*).[32] In short, the content of the nobility's rights and the nature of their relationship to the Crown were not fixed, but expressly negotiable.

Conclusion

The ancient constitution was an invention of the late eighteenth century. Before this time, all that may be said is that *rex* and *regnum*, king and political community, were competing subjects of right, each possessed of what they considered to be separate and self-generating rights. Their relationship allegedly rested on customary principles, but these were, like all of customary law, uncertain, malleable and open to new constructions. What the constitution was at any one moment depended upon political circumstance, which worked against the establishment of norms around which a lasting consensus might be obtained. Institutional rules and the content of the kingdom's public law were thus, until the nineteenth century, principally determined by temporary and shifting relations of power. Under these circumstances, there could be no stable construction or set of agreed norms sufficient to merit the name of a constitution. In place of an 'ancient constitution', there was only an ancient contestation.

Further Reading

Bak, János M., *Königtum und Stände in Ungarn im 14.–16. Jahrhundert* (Wiesbaden, 1973).
Bak, János M. et al. (eds), *Decreta Regni Hungariae Mediaevalis/The Laws of the Medieval Kingdom of Hungary*, 5 vols (Bakersfield, CA, Salt Lake City, UT, Los Angeles, Idyllwild, CA, and Budapest, 1989–2012).
Engel, Pál, *The Realm of St Stephen: A History of Medieval Hungary, 895–1526* (London, 2001).
Macartney, C.A., *The Habsburg and Hohenzollern Dynasties in the Seventeenth and Eighteenth Centuries* (New York, 1970).
Murdock, Graeme, *Calvinism on the Frontier, 1600–1660: International Calvinism and the Reformed Church in Hungary and Transylvania* (Oxford, 2000).
Pálffy, Géza, *The Kingdom of Hungary and the Habsburg Monarchy in the Sixteenth Century* (Boulder, CO, and New York, 2009).
Rady, Martyn, *Customary Law in Hungary: Courts, Texts, and the Tripartitum* (Oxford, 2015).

Notes

1. Werbőczy's *Tripartitum* is now available with a parallel English translation in János M. Bak et al. (eds), *The Customary Law of the Renowned Kingdom of Hungary in Three Parts (The 'Tripartitum')* (*Decreta Regni Mediaevalis Hungariae*, 5) (Idyllwild, CA, and Budapest, 2005).
2. For the role of customary law in Hungary, see László Péter, 'Die Verfassungsentwicklung in Ungarn', in H. Rumpler and P. Urbanitsch (eds), *Die Habsburgermonarchie 1848–1918*, vol. 7 (part 1) (Vienna, 2000), pp. 239–540 (pp. 242–5); Martyn Rady, *Customary Law in Hungary: Courts, Texts and the Tripartitum* (Oxford, 2015); also Martyn Rady (ed.), *Customary Law in Central Europe* (Cambridge, 2003).
3. For the operation of the courts in pre-modern Hungary, see Martyn Rady, 'Judicial organization and decision making in old Hungary', *Slavonic and East European Review* xc (2012), pp. 450–81.

4. Martin Pilch, 'Rechtsgewohnheiten aus rechtshistorischer und rechtstheoretischer Perspective', *Rechtsgeschichte* xvii (2010), pp. 17–39.
5. Imre Szentpétery, *Scriptores rerum Hungaricarum*, vol. 1 (Budapest, 1937), p. 504.
6. Ralph E. Giesey, 'The juristic basis of dynastic right to the French throne', *Transactions of the American Philosophical Society*, N.S., li (1961), pp. 2–47 (pp. 3–4); Sir Thomas Malory, *Le Morte d'Arthur*, edited by Stephen H.A. Shepherd (New York, 2004), book 1, chs 7–8.
7. B.J. Sprujt, '"En bruit d'estre bonne luterien": Mary of Hungary (1505–58) and religious reform', *English Historical Review* cix (1994), pp. 275–307 (p. 275).
8. János M. Bak, *Königtum und Stände in Ungarn im 14.–16. Jahrhundert* (Wiesbaden, 1973), pp. 68–9.
9. Bak, *Königtum und Stände*, pp. 67, 118.
10. The text of the Rákos Declaration and relevant extract from the *Tripartitum* are given below in the Appendix.
11. Graeme Murdock, '"Freely elected in fear": Princely elections and political power in early modern Transylvania', *Journal of Early Modern History* vii (2003), pp. 213–44.
12. Robert Bireley, *Ferdinand II, Counter-Reformation Emperor, 1578–1637* (Cambridge, 2014), pp. 87–8.
13. The text of the relevant law of 1687 is given below in the Appendix.
14. László Péter, '*Ius resistendi* in Hungary', in L. Péter and M. Rady (eds), *Resistance, Rebellion and Revolution in Hungary and Central Europe: Commemorating 1956* (London, 2008), pp. 41–55 (p. 48).
15. Gyula Mérei and Károly Vörös (eds), *Magyarország története tíz kötetben, 1790–1848*, vol. 1 (Budapest, 1980), p. 88; Adam Wandruszka, *Leopold II*, vol. 2 (Vienna and Munich, 1965), pp. 275–314.
16. Thomas Lorman, *Counter-Revolutionary Hungary, 1920–1925: István Bethlen and the Politics of Consolidation* (Boulder, CO, and New York, 2006), pp. 14–15, 27–8, 69–72, 77–8.
17. The relevant extract from the *Tripartitum* is given below in the Appendix.
18. For Diets during the Jagello period, see János M. Bak, 'Diets and their decisions 1490–1526', in P. Banyó and M. Rady (eds), *The Laws of the Medieval Kingdom of Hungary – Decreta Regni Mediaevalis Hungariae*, vol. 4 (Idyllwild, CA, and Budapest, 2012), pp. li–lvi. See also János M. Bak and András Vadas, 'Diets and synods in Buda and its environs', in B. Nagy et al. (eds), *Medieval Buda in Context* (Leiden and Boston, MA, 2016), pp. 322–44.
19. Given in Georgius Pray, *Epistolae Procerum Regni Hungariae* (Bratislava, 1806), pp. 193–201.
20. Law 67 of 1790/1; Elemér Mályusz, *Sándor Lipót főherceg nador iratai 1790–1795* (Budapest, 1926), p. 120.
21. István M. Szijártó, 'The Diet: The Estates and the Parliament of Hungary, 1708–1792', in G. Ammerer *et al. (eds)*, *Bündnispartner und Konkurrenten der Landesfürsten? Die Stände in der Habsburgermonarchie (Vienna and Munich, 2007)*, pp. 119–39 (p. 127).

22. István M. Szijártó, *A diéta. A magyar rendek és az országgyűlés 1708–1792* (Budapest, 2005), p. 282.
23. János Zlinszky, *Az ügyvédség kialakulása Magyarországon és története Fejér megyében* (Székesfehérvár, 1976), p. 26.
24. Ignác Kassics, *Enchiridion seu Extractus Benignarum Ordinationum Regiarum*, 3 vols (Pest, 1825).
25. J.N. Kovachich, *Lectiones Variantes decretorum comitialium* (Pest, 1816), pp. 113–38, 461–517; Éva V. Windisch, *Kovachich Márton György, a forráskutató* (Budapest, 1998), p. 184.
26. Windisch, *Kovachich Márton György*, p. 190.
27. For the historical background to the Golden Bull and its legacy, see Martyn Rady, 'Hungary and the Golden Bull of 1222', *Banatica* xxiv/2 (2014), pp. 87–108.
28. The relevant text is given below in the Appendix.
29. The text of the relevant law is given below in the Appendix.
30. Péter, '*Ius resistendi* in Hungary', pp. 50–3; Elemér Balogh, 'The place of the Golden Bull in Hungarian constitutional history', in L. Besenyei, G. Érszegi and M. Pedrazza Gorlero (eds), *De Bulla Aurea Andreae Regis Hungariae MCCXXII* (Verona, 1999), pp. 203–24 (p. 223).
31. The text of the oath is given below in the Appendix.
32. László Péter, 'The primacy of consuetudo in Hungarian law', in M. Rady (ed.), *Custom and Law in Central Europe* (Cambridge, 2003), pp. 101–11 (p. 104).

CHAPTER 3

THE BIRTH OF THE CONSTITUTION IN EIGHTEENTH-CENTURY HUNGARIAN POLITICAL THOUGHT[1]

István M. Szijártó

This chapter seeks to explain the circumstances under which the idea of a Hungarian constitution was born in the eighteenth century, and to describe the historical moments that had a decisive impact in shaping the idea's evolution. To this end, a historical background is provided, one that highlights crucial long-term developments in Hungarian constitutional history, but that also outlines the structural contours of Hungarian politics in the nineteenth century and pays attention to Hungary's differences from the Habsburgs' other provinces. To begin, it seems convenient to take a well-known nineteenth-century fact as our starting point.

When Ferenc Deák presented his framework for the Austro-Hungarian Settlement on 16 April 1865, in his so-called Easter Article, he based his legal argument on the Pragmatic Sanction,[2] the solemn decree regulating the Habsburg succession to the throne, as accepted by the estates of Hungary at the Diet on 30 June 1722, and subsequently enacted as Articles 1–3 of Act 1723.[3] Deák did so despite the fact that earlier he took great pains to demonstrate the legal validity of the so-called April Laws of 1848 that thoroughly redefined the relationship of Hungary and its Habsburg king.[4] In political terms, however, he was completely right to take one step backwards and go back to 1722 to find a basis mutually acceptable both for Hungary and the Habsburg dynasty, for the appointment of an independent Hungarian government took place on 17 March 1848 under the direct influence of revolutions in Vienna and Pest.

The Pragmatic Sanction was, however, accepted by the estates of Hungary in 1722 without any second thoughts or resistance, in the optimistic political climate both of impending beneficial reforms prepared by the *Systematica Commissio* (1722) and, especially, of compromise; King Charles III (as Emperor Charles VI) was ready to guarantee noble rights. The Pragmatic Sanction was, first of all, a regulation determining the precedence of different successors of Leopold I to the throne, but also stipulated the 'indivisibility and inseparability' of Hungary and the other kingdoms and provinces of its Habsburg king.[5] It opened the way for Maria Theresa to ascend the throne of the kingdom of Hungary, as in 1687 the hereditary rule of the Habsburgs in Hungary had only been accepted for the male line of the dynasty.

This was an important step in the constitutional history of Hungary, bringing to an end the 150-year-long Ottoman occupation of the central territories of the country and the parallel existence of two Hungarian states: the kingdom of Hungary, ruled by the Habsburgs in the west and the north on the one hand, and the Ottoman vassal state of the Principality of Transylvania in the east on the other. As a result of the Ottomans' failure to take Vienna in 1683 and the serious defeat inflicted on them in open battle by the Christian coalition, Hungary was reconquered in the ensuing one and a half decades, and Transylvania was reincorporated under the Crown of St Stephen. The declaration by the Hungarian Diet in 1687 that it accepted the hereditary rule of the House of Habsburg in the male line, as well as renouncing the Hungarian estates' right to lawful resistance to their king, heralded a new era. The Pragmatic Sanction sealed this process.

But the constitutional and political conditions of eighteenth-century Hungary were not only set in the final years of the seventeenth century but also in the early eighteenth, especially by the war of independence led by Ferenc II Rákóczi (1703–11), triggered not by the self-defence of Protestants (mainly in Eastern Hungary) against the

Counter-Reformation, as was the case with the earlier Hungarian rebellions against the Habsburgs, but first of all by the overall dissatisfaction at the conditions created by the protracted war expelling the Ottomans (1683–99); the liberating imperial troops imposed a barely bearable burden for the populace on the one hand, and the political rights of the estates of Hungary were curtailed on the other – the rights of levying the *contributio*, the war tax, had been lost by them already in 1670 and also the nobility was taxed, as often but not always since 1526.

The Rákóczi rebellion was a fully fledged war of independence by Hungary, led by the greatest landowner of Hungary, Prince Ferenc II Rákóczi, elected Prince of Transylvania, and conducted in unofficial alliance with Louis XIV of France, waging the War of the Spanish Succession against the Habsburgs (1701–14). Although it ended in a military defeat with the country exhausted also by a severe plague, it still forced a conclusion on both parties involved: on the one hand it was a political reality that a dissatisfied Hungary could cause significant problems for the Habsburgs pursuing their dynastic interests in the West, and several imperial regiments had to be committed in Hungary while they were painfully missed in the main, Western theatre of war; on the other hand, the resources of Hungary were proved to be inadequate to attain full independence. Therefore, the Treaty of Szatmár (1711), which concluded the war, also stabilized the position of the Hungarian estates, restoring the earlier political structure in which the Crown and the estates were situated at two opposing poles of the field of politics.

This dualism was, by then, increasingly seen as an anachronism in the age of absolutism in Europe. Nevertheless, the Diet regained control over taxation, and noble elites (the aristocracy and gentry, in contrast to the masses of petty nobility) did not have to pay the *contributio* any more. Although the kings of Hungary were not elected, their coronation oaths and the *diploma inaugurale* issued by them before their coronation were still a result of bargaining with the Diet and conserved elements of the former *Wahlkapitulationen*.[6] Moreover, the estates preserved their monopoly on regional administration through the institution of the counties as well as significant rights in national administration and jurisdiction.

The Treaty of Szatmár was not just another of the many settlements in the long history of animosity between the Crown and the Hungarian nobility: it was the very cornerstone on which the status of Hungary in the Habsburg Empire had been constructed. Thus, Ferenc Deák saw it as advisable to reach back to it when the last important compromise, the settlement of 1867, was under construction. The settlement's importance is convincingly demonstrated by the fact that, in contrast to the kingdom of Bohemia, which elected Charles Albert, Elector of Bavaria, later Emperor Charles VII, as its king, Hungary stayed loyal to Maria Theresa in the War of the Austrian Succession (1740–8), saving her empire – or at least that was what Montesquieu claimed.[7]

The subsequent treatment of Hungary can partly be explained by Maria Theresa's sincere gratitude and partly by the sound insights of Viennese statesmen into the viability of the 1711 settlement. Thus, the kingdom of Hungary was excluded from the centralizing reforms enacted by Count Haugwitz, which sought to enhance Habsburg military power in order to reclaim Silesia from Prussia. In order to achieve this goal, taxation was reformed. Not only were more taxes collected from commoners, but also regular taxation was introduced for the clergy and the nobility. In addition, institutional changes bound the unreliable Czech provinces of the empire more closely to its core Austrian provinces.

In the long run, it is the Haugwitz reforms that can be identified as the beginning of the *Sonderweg* of Hungary within the Habsburg Monarchy, as Gyula Szekfű observed.[8] Hungary had always been a special case among the kingdoms and provinces of the empire but, from the mid-eighteenth century, these peculiarities took the form of a new political structure completely different from the rest of the Habsburg Empire. The establishment of the dual monarchy of Austria–Hungary in 1867 reflected this difference more than a century later. Hungary's distinctiveness within the empire can also be traced back to its separate system of counties, a regional organization of noble self-government, which served as the local representatives of the state. Peter Dickson pointed out that while the Diet could be ignored (until 1792, it was convoked only eight times after 1687, and not once between 1765 and 1790), the counties could not be bypassed. Thus, while the other provinces of the empire were administered by bureaucrats, Hungary was run by nobles.[9] R.J.W. Evans, moreover, suggests that this county administration, and its political expression in the Lower Chamber of the Diet through the county deputies, was an effective rival to the centrally appointed royal administration which transmitted imperial policy into Hungary. Political struggles in Hungary can therefore be interpreted as a battle between these two administrations.[10]

Taxes and Compromises

The political chessboard of Hungary had three characteristic arrangements in the eighteenth century; the first decades were markedly different from the bulk of the century, while its final years saw the emergence of a completely new pattern. The sessions of the Diet were roiled by religious debates in the 1710s and 1720s, culminating in the hefty clashes between Catholics and Protestants in 1729. In all these debates, the political game of the seventeenth century was turned around. While Hungarian Protestants were a majority and formed the backbone of anti-Habsburg resistance in the seventeenth century, by the eighteenth, reduced to a minority among the estates, they were often forced to look for support from Vienna, from the tolerant Charles III and especially from the almighty Prince Eugene of Savoy. On the other hand, Hungarian Catholics evoked the estates' privileges in their efforts to pursue a more severe Counter-Reformation. Tensions between the two denominations caused the religious question to be regulated by royal arbitration, with the so-called *Carolina Resolutio* (1731) even forbidding religious matters from being put before the Diet. Curiously, this also resulted in a swift agreement between the estates that bridged the denominational divide as representatives of all denominations formed a unified front against the Crown in Hungarian politics. Thus, the dualist model of king and estates can best characterize the political climate of Hungary in the mid-eighteenth century. In these decades, the question of the contribution and the extent of the nobility's privileges was central to politics, helping Catholics and Protestants to work together for both (what they perceived to be) the national interest and the interests of the aristocracy and the gentry.

In contrast to the situation in most of the sixteenth and seventeenth centuries, when noble taxpaying was the rule, the eighteenth century was characterized by the tax immunity of the nobility. This tax immunity did not, however, extend to the masses of the petty nobility; for the taxing of the group of *armalistae* see §4 of Article 6 of the Law of 1723, and for the taxing of other petty nobles see e.g. the practice of the

County of Somogy in the 1720s.[11] All strata of the nobility also helped fund the occasional *subsidia*, offered voluntarily by the Diet – although this occurred infrequently in the eighteenth century. Thus, it was only partial tax immunity. Nevertheless, it was certainly the most dearly held privilege of the Hungarian political class in the eighteenth century, and it was under threat from enlightened absolutistic rulers, who regarded this as an infringement on the common good.

The other constant topic of politics in this period was the extent of the annual *contributio*, paid by the *misera plebs contribuens*, masses of peasantry and other commoner taxpayers, but determined by the Diet. The Rákóczi rebellion had won back this right for the estates, and its form from 1722 was the following: after lengthy bargaining with the Crown, the Diet offered an increase in the existing *contributio*, which was then collected annually until Crown and Diet again agreed to a further increase. When the amount of Hungary's contribution over the entire period is considered, it becomes clear that the Rákóczi rebellion not only won back – albeit incomplete – control over taxation for the estates and secured their immunity from the most onerous taxes that had been imposed on the landed nobility in the seventeenth century, but it also won much lower taxes for the *misera plebs contribuens*. Their contribution fell from 3–4 million forints at the turn of the century to 1.5–2 million forints in the years after the conclusion of the Treaty of Szatmár. For the Crown, it took more than half a century of bargaining with the estates to return the annual *contributio* to the level it had reached around 1700.[12] The amount of the *contributio* clearly reflected the development of the power relationship between the estates and the Crown in Hungary. The Rákóczi war of independence won a very strong position for the estates, which was then gradually eroded up to the 1780s. The upheavals of the international position of the Habsburg Empire brought only temporary changes in this respect, for example in 1740/1 and in 1789/90.

In the meantime, however, a restructuring took place within the camp of the estates that was clearly reflected in the institutional development of the Diet, especially in the relationship of the two houses of the Diet, the development of the so-called *sessio circularis* and that of the voting procedures. The Lower Chamber, mostly composed of the deputies of the counties, royal free boroughs and ecclesiastical bodies, came to dominate the Upper Chamber, composed largely of bishops and magnates, while within the Lower Chamber itself, county deputies got the upper hand. The unofficial sessions of the *sessio circularis* developed into the main decision making foci by 1790, and in the Lower House, representatives of the clergy and the royal free boroughs were reduced to one block vote each. While the Hungarian estates were led by the aristocracy in the early eighteenth century, at the Diet of 1790/1 the well-to-do gentry, the *bene possessionati*, obtained the upper hand. This change was a manifestation of a broader social trend, for the growing influence of the *bene possessionati* had first become evident in the county assemblies before making itself felt in national politics.

The Diet of 1728/9 was a turning point not only in the relationship of the Upper and the Lower Houses. It was at this Diet that the authority of the aristocracy was publicly challenged for the first time and the *bene possessionati* launched their protracted but ultimately irresistible takeover. This Diet, with its heated confessional debates, also served as a milestone which marked the closing of the age of confessionalism in Hungarian politics and the beginning of the period in which constitutionalism became its dominant theme.

The Diets of 1751 and 1764/5 brought increasing tension with the Crown, because, to Maria Theresa's growing dissatisfaction, her proposals for the introduction of noble taxation were rejected. Increasingly, the defence of noble privileges, the stubborn resistance to raising the annual contribution, as well as the conservation of different elements of the political system, were, under the direct influence of Montesquieu, interpreted by Hungarians as defending the constitution of Hungary. This reinterpretation of what had hitherto been termed the customs, rights and privileges of the country, and was now termed a constitution, entailed the increasingly strong conviction that its defence was a question of principle rather than of interests that could be the subject of political bargaining. In practice, this meant a gradually accelerating erosion of that capacity for compromise that had been so important for the Hungarian political elite to manage political conflicts, thus bringing us to the final phase of the constitutional history of eighteenth-century Hungary.

Comparing eighteenth-century coronations, Ákos Barcsay has convincingly demonstrated that in these key situations there was always evidence of both a need for compromise and a potential to reach it.[13] Various tendencies in the late eighteenth century, however, clearly reduced this potential and increased the chance of open confrontation between the estates and the Crown of Hungary. The high office-holders of Hungary, the group situated at a crucial juncture in the political system as members of the government and entrusted by the Crown, resided in Vienna, but were still linked by a myriad of ties to the Hungary of the estates, and had fewer chances to work successfully towards a compromise.

Ruling uncrowned and without calling a Diet, Joseph II tried to impose enlightened reforms on Hungary. Among others, he abolished the autonomy of the counties, introduced German as the official language and made preparations towards introducing a general land tax abolishing noble tax immunity. When he died in 1790 and his regime collapsed, the high office-holders of Hungary successfully forged a settlement to resolve a potentially dangerous situation. The estates of Hungary sought to exploit the death of Joseph II to restructure politics and acquire a position vis-à-vis the Crown comparable to the privileges enjoyed by their Polish counterparts, but they were forced back to reality and accepted a settlement with Leopold II. The pendulum returned to a middle position after Joseph II's unconstitutional rule and after the spring of 1790, when the estates of Hungary imagined that they would be able to rewrite the country's constitution.

The Constitution and the Common Good

Following the removal of denominational disputes from the agenda of the Diet, and after their place was occupied by debates about the size of the *contributio* and the nobility's immunity from taxation, the *bene possessionati* took the leading role among the estates. Thus, after 1764, a demand for a certain kind of constitutionalism gradually came to the forefront of Hungarian parliamentary politics. This solidified into a new pattern on the chessboard of politics at the very end of the eighteenth century, characteristic of what was to follow in the first half of the nineteenth century. In this new pattern, politics was gradually polarized, characterized less by a willingness to compromise and more by conflicts. The incessant enumeration of grievances by the Hungarian estates became a fruitless way of doing politics, scornfully termed *sérelmi politika* by contemporary liberals, the 'politics of grievance', accompanied by constant references to the *ősi alkotmány*, Hungary's 'ancient constitution'.

Later, this focus on constitutional issues in politics became the core of the so-called *közjogi kérdés*, the problem of public law, which was dominated by the questions of Hungary's intergration into the Habsburg Empire, and it went on dominating Hungarian politics up to the end of World War I.

The new obsession with constitutionalism in Hungarian politics was the result of a reinterpretation of earlier problems such as the size of the yearly *contributio*, the extent of the nobility's immunity from taxation, and the intertwining question of the reform of the obsolete noble levy (as the Crown repeatedly intended to replace this by a regular army paid by the privileged) as constitutional questions. This reinterpretation was evidently reinforced by Joseph II's reforms, which affected the whole social–political order, and upset the complete constitution of the estates, but the roots of this reinterpretation can be found in earlier politics. In general terms, the influence of the Enlightenment was important in Hungary, while the impact of Montesquieu's ideas was decisive. He saw the Diet at work in 1728, then wrote about the Hungarian estates in very favourable terms. As a result, his *The Spirit of the Laws*, published in 1748, became very popular in Hungary. This book was the reason why the system of rights and privileges came to be interpreted in Hungary as a constitution. To quote László Péter, the Hungarian nobility 'discovered, not unlike Molière's burgher who learnt that he was speaking "prose", that what they possessed was a "constitution" rather than just a collection of customary rights'.[14]

It was at the end of the eighteenth century, as a result of this slow development, that the concept of a constitution came to play the central role in Hungarian history throughout the nineteenth century. József Takáts quotes Henrik Marczali, who 'makes a very important point, namely that the political language of referring to the ancient constitution, as we know it from the political texts emanating from the first half of the nineteenth century, was in use only from the late eighteenth century'. Earlier, texts simply spoke about rights, privileges, laws; *constitutio* as a complete building appears only from Joseph II's rule.[15] As Barna Mezey observed, the expression of *sarkalatos törvények*, the fundamental laws, is replaced by 'constitution' in Article 10 of the Law of 1791 for the first time.[16] Similarly, among the instructions issued by the County of Somogy to its deputies in the eighteenth century, the

The Birth of the Constitution

first to include the term 'constitution' was only issued in 1790.[17] It was only then that this term first appeared in the ceremonial speeches; and it was two years later that the term was used at the beginning of the Diet by the Chancellor, who presented royal propositions, and by the Archbishop, who received these in the name of the estates of Hungary. Archbishop József Batthyány, head of the Catholic Church in Hungary, called it a principal task of the incipient Diet to uphold the 'ancient constitution'. Half a page was consecrated in the published protocol of the proceedings of the Lower House to the speech given by the *personalis* József Ürményi, chairman of the Royal Court of Justice, also Speaker of the Lower House of the Diet. In this short text, the word 'constitution' features on no less than four occasions.[18]

An overview of the vocabulary of eighteenth-century political texts is also instructive on another point too. The secularized interpretation of the common good became a central point of reference for early modern monarchs inspired by Machiavelli and Jean Bodin. The ideal king of enlightened absolutism was one who not only ruled by the grace of God, but who also served his country. R.J.W. Evans claimed that the dominance of the Catholic Church was, from the 1740s, replaced by this variation of patriotism based on the common good (*allgemeines Wohlsein, das allgemeine Beste*) as the official ideology of the state. Theoreticians such as Karl Anton Martini and Joseph von Sonnenfels encouraged the teaching of these ideas in schools, and Leibniz's ideas were propagated by Christian Wolff. It was central to Martini's and Sonnenfels's thinking that the monarch represented the common good.[19]

State councillor Baron Egid von Borié insisted that the rights of the enlightened ruler were based on attaining the common good, and the common good was also emphasized when the estates of Hungary were put under pressure to make concessions and give up certain rights.[20] In the camp of the Hungarian estates, it was through the high office-holders that the concept of the common good was promulgated. For example, József Ürményi and Sándor Pászthory considered the laws of Hungary (but not its fundamental laws) modifiable in the interests of the common good.[21] From the correspondence of the latter with Count György Festetich a fully fledged concept emerges, stating that it is the common good that has to be served.[22]

The common good had, however, always been present in the other half of the field of Hungarian politics, too. The basic structure of the political language used by the estates in Hungary was shaped by classical republicanism, in which the common good had always featured prominently, as a positive counterpoint to (supposedly negative) private interests. By the late eighteenth century, however, the new interpretation of the common good by proponents of enlightened absolutism was accepted by the estates as well.[23] It is not without relevance that although the concept of the common good offered a firm basis for cooperation between enlightened absolutism and the estates of Hungary, this potential was never explored. Although representatives of the Hungarian estates, and especially those who held high offices, repeatedly referred to the common good in the second half of the eighteenth century, by the end of the century the stress shifted in the sphere of the values of republicanism from the common good to the ideal of liberty, understood as participation in public affairs.

This process happened in parallel with the growing tensions between the absolutist government and the estates, who redefined their rights and privileges as the constitution of Hungary. The language of classical republicanism was, therefore, complemented by references to the ancient constitution. This alteration fit perfectly with the defence of privileges, and was barely compatible with the concept of the common good. The political language of the ancient constitution was, basically, a distorted eighteenth-century Hungarian version of the political language of classical republicanism. It expressed the full opposition to the enlightened government, which monopolized the representation of the common good. Thus, Hungarian noblemen, and in particular the *bene possessionati*, who had obtained a dominant position in Hungarian politics, adjusted the Roman virtues learned at school and subsequently internalized them to conform to the social realities of their world.

Nation and Confrontation

The political speeches of the late eighteenth century also reveal how how these ideas developed and how these elements solidified into a new pattern of confrontational politics in Hungary.

Following the example of revolutionary France, the County of Szabolcs demanded a solemn oath from its *supremus comes* as well as his would-be deputies to the Diet in 1790, who were to represent the county in the Upper and the Lower House respectively. It contained a pledge to stand for the country and its rights and to renounce all government favours.[24] The oath is, however, more remarkable for the fact that the deputies and the *supremus comes* swore allegiance first to the 'free Hungarian nation' (*szabad magyar nemzet*) and only thereafter to the king. The nation was assumed, at least in the text of the oath, to possess complete legislative powers – without reference to the king, who actually shared this power with the estates of Hungary at the Diet, and the *regnum*, the country here renamed as the 'nation'. This was a reinterpretation of far-reaching consequences; while non-Hungarians could be members of the *regnum*, with the birth of linguistic nationalism they felt increasingly excluded from the nation – and from power, too. The term constitution did not, however, find its way into the text written in the spring of 1790; the customary term of 'fundamental laws and privileges' of Hungary was used.

The oath also demanded that the representatives of the County of Szabolcs in the Diet subordinate private to public interests, according to the republican understanding of the common good, and also barred them from accepting public office and other government favours. This latter demand is revealing of the worldview of the nobility of Szabolcs, or rather of the *bene possessionati* who were active in politics; they regarded national politics as a confrontation between two sides rather than as cooperation between the Crown and the estates. As, for most of the eighteenth century, a primary objective of county deputies to the Diet was being appointed to a royal office,[25] entailing both salary and power, this was a drastic change. So much so that this stipulation of the oath was supplemented with a clause: offices could still be accepted so long as the estates consented. Finally, the oath envisaged that the necessary agreement to reach the common good would occur 'among the patriots'. The role of the Crown was left unmentioned, as was the case where the oath discussed legislation. While this latter omission did not correspond to the realities of politics, the exclusion of the monarch from the Hungarian nation was to become a significant fact of politics in half a century.

When the Diet was finally opened, most of the deputies took an oath which was a milder and more detailed version of the one drawn up by the County of Szabolcs.[26] It served, first of all, to ensure that members of the Diet would not cross over to the side of the Crown in any clash with the Diet. It did not merely exclude the monarch from formulating legislation, it completely forgot about the competencies of the Crown — there is simply no mention of the monarch in the oath at all. Unlike in the oath formula of the County of Szabolcs, the sensitive question was evaded whether loyalty should be pledged to the crowned king only, to the ruler who had taken an oath to preserve the rights and privileges of Hungary. This was a burning issue loaded with significance after the nine-year rule of Joseph II, who was never crowned king of Hungary and who, accordingly, never issued a coronation diploma and never took an oath that would require him to conserve the political system of Hungary; and after the attempts of some leading representatives of the estates of Hungary who had invited a foreign prince to seize the throne.[27] Similarly to the Szabolcs County oath, the constitution was not mentioned in this oath either, but the concept of the nation was also omitted and the *regnum* continued to be used as the official term for the country.

The political climate of the eighteenth century is best characterized by the fact that the counties were represented at the Diet in large numbers by royal office-holders, members of the Royal Court of Justice, the Lieutenancy Council, the Hungarian Chamber or other offices and courts of law. Although these were royal offices, the central court of justice, the main royal governing body and the central organ of economic administration, no conflict of interest was seen here. As, however, politics became increasingly confrontational, not only the estates aspired to draw clear borderlines around their political camp, for example by using oaths like those referred to earlier, but also the government took steps to bar office-holders from appearing at the Diet as deputies who were increasingly viewed less as partners, and more as adversaries. In December 1791, a decree was issued which forbade royal officials from being elected as deputies to the Diet unless they had preliminary royal assent. This measure was meant to prevent councillors of the Lieutenancy Council, such as Imre Beöthy and József Vay, or the mayor of the royal free borough of Debrecen, Lajos Domokos, from being elected as deputies to the coming Diet — all prominent leaders of the opposition.[28]

Although the radicalization provoked by the French Revolution and the outbreak of the war against revolutionary France caused strains in the relationship between the estates and the Crown, and the retaliation following the failed Jacobin conspiracy led by Ignác Martinovics established an atmosphere of fear, there is evidence that the concept of politics as crystallized in 1790 was preserved. In 1796, Pál Czindery, *substitutus vicecomes* of the County of Somogy, was elected as a deputy to the coming Diet in place of the *supremus comes*'s official candidate. This was a direct result of his speech, in which he suggested that the deputies should be instructed to present all of the grievances of Hungary to Francis I – while his letter of invitation named the *subsidium*, the extraordinary tax to be paid by the privileged and intended to help the war against France, as the sole subject which would be addressed by the Diet.[29] Within a fortnight, Francis I invalidated Czindery's election as one of the two deputies of the County of Somogy and instructed the county to elect another in his place. Finally, a single deputy represented Somogy at the Diet, but when even he tried to argue for Czindery's innocence and advocate his acceptance as a deputy, the estates turned a deaf ear to him and avoided conflict with the Crown.[30]

In his scandalous speech that provoked the retribution of the Crown, the *subsitutus vicecomes* defended the Hungarian constitution, without using this term. He protested against the idea that a Diet could serve exclusively as a means to provide the Crown with the necessary finances, without demanding remedies for the country's grievances. Czindery clearly regarded politics as confrontation; the Hungarian estates should grasp the opportunity, he argued, to exploit the dire situation of Francis I to find lawful redress – and he presented a long list of the government's unlawful measures. He suggested that the Diet help the King, but on condition that a deadline was set for the redress of grievances, when the Diet should convene automatically, without royal convocation, four years after a future peace treaty had been signed with France.

Czindery insisted on the independence of Hungary, that its particular political system should be recognized, and, as a part of this, that the estates' political rights should be conserved. The implication was also that if the Crown wanted something from Hungary, it should offer something in return. But, tellingly, for him, the king's partner in this *tractatus diaetalis* was not the country, but the nation. A conspicuous characteristic of the speech is the frequent use of the word 'Hungarian', or 'the Hungarians'. For the *substitutus vicecomes*, the twin poles of politics were not the king and the *regnum*, but the king and the Hungarians or 'king and nation'. Although Czindery claims that these are not two contrasting loyalties, this theoretical possibility is encoded into his thinking – to become a political reality within decades.

It is the marked confrontation, characteristic of this speech, that must have induced the violent reaction of the King and his government in Vienna. Czindery spoke in terms of a zero-sum game, in which Hungarians could only win something if they took it from their monarch. The enthusiastic support the *substitutus vicecomes* of Somogy won for himself at the general assembly of his county testified to this fact. The attention the estates paid to their constitution had rearranged the way politics was understood in Hungary. This concept was, then, bequeathed to the nineteenth century.

Specific factors led, therefore, to the restoration and subsequent consolidation of the duality of Crown and estates in Hungary in the first half of the eighteenth century, while the second half of it brought an increasing polarization of politics, when also the cornerstones of Hungarian politics, earlier referred to as customs, rights and privileges, were more and more frequently referred to as 'constitution'. Confrontational politics was to be the mark of Hungarian noble opposition from the end of the eighteenth century, and the ancient constitution of the country was to be on its flag.

Notes

1. The author would like to acknowledge the financial assistance of the project NKFI K 116166.
2. György Szabad, 'Az önkényuralom kora (1849–1867)', in E. Kovács and L. Katus (eds), *Magyarország története, 1848–1890* (Budapest, 1979), p. 736.
3. Kálmán Benda (ed.), *Magyarország történeti kronológiája*, vol. II (Budapest, 1982), pp. 559–60. Cf. Dezső Márkus (ed.), *Magyar törvénytár Vol. iv: [Az] 1657–1740. évi törvényczikkek* (Budapest, 1900).
4. Ferenc Deák, *Adalék a magyar közjoghoz. Észrevételek Lustkandl Vencel munkájára: "Das ungarisch-österreichische Staatsrecht" a magyar közjog történelmének szempontjából* (Pest, 1865). Cf. Szabad, 'Az önkényuralom kora', p. 731.
5. Győző Ember, 'Magyarország a Habsburg birodalomban', in Gy. Ember and G. Heckenast (eds), *Magyarország története, 1686–1790* (Budapest, 1989), pp. 382–5; Győző Ember, 'Az országgyűlések', in Gy. Ember and G. Heckenast (eds), *Magyarország története, 1686–1790* (Budapest, 1989), p. 404.
6. From 1387, rulers usually promised in writing before their coronation that they would keep the constitution of Hungary. This *Wahlkapitulation* took the form of the *diploma inaugurale* later, which was enacted as an article of the king's first *decretum* from the time of Ferdinand II.
7. Montesquieu, *Esprits des lois*, book viii, chapter ix.

8. Bálint Hóman and Gyula Szekfű, *Magyar történet*, 5 vols (Budapest, 1935), vol. IV, p. 510.
9. Peter Dickson, 'Monarchy and bureaucracy in late eighteenth century Austria', *The English Historical Review* cx (1995), p. 350.
10. A statement formulated originally for the period 1790–1848 by R.J.W. Evans, *Austria, Hungary and the Habsburgs. Essays on Central Europe, c. 1683–1867* (Oxford, 2006), p. 183.
11. István M. Szijártó, *Nemesi társadalom és politika. Tanulmányok a 18. századi magyar rendiségről* (Budapest, 2006), p. 157.
12. István M. Szijártó, 'The Rákóczi revolt as a successful rebellion', in L. Péter and M. Rady (eds), *Resistance, Rebellion and Revolution in Hungary and Central Europe: Commemorating 1956* (London, 2008), pp. 71–3.
13. Ákos Barcsay, *Herrschaftsantritt im Ungarn des 18. Jahrhunderts. Studien zur Verhältnis zwischen Krongewalt und Ständetum im Zeitalter des Absolutismus* (St Katharinen, 2002), pp. 267–75.
14. Miklós Lojkó (ed.), *Hungary's Long Nineteenth Century. Constitutional and Democratic Traditions in a European Perspective. Collected Studies of László Péter* (Leiden and Boston, MA, 2012), p. 156.
15. József Takáts, 'Magyar politikai beszédmódok a XIX. század elején. A keret', in M. Szajbély (ed.), *Mesterek, tanítványok. Ünnepi tanulmánykötet Csetri Lajos tiszteletére* (Budapest, 1999), pp. 231–2.
16. Barna Mezey, 'Jogalkotás a 16–19. századi Magyarországon', *Rubicon* vii/1–2 (1996).
17. Gyula Melhárd, *Somogyvármegye a rendi országgyűléseken I. 1661–1812* (Veszprém, 1906), p. 60; István M. Szijártó, *A diéta. A magyar rendek és az országgyűlés, 1708–1792* (Budapest, 2005), pp. 388–91.
18. István M. Szijártó, *A 18. századi Magyarország rendi országgyűlése* (Budapest, 2016), pp. 156, 198–200.
19. Győző Concha, *A kilenczvenes évek reformeszméi és előzményeik. Irodalomtörténeti vázlat* (Budapest, 1885), pp. 10–11, 15–16.
20. Ferenc Strada, 'Izdenczy József, az Államtanács első magyar tagja', *A Gróf Klebelsberg Kunó Magyar Történetkutató Intézet Évkönyve* x (1940), p. 60.
21. Ambrus Miskolczy, *Kazinczy Ferenc útja a nyelvújítástól a politikai megújulásig. I. Orpheus világában, avagy a magyar demokratikus politikai kultúra kezdetei* (Budapest, 2009), p. 50.
22. György Kurucz, 'Kényszer és szolgálat. Portrévázlat Festetics Györgyről', *Századok* cxl/6 (2006), p. 1350.
23. Concha, *A kilenczvenes évek*, p. 35; Géza Ballagi, *A politikai irodalom Magyarországon 1825-ig* (Budapest, 1888), pp. 726–7.
24. Quoted by Éva Kujbusné Mecsei, 'Az 1790–91-es diétai történések a szabolcsi követjelentések tükrében', *Szabolcs-Szatmár-Beregi Levéltári Évkönyv* xii (1997), p. 124.

25. István M. Szijártó, 'Emberek és struktúrák a 18. századi Magyarországon. A politikai elit társadalom- és kultúrtörténeti megközelítésben', DSc dissertation, Budapest, 2017. Manuscript.
26. *Naponként-való jegyzései az 1790dik eztendőben felséges IIdik Leopold tsászár, és magyar országi király által, szabad királyi várossába Budára, Szent Jakab havának 6dik napjára rendelt, 's Szent András havának 3dik napjára Posony királyi várossába által-tétetett, 's ugyan ott, következő 1791dik esztendőben böjt-más havának 13dik napján bé-fejezett magyar ország gyűlésének; mellyek eredet-képen magyar nyelven írattattak, és az ország gyűlésének fő-vigyázása alatt, hitelesen deák nyelvre fordíttattak* (Buda, 1791), pp. 63–4.
27. Robert Gragger, *Preussen, Weimar und die ungarische Königskrone* (Berlin and Leipzig, 1923).
28. Anita Kiss, János Nagy and Adrienn Kapitány (eds), *Pest-Pilis-Solt vármegye országgyűlési követutasításai a 18. században* (Budapest, 2015), p. 149.
29. *Dictio d[omini] v[ice] Comitis Pauli Czindery in generali congregatione comitatus Simighiensis habita 20 octobris 1796 in oppido Kaposvár*. A Magyar Nemzeti Levéltár Győr-Sopron Megyei Levéltára, Soproni Levéltár XIII. 11. A felsőbüki Nagy család levéltára, Box 6. Felsőbüki Nagy József iratai.
30. Ede Reiszig, 'Somogy vármegye története', in D. Csánki (ed.), *Somogy vármegye* (Budapest, s.d. [1914]), pp. 501–2.

CHAPTER 4

RESURRECTING THE PAST, RESHAPING THE FUTURE: THE RISE OF THE 'ANCIENT CONSTITUTION' AT THE DIET OF 1790/1

Philip Barker

There is a teasing imprecision about the phrase the 'ancient constitution', as it tends to suggest the existence of a 'fixed' constitution, as well as a Golden Age of liberty and constitutional perfection that prevailed in the distant past.[1] Certainly, this must have appeared to be the case to many of the nobles who argued for the restitution of ancient laws in late eighteenth-century Hungary. But as Henrik Marczali observes, even the abstract use of the term *constitutio* and its translations to refer to an overarching 'body' of laws (as opposed to individual decrees, edicts and privileges) was itself a rhetorical innovation in late eighteenth-century Hungary, one that was inspired by two key factors. The first was news from revolutionary France, where the National Assembly had called itself a *constituante* assembly, and promised not to disperse until a new 'constitution' had been established. The second was the whirlwind of political reform during the reign of Joseph II that saw a fresh understanding of domestic laws as constituting a 'whole, a work of creation'; this had 'only became apparent to the nobility after Joseph had attacked not just individual laws, but all of them in their entirety'.[2]

Marczali's observations are correct, although in response to Joseph's tumultuous programme of reform Hungarian nobles had also been looking elsewhere, in particular to England, for 'constitutional' ideas. Furthermore, Marczali conflates two distinct abstract meanings of the term 'constitution' that existed – both in Hungary and elsewhere – before and after the French revolutionary break. The first, earlier sense referred in a broad, descriptive manner to the overall 'state' or 'condition' of a country as determined by its population, geographical conditions and division of power, including the various 'fundamental' or 'cardinal' laws that determined its basic socio-political structure. This was not an explicit reference to the laws themselves, but rather a 'body politic' metaphor that foregrounded how a polity – much like a human body – possessed a particular form of 'physical disposition' or socio-political 'character'. The second understanding of the term 'constitution' involved a more clearly normative vision of law, one that became associated with the tenets of the written constitutions of America and later France. Here, the constitution was a comprehensive set of higher legal norms that were conveniently embodied in a single document. Such constitutions, specifically designed to establish and regulate public power, did not merely emanate from the whim of a ruler, but from an authority outside and above the order they established. This authority was the 'people', whose ratification was required to legitimate the constitution itself. Legislation was thus intended to be reflexive: the will of the people was to bind government by regulating its creation and application of laws, laws that in turn bound the people to specific commitments and obligations. Thus, when in *Common Sense* Thomas Paine stated that 'in America the law is king'[3] he was claiming that law was prior to government and that it constrained the caprices of self-interested, momentarily empowered rulers. Furthermore, this law was not the 'common law' so often touted by judges; nor was it a body of purportedly unchanging and universal moral principles known as 'natural law'. Rather, it derived from a combination of what Paine considered to be democratic and republican principles: democratic in that the law was expressed by representatives who acted upon the will of the people, and republican in that they acted unswervingly toward the common good of *all* people.[4] Inspired by thinkers such as Locke, Montesquieu, Rousseau, Voltaire and Beccaria, the American constitution was for Paine, as it was for many, the culmination of 'a revolution in the principles and practice of government'.[5]

But while the written American and French constitutions – symbols of popular liberation and revolution – came to represent a radical break with the ideals of tradition and the political realities of the *ancien régime*, it was from roughly the turn of the 1780s–90s that the Hungarian nobility began to speak of an *ősi alkotmány* ('ancient constitution'),[6] a term that not only looked to the past rather than to the future, but that also survived to become a 'master noun' in the political rhetoric of the nineteenth century and beyond, despite there being no universally agreed-upon definition of its tenets.[7] This leads us to a third kind of understanding of the 'constitution', which was also common in seventeenth- and eighteenth-century Europe and the English colonies.[8] To refer to an 'ancient constitution' was not to blandly refer to the overall 'composition' or 'disposition' of the body politic (e.g. as a 'monarchy', 'oligarchy' or 'aristocracy'); nor was it to foreground the creation of a novel political order. Rather, it was to invoke the existence of a collection of traditional laws, practices and institutions that had supposedly evolved in a continuous process, and that derived their authority from sheer antiquity and the presumed wisdom of long-standing conventions.[9] Indeed, the language of ancient constitutionalism was often based upon a customary vision of law that emphasized how certain legal practices and arrangements were so long-established that they could be considered as the 'nature' of a given community. The ancient constitutional 'vision' thus resembled an evolutionary model of the early 'body politic' concept: local practices established over time formed the identity of the polity in the same way that one's past development and physical make-up comprised one's overall 'constitution'.[10]

Thus, to talk of an 'ancient constitution' was not merely to theorize about the historical past. By idealizing the antiquity of laws and the desirability of continuity over time, the idea of an 'ancient constitution' also presented a vision for a constitution in the present, one that was characterized as resting upon desirable ancient foundations, and that was therefore to be preserved – or indeed reconstructed – for the benefit of the polity. And it is in this aspect of ancient constitutional thinking that we may discern one of its key normative – and potentially polemical – features. Because, it was argued, customary law had been tried and tested over vast periods of time, it embodied a form of enduring, communal wisdom that could not be rivalled by any single man, legislator, or indeed generation. Following this assumption, it could be argued that ancient laws constituted a form of authority that was both *antecedent* and morally *superior* to the authority of certain claimants to power and right – such as monarchs, who claimed the 'divine' right to rule. From this perspective, 'ancient constitutional' reasoning provided a convenient theory of resistance for those who saw the rule of absolutist monarchs (or indeed powerful legislative bodies) as being high-handed and unjust. Indeed, proponents of the 'ancient constitution' often identified exercises of royal power or state centralization as novel or artificial 'innovations' that ran contrary to the wisdom of ancient custom. In doing so, they sought to delegitimize new rulings as undesirable or illegal encroachments upon the historically accrued rights and privileges of certain individuals and corporate groups in the pre-modern state. These 'ancient' rights were of course not universal in scope; nor were they codified in a single written document. They were rather evidenced by a wealth of evolved institutional practices, customs, feudal oaths, as well as written agreements, charters and codes, some of which were described at political assemblies as 'fundamental' or 'cardinal' laws.[11]

This leads us to a perplexing difficulty of the common law understanding of the 'ancient constitution': because in their idealized form customary rights were enjoyed through the durability of long-standing practices as opposed to the dictates of positive law, they were only rarely, or partially, codified in written legislation. One upshot of this was that proponents of 'ancient constitutionalist' arguments often became engaged in the self-consciously antiquarian study of law in the attempt to demonstrate the ancient provenance of certain practices or customs. This would in the long run contribute to the increased sense of historicity that played a vital role in the formation of modern nationalisms. But when engaging with their histories, writers did not always seek to prove the reasonableness of their assertions as modern historians do in the light of suitable evidence. Rather, speculative interpretations of the past were pressed into the service of present concerns, and imagined histories were often skilfully blended with verifiable historical fact in the creation of potent – if highly contestable – medieval and ancient mythologies. Thus, instead of denoting a coherent philosophy, the idea of an 'ancient constitution' could serve up a wealth of *a posteriori* justifications for a variety of political positions, in addition to the common argument that the powerful were obliged to respect ancient laws.

The applications of ancient constitutionalist rhetoric in late eighteenth-century Hungary share many of the above features. At the Diet of 1790/1, for example, the component elements of the 'ancient constitution' were often claimed to be *gyökeres törvények* (lit. 'rooted' or 'radical laws', often to translate *leges fundamentales*), and *sarkallatos törvények* (*leges cardinales*).[12] Characterized as rulings of time-worn provenance, these were often decrees or high-level legal pacts that had emerged, however forcibly, through negotiations between monarchs and estates in the bipolar, dualist system of rule. Often, these ancient laws were further characterized using organic metaphors: for example, the above conceptualization of the law as a 'rooted', 'living' entity, bound to the soil of the realm, not only suggested an 'evolutionary', rather than 'revolutionary', idealization of legal development, but also implied a conceptual opposition between the 'indigenous' laws of the Hungarian kingdom, and the royal court's 'foreign' and man-made 'innovations'. Thus it could be suggested that foreign and 'artificially' imposed legislation of the king threatened the 'injury' or 'death' of the 'natural' constitutional organism, and with it the irreversible collapse of the political order. A complementary organic metaphor was that of the nobility's *sérelmek* (literally 'injuries', translated from Latin *gravamina*, this term is often rendered as 'grievances' in English); this underpinned the restitutive character of legal negotiations at the Diet by suggesting that damage had occurred to an individual or corporative 'body', and that the situation was to be remedially addressed through negotiation with the king.

However, while some of the 'ancient' laws that campaigners referred to were indeed archaic, others were more recent innovations, and none were anywhere definitively listed or codified.[13] Furthermore, the ancient constitutional model did not merely support the rights of the nobility, as it was based upon the dualist, monarchical system of rule, whereby power was shared between king and country (*ország*, 'country', but also 'nobility').[14] In this way, the 'ancient constitution' could also be seen to include a number of historical legislative developments that enshrined the rights of monarchs. This created much wiggle room for lawyers and political activists to sift through the *Corpus Juris* and other legal compendiums and retroactively select different laws – often in line with their particular politico-legal outlooks – as central elements of the 'ancient constitution'. In light of the above considerations, the remainder of this chapter will illustrate some of the broad deployments and trajectories of 'ancient constitutional' rhetoric at the Diet of 1790/1, with a particular emphasis on the polemical uses of history in the era's political interactions.

The Ancient Constitution versus Josephinian Absolutism

A key work that spurred thinking on how certain laws influenced the overall 'constitution' or character of the Hungarian body politic was Montesquieu's De l'esprit des lois.[15] Paying attention to the interrelatedness and development of socio-political phenomena, Montesquieu famously argued that undermining groups or institutions that constrained monarchical power, such as the nobility, would not actually strengthen a monarchy, but rather transform it into an unstable and abhorrent form of 'despotism'.[16] This, along with Montesquieu's expression of sympathy for the Hungarian nobility in their struggle against Habsburg oppression, inspired the Hungarian estates to cite De l'esprit in defence of their noble privileges during the years of Joseph II's reign.[17] Furthermore, in lauding the 'balanced' English model of government, Montesquieu's idea of divided powers seemed only to justify the separation of king and Diet outlined – inter alia – in the Golden Bull of 1222 and Werbőczy's Tripartitum, cornerstones of traditional customary law that were seen to parallel English constitutional structures, and that would soon be claimed as pillars of the newly coined, but historically conceived, 'ancient constitution'. Following these ideas, references to an 'ancient constitution' could serve to legitimate the separation of powers between the king and the Hungarian Diet, as well as the nobility's right to participate in legislation and the resolution of gravamina. Re-establishing these phenomena as political realities would, however, involve the 'restoration' of the constitutional organism to its pre-Josephinian condition.

Indeed, thus conceived as a customarily evolved body politic that embodied a Montesquieuan division of powers, it is chiefly in opposition to the tenets of Josephinism that we may see how the idea of an 'ancient constitution' served both as a counter-concept to the ideas of absolutism and state centralization, and as a legitimizing argument for the restoration of the pre-Josephist status quo. While, for example, the Josephinian *Staat* was the absolutist princely state, ruled by unilateral decree and acts of 'individual' will, ancient laws were a product of communal, social evolution, not the product of any one legislator; while Joseph's rule was characterized by the rationality and 'dangerous innovations' of 'modern' Enlightenment, the Hungarian constitution was 'ancient', customary, tried and tested through history; while Joseph attempted to undermine the feudal system, the ancient constitution provided recognition of ancient corporate rights and privileges, and while Josephinian rule was imported from abroad, the ancient constitution was an organic product of 'natural' autochthonous growth. The idea of the 'ancient constitution' thus defined the Hungarian nobility's counterposition to Habsburg absolutism by using conceptual criteria that automatically contradicted the Habsburgs' absolutist stance.[18]

As Joseph's opponents sensed he was further losing his grip on his empire they invoked a yet broader panoply of Enlightenment ideas and keywords in their defence. But imported Enlightenment vocabularies were frequently complicated by earlier ideas that were now being claimed as pillars of the 'ancient constitution'. References to the 'rights of man' and Rousseau's *Social Contract*, for example, appeared in pamphlets and county communiqués in defiance of Habsburg absolutism. But universal 'rights' were frequently confused with particularist, noble 'rights', and Rousseau's 'people' was here interpreted in the sense of Werbőczi's *populus*, i.e. in the restricted sense of 'nobility'. In this way, through a rhetorical sleight of hand, the tenets of 'universal' natural law were now being invoked to legitimate the nobility's claim to power. Similarly, Hungarian *egyenlőség* 'equality' was less equated with 'universal' equality than it was with Werbőczy's concept of *una eademque libertas*, which touted the legal equality of all nobles (and usually the 'upwards' equality of the middle nobility with the magnates). In religious discourse the same term appeared in connection with the Protestant nobility's demands for religious equality, often as a counter-concept to 'tolerance', a term which could also imply the dominant Catholic faith's 'sufferance', as opposed to legal recognition, of other religions in the realm. Only in the writings of a handful of reformers was equality equated with the extension of 'downwards' equality to the lower orders.[19] Thus, while campaigners frequently invoked revolutionary keywords such as *szabadság* 'freedom', *népfelség* 'popular sovereignty', *hazafiság* 'patriotism' and *alkotmány* 'constitution', Ferenc Eckhart aptly noted how the Hungarian noble opposition deployed the slogans of the French Revolution to reinforce their own position, 'holding Montesquieu and Rousseau in one hand, and the *Tripartitum* in the other'.[20]

From this perspective, some of the above rhetorical innovations may be seen to demonstrate how certain 'new' ideas were not merely adopted, but rather adapted to suit 'ancient' or pre-existing concepts. But just as the 'new' could be pressed into legitimating the 'past', so too could the 'past' be used to sanction the 'new'. Indeed, it would be a mistake to suggest that the idea of the 'ancient constitution' was exclusively deployed for restorative ends, or to bring about a complete *restitutio in integrum* to the pre-Josephinian era. As we shall see, some forms of ancient constitutionalist argument were in fact radical, dressing unprecedented forms of legal change in the rhetorical garb of custom and tradition. Furthermore, outside of its anti-Josephinian applications, the idea of an 'ancient constitution' was not a consolidated, but rather a contested concept, and by the time of the 1790/1 Diet, both supporters and opponents of the King, different religious representatives, and even proponents of language reform were invoking a variety of historical

Figure 4.1 A contemporary depiction of the arrival of the Holy Crown in Buda on 21 February, 1790.[21]

arguments, each voicing different ideas on desired or existing relations between past and present, to justify their claims. In this context it was less clear whether the 'ancient constitution' – with its acceptance of unequal rights and privileges in a socially, linguistically and religiously fragmented population – could provide a clear-cut framework around which the noble 'nation' could rally in opposition to the king.

The Ancient Constitution of the Middle Nobility

Retreating from his programme of reform, Joseph's famous rescript of 28 January 1790 stated that the Emperor wished to return the country to the condition of its standing in 1780; only his patents of toleration, peasant emancipation, and 'livings' (which dissolved certain religious orders and founded new schools on their lands) were to remain. Joseph also promised to convoke a Diet, and ordered the return of the Holy Crown, which he had removed to Vienna in 1784, to Hungary.[22] In preparation, noble *banderia* or militias[23] were formed to escort the venerated artefact on a tour back to Buda,[24] and the months preceding the Diet of 1790 saw outpourings of noble solidarity against 'German' influence, often expressed through demands to use Hungarian as the language of governance and the donning of extravagant Magyar dress.[25] Three weeks after issuing his rescript, and with the country in celebration, Joseph died on 20 February 1790.

Amid great uncertainty Joseph's brother, Leopold II, called the Hungarian Diet into session, the first for 25 years, with the intent of being crowned king of Hungary and restoring order to his dominions. In Hungary, agitation was no doubt the result of a combination of factors, including revolt in the Austrian Netherlands, the war against Turkey and Russia, tension with Prussia, and last but not least, news of the French Revolution. But the joy felt at Joseph's downfall had now galvanized into a resolve to cast off the Habsburg yoke, and by March 1790 a feudal revolt appeared to be taking shape. This was comprised of four connected events: the *banderium* movement, agitation at the Diet, the expression of proto-nationalist sentiments in Hungarian army regiments, and noble collusion with the Prussian government to provide (in typically contractarian terms) a 'guarantee' for Hungary's noble constitution.[26]

A significant development in this context was that the *banderia*'s oratories now not only suggested that the bannermen were prepared to defend the Holy Crown with their lives because it was the chief *palladium* of noble liberty and legitimate monarchical rule,[27] but also that it was to be safeguarded from danger along with three other elements of the noble-nation's ancestral heritage. These were 'language', 'clothing' and 'law', a triad of idealized identity markers that were seen to constitute the nobility's historically conceived 'national character',[28] and that thus possessed 'ancient constitutional' value, even if they represented more a sense of emerging 'national' consciousness than they did any clear-cut legal conception of constitutionalism.

Undoubtedly, late eighteenth-century Hungary had seen a rise in proto-nationalist sentiment. This had been shaped in part by the socio-political cleavages that existed between the middle and lesser nobility, who were usually tied to the land, and the wealthy and powerful magnates who were associated with the royal court in Vienna. Against this backdrop, the sod-bound middle nobility often claimed to be true Magyar *hazafiak* ('patriots', lit. 'sons of the homeland'), while simultaneously deriding their loyalist counterparts for aping the *módi* 'modish' German – and indeed French – fashions popular at the royal court in Vienna. Certainly, as Joseph's rule became increasingly unpopular in the 1780s, rhetoric lambasting foreign 'modish' fashions increased alongside appeals in the classical republican vein to the virtues of simplicity and the need to uphold the moral codes of the nation's ancestors.[29] But the antagonism between the 'autochthonous' middle nobility and their 'heterochthonous' counterparts was being further exacerbated as the very historical core of noble 'Magyar' identity was itself being contested in the era's literature. On the one hand, the publication of medieval chronicles such as Anonymus's *Gesta Hungarorum* (in 1746) and Simon of Kéza's *Gesta Hunnorum et Hungarorum* (1781) had broadly popularized the idea of the nobility's proud and warlike Hunnish–Scythian ancestry. In contrast, works by the era's linguists, such as János Sajnovics, had claimed the linguistic kinship of the Magyars with apparently more sedentary 'Lappic' peoples, an idea that was perceived as an attack on the noble class's martial ethos and the myth of their warrior pedigree.[30] It is thus perhaps no surprise that at the Diet, military-style clothing became a prominent symbol of noble-national identity for the self-styled 'patriots'. Even so, while many *banderia* members may have boasted about their martial virtues and their privileged role in guarding the Crown, the high costs of acquiring weapons and traditional hussar-style uniforms ruined many of the poorer nobles.[31] Eventually, a proposal to enact legislation – binding Hungarian noblemen and -women to wear 'national' dress in public – was rejected at the Diet. The chancellery argued that nobody could be forced to don or doff clothes against their will. Later, many nobles were satisfied when Leopold himself wore Hungarian clothes to his coronation, displaying his allegiance to the nation. Further discussions of the question were postponed.[32]

The inclusion of the vernacular language as part of the constitution may have stemmed in part from the Hungarian 'language reform' (*nyelvújítás*), usually dated from the early 1770s. This programme saw a variety of attempts to codify and standardize the Hungarian language so that it might displace Latin as the main medium of erudition and science. However, following Herder, language was also becoming considered as the chief identifying 'characteristic' of the 'nation'. Thus, one's use of language – just like one's choice of clothing – was a powerful symbol of difference or assimilation, of loyalty or allegiance to the Hungarian noble-nation, or of disloyalty, un-patriotism and Viennese 'cosmopolitanism'. Indeed, in the pamphlets of the era, many calls were made for foreigners who ate 'Magyar bread' to speak the Hungarian language. Here, language was being linked to affection for the soil, and part of the 'constitution' that arose from the interplay of geography and humanity. Yet strident expressions of linguistic imperialism such as these point only to the later problems of imposing Magyar linguistic uniformity in a country where Hungarians constituted but a relative majority.

A further, more overtly political demand was made at the Diet of 1790/1 for the introduction of Hungarian as the official language of government. This was partly a reaction to Joseph's language decree of 1784, which had introduced German as the language of administration, and which was often seen as part of a broader attempt to impose 'German' political and cultural hegemony upon Hungary. However, while the middle nobility claimed the use of Hungarian as a pillar of the 'ancient constitution' (i.e. as a historical right of the ethno-linguistically conceived noble 'nation'), they met with stern opposition at the Diet. Many opponents claimed that Latin was the *de facto* language of the ancient constitution, as it was the language in which all legislation had been recorded since the foundation of the *regnum*: calls for the use of Hungarian were based upon anything but historical precedent. In some cases, the admonitions of St Stephen were cited in opposition to the idea (*Nam unius linguae uniusque moris regnum, imbecille et fragile est* 'a realm with one language and one [set of] custom[s] is weak and feeble'). Hard-line Catholics suspected a ruse by Protestants to allow them greater access to positions of privilege within government (Protestants in turn retorted that Catholics favoured Latin as they were un-Magyar). Representatives of other nationalities, such as the Croats, also opposed the move, claiming it would impede their participation in political affairs. But in the proto-nationalist mindset of the middle nobility, the language question was already being interpreted as a surrogate emancipation movement: in a situation where direct political resistance against the Habsburg Empire was fraught with danger, the struggle to have the 'native' Hungarian language recognized as the sole language of state had already become symbolic of the Hungarian nation's struggle to free itself from 'foreign' influence and achieve political autonomy. In the end, ethno-'national' loyalties won: of the 49 counties that sent deputies to the Diet, 22 voted for Magyar as the official language, 19 to retain Latin, and 8 for the use of both languages.[33] Because of the narrow vote, and also due to opposition from the Croats, the Diet of 1790/1 marks the beginning of an era in which the official records of the assembly were recorded in Hungarian and Latin. In hindsight, this represented a significant step in the later nationalist drive to create a unilingual and unitary 'nation state'. In the extreme, the demand for 'law' could be interpreted along multiple lines.

Abstract in the extreme, the demand for 'law' could be interpreted along multiple lines. Often paired with the references to 'custom', it could refer, *inter alia*, to the restoration of earlier laws sanctifying noble rights and privileges or 'Magyar Freedom(s)', and to the noble right to participate in legislation at the Diet. But it could also refer, in a more seditious sense, to the wish for 'domestic' rule, and exclusively 'Magyar' laws for the 'Magyar' kingdom, perhaps through the drafting of a new written constitution, written by the noble 'people', and based upon ancient foundations. While, as we shall see below, some reform-minded members of the nobility looked to foreign constitutional developments to provide inspiration for a new constitution, it was chiefly for the middle nobility that the historical-nationalist vision of the 'ancient constitution' seems to have possessed an almost mystical appeal as a symbol of hierarchical and traditional order. As Marczali claimed, its 'magic' derived from its multiple allusions, to the nobility's sense of pride and class distinction, from the desire for their laws and freedoms to have ancient provenance, and from the allusion to the historical greatness of the Magyar homeland.[34]

Ürményi's Speech on the Ancient Constitution

A more theoretical account of the 'ancient constitution' as a constitutional monarchy resting upon ancient foundations was delivered by the king's *personalis*, József Ürményi, in his opening speech to the lower table at the Diet.[35] Loyal to both king and country, Ürményi sought to negotiate the middle ground between the incoming monarch, Leopold II, and the various factions of the Hungarian nobility.[36]

In his speech Ürményi expresses delight that 'divine providence' has, after 25 years, enabled the assembly to freely exercise its 'ancient and centuries-old legislative power'. But he also expresses surprise that so many vicissitudes have befallen the 'trunk and roots' of the 'ancient constitution' over the years. The constitution, he explains, was formed by the nobility's 'glorious elders and forebears', who entered into a 'civil society', and sealed an indissoluble pact with the prince. This pact recognized both the sovereign rights of the prince *and* the nobility's freedoms, and also provided for the 'happiness' of the people at large.

Thus drawing upon the idea of the 'social contract', Ürményi conceptualizes the constitution as an 'original contract' that can be traced back to the very foundation of the political community. This contract respected both the hereditary right of the king *and* the rights of the nobility (including their right to partake in legislation at the Diet), and as such stood in contrast to the pro-Habsburg, absolutist theories of Joseph von Sonnenfels and Carl Anton von Martini, who used similarly historical-contractual arguments to place absolute legislative right in the hands of the monarch.[37]

However, a peculiar aspect of Ürményi's speech is the way in which he reverses the legitimizing role of time: perhaps unsurprisingly, he alludes to the injurious rule of Joseph, claiming that the 'rooted Constitution' had, over the years, fallen into a state of decline and, in recent times, near 'ruin'. But he does not stop there: ever since the very enactment of the 'constitution', he claims, the passing of time has seen discordant and selfish individuals act for 'personal gain'; the result was that the laws of Andrew II (i.e. the Golden Bull of 1222), and the other 'chief branches' of the 'lawful constitution' had come to be tarnished by many imperfections. For Ürményi, time is now the chief source of constitutional 'erosion' as opposed to legitimacy. Following his frequent use of organic metaphor, it appears he intends for past laws to be 'weeded' at the Diet. But how could this be achieved without rejecting the very authority of ancient custom and the old definitions of law?

Ürményi goes on to provide a rubric by which legal precedents may be evaluated and discarded at the Diet. First, he claims the law's chief purpose is to provide public security. But security can only be safeguarded insofar as 'trust' exists between the prince and the estates, and so long as the public feel 'affection' towards the 'legislative' and 'executive' powers. To achieve this state of affairs, the nobility must first carefully consider the 'origins and foundations' of the ancient laws, their 'natural progression', and their 'utility' for each member of 'civil society' (here referring to the political elite). Then, secondly, once the nobility have established the causes of their *sérelmek* ('grievances', lit. 'injuries'), they must adhere to 'remedial' and 'reparative' means in their negotiations, without the 'pursuit of private interest'. Thus, justice is not only to be found in acts of legal restitution, but also in consideration of the law's communal utility and historical development. By opening up the 'rooted' laws to scrutiny, Ürményi claims the nobility can expunge the many 'improper customs' that have 'slipped into use', customs that are contrary to the 'true sense' (*igaz értelme*) of the 'rooted' laws.

History, community, utility; these are the three benchmarks against which legislation is to be assessed and deleterious customs expunged. But what does Ürményi mean by the 'true sense' of the law? On the one hand, the law's true essence appears in Ürményi's speech as something external to human activity, as part of a set of timeless, immutable truths that transcend mere temporary arrangements or prior written laws. 'Rooted' in the logic of time-worn inheritance and tradition, the 'true sense' of the law is, we may infer, an unwritten truth, one whose rationality belongs to the immemorial authority of customary law and to what Ürményi calls the 'spirit' of the constitution. By describing the law in these terms, Ürményi urges the nobility to see that they were 'discovering' the law, rather than engaging in its creation.

However, while Ürményi claims the Diet's primary function was to address noble 'grievances' and create 'trust' between king and nobility, he goes on to raise a more contentious set of issues when outlining the 'spirit' of the constitution. The assembly's second task, he says, is to ensure the 'affection' and 'confidence' of the country's lower orders. This can only be achieved by making them 'happy', by eradicating every trace of lawless rule and by sharing 'public burdens' among the different estates proportionately; these goals, in addition to religious and class tolerance, comprise the 'marrow and soul' (*veleje és Lelke*) of the laws, and create a unique form of security that was always 'rooted in the chief constitution of our laws'. If the nobility ensures that this 'true sense' of the root laws is not misinterpreted then they

> will surely enjoy the trust and affection of our king, as well as the gratitude of our fellow compatriots and descendants, and rightly boast of an eternal constitution (*örökös Alkotmány*) that serves as a memorial to the homeland's perpetuity.

Despite Ürményi's grandiose conclusion, his conception of the 'ancient constitution' was combined with elements of Joseph's eudaemonistic programme of enlightened government. Furthermore, the rebellious middle nobility did not wish to hear about the king's automatic right of succession, and were claiming their right to elect a new monarch. The opening ceremony was thus followed by an uproar. Because Ürményi and Judge Royal Károly Zichy, who presided over the upper table, had been appointed during the reign of Joseph II, members of the *bene possessionati* at the lower table called for them (and others) to be removed from their posts.

Draft Constitutions for the Diet

In spire of the furore, the nobility were not united in their conception of the 'constitution', be it ancient or modern. Divided loyalties, disagreements over the correct path of political reform, and fears of popular revolution saw three political groupings or 'voices' emerge at the Diet, each with differing attitudes to the old laws: the first group, mostly enlightened aristocrats, favoured moderate reform instead of radical change; the second, a more marginalized group of intellectuals who in some cases had worked under Joseph, believed in more widespread reform and emancipation of the peasantry; the third, often associated with the *bene possessionati*, sought to reaffirm noble liberties and privileges, even if it meant taking up arms to create a noble-led republic.[38] These groupings are thought to be reflected by three quasi-constitutional manuscripts that were drafted in preparation for the Diet and circulated in secret among members of the nobility.[39] The stakes were high: the potentially anti-monarchical and even revolutionary connotations of drafting or demanding a written 'constitution' were becoming increasingly apparent, especially considering developments in France. What follows is a brief description.

The first text is Count Ferenc Széchényi's unpublished manuscript *Unpartheyische Gedanken über den 1790. abzuhaltenden Landtag* that was circulated among the magnates.[40] Széchényi felt the 'noble opposition' were rash in demanding a new constitution, with Leopold embroiled in foreign politics.[41] He questioned the philosophical principles of new constitutionalism, seeing a lack of satisfaction where centuries-old constitutions had been toppled. The peasants, he claimed, were incapable of composing a new constitution, and any radical constitutional transformation would lead to bloodshed. Thus, it was preferable to restore the old laws. But Széchényi did begrudgingly admit that Joseph had revealed the path to reform, although he had used the various 'imperfections' of the Hungarian constitution (i.e. divisions over religious matters, the peasantry and Protestant freedoms) as leverage in order to undermine the nobility's privileges. He called for equality between the religious orders and, significantly, between the aristocracy and middle nobility. If the nobility were united, the peasantry would remain loyal. But a 'sacrifice' was required: the nobility must shoulder part or all of the military tax to reduce the burden upon the peasantry and deflect the criticism that the nobility contribute nothing to the 'common good'. Széchényi called for a Diet every two years, with or without royal consent, and suggested that tax rates should be fixed for a two-year period with noble checks. Through scientific advances, language reform and the establishment of committees to reform public law, Széchényi claimed a new constitution could be introduced in ten years.[42]

The second text is *Gedanken eines ungarischen Patrioten über einige zum Landtag gehörige Gegenstände*, published anonymously in March in Vienna, and penned by Széchényi's secretary, József Hajnóczy.[43] Hajnóczy was the most radical of the three authors (his support for the Jacobin movement eventually led to his execution in 1795).[44] Nevertheless, this early pamphlet is less radical than his later works.

Although barred from the Diet as an ignoble, Hajnóczy, too, claimed the maintenance of the current *Staatsverfassung* 'state constitution' was a priority.[45] He did, however, propose a more radical extension of rights to landed non-nobles, who should be allowed to run for office. He also claimed that landless ignobles could hold lower offices, so long as they were born Hungarians. The nobility's right to a hearing in the royal courts should be extended to all the country's inhabitants, and the tithe (to the Church) and ninth (to their lords) should be eliminated. Religious 'tolerance' should be replaced by equal rights for denominations, and magnates should renounce their personal voting rights, which they obtained from custom, and their hereditary right to the lord-lieutenancies of the counties.

The final anonymously written text was penned by Péter Balogh of Ócsa, chief ideologue of the rebellious middle nobility.[46] Highly influential in the county assemblies, Balogh's ideas provided the backbone of ideological resistance to the Crown, especially through his introduction of the *filum successionis interruptum* argument: because Joseph had refused coronation and died with no direct heirs, the line of hereditary succession, it was claimed, had been broken. And following Rousseau's *Social Contract*, the right to elect a new monarch had been passed back to the 'people'. But here Rousseau's 'people' was understood in the Werbőczian sense of 'nobility'; Balogh's frequent references to the 'social contract' thus amounted to little more than the rehashing of traditional feudal relations in 'revolutionary' vocabulary.

Balogh's document, circulated by Freemasons, set out the following radical demands: the Diet should meet at Pest annually and vote on taxation; the Crown's power of veto should be removed; a 'senate' should oversee the executive branch of government; the chancellery should be returned from Vienna to Buda, and the chancellor should be responsible to the Diet; prefects appointed by the king should be chosen from candidates elected by the counties, and all appointed office-holders should be selected from candidates nominated by the senate; Hungary should have its own national army, commanded by appointees from the middle nobility, and independent of the War Council in Vienna; the Palatine, head of the army, should receive orders from the senate; the *jus resistendi* or right of insurrection, abolished in 1687, should be reinstated. Similarly to the Polish constitution of 1791, Balogh's proposal did not grant any rights to the peasantry, who were to be kept in a state of servitude. Even so, a Lutheran, Balogh did believe Protestants should be granted equal rights on the basis of the Peace of Vienna (1606) and the Treaty of Linz (1645). For Balogh, these were multilateral 'contracts', signed by foreign powers, that could only be changed with the full agreement of the contracting parties, and thus not changed unilaterally by the king or the Diet alone.

Balogh claimed that not one part of the ancient constitution, 'tested throughout centuries of practice', must be changed in any way, unless its 'security' or 'expansion' demanded otherwise. Yet despite this historicizing language, the text somewhat anachronistically combined 'ancient constitutional' arguments with elements of 'national' republicanism, notions of religious 'tolerance' and the idea of the social contract. Unsurprisingly, in negotiations over the *diploma*, the court rejected many of these claims on similarly historical grounds: the law did not support the *filum sucessionis interruptum* argument, and made no clear mention anywhere of a historical Hungarian 'senate'.[47] The right of insurrection had been abolished for over 100 years, and the nobility's claims that constitutional rights were bilateral 'contracts' that could not be unilaterally altered were contradicted by their attempts to unilaterally reject, inter alia, Leopold's right of succession. Despite all the talk of an 'ancient constitution', it appeared to the royal court that the estates were in fact attempting to overturn the historically evolved state in order to unilaterally transfer sovereignty to their own class.[48]

Religion

While the Lutheran Balogh and the *bene possessionati* held sway over the Diet during the drafting of the royal *diploma*, early negotiations almost ground to a halt as Catholic prelates refused to swear an oath of allegiance to the 'constitution', and tensions arose over questions of religious rights. Although Joseph had not revoked his Edict of Tolerance, public attention was focused upon whether it would remain a permanent feature of Hungarian law or whether the Diet would consign it to oblivion. At the Diet, the Protestants wanted their rights to be explicitly included in the draft *diploma* (with what we might call 'constitutional' effect). But hard-line Catholics opposed this line and argued that any such laws should be included in normal legislation. This would mean that the rights of other religions would remain dependent upon normal legislative processes, and thus negotiable at future diets.

The Catholic prelacy were, by way of concession, prepared to renounce the older use of the descriptive term 'dominant' in descriptions of the Catholic Church's status. But they insisted it should instead be described as the *prima et praeeminens* religion, and retain its right to preside over cases of apostasy, marriage and divorce, and also determine the religion of children of mixed-faith marriages. The legitimacy for these claims was born of ancient constitutionalist reasoning: the Catholic Church, they claimed, had been *in situ* for 800 years in Hungary, whereas Protestant denominations (foreign imports from Germany) had only been recognized since 1608. Indeed, they argued that the laws of the land had sanctified the Catholic Church ever since the foundation of the State by St Stephen, and that other religions, proven by law to be 'false', had merely been granted a degree of amnesty due to changing circumstances. Furthermore, as inheritor of the title of 'Apostolic King' from St Stephen, it was said to be the king's duty to maintain Hungary's status as the *Regnum Marianum* or 'Kingdom of Mary'. Protestants, it was claimed, were wrong to believe that the (old, if not ancient) treaties of Vienna and Linz were, as bilateral treaties, superior to unilaterally declared law: by allowing foreign nations to intervene in Hungary's internal politics, they were attempting to undermine the sovereignty of the realm. A final ancient constitutionalist argument was aimed at the 'soul' of the nascent Magyar 'nation'. While non-Catholics might be Magyar, they were only Magyar in body, it was argued. Catholics, however, were 'true Magyars', both in body *and* spirit. This was because Hungary was the *Regnum Marianum*, and the Catholic faith was linked to the ancient laws of the land.[49] Thus, not only was the Catholic Church claimed to be the true representative of God; it was also said to be the true and spiritual representative of the 'nation'. This was, of course, little more than an attempt to deny the full 'national' and 'patriotic' status of the Protestants.

Religious disputes proved intractable at the Diet, and were referred to the king on the basis of Law XXX of 1715. When Leopold stated that he wished to continue in the spirit of Joseph's *Toleranzedikt*, the Diet approved. The Catholic hardliners, however, remained intransigent, and recorded their protests in the law, even if it was noted that their objections possessed no perpetual validity.

Conclusions

The Hasburgs' consolidation of peace with the Prussians was the turning point at the Diet. With his position strengthened following the peace of Reichenbach, Leopold accepted no limitations upon his powers other than those outlined in the *diplomas* of Charles VI (Charles III of Hungary) or Maria Theresa. The Diet, with the rebels chastened by the loss of any foreign support, agreed to Leopold's coronation. The *personalis* Ürményi and Károly Zichy attempted to save what demands of the nobility they could in negotiations over the *diploma*, but with the coronation looming and enthusiasms waning, a full-scale elaboration of Hungarian law was eventually entrusted to nine committees, the *deputationes regnicolares*, which were charged with providing a comprehensive legal framework for the entire country.[50] As Leopold had demonstrated that he wished to work with the consent of the Diet in legislative matters, the nobility finally accepted Leopold's son, Alexander, as Palatine, entrusting the previously empty post to a junior member of the Habsburg dynasty.

Although no written constitution was enacted by that name at the Diet of 1790/1, a number of 'new' laws did emerge, many of which were later seen to provide 'constitutional' precedent for Hungarian legal development in the 'Reform Age' of 1825–48.[51] These included the delaying of monarchical prerogatives until the king's lawful coronation and oath, which was to take place within six months (Article III); the right to elect a Palatine (Article V); the housing of the Holy Crown in Buda (Article VI); the constitutional status of Hungary as an independent kingdom (Article X); the shared right to compose, annul and interpret the laws with the king, and the exclusion of rule by decree or patent (Article XII); the use of Hungarian in public institutions, and the appointment of grammar teachers in gymnasia and the University of Pest (Article XVI); religious freedom, including the right of Protestants to own property and take up official posts (Articles XXVI–XXVII); the free movement of serfs (Article XXXV); the right of Jews to relocate to all areas of Hungary (apart from mining towns) from where they had been expelled (Article XXXVIII); the banning of torture (Article XLII); and the right of non-nobles to appeal against capital punishment or other serious sentences (Article XLIII).

Because only some of these laws had ancient historical precedents, it was clear that the 'ancient constitution' had undergone substantial modification, and had not been returned to the *status quo ante*. In keeping with ancient constitutional rhetoric, however, none of the legal changes were conceptualized as 'innovations', and certainly no mention was made of how some laws were merely reworkings of Joseph II's earlier patents. Overall, it seems, a degree of legal change suited the nobility. The reason was that on one level, the laws of 1790/1 marked a significant retreat from the programme of enlightened absolutism. On another, the dominant influence of the middle nobility had left the feudal system largely intact: the peasantry were granted little more than the confirmation of Maria Theresa's *Urbarium* and the right to change their domicile. Even if religious matters had been settled by the court,[52] Protestants and moderates were satisfied with the reaffirmation of religious liberties. Yet despite the codification of these and many other changes into positive legislation, the law omitted any reference to the existence of or indeed restoration of an 'ancient constitution'. What then would be the significance of this concept for future generations?

In its broadest manifestations, the 'ancient constitution' would become a byword for gradual, as opposed to rapid, alteration to the law; it symbolized noble resistance to the claims of Habsburg centralization, and the preservation of noble privilege and dominion over the peasantry. At the same time, however, talk of the 'ancient constitution' as a single overarching *lex terrae* had resulted in a new kind of problem in late eighteenth-century Hungary, that of consistency with collective historical definition. This was because 'ancient' political structures not only accepted monarchical rights, but also regional and social diversity among the bodies into which the populace was divided.

Yet just as the organic concept of the 'ancient constitution' was born during the revolutionary era, so too was the identity of the community itself being reshaped along linguistic and ethnic lines. Indeed, it is at the Diet of 1790/1 that an abstract concept of 'nation' also stakes its first claim to sovereignty. The significance of the middle nobility's claim to represent the 'people' in a fragmented and multi-ethnic kingdom, however contradictory and assumptive that claim may have been, was that it was based upon an argument born of a proto-nationalist strain of ancient constitutionalist argumentation. Hungary, they claimed, was a separate country, named after the Hungarians who rightfully possessed it through ancient conquest. And they, the middle nobility, represented the 'people' of Hungary, not merely because they were patriotic and noble, but because they were the most 'Hungarian' element of the population, free from German and other forms of cosmopolitan influence. Here a significant conceptual switch was taking place. The older conception of the *ország* and its constitution revolved around the protection of multiple, territorially held corporate rights vis-à-vis the king. But the newer ethno-national concept shifted the emphasis. It focused upon the primacy of one ethno-national group in the history of the territory over which sovereignty was claimed. Now, disputes over the constitutive elements of the ancient constitution were rapidly becoming struggles to control the collective 'narrative history' of the ethnically and culturally conceived 'national' community. For the foreseeable future, however, the 'nation' would be characterized chiefly along feudal, noble-national lines. This was partly because politics took a reactionary turn following Leopold's sudden death in 1792 and the accession of Francis II. The trial of the Hungarian Jacobins, the execution of their leaders (including Hajnóczy) in 1795 and the imprisonment of many enlightened intellectuals took place amidst fears of popular revolution and French military advancement, stifling the voice of egalitarianism until the nineteenth-century Reform Age.

In hindsight, it was Law X of 1791 that was to prove significant for later generations in their claims for 'national' independence. This law stated that Hungary was a 'free and independent kingdom' that 'submitted to no other kingdom or people'; Hungary was thus not to be considered as a lesser entity, as a mere province that could be incorporated into the Habsburg state. This, along with the provisions of Article XII on the sharing of powers, represented a significant retreat from Joseph II's absolutism. But in further stating that Hungary was 'possessed of her own consistence and constitution', Leopold II was merely stating that the Hungarian lands possessed their own legally constituted 'character' or 'disposition', in accordance with the older meaning of the term.[53] This did not entail the recognition of a separate and unassailable body of 'national' laws that, for example, contradicted the royal *diploma*, or that stood as a codified document of laws symbolizing the foundation of an independent 'national' state. Indeed, the *diploma* stated that Hungary was to be ruled in accordance with her own laws and customs *by hereditary monarchs*. Thus, Law X was more a

Figure 4.2 A Hungarian peasant and nobleman in their 'national' dresses.[54]

statement of how Hungary constituted an organic political entity that retained administrative autonomy under Habsburg direction. But for later generations, this law was seen as a preliminary step on the path to full national independence. Even if no written constitution arose from the Diet of 1790/1, the late eighteenth century marks a period of transition in which a new narrative began to unfold: this was the story of the Hungarian ethnic nation's 'ancient constitution'.

Figure 4.3 Hussar-style noble-national costumes from 1790.[55]

Notes

1. Glenn Burgess, *The Politics of the Ancient Constitution* (University Park, PA, 1993), p. 19.
2. Henrik Marczali, *Az 1790/1. Országgyűlés*, 2 vols (Budapest, 1907), vol. 1, p. 110.
3. Thomas Paine, *Paine: Political Writings*, edited by Bruce Kuklick (Cambridge, 1989), p. 28.
4. Robin West, 'Tom Paine's constitution', *Virginia Law Review* lxxxix/6 (2003), pp. 1413–61 (p. 1416).

5. Gordon S. Wood, 'The American revolution', in M. Goldie and R. Wokler (eds), *The Cambridge History of Eighteenth-Century Political Thought*, reprint edition (Cambridge, 2016), pp. 601–20 (p. 601).
6. The term *ős* means 'ancestor', hence the adjective *ősi* 'ancestral, ancient'; *alkotmány* derives from the verb *alkot-* meaning 'to create, manufacture', and may literally be translated as 'creation'. In the period's literature, the term was used to describe, inter alia, the 'constitution' of the human body and man-made objects. But it was also used to refer to God's 'creations', including the natural world and its creatures. This latter usage, often following the Augustinian concept of *ordo*, denoted the divine and hierarchical order of the universe, whereby God's creatures (including humans) were assigned a 'position' within the cosmic hierarchy. As such, *alkotmány* was often used to signify a feudal, estates-based view of the body politic, where the different classes of feudal society occupied their divinely ordained places, from king, through nobility, to peasant. This, of course, stood in stark contrast to more jurisprudential, secular and egalitarian understandings of constitutionalism.
7. József Takáts, *A megfelelő ötvözet* (Budapest, 2014), p. 57.
8. Jacob T. Levy, 'Ancient constitutionalism', in M. Bevir (ed.), *Encyclopedia of Political Theory* (London, 2010), pp. 44–6.
9. John G.A. Pocock, *The Ancient Constitution and the Feudal Law* (Cambridge, 1987), pp. 47–9, 171–3.
10. Charles Howard McIlwain, *Constitutionalism, Ancient and Modern* (Ithaca, NY, 1947), p. 27.
11. Heinz Mohnhaupt and Dieter Grimm, *Verfassung. Zur Geschichte des Begriffs von der Antike bis zur Gegenwart, Zwei Studien* (Berlin, 1995), p. 63.
12. The Hungarian term is derived from the verb *sarkallik*, 'to pivot upon sg', and thus, similarly to its Latin counterpart, signifies how a law is of 'pivotal' or crucial importance.
13. István M. Szijártó, *A diéta: a Magyar rendek és az országgyűlés, 1708–1792* (Budapest, 2005), p. 203.
14. The term derives from *uru* 'lord' and *-szág* '-ship', meaning 'dominion' or a collection of feudal territories assigned to lords, cf. German *Herrschaft*, French *seigneurie* etc.; see Loránd Benkő (ed.), *A magyar nyelv történeti-etimológiai szótára* (Budapest, 1967), vol. 2, p. 1095.
15. László Péter, 'Montesquieu's paradox on freedom and Hungary's constitutions 1790–1990', in Miklós Lojkó (ed.), *Hungary's Long Nineteenth Century: Constitutional and Democratic Traditions in a European Perspective. Collected Studies* (Leiden and Boston, MA, 2012), pp. 152–82.
16. Charles de Secondat Montesquieu, *The Political Theory of Montesquieu*, selected and translated by Melvin Richter (Cambridge, 1977), p. 77.
17. Béla Köpeczi, 'A Francia és Magyar felvilágosodás', *Irodalomtörténet* xiii/1 (1986), pp. 3–26 (p. 11).
18. See Chapter 3 in this volume.

19. Marczali, *Az 1790/1-diki országgyu?lés*, vol. I, pp. 112–14. As discussed below, the writings of József Hajnóczy and the marginalized Hungarian Jacobins embraced the emancipatory ideals of the French Revolution.
20. Ferenc Eckhart, *A szentkorona-eszme története* (Budapest, 1941), p. 254.
21. Hungarian National Library, Collection of Images (Képtár).
22. Joseph ignored the Diet during his reign and ruled instead by patent to avoid power sharing with the estates. He also refused coronation to avoid swearing the traditional inaugural oath that guaranteed the nobility's rights and privileges.
23. In medieval Hungary, the high nobility were obliged to muster troops under their own banner to defend the homeland, hence the name applied to such cohorts.
24. Ernő Taxner, 'Tudósítások a szent korona 1790-es diadalútjáról', *Magyar Szemle* xxi (2012), pp. 111–20.
25. Endre Arató, 'A magyar "nemzeti" ideológia jellemző vonásai a 18. században', in *Nemzetiség a feudalizmus korában* (Budapest, 1972), pp. 130–81.
26. Béla K. Király, *Hungary in the Late Eighteenth Century* (New York, 1969), p. 174.
27. Without coronation, many Hungarian nobles argued they owed Joseph no allegiance; he was famously stigmatized as the 'hatted king' by the sentimentalist poet and monk Pál Ányos, who wrote 'Terrible power! 'Tis here an unknown thing, that crownless be our king.' On the oratories of the bannermen see Sándor Márki, 'A Koronaőrző nemesek naplója 1790-ből', *Századok* xv/4 (1881), p. 337.
28. Tibor Porkoláb and Ágoston Nagy, '"Ősi ruhát, igét, szívet meg tartotok": A nemzeti viselet és a koronaőrző bandériumok a 18. század végi politikai diskurzusokban', in *Docendo Discimus* (Miskolc, 2013), pp. 30–9.
29. Ferenc Bíró, *A fiatal Bessenyei és íróbarátai* (Budapest, 1976), pp. 215–16.
30. Gábor Klaniczay, 'The myth of Scythian origin and the cult of Attila in the nineteenth century', in *Multiple Antiquities, Multiple Modernities: Ancient Histories in Nineteenth-Century European Cultures* (Frankfurt, 2011), pp. 183–210 (pp. 196–7).
31. See Figure 1 and Figure 2 at the end of the chapter.
32. Henrik Marczali, *Magyarország története a szatmári békétől a bécsi congressusig 1711–1815* (Budapest, 1898), p. 532.
33. Robert A. Kann and Zdeněk V. David, *The Peoples of the Eastern Habsburg Lands, 1526–1918* (Seattle, WA, 1984), p. 227.
34. Marczali, *Az 1790/91. országgyűlés*, vol. 1, p. 111.
35. A distinguished servant of the Crown, Ürményi (1741–1825), was appointed to a string of high offices throughout his career. He is perhaps best known for his role in co-authoring the *Ratio educationis* (1777), an administrative blueprint that influenced the financing and curriculum of a 'national' system of Hungarian education until 1848. Ürményi attempted to balance loyalties between Crown and country (he was also a Freemason), and while he believed in enlightened reform, he also sought to maintain Hungary's ancient constitution, with rule shared between monarch and Diet, and feudal

hierarchies left intact. Thus, Ürményi often found himself compromised by Joseph's attempts at centralization. In 1795 he fell out of favour with the court, and withdrew from public life until 1801, when he became governor of Galicia. In 1806–25 he served as Judge Royal. See Sándor Pruzsinszky, *Ürményi József* (Budapest, 1990).

36. The speech may be found in the official records for the Diet. *Naponként-való jegyzései az 1790dik esztendőben* (Buda, 1790), pp. 2–8.

37. The theories of Carl Anton von Martini and Joseph von Sonnenfels were highly influential during the Josephinist period, particularly through their interpretation of the 'social contract'. Sonnenfels claimed that the social contract had been sealed not between the ruler and individuals, but with society as a whole. Thus, the general welfare of one uniform social class of citizenry took precedence over the interests of particular classes or factions, and in order to identify and promote the 'general' welfare, the ruler must be granted absolute authority to govern effectively. Sonnenfels also believed that the productive classes were the State's chief economic resource, and that their numbers should be increased to enhance State power and prosperity. Similarly, Martini claimed that the State originated not from God's grace, but from a pact of unity (*pactum unionis*) between family heads who agreed to enter into a 'civil society'. Despite asserting that democracy was the original form of government that existed in the 'state of nature', Martini argued that the 'people' had decided whether they wanted to submit instead to an oligarchy or monarchy. The people of Austria had chosen monarchy, and had thus voluntarily transferred their sovereignty to the monarch in a 'pact of subjection' (*pactum subjectionis*). Thus, while the rule of the sovereign derived from the general will and consent of the people, Martini rejected popular sovereignty, as in his view the people had renounced all their claims upon government – including the right to revolt – after entering the *pactum subjectionis*. This forfeiture of rights was legitimized by the eudaemonistic obligations of the sovereign, who was impelled to introduce enlightened reforms through positive legislation that conformed with natural law – a purportedly 'universal' law that reflected God's divine rationality. Martini's social contract was thus designed around a form of 'rational' monarchical rule, one that was ultimately sanctioned by God, but that also possessed a distinctly secular character, as the ruler had supposedly been granted a popular mandate to bring about change for the good of man. See Walter W. Davis, *Joseph II: An Imperial Reformer for the Austrian Netherlands* (Dordrecht, 1974), p. 103. Also, Teodora Shek Brnardić, 'Modalities of enlightened monarchical patriotism in the mid-eighteenth century Habsburg monarchy', in *Whose Love of Which Country? Composite States, National Histories and Patriotic Discourses in Early Modern East Central Europe* (Leiden and Boston, MA, 2015), pp. 631–62.

38. István Schlett, 'Elszalasztott lehetőség vagy zsákutca?', *Politikatudományi Szemle* v/1 (1996), pp. 7–42 (p. 23).

39. Henrik Marczali, 'Alkotmánytervezetek 1790-ben', *Budapesti Szemle* 125.351 (1906), pp. 393–422.

40. For a partial Hungarian translation see Gábor Pajkossy, *Magyarország története a 19. században. Szöveggyűjtemény* (Budapest, 2006), pp. 34–8.
41. Count Ferenc Széchényi (1754–1820) was born into a Catholic family of firm Habsburg loyalty, and was one of the wealthiest noblemen of eighteenth-century Hungary. He fathered the well-known reformer István Széchenyi, and also founded the Hungarian National Library and National Museum in Budapest by donating his private collections to the nation in 1802. Initially a supporter of Joseph II's autocratic but enlightened reforms, Széchényi received high office from the monarch in 1785, but resigned a year later, disenchanted with Joseph's methods. Following the monarch's death, Széchényi associated with other nobles who sought to introduce social reforms, even at the expense of their own privileges. He was, however, shocked by being blacklisted as a potential traitor by the court during the 1790/91 Diet. Unsettled by his wife's poor health and the execution of the Hungarian Jacobins in 1795, Széchényi succumbed to depression. He later recovered, and served under the reactionary Francis II; however, the former Freemason was now a Catholic bigot with an unswerving respect for authority. On retiring in 1808 he was awarded the Order of the Golden Fleece, the highest honour of the Habsburg Empire. See László Bártfai Szabó, *A Sárvár-Felsővidéki gróf Széchenyi-család története*, vol. II (Budapest, 1911).
42. Marczali, *Az 1790/1-diki országgyűlés*, vol. 1, pp. 83–8.
43. For the full text see Kálmán Benda, *A magyar jakobinusok iratai*, 3 vols (Budapest, 1952–7), vol. 1, pp. 50–60.
44. Born of an ignoble Lutheran family, József Hajnóczy (1750–95) studied law in Bratislava, and spoke several languages, including English. He worked as a secretary, most notably for Count Ferenc Széchényi in 1779. He was appointed as vice-lieutenant of Szerém County in 1786, but due to his ignoble status, lost his post after Joseph died. Hajnóczy had supported Joseph II in opposition to domestic feudalism, but turned to the ideas of enlightened constitutionalism and the French Revolution at the Diet of 1790/1. However, as a progressive, he became disillusioned with the noble-national movement of 1790/1; in 1791 he met Josephinist (and secret agent for Emperor Leopold II) Ignác Martinovics through the Freemasons. Hajnóczy's views became increasingly radical, especially following the reactionary politics of Francis II, and in 1793, Martinovics made him a prominent member of the Hungarian Jacobin movement. Martinovics's Jacobins planned a two-phase revolution: the first, led by the secret 'Society of Reformers', was intended to manipulate the feudal nobility into revolting against the Habsburgs. The second, led by the 'Society of Freedom and Equality', was to eliminate the members of the first feudal society. Insurrection was thus intended to remove both external and internal obstacles to reform. Finally, the Jacobins sought to establish an independent republic with a bicameral parliament, introduce press freedoms, emancipate the peasantry, abolish restrictions on domestic and foreign trade, and somewhat remarkably, transform the kingdom of Hungary into a federation of free

nations, each possessing its own constitution. In July 1794, however, both societies (somewhere between 200 and 300 people) were uncovered by the police. Following their trial, headed by József Ürményi, seven of their leaders, including Martinovics and Hajnóczy, were executed in 1795, and many of the Hungarian literati were imprisoned, including the language reformer Ferenc Kazinczy; fears of revolution and the advance of French armies galvanized noble support for the war effort against France, silencing the voice of reform for many years. For an exhaustive account of the Jacobins see Benda, *A magyar jakobinusok*; on Hajnóczy, see György Bónis, *Hajnóczy József: 1750–1795* (Budapest, 1954).

45. Benda, *A magyar jakobinusok*, vol. 1, p. 51.
46. A Lutheran, Péter Balogh (1748–1818) began work as a Nógrád County official in 1769 and became the county's vice-lieutenant in 1783. During the reign of Joseph II, who allowed Protestants to enter high office, he was appointed as a judge on the Royal Table in 1786, and on the Septemviralis Court or court of appeal in 1788. However, he opposed the tenets of Josephinian absolutism, and was removed from his post on the Septemviralis Court in 1789 after delivering a controversial speech in Nógrád. At the Diet of 1790/1 he became one of the main ideologues of the noble opposition as a representative for Nógrád County and a promoter of Protestant rights. His plan was supported by Protestants and Catholics alike, and even by some magnates, but was more influential among the eastern counties, as the Transdanubian counties remained more loyal to the King. As passions subsided at the Diet, Leopold II appointed Balogh as the lord-lieutenant of Torontál County. He worked as a court councillor in Vienna between 1793 and 1795, but returned to the Septemviralis Court in Pest due to ill health – a move that was thought to have implicated him in the Martinovics conspiracy. However, as the French Revolution progressed during the reign of Francis II, Balogh remained loyal to the court. See István Horváth, 'Balogh Péter', in *Nógrád Megyei Múzeumok Évkönyve* XX (Nógrád, 1995), pp. 11–31.
47. This was a politically motivated anachronism, as the law referred instead to a 'royal council'. Marczali, *Az 1790/1-diki országgyűlés*, vol. 2, p. 11.
48. Ibid., p. 154.
49. Ibid., vol. 1, pp. 230–9.
50. Many ideas, however, were shelved, and only resurfaced in the Reform Age. Martyn Rady, *Customary Law in Hungary: Courts, Texts, and the Tripartitum* (Oxford, 2015), pp. 218–20.
51. R.W. Seton-Watson, 'The era of reform in Hungary', *The Slavonic and East European Review*, American Series, ii (1943), pp. 145–66 (p. 148).
52. Ernst Wangermann, *From Joseph II to the Jacobin Trials* (London, 1959), p. 88.
53. A translation of Laws X and XII is given in the Appendix.
54. From Robert Townson, *Travels in Hungary, with a Short Account of Vienna in the Year 1793* (London: G.G. and J. Robinson, 1797), p. 2.
55. Henrik Marczali, *Magyarország története a szatmári békétől a bécsi congressusig (1711–1815)* (Budapest: Athenaeum, 1898), p. 409.

CHAPTER 5

REFORMING OR REPLACING THE HISTORICAL CONSTITUTION? LAJOS KOSSUTH AND THE APRIL LAWS OF 1848

Ferenc Hörcher

This chapter will reconstruct the events leading to the birth of a new, post-feudal parliamentary regime in mid-nineteenth-century Hungary, in order to reinterpret the original intentions of Lajos Kossuth, one of the founding fathers of the April Laws, the legal document on which the new regime was based. Between 3 March and 11 April 1848, the Hungarian Diet, the lawful organ of legislation in the Hungarian kingdom, peacefully convinced (or blackmailed, to use a stronger word) the lawful ruler of the country, King Ferdinand V, to sign 31 laws, establishing the new legal framework of a quasi-sovereign Hungarian kingdom under Habsburg rule.[1] The country before and after the April Laws was and remained in a peculiar legal relationship with the Habsburg Empire, sharing the persona of the ruler who ruled both territories from the royal court in Vienna, while the Hungarian kingdom had to be governed in accordance with the Hungarian constitutional tradition. The promulgation of the list of new laws unsettled the status of the historical constitution, and initiated a new phase of constitutional thinking in the political elite of the reform camp.

In fact, the April Laws of 1848 turned out to be the crowning moment of decades of political and constitutional struggle within the country and, much more emphatically, between the country and the Crown. The period between 1825 and 1848 is described in Hungarian historiography as the Reform Era, when the political elite tried to reconfigure the rules which framed political, economic and social life in the country, by introducing new legislation. This effort, however, was strongly opposed by the Habsburg court, because of the fears in Vienna of the efforts to gain 'independence' by the Hungarian political elite. When the April Laws were introduced, following a very short preparatory period, in the shadow of a Europe-wide wave of revolutions, they went well beyond the earlier expectations of the elite of the Reform Era, and yet their acceptance by the court could not prevent – in fact, as it turned out, they prepared the way for – the declaration of independence.

This chapter will deal with the birth of the April Laws, searching for the original intentions behind the document. It answers the following rather simple and yet very difficult question: should the April Laws be interpreted within the framework of the well-established 'ancient constitution' of *ancien régime* Hungary or should they be regarded as the expression of the nation's will to break with the past, giving up the centuries-long continuity of the historical constitution? The question seems to be simple, but to find the right answer is complicated by the fact that already on 15 March, according to contemporary descriptions, a public demonstration (revolution?) was taking place on the streets and squares of Pest–Buda (from 1873 Budapest), the social and economic centre of the country. Politically active youngsters were able to drum up public support for the new legislation prepared in Pozsony, the venue of the last *ancien régime* Diet. The street protest sparked off a 'bloodless' revolution (a term of which Hungarians were and have remained quite proud). This happened in the immediate aftermath of a prompt and loud conflagration of violent battles on the streets of major cities in Italy, France and Austria between the inhabitants and oppressors, which helped to push the demands forward in Hungary, too.

The April Laws were accepted and promulgated by due process, in accordance with the customs constraining legislative activity in the kingdom, supported by both the Lower and the Upper Houses of the Diet, and signed by the Crown as well. Their promulgation was followed by a lawful national election of parliamentary representatives. The new regime, however, could not stabilize its power, as both parties drifted away from their original position when the April Laws were promulgated and the tension soon provoked the armed attack of the troops of the Croatian Ban Count Josip Jelačić, most probably encouraged by the Viennese court, which caused the outbreak of what came to be called the war of independence in the country, which led step by step to the declaration of independence ritually proclaimed by the governor (*kormányzó*), Lajos Kossuth, in the Protestant stronghold of Debrecen in eastern Hungary. The line of dramatic events which led to this proclamation was concluded by the intervention of the Russian tsar in accordance with the agreements of the Holy Alliance of the European powers, ending what was by then a war of independence. The armed defeat of the independence efforts pushed the country back into a 15-year-long passive resistance, which led to the reopening of the negotiations establishing the Austro-Hungarian Dual Monarchy in 1867. The Hungarian part of the Dual Monarchy was ruled from then on in accordance with the principles of the April Laws from 1867 up until the end of World War I.

This chapter cannot give a detailed account of the perplexing constitutional history of mid-nineteenth-century Hungary. Neither is it an exercise in historical constitutional interpretation. Rather, it is concerned with a question recurring in the intellectual historical reconstructions of the period: what was the original intention behind the new legislation of April 1848, and how did it relate to the long-standing constitutional culture of the country? Compounding this problem is the question of how the protagonists (and especially the key player, Lajos Kossuth) understood their own roles. To answer these questions, the political manoeuvres which led to the drafting and promulgation of the new legislature will be reconstructed. This method is based on the assumption that by interpreting participants' political actions, together with the texts they have left behind, their way of thinking can be reconstructed as well as their view of the relationship of the new legislation to the constitutional traditions of the country.[2]

The Historiographical Issue and Eyewitness Accounts of Early 1848

The historiographical issue this chapter addresses concerns, in other words, the evaluation of the April Laws. Due to the bloodless revolution of Pest–Buda on 15 March it is hard to avoid applying the tempting label of revolutionary legislation. Interestingly enough, some of the most influential interpreters try to balance our understanding of these events. István Deák for example, the author of an influential monograph on 1848, which has been published in English, Hungarian and German, tried to rephrase the relationship between the March and the April events by introducing the label 'lawful revolution' (*törvényes forradalom*).[3] Although this expression seems to be a contradiction in terms, it serves very well the interpretative strategy to make sense of the revolutionary potential as well as the lawful procedural nature of the legislative process. In order to see both sides of the coin, it is worth recalling how Deák described events in his classic analysis.

As he claimed in the introduction to his work, in the spring of 1848 the Hungarian political elite managed to obtain a new constitution from the ruler. It is important to note that with this claim Deák described the April Laws as a new constitution, but he also adds that this achievement was made without bloodshed, which leads to the conclusion that if it was a revolution, it should be distinguished from the majority of such political events by calling it a lawful one. In his view, however, there were two further aims on the agenda of the Hungarian leaders: to win a leading position within the Habsburg Monarchy, and to gain control over the national minorities within the country's own territories. These further aims brought together their opponents – the Habsburg House, the Austrian government and the minorities – and the war that broke out made it unavoidable that 'in September 1848 the remaining Hungarian leaders stepped over from the road of reforms to the road of the revolution, still emphasizing that they did so out of necessity and not out of an ideological conviction.'[4] A further interesting twist of Deák's interpretation is that he thinks that although the war of independence was lost, the peace was won. He is referring with this expression to the Settlement establishing the Dual Monarchy in 1867, which in fact sanctified the victory of the Hungarian nobility, securing an equal stance in the Austro-Hungarian Empire.

Let us see another key player in the recent historiography of 1848. In an essay entitled 'The civil constitutional regime in 1848' ('A polgári alkotmányos államrendszer 1848-ban')[5] historian András Gergely presents the following case. First he refers to the contemporary judgement of the Hungarian royal chancellery, which claimed that the first drafts of the April Laws, which were under consideration in early 1848, 'did nothing more than concretize (at certain points developed) the immemorial constitution (*sok évszázados alkotmányt*)'.[6] In other words, they secured continuity between the historical constitution and the achievements of 1848. On the other hand, the *Staatskonferenz* held the view that the proposal was about 'a new constitution for Hungary', and its signing 'would mean the abdication of the king'.[7] Gergely's point here is to pose the question 'Was a new constitution born, or was the earlier one merely improved?' His answer departs from the fact that the new laws had no unifying structure, and this leads him to claim that 'no new constitution was drawn up', as they did not want to prepare a 'charter', but simply enact additional legislation. He compares this compromised development of a historical constitution to the British example, finding a number of common traits. The Hungarian nobility's aim was to develop the constitutional tradition of the estates into a proper constitutional parliamentary structure.

On the other hand, Gergely defends the notion of 'the constitution of 1848'. The reason for this is partly that a number of fundamental laws were enacted in 1848, and partly that the discrepancies between the valid legal framework and the *de facto* character of Habsburg rule over Hungary excluded the possibility of reinterpreting the institutional structure of the feudal constitution and smoothly transforming it into a guaranteed framework for a democratic parliamentary system. Therefore, Gergely argues, a complete break (which, however, was both legal and legitimate) with the world of the estates and its noble prerogatives was required. Gergely's narrative also, however, lays great emphasis on the fact that the actual content of the laws was to a large extent compromised, due to the 'urgency of the circumstances'.[8] At the same time, the small circle of the Hungarian political elite who actually took part in the process clearly committed themselves to 'lay the foundations of an evolving civil constitutional system (*polgári alkotmányos rendszer*)'.[9] For that very reason Gergely (who himself in this respect followed the path opened up by György Szabad) finds the expression 'the constitution of 1848' well-founded.

Let us turn to a third interpretation of the 1848 events. Professor László Péter had very fine historical judgement, and his analysis was also balanced. His essay on the events of 1848 was entitled 'Lajos Kossuth and the conversion of the constitution'.[10] Here the term 'conversion' is meant to present Péter's answer to the question of the continuity or discontinuity of the constitutional tradition in 1848. He puts it bluntly: 'The Hungarian constitution, in the widest sense of the term, was undoubtedly transformed in 1848.'[11] In his understanding, this conversion meant that 'the system of privileges was to be replaced by a social order based on legal equality.'[12] It also meant 'the transition from the customary constitution based on the bipolarity of the *ország* and the Crown to the all-embracing legal system, called the State, created by statute law'.[13] But this programme of '*alkotmányos kifejlés*' (constitutional development) was not fully realized, and even when it was, it was achieved through '*érdekegyesítés*' (interest-amalgamation) and '*jogkiterjesztés*' (extension of rights).[14] And even where it was realized, this was done gradually, and most importantly, he asserts 'the Hungarian position became more radical after the collapse of the Metternich system.'[15] The failure to complete the conversion was, however, occasioned by the competing interpretations of the actual content of the laws. 'Kossuth and Prime Minister Batthyány read "personal union" into the April Laws,' while 'the Austrian response was the claim to the existence of a *Gesamtstaat* (united state), read into the Pragmatic Sanction, which then justified the demand for the revision of the April Laws.'[16] In other words, both parties read the accepted laws as their own constitutional tradition and reason of state demanded. To be sure, the whole long nineteenth century of the Habsburg–Hungarian relationship is characterized by total incomprehension caused by talking at cross-purposes: the Habsburgs had to take care of the whole of their realm, while the Hungarian nobility defended their own freedoms and privileges, which were connected in their discourse with the liberty and constitutional self-standing of their country. These contrasting interpretations of the constitutional standing of Hungary in relation to the court led to an 'intractable constitutional conflict',[17] and ultimately war. There is no doubt that the two parties shared responsibility for the radicalization of the situation, but Péter emphatically criticizes

Kossuth's unrealistic hopes. In Péter's reading, Kossuth was not striving to restore the 'Hungarian State'; he rather sought to be its 'creator' as he intended to convert the constitutional standing of the *ország* into that of the state. The April Laws need, in this reading of 1848, to be distinguished from Kossuth's own ambitions.

Finally, mention should be made of a recent publication on the political languages of constitutionalism in 1848/9.[18] György Miru follows the research methods of the Cambridge historians of political thought, and Koselleck's school of conceptual history, by reconstructing the 'political languages' or discourses and analysing the meaning of the concepts used to debate the April Laws. He claims that the recurring question of whether a new constitution was born in 1848 is not tenable anymore, as the facts are clear: Hungarian legislators did not create a written, constitutional charter. He insists that Hungarian legislators did not want to codify the constitutional basic principles in the form of a systematic fundamental law, not only because of the lack of time. A further reason was that they were proud of their historical constitution, and they preferred to follow the norm-creating procedures employed earlier, interpreting and modifying the law as it appeared in custom and statute, in accordance with the requirements of the day.[19]

While stressing this continuity, Miru nevertheless repeatedly emphasizes that in introducing a new constitutional arrangement they not only established a new set of principles for the social system, but changed the political system as well.[20]

In what follows, inspiration taken from these historians will be used to show that even if the April Laws themselves were revolutionary in relevant respects (introducing the institutions of 'responsible government' (*felelős kormányzat*)[21] and the principle of popular representation, the abolition of serfdom and the eradication of unfair discrimination by the nobility), they were not conceptualized as a dramatic break with the past, as was the case with the French Revolution of 1789. Rather, the claim was that the achievements of the April Laws could easily be reconciled with the past, as they in fact grew out of the country's earlier constitutional traditions.[22] This claim was later empirically verified and reaffirmed by Ferenc Deák's use of the principles of the April Laws as the foundation of the settlement of 1867.

To formulate its thesis more precisely, this chapter will argue that while the formal aspects of the April Laws were mostly unassailable, their legal substance, namely the institutions they eliminated or created, as well as the new constitutional principles they involved were genuinely new. The further point will also be made that by keeping the formal aspects of a constitutional tradition intact, the April Laws reformed the substance of the historical constitution while preserving the continuity of the constitutional tradition. Nevertheless, these abrupt and daring institutional and conceptual innovations also risked the elimination of the constitutional tradition itself.

In order to substantiate the above point it is necessary to reconstruct the actual process which led to these unprecedented achievements. First of all, let us see those eyewitness reports which show that the events were experienced by their protagonists as a milestone in Hungarian history. Let us, for example, recall the radical voice of one of the youngsters who participated in the street demonstrations of 15 March. The words of the revolutionary poet Sándor Petőfi demonstrate that the 'Youth of March' (*Márciusi ifjak*) saw this day as a real historical turning point. He wrote in his diary:

> This was 15 March. Its results make this day for ever celebrated in Hungarian history. As a continuation of events, it would be, without doubt, ordinary; but if we take it as it was, as a beginning, it was great and glorious.[23]

His friend the novelist Mór Jókai, another famous protagonist of the events of this memorable day in Pest–Buda, shared this view. He claimed that 'the liberty of the Hungarian nation starts from this day. In the history of the Hungarian nation this was the epoch-making day.'[24]

But are these romantic writers reliable witnesses of the events that they participated in? No doubt their words were emotionally charged, which suggests that they should be read cautiously when trying to assess the historical significance of the political–legal transition of the spring of 1848. No doubt they played very important symbolic roles: they were among the first members of the public, of the fledgling civil society that was created in those moments, together with the unnamed citizens of and visitors to Pest–Buda, who in fact seized the political initiative on that very day. But none of them was actually involved in the institutional struggle that led to the birth of the April Laws.

Arguably, those who were somewhat older, and politically more experienced, namely the professional politicians, are more reliable guides. What did these people think of the events of 15 March from their places, not in the streets, but in the halls of the Diet and at the negotiations with the court? Let us consider the eyewitness report of Lajos Kossuth himself, the driving force behind the whole series of events that led to the passing of the April Laws. A very agile journalist and lawyer, with an exceptional capacity to influence both houses of parliament, the representatives of the nobility and the members of the aristocracy, Kossuth recalled that

> the logic of history is sometimes stranded for a long time, but sometimes in a minute it steps forward centuries. It has such a long footstep that the short-sighted only cries 'Who would have thought so?', and talks about an accident.[25]

One can certainly quote a number of further reports. Most of them would later agree that the political events of the spring of 1848 were exceptional, and that they had a long-term effect on Hungarian constitutional history. Even those who endorse the interpretation of the Reform Era of 1825–48 in the framework of an organic development of constitutional reforms would accept that 1848 in many ways brought an abrupt change: what was indeed desired by earlier generations had become true in the course of a few days, and even more.[26] The next question is: what made this breakthrough possible? Thinking through the possible causes of this breakthrough suggests that the direct and indirect influence of European affairs is not negligible. Let us now glance at the Continental panorama in early 1848.

Hungary and Europe in 1848: Parallels and Differences

The spring of 1848 brought a series of Europe-wide revolutions. This was not simply a coincidence as the continent's radical reform movements were mutually influenced by each other. Revolutionary ideals reverberated (for example, the slogans of the French Revolution) and spread the sparks of active political engagement. No doubt, the earlier constitutional experiments of the United States and the repeated efforts of the French to modernize their country's constitutional structure provided an impetus, too; one that was intensified by the exchange of ideas between networks of European progressive intellectuals. French authors with a lasting influence included such giants as Alexis de Tocqueville, the French aristocrat who traversed the new American republic, and penned his impressions in a thoughtful and influential way; Benjamin Constant, one of the key intellectual spokespersons of the new, revolutionary era; and François Guizot, a French statesman and historian. Paris, as a continental cultural centre, attracted a number of Hungarian noble intellectuals. Some of them even travelled as far as the US, such as the young Sándor Bölöni Farkas, who in 1831 published his experiences of the political culture of North America in a book which was widely read and discussed in contemporary Hungary.

Further external impacts on Hungary can also be discerned. After the dissolution of the Holy Roman Empire, and the establishment of the German Confederation in 1815, a number of new constitutions were drawn up, including those of Baden and Bavaria in 1818, Württemberg in 1819, Hessen–Darmstadt in 1820, and Brunswick, Hesse and Saxony in 1831. In fact, developments in the German states were even more appealing to mid-nineteenth-century Hungarian noble-politicians than the French example. This was partly due to similarities in the respective political cultures, and to the German political class's reputation for caution and moderation, qualities which dovetailed with the hesitant and risk-averse Hungarian nobility. It is therefore remarkable that, in spite of its earlier reservations, the Hungarian nobility gave up most of its privileges in 1848, which suggests that they were not as hopeless as they are preserved in the memory of the Hungarian public.[27]

For some of the best minds of the age, however, there were further examples of good practices – including the parliamentary monarchy of the British Isles, where a number of Reform Bills had been introduced in the first half of the nineteenth century. Some historians have noted the deep sympathy for the British constitutional system that inspired the events of 1848 in Hungary. As Gergely declared, 'what was created in 1848 was less a constitutional monarchy, but rather a parliamentary monarchy following the English system, based on the overwhelming power of the parliament.'[28]

The Belgian constitution of 1831, a model constitution which tried to unite the merits of the French, Dutch and British models, was also influential. It is noteworthy that the British constitutional theorist A.V. Dicey went as far as to claim that the Belgian constitution 'comes very near to a written reproduction of the English constitution'.[29] According to the recent historiography of 1848, this might have been the most influential inspiration for the founders of the 1848 'constitution'.[30]

In the run-up to the Hungarian constitutional moment of 1848, the revolutionary movement spread from Sicily in January, arrived in Paris on 22 February and reached Vienna on 13 March, one day before the Diet of Pozsony reconvened, in turn just one day before the events of 15 March in Pest–Buda. There can be no doubt that the Youth of March, who initiated the street protest in Pest–Buda, were inspired by the continental flow of revolutions. It is also beyond reasonable doubt that the events in Hungary could not have occurred without the external support they received from this international revolutionary movement, and the pressure it exercised on the Viennese court.

The temporal dimensions of the Hungarian constitutional process appear to be brief, beginning in January and concluding with the moment when the April Laws were authorized by the court's administration, giving in to the political pressure of the street and to the legal demands of the Diet. However, from a *longue durée* perspective, the Hungarian elite had already started work on these items of legislation during the reform Diets of the very early 1790s, and only returned to them after decades of stagnation in which the constitutional life of the country was suspended and frozen by the decision of Vienna. There is insufficient time here to follow events on this grand historical scale. Instead, this chapter will concentrate on the short-term perspective: on the last feverish days of the Diet, when the texts of the new laws were prepared, and the obligatory 'nihil obstat' was obtained from all constitutional parties involved. This approach is based on the assumption that by slowing down the pace of history, as we slow down the projection of a film, in order to see the individual frames one after the other, the details that are lost during the normal, real-time tempo of the events become clearer. This chapter seeks to provide a clearer picture of the intentions of the participants by interpreting their actions as reactions to the earlier deeds of others. After all, politics is a large-scale strategic game, in which most often action is followed by reaction and vice versa. One needs to take account of this interaction between the players to make sense of their occasionally original way of thinking.

The Last Days of the Process that Led to the April Laws

To understand the essence of the new legislation, the immense political pressure of the moment has to be reconstructed in order to appreciate Lajos Kossuth's brilliant rhetorical and political moves, his reactions to the particular needs of the moment. In this section we show how his practical genius was alert to every unexpected opportunity, and how – as a good lawyer – he never made a mistake in when and how to advance his case. It will be argued that it was basically his skills, as well as the efforts of the Palatine of Hungary, Stephen Francis Victor, who rather unexpectedly stood up for the Hungarians, that made the constitutional moment of 1848 so productive in Hungary.[31]

At the beginning of 1848 a balanced political situation characterized the Diet's Lower House, controlled by the nobility: the opposition and the pro-government forces had equal power, and the distance between their positions looked unbridgeable. After receiving news of the Italian revolutionary movements, Kossuth proposed that the opposition should introduce a bill with a demand which could achieve a conclusive breakthrough, but this was then still rejected by the leaders of the opposition factions.

On 1 March the news of the Paris revolution reached Pozsony, and the members of the Diet anxiously debated the thrilling events. As a result of these discussions the opposition was ready to support Kossuth's new proposals for reform with enthusiasm. On 3 March, building his argument on the facts of the financial crisis of the empire, Kossuth gave a dramatic speech in the Lower House, in which he put forward a whole list of demands in a draft Address (*felirati javaslat*) from the Diet to the Crown. The starting point was the claim that 'the actual cause of the breaking up of peace in the monarchy, and of all the evils which may possibly follow from it, lies in the system of Government,'[32] very cleverly drawing the picture of a century-long opposition between the absolutist system of government of Vienna and 'the constitutional direction of the Hungarian nation' (*a magyar nemzet alkotmányos iránya*). After this introduction he did not hesitate to mention most of the major demands of the opposition reformers, debated by the reform Diets of the last two decades, including the abolition of serfdom, the sharing of social burdens, a parliamentary system with popular representation, and a system of responsible government. He did not address the issue of the independence of Hungary, did not question the legitimacy of the Hungarian Crown, and certainly kept his proposals within the confines of the constitutional tradition of the country, even taking care not to disregard the interests of the House of Habsburg. What he did, however, was to refer to the introduction of new constitutional measures as the key to solving the crisis within the empire, claiming 'that bond of Constitutionalism which can produce a kindred feeling'.[33] In a prophetic voice he also heralded the personal consequences of the recent European wave of revolutions, warning that 'in a few days the men of the past will descend into their graves,' and he also touted (perhaps in this case tactlessly) the name of the Archduke as a future occupant of the Hungarian throne:

> for that scion of the House of Habsburg who excites such great hopes, for the Archduke Francis Joseph, who with his first appearance earned the love of the nation – for him there waits the inheritance of a splendid throne which derives its strength from freedom.[34]

The astonishing result of this combination of compromise and blackmail was that the deeply divided Lower House offered its unanimous support to Kossuth. However, for the moment, the Address could not be sent to the Upper House for approval, as all the main dignitaries of the country, including the Palatine (*nádor*) and the Chief Justice (*országbíró*) – who normally presided over the Upper House – were cautiously ordered to Vienna for an emergency meeting. Court circles considered the option of disbanding the Diet, while one of the most prestigious reform politicians, Count István Széchenyi, who at this time was sharply opposed to Kossuth's radicalism, volunteered to take control of the Diet as a plenipotentiary royal commissioner, but even he was not trusted by Vienna in this strained situation.

It was during these nerve-breaking moments of waiting and seeing that József Irinyi, a representative of the Pest-based civil initiative of young intellectuals called the Opposition Circle (*Ellenzéki Kör*), arrived to meet Kossuth in Pozsony. He and the circle he represented publicly supported Kossuth's 'Address' to the Lower House by collecting signatures from sympathizers all around the country. It was after their exchange of views that Irinyi finalized the famous 12 points of 12 March, which presented the reform agenda in a popular format to the participants of the signature-collecting campaign. As it turned out later, his short list of radical political demands was the inspiration behind the 15 March street demonstrations in Buda and Pest, along with the poem 'National Song' (*Nemzeti dal*) written for this occasion by Petőfi, the most radical and popular of the young poets and intellectuals. Both of these short pieces were printed illegally, by the printing machine of Landerer and Heckenast, seized in the name of the people on 15 March (with the support of the owner himself). This symbolic and practical deed was the first expression of the demand for the freedom of the press. However, to bring popular enthusiasm to fruition a further external influence was required.

On 14 March Hungarians received the news that revolution had also broken out in Vienna.[35] The people of that city, together with the local administration and the provincial assembly (*Tartománygyűlés, Provinzversammlung*), called for the guiding statesman of the empire, Prince Metternich, to be dismissed and – in keeping with Kossuth's oration on 3 March – a new constitution was demanded by the revolutionaries to sate the passions of the people. The excitement of the Viennese revolutionaries was fuelled by the street distribution of the German version of the text of Kossuth's great speech in the Hungarian Diet on 3 March. It was translated by 4 March, giving impetus to the mobilizing activity of the *Juristischer Leserverein*,[36] demonstrating that the revolutionary spirit could be transferred back and forth, from Pozsony to Vienna as well as from Vienna to Pozsony.[37] In contrast to the bloodless nature of the 15 March demonstration in Pest–Buda, the army opened fire on the crowds in Vienna, barricades were raised, fires were lit and factories were demolished. The court dismissed Metternich, promised a constitution, permitted the organization of a militia and proclaimed the liberty of the press.

In the meantime, Archduke Stephen, Palatine of Hungary, travelled to Pozsony in a futile effort to stave off revolution. He summoned the representatives of the Diet's Upper House, and let them approve Kossuth's draft Address. Apparently the Habsburg administration thought that this was the lesser of two evils, and would take the wind out of the Hungarian sails.

If the aim was to calm passions, the move was not successful. On 15 March the Diet sent a delegation of 100 from Pozsony to the capital, Vienna, where it was received by a celebrating crowd, while at the same time Irinyi, Petőfi, Pál Vasvári and the other members of the Opposition Circle provoked a public demonstration in the streets of Pest–Buda, and by the end of the day they could claim to have initiated what was regarded as the revolution of 15 March. The institutions of public administration (the City Council and the Council of the Palatine, *Városi és Helytartótanács*) gave in and accepted the demands of a crowd of 20,000, conveyed to them by the newly appointed Revolutionary Committee (*Forradalmi Választmány*).

The next day Viennese court officials met the delegation of the Hungarian Diet, and accepted Kossuth's Address, which was by now supported by both the Diet's houses. The following evening, on 17 March, the main decision making body of *ancien régime* Austria, the *Staatskonferenz*, met for the last time. It received the news of the revolution in Pest–Buda. The *Staatskonferenz* decided to make the concession to the Hungarians that the King would accept Kossuth's Address. But the resolution of the Crown only referred to the Archduke's official assignment as Palatine, but not to that of Batthyány as prime minister. It also contained a summons for the Palatine to prepare a bill for the establishment of a responsible ministry.

After his talk with Kossuth and Batthyány, however, Archduke Stephen seized the initiative (with the oral agreement of the monarch, his nephew, Ferdinand V) and on 17 March appointed Lajos Batthyány as prime minister of Hungary.

After this decision, from 18 March onwards, reform laws were drafted amidst much animated and heated discussion in Pozsony. Hesitant aristocrats were intimidated by false reports of peasant uprisings in the countryside, and by rumours that Petőfi had assembled a peasant army outside Pest. They accepted the social reforms, including the abolition of serfdom, without any further reservations.

This move was affirmed by Prime Minister Batthyány, who sent out a circular on 23 March in which he informed the county assemblies of the new legislation on the abolition of serfdom. Unfortunately and against the law, this circular preceded the actual decision of the Diet, which should have enacted this policy.

The Diet had good reason to speed up the process. A counter-attack from the Court tried to delay the abolition of slavery and the establishment of the responsible government on 28 March. However, strong reactions came both from Pest and Pozsony, and when the Austrian officials received news of the outbreak of hostilities between the Italian revolutionaries and Austrian soldiers, an agreement was swiftly reached between the Diet and the Crown. The April Laws were accepted by the Emperor on 7 April, and he had no option but to appoint the remaining ministers of the Hungarian government.

As a final ritual act, on 11 April the laws were promulgated in the presence of the Emperor, and with that the last feudal Diet (and the last parliament in Pozsony) was closed down. The feudal structure of society was demolished, and a new, constitutionally legitimized responsible government took control of the country. The institution of the Palatine's Council was dissolved, and Hungary was not run by the organs of the empire anymore, even if Hungary remained a part of the empire as far as its external policies were concerned – including military organization, foreign affairs, the budget and the common issues of the empire.

Conclusions Drawn from the Slow-Motion Historical Narrative

Let us try to draw generalized conclusions from the above narrative. As it seems, Kossuth had an unparalleled political genius, which helped change the entire political landscape: he led the reformist elite of the Hungarian Diet to victory, inspired the Pest–Buda and Viennese revolutionaries, and later mesmerized ordinary people. He was a charismatic leader who had no scruples, and risked everything if he saw at least a minimal chance for a breakthrough. But the international background offered unparalleled help to him in this struggle.

One should also point out that he had not yet become a revolutionary. He had the necessary skills to orchestrate the breakthrough, but there was no need to use unwarranted political means to bring it about. He easily and promptly adapted to the situation when external effects changed the political landscape. Whenever he experienced deadlock, as on 3 March, 17 March and during the final stages of the process, he employed new techniques to vindicate his political will. He was very good at combining promises and praise with intimidations and threats. He had a number of personal enemies, and yet the elite as a whole, faced with his fanatical supporters, taken together, was not strong enough to turn against him. But he did not push the reformist agenda beyond the threshold of revolution. He was well aware that he and Batthyány needed to preserve constitutional norms so long as they could be used to create the new government.[38] He wanted to safeguard the economic and political interests of the nobility, which was seriously afflicted by the abolition of serfdom. Therefore, he did not want to introduce a properly bourgeois constitution. His main support came from the traditional political class in the countryside; this is why he avoided a reform scheme to annul the anachronistic county-system. Instead, he was obliged to rely on his hinterland, and did not want to take on unnecessary burdens and risks. This might have been the cause of his hesitancy to introduce constitutional measures to satisfy the demands of the ethnic minorities or of the Jewish part of the population: his popular mandate might have been endangered by these measures, and he wanted to avoid empowering his opponents. Although he was convinced of his own 'truth', his ideology did not blind him. He calmed the fears of the court by downgrading the chances of a secessionist movement in Hungary, and persuaded the Archduke to stand up for the Hungarian cause by promising to maintain the throne of the country. His alliance with Batthyány also turned out to be a sound tactical move: he could directly influence the government's political direction through his personal relationship with the Prime Minister. In these days the cautious Deák was just as much on his side as were the revolutionary youth of Pest–Buda. And yet he did not seek a major post in the first government. He knew he had to wait for his moment, and it arrived soon enough. For the time being, therefore, he remained a constitutionally legitimate political force within the political elite.

Most importantly, it was Kossuth's situational acuteness which made the lawfully revolutionary April Laws possible. As a result of his practically wise tactics, the new legislation was daring, but not unrealistic; courageous but also very circumspect; in line with the revolutionary movements of Europe, while still preserving the essence of the ancient constitution.

Continuity or Break? 1848 and the Constitutional Tradition in Hungary

As the above analysis of the endgame of the feudal Diet shows, Lajos Kossuth was one of those rare talents in politics who are able to articulate popular demands, and translate them not only into political action, but also into a constitutional rearrangement or reshuffling. However, according to his fiercest opponents, including Count Széchenyi, or his earlier allies and later critics, like Zsigmond Kemény, he could not be satisfied with this outcome.[39] Already, prior to the revolution, his greatest opponent, Széchenyi, discerned in him a revolutionary dogmatism which was already apparent at the beginning of the 1840s, and would eventually lead him to disregard political reality.[40] However, without Kossuth the April Laws could not have been drawn up in 1848, and the government of Batthyány could not have been established. While Széchenyi himself had an admirably realistic attitude in his civil projects, exemplified by his philanthropic and construction activities, such as the donation to establish the Academy of Sciences and the National Casino, yet his daily political practice lacked the skills which Kossuth employed in this period. An exceptionally acute sense of politics was required to rule the Diet in a divided society like that of nineteenth-century Hungary. Nevertheless, his prediction that the radicalism of Kossuth would lead the country into a revolutionary disaster turned out to be correct, according to most of the survivors of the conflict that broke out at the end of 1848 between Hungary and the Crown, as well as according to many historians of the period. In the aftermath of the lost war of independence, Zsigmond Kemény, one of the brightest intellectuals of the age, while defending his own role in the gradual radicalization of the wartime government, also accused Kossuth of possessing a revolutionary fervour which set the nation afire, and led directly to the shock and terror after the war of independence was crushed by the overwhelming preponderance of the Russian Tsar's troops.[41] This might be an exaggeration, but to most of his critics, Kossuth was a populist politician who had inbuilt autocratic tendencies, and as president of the Committee of National Defence (*a Honvédelmi Bizottmány elnöke*) was destined to grasp the executive power at a certain point, and to proclaim the independence of the country from the

Habsburg House, because 'the House of Habsburg–Lorraine, perjured in the sight of God and man, had forfeited the Hungarian throne.'[42] This straightforward and abrupt move determined the fate of the reform movement, made any further concessions by the Habsburgs impossible, and legitimized their interference in Hungarian affairs which culminated in the complete reincorporation of Hungary into a newly centralized empire.

The April Laws must, however, be distinguished from these later developments, just as the Kossuth who fought for these laws must be distinguished from the Kossuth who turned into the autocratic leader of the Hungarian independence movement. The April Laws were the result of a legally spotless procedure (except for Batthyány's decision to announce the abolition of serfdom before it was actually enacted by the Diet), and no neutral critic has ever questioned their legitimacy. Therefore, it cannot be claimed that they broke constitutional continuity. It was due to the laws' formally spotless birth that the historian István Deák could call this achievement a 'lawful revolution'.[43] The fact that this phrase is a contradiction in terms calls attention to the Janus face of the event. The April Laws dramatically changed the content or substance of the law but formally they were continuous with earlier constitutional arrangements. As Kossuth argued in his great speech of 3 March:

> Your Majesty's imperial government – not being constitutionally directed – paralysed the autonomy of our government as well as our constitutional life. So far, this direction has only hindered the development of our constitutionality, but now we see, that if it is continued this way and is not brought into harmony with constitutionality, Your Majesty's throne and your empire, brought together with us by beloved bonds through the Pragmatic Sanction, will face incurable consequences, and cause our homeland unutterable damages [...] Your Majesty has summoned us to reform, we saw it as fulfilling our old expectations, and we are ready to work industriously.[44]

From Kossuth's perspective, the April Laws were not intended to be revolutionary, but whether their legally undisputed birth also implies that they were meant to be integrated into the largely uncodified historical constitution of Hungary, or whether they were intended to mark a new beginning in Hungary's constitutional history, remains controversial.

One can approach the issue of the legitimacy of Kossuth's constitutional hyperactivity from another angle, too. The question raised from this perspective is whether what Kossuth achieved can be said to have originated from the will of the people. It might be possible to forcefully argue that the April Laws had the support of a large majority of the people. Due to the fact, however, that the ancient constitution was still in power when these laws were being formulated, they had to be drafted by the delegates to the Diet rather than the people. Under the earlier regime, the nobility, who dominated the Diet, enjoyed a privileged constitutional status. And yet this fact did not prevent their representatives passing the April Laws, which in the short run was against their interests. After all, they had to surrender a lot of their constitutional privileges in order to rally the people behind the fortification of the constitution. Notice that the Preamble of the Laws uses expressions such as

> to unite the whole Hungarian people's rights and interests' [...] 'to secure lawful autonomy for the country (*ország*)' [...] 'the lawful relations to the provinces of the empire to which by virtue of Pragmatic Sanction the *ország* was indissolubly connected' [...] 'to give voice to the constitutional life of the nation, the requirements of the age, the urgency of the circumstances; and the ardent concord of the spiritual powers and material talents.'[45]

Anyone ready to admit that the masterful skills of Kossuth were used here to give voice to the demands of ordinary people should also admit that this was a legitimate justification for his political actions. Naturally, it was the political leader's alertness that was required to operationalize the resentment of the bulk of the population, who for centuries had been excluded from participating in the nation's politics and economy. As always, when a window opens on the future, someone has to grasp the *kairotic* moment, and Kossuth's accomplishment was to find the right arguments for it by exploiting both the internal and the external context, to guide the Diet as it drafted the actual wording of the laws, and then put in motion the somewhat rusty but still working cogwheels of the Diet's venerable decision making mechanisms one final time.

Once More on Péter's Views and The Enduring Relevance of 1848

In his posthumously collected volume of essays, *Hungary's Long Nineteenth Century*, Péter, in his characteristic non-Whig style of history writing, claimed that in Hungary, during the nineteenth century, a 'long, discontinuous process' took place, namely 'the conversion of the constitution'.[46] He describes this conversion as one in which a 'system based largely on customary rights was transformed into one partly based on statute law'.[47] As he saw it, the issue was more than the form of the law. It had clear consequences for the substance of the law. The April Laws also brought about basic institutional transformations of society, for, as Péter explained, 'the segmentary "feudal" society, based on a hierarchy of privileges, was replaced by a social order founded on a unitary legal system."[48] This sounds like a rather dramatic social reformulation, but the delegates to the Diet tried their best to soften the effects of the drastic new legislation. They were well aware that they neither could nor should change social reality abruptly, and they had in fact no such intention. Péter states the case very clearly when he notes that 'the programme did not include the creation of a society led by the bourgeoisie.'[49] This is because although the nobility was prepared to give up its immunities, even the most radical part of this stratum, including Kossuth and his closest allies, wanted 'to preserve the ascendancy of the nobility in society'.[50] In fact, they worked with the well-educated, sociable and productive members of the bourgeoisie, but never thought to give up their (the nobility's) traditional leading political role to achieve their ambitions.

In the political arena the real change was that politics was removed from the level of 'the loyal aristocracy' and from the court authorities, councils and bureaus, which were dependent on the Crown, and was now conducted by the nobility (the Lower House of the Diet) and its organ, the government in Pest–Buda. The nature and composition of this politically active nobility are readily explained by Péter's description of them as the *'bene possessionati'*, the well-to-do landed nobility (*birtokos köznemesség*).[51]

In spite of the new content of the law, Péter convincingly argues that there was nothing revolutionary in the April Laws: first of all, internally, because of the procedural smoothness of the transition and secondly, externally, because the Hungarian elite did not strive for secession from the empire. He notes that 'the April Laws of 1848 made abundantly clear that Hungary was to remain a part of the empire.'[52] Moreover, the social consequences of the April Laws were not at all radical; the civil society that the laws sought to create was understood in the pre-Hegelian rather than in the Marxist sense. There is nothing in the April Laws that echoes the language of the *Communist Manifesto*.[53] In other words, neither in their form nor in their content were they a revolutionary piece of legislation. In this sense the procedure that brokered them was not only lawful, but also constitutionally orthodox and legitimate.

But if they were not revolutionary, why did the political edifice constructed by the April Laws collapse so rapidly? Péter offers his own explanation why the compromise of 1848 could not hold, when he writes that 'the Hungarian political elite and the politicians in Vienna did not keep to their terms.'[54] According to this argument, if the April Laws had been observed on both sides of the conflict, it could have been advantageous for both parties. It was the voluntary transgression of the laws by the two partners that led first to the armed conflict, later to the declaration of independence and finally to the tsarist invasion and the absolutist rule of Vienna in the 1850s. Péter is refreshingly unbiased: he is aware, and makes us aware, of the responsibility of both parties for the deadlock. The new constitutional settlement of 1848 failed to endure not because of the inherent content of the April Laws, but because the spirit of compromise and settlement that had led to their enactment was abandoned by the two opposing poles of the constitutional arrangement itself.

It is noteworthy that in spite of his critical tone, Péter is not really pessimistic about the long-term effects of 1848. First of all, in his view, Ferenc Deák could not have negotiated with Francis Joseph to achieve what Péter consistently calls the 1867 settlement (and not the 1867 compromise) without the standards provided by the April Laws.[55] If, on the other hand, one argued that 1867 itself was not a long-lasting achievement, he would reply with a second argument about the long-lasting relevance of 1848: 'Although the April Laws failed as a settlement, they, and above all the new claims read into them, set political standards that survived even after the collapse of the Habsburg Monarchy at the end of World War I.'[56]

To measure the durability of these standards and to comprehend the influence of the April Laws on Hungarian public mentality, an obvious point of reference is to see how the transition in 1989–90 recycled its basic values. On 15 March 1989, when a huge mass demonstration was held in Pest, leading to the symbolic public occupation of the headquarters of the state television (on Liberty Square, opposite the American Embassy), a popular actor, György Cserhalmi, read out to the crowd an updated version of the 12 points, connecting 1848, 1956 and 1989. Among these basic demands were the call for multi-party elections, the establishment of the rule of law, freedom of speech and liberty of the press, as well as the liberation of the country from Soviet rule.[57] This was an elevating moment: in spite of all the petty debates among the new political parties which tried to capitalize on the evaporating power of the governing Hungarian Socialist Workers' Party (*Magyar Szocialista Munkáspárt*), participants in the mass rally were enthusiastic about the 12 points and showed their support for a change of system. Then, again, events gathered speed. Within a week, the Opposition Round Table (*Ellenzéki Kerekasztal*) was called together, and by 10 June an agreement had been signed with the ruling party to initiate the National Roundtable Talks (*Nemzeti Kerekasztal Tárgyalások*), the platform which discussed the lawful transition from a totalitarian to a democratic regime.[58] The lost hopes of 1849 and 1956 had once again been revived.

Having identified the main pillars of its public memory, a short historical overview of how '48 kept influencing later Hungarian political and social history might be useful. The example of 1848 had already become a reference point for the Hungarian public in the 1860s. The common saying, '*Nem engedünk a negyvennyolcból!*' ('No backsliding from the achievements of '48!'), was a very successful slogan of the Independence Party in the debates about Deák's 1867 settlement.[59] After the Treaty of Trianon in 1920, when the Dual Monarchy was officially declared dissolved by the international community, the historical kingdom of Hungary ceased to be and its legitimate king departed, with the loss of the larger part of its territory and a significant portion of its inhabitants, a reference to 1848 meant a harking back to a Golden Age when the country was still ready to stand up to defend its constitutional integrity. But 1848 was also exploited by the propaganda machinery of the neo-Baroque Horthy regime of the interwar period just as much as by the new, Communist totalitarian regime after World War II. To exaggerate the revolutionary character of 1848 served propaganda functions for the Stalinist Rákosi regime in Hungary: it was presented as an unprecedented social upheaval, and the nationalist element of it was downplayed. And yet the anti-totalitarian 'people's uprising' (*népfelkelés*) of 1956 (as it was famously called by Imre Pozsgay in 1989)[60] consciously traced back its connections to the youth movement of '48. Therefore the mass rallies of the late 1980s were often connected to this highly symbolic national holiday: 'in 1988 [...] the regime broke up the demonstrations organized by opposition groups to commemorate symbolic anniversaries such as the revolution of 1848 in March, Imre Nagy's execution in June, and the 1956 uprising in October.'[61]

As was pointed out earlier, the most compelling genealogy of 1990 connects the following three historical data: 1848–1956–1989/90. The presumption of this overarching meta-narrative is that there is a continuity in Hungarian political history, which links the youthful and revolutionary character of each new generation as it strives (often in vain) for liberty. As A. Körner points out, 'in 1956, and again in 1989, it [i.e. 1848] was the model for national uprisings.'[62] Paradoxically, 1990 also turned out to be a lawful revolution, as 1848 was. In fact, the first prime minister of the post-transition period, the historian József Antall, famously complained to his disgruntled parliamentary fraction, who were dissatisfied with the pace of change, 'if only you had made a revolution!'

As this example shows, public imagination in Hungary still preserves something of the revolutionary overtones of the cult of 1848. The national tricolor has been preserved since 1848. After the transition, the Kossuth coat of arms was a strong contender to become the official coat of arms of Hungary, only finally overcome by a parliamentary majority voting for the medieval one. When in 2010 Fidesz won a two-thirds majority, the Prime Minister claimed to have pulled off a 'ballot box revolution', most probably pointing back to the peaceful nature of both 1848 and 1956.[63]

When in 2012 the new Fundamental Law of Hungary came into force, it was seen as a legal–political document which tried to rebuild the ancient architecture of Hungarian constitutionalism, incorporating the best moments (constitutional achievements) of the nation's struggle for survival, including 1848. Constitutional continuity is an important building block in the historical narrative of the preamble to the newly accepted Fundamental Law, too: its text contains elevated references to the most important national holidays, including 15 March 1848, 20 August (St Stephen the King's day), and 23 October, commemorating the outbreak of the 1956 Revolution.

In an important sense the public memory of Hungary still preserves a revolutionary identity. If historians try to demystify these turning points, it is a question of identity for most members of the political mainstream to defend the heroic aspects of the past of the political community, even if professional research has revealed their fictitious nature. Memory politics, of course, wages wars to occupy the major points of a tragic history. However, there are hardly any responsible participants in the political life of the country who would not regard 1848 as one of the glorious moments of our common history. This is, in itself, a sign that 1848 could find its place in the continuity of the country's constitutional life. In fact, it has turned by now into one of the most stable foundation stones of the community's self-perception.

Notes

1. For the origin and ideology of the Diet, as the institutionalized expression of the country, see István M. Szijártó, 'The Diet: The estates and the parliament of Hungary, 1708–1792', in G. Ammerer et al. (eds), *Bündnispartner und Konkurrenten des Landesfürsten? Die Stände in der Habsburgermonarchie* (Vienna and Munich, 2007), pp. 119–39.
2. This method owes a lot to, but does not simply take over the one used in, the work of the late Professor László Péter, which tried to identify 'constitutional forms and ideas' in a wide sense. See 'Introduction', in Miklós Lojkó (ed.), *Hungary's Long Nineteenth Century: Constitutional and Democratic Traditions in a European Perspective. Collected Studies of László Péter* (Leiden and Boston, MA, 2012), pp. 1–14. It is also influenced by John G. A. Pocock's writings on the ancient constitution, and by the nuanced historical reconstructions of early modern political debates by István Hont.
3. István Deák, *The Lawful Revolution. Louis Kossuth and the Hungarians, 1848–1849* (New York and London, 1979). The Hungarian language version: *A törvényes forradalom. Kossuth Lajos és a magyarok 1848–49-ben*, translated by Éva Veressné Deák (Budapest, 1994).
4. István Deák, 'Introduction', in Deák, *The Lawful Revolution*.
5. András Gergely, 'A polgári alkotmányos államrendszer 1848-ban', originally published as 'Az 1848-as magyar polgári államszervezet', in A. Csizmadia et al. (eds), *A magyarországi polgári államrendszerek* (Budapest, 1981), pp. 50–80,

republished with a new title in András Gergely, *Egy nemzetet az emberiségnek. Tanulmányok a magyar reformkorról és 1848-ról* (Budapest, 1987), pp. 380–430. It is important to note here that the Hungarian word *polgár* (just like German *Bürger*) has two different meanings: it can be used in a social-political context to refer to the citizen or burgher, the member of a political community, or in an economic context it can refer to the figure of the bourgeois, one who is (self-)employed in urban economic–financial activities, like commerce or industry, and who is associated with the idea of the entrepreneur.
6. Ibid., p. 380.
7. Ibid. Gergely quotes these views from Árpád Károlyi, *Az 1848-diki pozsonyi törvénycikkek az udvar előtt* (Budapest, 1936), pp. 58, 70. He also refers to E.W. Stroup, *Hungary in Early 1848: The Constitutional Struggle against Absolutism in Contemporary Eyes* (New York, 1977).
8. Gergely refers here to the foreword (*Előbeszéd*) of the April Laws, which uses the following term: 'a körülmények sürgős volta'. *1848. évi törvénycikk. Előbeszéd*, available at https://1000ev.hu/index.php?a=3&param=5268 (accessed 3 March 2018).
9. Ibid., p. 382.
10. Péter, in Lojkó, *Hungary's Long Nineteenth Century*, p. 199.
11. Ibid.
12. Ibid., p. 201.
13. Ibid.
14. Ibid., p. 202. 'In the preamble of the April Laws, the estates [...] listed [...] the intention "to unite the interests, under the Law, of the whole Hungarian people".' *Előbeszéd, 1848–1849. évi törvények*, quoted by Péter in Lojkó, *Hungary's Long Nineteenth Century*, p. 207.
15. Ibid., p. 206.
16. Ibid., p. 208. In fact Péter claimed that both partners to this conflict of the *Gesamt-Monarchy* and the *magyar álladalom* 'trampled on centuries-old traditions although they were dressed up in historic guise'.
17. Ibid., p. 209.
18. György Miru, *Az alkotmányozás politikai nyelve 1848–49-ben* (Budapest, 2015).
19. Ibid., p. 12.
20. Ibid., p. 13.
21. Before 1848 Hungary was practically governed from the administrative offices of the Habsburg court called *Helytartótanács* (Locotenential Council).
22. Gergely, "A polgári alkotmányos államrendszer 1848-ban", p. 382. He compares this Hungarian development to the 'English development'.
23. 'Ez volt március 15-ke. Eredményei olyanok, melyek e napot örökre nevezetessé teszik a magyar történetben. Események folytatásának ez közönséges volna, kétségkívül, de tekintve annak, ami volt, kezdetnek nagyszerű, dicső.' (Sándor Petőfi, *Összes prózai művei és levelezése* (Budapest, 1960), p. 409.) Quoted by Gábor Gyáni, 'A történelmi esemény fogalma', *Magyar Tudomány* clxxii/11 (2011), pp. 1324–32 (p. 1324). One should note that Petőfi took his own

words so seriously that he was ready to sacrifice his life on what he regarded as the altar of the war of independence (*szabadságharc*) in one of the last battles of 1849.
24. 'A magyar nemzet szabadsága e naptól kezdődik. A magyar nemzet történetében ez volt az epochális nap.' (Ferenc Bay (ed.), *1848–49 a korabeli napilapok tükrében* (Budapest, 1943), p. 13, quoted by Gyáni, 'A történelmi esemény', p. 1324.)
25. Lajos Kossuth, *Kossuth Lajos iratai VII.* s. a. r. Kossuth Ferenc (Budapest, 1900), pp. 203–4, quoted by Gyáni 'A történelmi esemény', p. 1327.
26. On the historiographical debate about whether the Reform Era lasted only 25 years, or should be counted from 1790, see Ferenc Hörcher, 'Enlightened reform or national reform? The continuity debate about the Hungarian reform era and the example of the two Széchenyis (1790–1848)', *Hungarian Historical Review* v/1, pp. 22–45.
27. In some respects, Hungarian poetry and fictional narrative is responsible for these rather critical views; see the poems of Petőfi or the novels of Eötvös. On the other hand, 1848 had its own cult, again fuelled by literature, as the novels of Jókai show.
28. Gergely, *Az 1848-as parlament*, p. 329.
29. Albert Venn Dicey, *An Introduction to the Study of the Law of the Constitution* (London, 1885).
30. Gábor Erdődy, 'A reformkori magyar parlamentarizmus mintái Nyugat-Európában', in T. Dobszay et al. (eds), *Rendiség és parlamentarizmus Magyarországon. A kezdetektől 1918-ig* (Budapest, 2013), pp. 337–43, especially pp. 341–2. For a longer overview of the Belgian constitutional regime, see G. Erdődy, 'Szabadságot mindenben'.
31. In what follows I will rely on the summary of the events of early and mid-March given by András Gergely in A. Gergely (ed.), *19. századi magyar történelem 1790–1918* (Budapest, 1998), pp. 249–52. See also his 'Az 1848-as parlament', in Dobszay (ed.), *Rendiség*, pp. 329–36. A short overview of the period is available in English as well: C.A. Macartney, *Hungary. A Short History* (Edinburgh, 1962), chapter 7, 'Revolution and reaction'. For further English-language accounts of the March–April events, see Edsel Walter Stroup, *Hungary in Early 1848: The Constitutional Struggle against Absolutism in Contemporary Eyes*, foreword by Steven Bela Vardy (State University College at Buffalo, Program in East European and Slavic Studies Publication no. 11) (Buffalo, NY, 1977), as well as István Deák, *The Lawful Revolution: Louis Kossuth and the Hungarians, 1848–1849* (New York, 1979), chapter 2, 'Reform triumphant: March–April 1848', pp. 63–106.
32. 'A birodalombeli nyugalom bomladozásának, s az ebből eredhető minden balkövetkezéseknek valódi kutfeje a bécsi kormány rendszerben fekszik.' KLÖM XI. Available at http://www.arcanum.hu/hu/online-kiadvanyok/Kossuth-kossuth-lajos-osszes-munkai-1/kossuth-lajos-osszes-munkai-xi-CE85/

kossuth-lajos-184849-ben-i-kossuth-lajos-az-utolso-rendi-orszaggyulesen-184748-CE8D/iii-harc-a-polgari-alkotmanyert-1848-marc-3marc-17-DB4A/ 144-pozsony-1848-marcius-3-kossuth-nagy-beszede-es-felirati-javaslata-az-orszaggyulesi-teendok-targyaban-DB4B/ (accessed 3 March 2018). English translation: C. Edmund Maurice, *The Revolutionary Movements of 1848–9 in Italy, Austria–Hungary, and Germany. With Some Examinations of the Previous Thirty-Three Years* (New York, 1969), p. 227.

33. 'ezen egyesülést [...] csak az alkotmányosság érzelem rokonitó forrasztéka teremtheti meg.' KLÖM XI. Available at http://www.arcanum.hu/hu/onlinekiadvanyok/Kossuth-kossuth-lajos-osszes-munkai-1/kossuth-lajos-osszes-munkaixi-CE85/kossuth-lajos-184849-ben-i-kossuth-lajos-az-utolso-rendi-orszaggyulesen-184748-CE8D/iii-harc-a-polgari-alkotmanyert-1848-marc-3marc-17-DB4A/144-pozsony-1848-marcius-3-kossuth-nagy-beszede-es-felirati-javaslata-az-orszaggyulesi-teendok-targyaban-DB4B/ (accessed 3 March 2018).

34. 'A mult kor emberei egy két nap után sírba szállanak, de a Habsburg ház nagy reményü ivadékára, Ferencz József főherczegre, ki első föllépésekor e nemzet szeretetét magáévá tette, egy fényes tronus öröksége vár', ibid., quoted by Maurice, *The Revolutionary Movements*, p. 227. Interestingly, Maurice argues that if Kossuth had been able to preserve this tone of his rhetoric, he could have united the liberals of the empire: 'Had Kossuth remained true to the faith which he proclaimed in this speech, it is within the limits of probability that the whole Revolution of 1848–9 might have had a different result', ibid., pp. 228–9.

35. On the cooperation between the Hungarian and Austrian opposition, see Ágnes Deák, 'Együttműködés vagy konkurencia, Az alsó-ausztriai, a csehországi és a magyarországi ellenzék összefogási kísérlete 1847–1848-ban', *Aestas* xiv/1–2 (1999), pp. 43–61. Available at http://epa.oszk.hu/00800/00861/00011/1h-02.html (accessed 3 March 2018).

36. 'Of the many Vormärz reading associations, historians have devoted particular attention to the Vienna Legal-Political Reading Association, partly because its membership reads like a "Who's Who" of post-1848 cabinets and ministries and partly because its location in Vienna put it at the centre of several political conflicts. Founded in 1841 as a discussion club, the association counted over 200 dues-paying members by the end of 1847.' 'Despite the repeated attempts by the Viennese police to close it down, the association remained open, thanks ironically to the efforts of those members who themselves occupied prominent posts in the government.' Pieter M. Judson, *Exclusive Revolutionaries: Liberal Politics, Social Experience, and National Identity in the Austrian Empire, 1848–1914* (Ann Arbor, MI, 1996), pp. 21–2, referring to the research of Engekl-Jánosi and John Rath.

37. James J. Sheenan, *German History, 1770–1866* (Oxford, 1989), p. 662.

38. For a summary of the operation and functions of the responsible government, see Gy. Szabad, 'A kormány parlamenti felelősségének kérdése', in Gy. Szabad (ed.), *A magyar országgyűlés 1848/49-ben* (Budapest, 1998), pp. 92–111.

39. As examples of full-blown criticisms of Kossuth, see Széchenyi's pre-1848 pamphlet (Széchenyi 1841), or the post-1848 essays by Zsigmond Kemény (Kemény, *Forradalom után*, Kemény, *Még egy szó a forradalom után*).
40. For a short monograph on this exchange see M. Lackó, *Széchenyi és Kossuth vitája* (Budapest, 1977).
41. The Russian Tsar was arguably following the obligations of the peace treaty of Vienna.
42. *Hungarian Declaration of Independence*, 1849.
43. István Deák, *Lawful Revolution*.
44. 'Ennek oka, hogy Felséged birodalmi kormánya nem lévén alkotmányos irányu, ugy kormányunk önállását mint alkotmányos életünket paralisálta. Eddig ezen irány csak alkotmányosságunk kifejlődését hátráltatta, most ugy látjuk, hogy ha tovább is folytattatik és az alkotmányossággal öszehangzásba nem hozatik, Felséged trónját s a pragmatica sanctionál fogva kedvelt kapcsokkal hozzánk kötött birodalmát elláthatlan következményekbe bonyolithatja, hazánkra kimondhatlan kárt áraszthat. Felséged minket reformokra hivott öszve, mi régi óhajtásunkat láttuk ez által telyesedve, s buzgó készséggel fogtunk a munkához.' KLÖM XI. (Budapest, 1951), pp. 623–8.
45. 'Az összes magyar népnek jogban és érdekben egyesítése [...] az ország törvényes önállása, – s függetlensége [...] a pragmatica sanctio által vele válhatlan kapcsolatban álló tartományok iránti törvényes viszonyai [...] a nemzet alkotmányos életének, a kor igényei, s a körülmények sürgős volta által szükségelt kifejtése [...] s a szellemi erők és anyagi tehetség azon lelkesült összhangzásának ez alapokoni élénkítése halaszthatatlanul megkívánt.' *Előbeszéd. Az 1848–1849. évi törvények*. Available at https://1000ev.hu/index.php?a=2&k=3&f=5268 (accessed 3 March 2018).
46. Péter, *Hungary's Long Nineteenth Century*, p. 6.
47. This claim could have been easier to defend if the text of the April Laws had been united into one statute.
48. Ibid., p. 6.
49. Ibid.
50. Ibid.
51. For a description of the eighteenth-century prehistory of this group, see István M. Szijártó, 'A vármegye és a jómódú birtokos köznemesség a 18. században', *AETAS* xiii/2–3 (1998), pp. 107–42. One can also consult Péter's German-language study: László Péter, 'Verfassungsentwicklung in Ungarn'. German language manuscript (1995), chapter 1, note 32. A publication from this manuscript (with the same title as the manuscript) appeared in H. Rumpler and P. Urbanitsch (eds), *Die Habsburger Monarchie, Vol. 8 (Verfassung und Parlamentarismus*, 2 parts) (Vienna, 2000), pp. 239–540.
52. Péter, in Lojkó, *Hungary's Long Nineteenth Century*, p. 7.
53. Karl Marx and Friedrich Engels, *Manifest der Kommunistischen Partei* (London, 1848).
54. Péter, in Lojkó, *Hungary's Long Nineteenth Century*, p. 7.

55. As he puts it: 'Arguably, without the first attempt at constitutional conversion in 1848 and the War of Independence in 1849 Deák would not have been able to secure a lasting settlement in 1867,' ibid., p. 8.
56. Ibid.
57. *Mit kíván a magyar nemzet? Szabad, független, demokratikus Magyarországot* [What is the wish of the Hungarian nation? A free, independent, democratic Hungary], 1989. A copy of the original leaflet is available at http://m.cdn.blog.hu/re/retropol/file/13-mitkivan1.jpg (accessed 3 March 2018).
58. For an overview of the political process, see András Bozóki (ed.), *The Roundtable Talks of 1989. The Genesis of Hungarian Democracy. Analysis and Documents* (Budapest, 2002).
59. Beside 1848, another date of ardent political debates in Hungarian history was going to be 1867. Deák's pragmatic deal was regarded, and continues to be regarded by some, as a betrayal of the ideals of 1848 and the heroes of 1849, while others claim that Deák was a pragmatic politician who achieved the maximum in his negotiations with the ruler to save the principles of 1848.
60. 'Pozsgay eventually addressed this issue head-on, by announcing the Party's re-evaluation of the events of 1956.' R. De Nevers, *Comrades, No More. The Seeds of Change in Eastern Europe* (Cambridge, 2003), p. 146.
61. Ibid.
62. Axel Körner, 'The European dimension in the ideas of 1848 and the nationalization of its memories', in A. Körner (ed.), *1848 – A European Revolution? International Ideas and National Memories of 1848* (Houndmills, 2000), p. 19.
63. Ferenc (Horkay) Hörcher, 'Töprengések a szavazófülkés forradalomról', *Kommentár* 2010/4, pp. 53–63.

CHAPTER 6

REFORM FEVER AND DISILLUSIONMENT: CONSTITUTIONAL CODIFICATION FIASCOS OF THE HUNGARIAN LIBERALS AFTER THE SETTLEMENT OF 1867

András Cieger

Figure 6.1 The opening of the Parliament by Francis Joseph in the Buda Castle Palace on 11 December 1865.[1]

A Constitutional Moment in 1867

In 1867, the Austro-Hungarian Settlement took shape as a result of a series of negotiations. For the first time since the establishment of the Habsburg Empire, the complex legal and political relations of the Austrian Empire and the Kingdom of Hungary were regulated. The codification of the settlement (Law XII of 1867) took place after Hungarian constitutionalism was restored (as Ferenc Deák, the intellectual force behind the settlement, had insisted on regime change) and after the appointment of the government led by Gyula Andrássy on 20 February 1867. It was followed by the coronation of Francis Joseph as king of Hungary on 8 June, and, with formal royal assent for the law, Hungary regained its legislative and governmental autonomy, even though the new political establishment significantly increased the ruler's prerogatives.[2]

Although the leader of the 1848/9 Hungarian revolution against the Habsburgs, Lajos Kossuth, opposed the settlement and remained in exile, many members of his inner circle decided to return to Hungary in order to actively influence domestic politics and assist the establishment of the political and legal structure of the modern civic state.

A fever for reform affected almost the entire political elite and the politically concerned public sphere, given that after centuries of waiting – with the brief exception of the turbulent months of 1848/9 – the opportunity had finally arisen for the Hungarian elites to rule the country and shape the various institutions of their state within a state according to their own vision. This endeavour naturally had a long history that owed much to the development of state theory from the last third of the eighteenth century onwards as well as the great reform debates of the Diet in the 1830s and 1840s.

At the time of the settlement, virtually all Hungarian liberal politicians knew the famous French and American declarations of rights and constitutions. Moreover, they broadly endorsed the principles of equality before the law, the right to human dignity and to privacy, freedom of press, religion, assembly, the right to association and the freedom of expression.[3]

These topics became central issues in Hungarian political discourse from the last third of the eighteenth century onwards, resulting in the theoretical legacy of the Enlightenment and the practical influence of Josephinism. Some of these principles were already raised by deputations at the 1791 and 1827 Diets, and especially at the session in 1843/4. In the course of these sessions, the MPs closely scrutinized the Code Napoléon and penal codes of the German and American states and consulted Carl J.A. Mittermaier, Professor of Law at Heidelberg, in order to ensure that their ideas conformed to European liberal legal standards. Even though the drafting of the penal code failed due to lack of support from the conservative aristocracy and the Crown, the lessons from these debates concerning liberties were ingrained in the Hungarian liberals' memory.[4]

The zest for home rule was indeed palpable around 1867, as revealed by the large number of pamphlets published in this period. One legacy of the 1848 propositions was that the basic demands of all Hungarian politicians in 1867 included an independent Hungarian parliament, responsible government, the restoration of municipal autonomy and the territorial integrity of Hungary. These demands were granted by the fundamental laws of the settlement, as a consequence of the long and fruitful negotiation process. Nevertheless, the task of creating the legal safeguards and the appropriate power relations among the new political institutions, as well as the establishment of a modern civil constitutional order that regulated the life of both the state and the society, had to be established by the liberal elite who came into power in 1867.

At the same time, a polyphonic political and professional debate started about the features of the modern state. Legal journals and law societies mushroomed and the first national assembly of jurists took place in 1870, which discussed 13 legal reform proposals. Review articles were published concerning foreign political institutions and legal systems, contemporary books on state theory were translated en masse, while the Hungarian pamphlet literature on this topic expanded yet further. The public was well informed by the popular press and the parliamentary records about the government's preparatory work. Government ministers also held regular meetings, attended by a range of experts who could voice their opinions about future regulations, and which were aimed at formulating a consensus over both the need for and the scope of each reform.

The opposition was active as well. They drafted bills concerning topical issues and presented various concrete proposals for reform to the government. If that proved to be unsuccessful, the opposition was ready to mobilize the populace through public rallies and the gathering of petitions. The county assemblies were also vocal participants in the reform process. They communicated with the government via official letters, and there is also evidence of individuals voluntarily drafting proposals without any prospect of remuneration.

The contrast with the turbulent atmosphere in the spring of 1848 is striking. In 1848 the political elite — despite incongruences — secured numerous individual and political rights. They also, however, deliberately refused to engage in open and comprehensive constitution making and strove instead for the temporary regulation of political institutions as they believed that the permanent reform of Hungary's constitution should only be carried out by a parliament based on popular representation.

A more apt basis for the completion of the rule of law in 1867 was the so-called 'Reform Age' (1825–48). This was especially the case as the theoretical questions of individual and collective rights (mostly drawing on J.S. Mill) constituted a favoured topic in Hungarian political thought after 1867.[5] Still, negative critiques emerged concerning this field as well. As one of Hungary's shrewdest political commentators, Gusztáv Beksics, observed, 'Political freedoms won a final victory in this century. However, individual freedom lagged behind the great achievements of liberalism almost everywhere, including Hungary, though it could function under political repression as well. Individual freedom fell behind, despite the most elaborate charters.'[6] The gradual falling behind of Europe was best illustrated by the Austrian example: there, one of the basic laws of the *Dezemberverfassung* in 1867 (following the constitutional preludes of 1849) listed the catalogue of liberties in 20 entries.[7] Then, in 1873, the Criminal Procedure Code was passed, which regulated in detail, among others, the process of arrest, hearing and perquisition. The lack of similar legislation in Hungary led Beksics to wryly note that 'in Austria, individual freedom has its own liberal guarantees. Yes, in Austria, compared to which Hungary always considered herself more liberal — and rightly so — and had been seen as more liberal by the world [...] And this Austria dared to establish the guarantees of individual freedom already in 1873, while these are still entirely absent up to now from our legislation.'[8]

Still, the codification programme of the government was ambitious: the short-term plans included the promulgation of a new civil and penal code, the establishment and regulation of the system of jurisdiction, the guarantee of various personal freedoms, the modernization of local administration and the House of Lords, a reform of both education and the tax system, and the reorganization of Hungary's military units (the *honvédség*). In short, the government pursued a broad-based reform of the state. This programme, though, had to be carried out by exploiting the central government's freedom of manoeuvre while simultaneously ensuring that it did not overburden itself and, at the same time, observed the legal and political limits set by the settlement.

In retrospect, the achievements of the liberal government in the first years after 1867 were spectacular. Already in 1868, 58 laws were enacted, which was surpassed in 1871 when 68 laws were placed on the statute books. A remarkable number of decrees were also issued by the various ministries, especially the Ministry of Justice. Successive governments also established multiple levels of civil jurisdiction, and passed laws concerning public administration, public education, the rights of minorities, and the status of the Hungarian branch of the armed forces. In spite of these accomplishments, many contemporaries of various political backgrounds were disappointed by the results of the period between 1867 and 1875. The editor of a legal journal wrote:

> The aims for the 1867th year were: to establish the rule of law in Hungary, to bring in all the institutions that are the accomplishments of liberal progress and the development of the law. These aims were unattained, moreover, our jurisdiction and our general legal progress faces a more depressing future than ever [...] Nothing exemplifies the real progress of Hungarian legal relations in the past thirteen years. The achievements remained on paper, they did not become part of the public domain.[9]

One opposition politician claimed the following:

> Neither in 1848, nor later have our legislatures harmonized our state institutions with the needs of the age [...] Ten years have since passed. We organized ourselves unworthily. We managed our own affairs poorly. We almost destroyed the credibility of our proudly proclaimed political maturity in front of cultivated foreign lands, nay, in front of ourselves.[10]

As an influential member of the government, the former Minister of Finance, confessed: 'When I take a look at my notes written about the notable year of 1867, the year of the coronation and the achievement of the settlement, I see the hope in our future and the trust in our viability [...] Was there intellectual progress, has the country flourished since then? The results give no favourable answer to these questions.'[11] The delay is obvious considering the prelude of the Reform Age and the promises that were given in 1867. Instead of analysing the psychological components of this disappointment, it will now be shown why and how the constitutional moment passed by swiftly and almost without any traces.

The Years of Change

The Hungarian liberals' sudden loss of confidence and the end of the fever for reform did not occur, of course, in a single moment. Nevertheless, many of the factors that contributed to this disillusionment were evident at a cabinet meeting that took place on 25 March 1869. The Andrássy government held a tense meeting in the immediate aftermath of the first parliamentary elections to take place after the signing of the 1867 settlement. It was obvious to both the government and the opposition that voters had expressed their opinion not only of the governing elite but also of the settlement itself. Therefore, the government party's loss of about 60 MPs was an embarrassment, while the number of those in parliament who were opposed to the settlement dramatically increased. Moreover, it was rumoured within the governing party (revealingly named after the architect of the settlement, Ferenc Deák) that the opposition had been secretly supported by Otto von Bismarck, chancellor of the North German Confederation, in order to weaken the position of the Austro-Hungarian Monarchy.[12] The depression that accompanied the meeting of the government was exacerbated by the fact that a member of the government, István Gorove, the minister for agriculture, industry and trade, had lost his bid for re-election.[13]

Socio-political movements in the aftermath of the settlement signalled the constant presence of a critical mass that rejected the new political establishment. The enduringly popular Kossuth, whose open letters circulated widely in Hungary, denounced this compromise on moral grounds. He accused Deák of misleading the nation and abandoning the accomplishments of 1848. He also claimed that the principles which the government had employed to legitimate the settlement were simply false. Both Hungary and Austria, Kossuth argued, had only pseudo-constitutional regimes which could not bring lasting peace and sowed dissension and animosities among the peoples of the empire. He even claimed that the settlement was a death warrant for the Hungarian nation. The opposition popularized these criticisms through various actions: they started to organize so-called 'democratic clubs' (the *demokrata körök*), which demanded the full restoration of the 1848 laws and took the leading part in several local demonstrations against the central government. These demonstrations and speeches even contributed to the emergence of some local peasant movements which demanded land reform.[14]

The government reacted harshly to every endeavour that questioned the validity of the settlement. The network of democratic clubs was banned – for undermining the constitutional order – and the self-government of the rebellious counties was temporarily suspended; royal commissioners were sent in to restore order, and the most intransigent local officials were dismissed. A libel suit was also initiated against the editor of the *Magyar Újság*, the daily newspaper which had published the letters of Kossuth. All of this did not, however, enhance the public's view of the government. Trust in the political system was further eroded by a financial crisis that broke out in the autumn of 1869, bringing down dozens of recently established corporations. The prime minister, Gyula Andrássy, allegedly told his party around this time that 'even though 9/10 part of the people is against us, 9/10 part of the intelligentsia is with us but we lose ground day by day.'[15]

This political context influenced the way in which individual freedoms were codified. The uncertain legitimacy of the regime, the relative weakness of the government, as well as the fear of social protest and an increasingly defensive attitude produced a transformation in the thinking of the governing liberal party. Instead of striving for the extension of civil liberties, the imposition of limits on freedom became a priority. This is evidenced by the way that members of the government at the aforementioned meeting discussed various proposals about civil liberties (concerning the freedom of the press, assembly and association, and reform of the franchise, penal code and the Budapest police) but eventually opted to enhance the efficiency of the state's control of wider society. Considering the complexities of these legislative processes, this chapter will focus on how two important bills pertaining to liberties took shape. The following section discusses the ways in which the penal code and the police Act were born.

Penal Code

About two months after his appointment as Minister of Justice, Boldizsár Horvát assembled a group of lawyers, professors of the Faculty of Law, members of the Hungarian Academy of Sciences (HAS) and ministry staff to lay the groundwork for a new penal code. Horvát assigned to his former professor, a member of the HAS, the task of drafting the bill in its final form. Imre Csatskó immediately tried to gain access to the most up-to-date foreign literature on the subject since the Reform Age, and studied the laws that had recently been enacted across Europe (especially those in the German language). He handed over the general part of the proposal to the Minister in April 1868, the text of which was permeated by the liberal agenda of the Reform Age.

Horvát promised, in response to a parliamentary question in November 1868, that he would soon submit the bill, but that only took place six (!) years later. The version of the penal code that was eventually put before parliament in the autumn of 1874 was based on entirely different principles. The new version was drafted in large part by the state secretary for justice, Károly Csemegi, while Csatskó donated his own draft to the library of the HAS.[16]

One of the possible grounds for this change was the political expectation which already surfaced in the course of the above-mentioned government meeting in 1869, expressed by the Prime Minister:

> Count Andrássy particularly emphasized that since the greatest power of the ministry lies in the fact that it has the trust of the ruler [Francis Joseph], this can only be sustained if the ministry proves its capacities to maintain order and to counter unrest in time, therefore he [Count Andrássy] asked the Minister of Justice when the new penal code would be ready. Its preparation is the more important because the old laws do not have a precise definition for the cases of disruption of public order, revolt and high treason.[17]

Clearly, the intentions of the lawmakers had changed significantly compared to those in the Reform Age. While the main purpose of the 1843 proposals was to keep the penal power of the state in check and to humanize jurisdiction, after 1867 new priorities emerged: preservation of royal trust and efficient legal limitation of any attack on the new establishment.

The penal code was passed as late as 1878 (Law V of 1878). It preserved capital punishment (in cases of regicide and premeditated murder) despite opposite international tendencies and the opinion of the majority of Hungarian lawyers. It also prescribed minimum penalties, terminating the possibility of judges easing them limitlessly. It was argued in justification that all this was necessary because of lenient judicial praxis. In line with the expectations of the government, the code penalized incitement against Hungary's legal and political relations with Austria, and regulated various political crimes in detail. Still, the well-constructed and logical paragraphs of the penal code defended multiple freedoms as well (e.g. personal freedom, inviolability of home, privacy of correspondence, freedom of religion, free exercise of the right to vote).[18]

It is clear, though, that the guiding principle of the penal code became the legal protection of the state and of the dual political system, instead of the individual or the citizen. Supposedly, the abolition of capital punishment fell victim to this very change, as did the anticipated early prohibition of corporal punishment.

After 1867 the Minister of Justice tried to postpone the abolition of corporal punishment until the submission of the penal code, which it was promised would happen soon. Naturally this does not mean that the governing liberals approved of corporal punishment. However, this tactic of procrastination may have been influenced by the intention not to weaken the police and the judiciary in their daily struggle for public safety.

The government, it seems, regarded all oppositional efforts as anti-regime attacks if they strove for any reform of the legal system, including initiatives for the protection of personal freedom. The radical opposition led by Dániel Irányi not only kept the settlement on the agenda but pursued democratization and modernization. Their interpellation and the bills they submitted aimed at forcing the government and the governing party to codify liberal-democratic principles concerning the freedom of religion, civil marriage, abolition of capital punishment and corporal punishment, the development of popular education and the introduction of a luxury tax. Though all political entities agreed on the necessity to remove corporal punishment from jurisdiction, the codification of one of the most basic freedoms emerged as a central issue in the debates between government and opposition. The bill on the abolition of corporal punishment in judicial practice was only passed four years after the settlement (Law LII of 1871).

Police Act

The necessity to draft a police Act was also voiced at the cabinet meeting of 25 March 1869. In this case again, the government had an interest in extending its room for manoeuvre and controlling society and opposition.

Guarding public safety traditionally belonged to the responsibilities of municipalities. However, their efficiency was rather poor due, inter alia, to financial restraints, urbanization and the sudden multiplication of public administration-related tasks. Moreover, some municipalities deliberately opposed the will of the central government. The establishment of a state police force under the direction of the central government for public safety and political reasons (e.g. controlling the movement of foreigners and labour) was especially desirable in the capital.

The Ministry of the Interior familiarized itself with other European police Acts and prepared the first draft bill to establish a police force in the capital in 1868. The government discussed the draft in detail in the autumn of 1869. After the cabinet meeting, a member of the expert committee went on a research trip in order to gain firsthand experience of the functioning of European police organizations (especially that of London). Based on these inputs, the draft was prepared in 1871. In accordance with the governmental decision, the bill intended to place the capital's police force under the control of the central government, but without conferring jurisdiction on that body. Following the English example, the draft planned to assign tasks such as those regarding petty offences to justices of the peace and later to civil courts.[19]

In order to protect freedoms, the draft declared that 'perquisition should always be conducted by a capable [quick-minded, proficient] police officer,' in the presence of witnesses, 'perquisition should be carried out with the greatest care towards the one affected, avoiding any unnecessary action that is not required by the aims established by the law and which would bother the inhabitants of the house needlessly.' Records had to be made of the proceedings. 'The justice of the peace as well as the police in their own capacities have to conduct interrogation dispassionately and ought not use promises, lies, violence or threats to make the accused confess or give any declarations.'[20]

However, no stand-alone police Act was submitted and debated by the parliament. Instead, two paragraphs of the law on the unification of the capital (Law XXXVI of 1872) addressed the issue in general terms. On the one hand, the government tried to capitalize on the political consensus that crystallized regarding the unification Act, which was long-awaited and inevitable in order to further develop Budapest. They deemed that the tacit inclusion of state control in this specific Act was less risky: 'it is desirable for the government to be able to rely on laws when carrying out such actions, considering that public support is highly unlikely for the establishment of a police organization.'[21] Still, the oppositional press interpreted the paragraphs as additional developments in the overt concentration of power in the hands of the state, in opposition to society: 'Power and centralization everywhere – at all costs! This is the motto, the basic principle of the government [...] The public of Pest is mighty and democratic; therefore these institutions are disguised.'[22] On the other hand, one can assume that the changes regarding the penal code draft influenced that of the police Act as well, and politicians may have wanted to wait for its codification before finalizing the police Act.

Another ten years passed before the drafting of the police Act. The government secured itself more latitude to police its citizens via decrees and regulations during the long interim period.

The final version of the Act concerning the Budapest police (Law XXI of 1881) did not include – beyond general utterances – the protection of civil liberties (e.g. in the course of perquisition, arrest and detention), it was more preoccupied with empowering the police (e.g. it was entrusted with judicial power). A paragraph about legal remedies concerning police abuse was only added as a result of a decision of the parliament (43§), and another which regulated cases of conflict of interest regarding police officers (44§).

In turn the opposition had visions of an emerging police state: 'we are deeply concerned by the groundless limitation of freedoms, moreover, their disablement, as well as by the overstretching police power [...] In times like this, when overall centralization of state and the extension of governmental power is underway, it is to be emphasized: we have to beware twice as much of the unnecessary increase of police power.'[23] Obviously, this sense of danger was exaggerated, but the fears were understandable. For example, the gendarmerie Act (Law III of 1881) comprised only 12 paragraphs and contained no legal guarantee whatsoever concerning the functioning of an armed body that was present throughout the country with the exception of the capital.[24]

A greater recognition of civil liberties as opposed to legal procedures only occurred around the turn of the century, with the passing of the Act on criminal prosecution (Law XXXIII of 1896).[25]

Two Models of State: Aristocracy or Democracy?

Ferenc Deák appraised the importance of the 1848 constitutional turn as follows: the lawmakers of 1848, understanding the zeitgeist, placed the privilege-based political and legal system on the foundation of equality of rights. Therefore,

> we should not make any such suggestions which would disturb the democratic spirit of the 1848 laws that would abolish equality before the law or would restore the hated inequality between classes; to cut it short, even temporarily, would mean an unwarrantable setback and would prevent the nation's pursuit which was directly expressed in 1848 to raise the Hungarian political nation to the level of cultivated European nations through equality before the law,

warned Deák.[26]

His democratic views, however, were not unanimously shared by his followers. They agreed on the sustenance of equality before the law, but instead of significantly expanding freedoms, they were busy securing political and legal means to protect the legitimacy of the 1867 regime and the supremacy of Magyars against those who opposed them, as well as benefiting those cultivated and well-off social strata which were mostly loyal to the regime. The later Minister of Finance wrote to his brother about the revision of the 1848 laws: 'Its restitution with corrections, not in a democratic but a liberal aristocratic form.'[27] Menyhért Lónyay definitely refers here to the tightening of the franchise, the significant decrease in the number of MPs and the introduction of property-based political privilege, virilism[28] (Deák opposed all of them). Gyula Andrássy declared the following about the expected formulation of Austrian and Hungarian governments: 'Regarding the personnel, he wishes them not to be purely of democratic orientation because he does not want democratization in Hungary, and the democratic principle in Cisleithania would influence Hungary too.'[29] No wonder that citizens of the capital criticized the Andrássy government in May 1868, among other reasons, precisely because 'this ministry [is] too aristocratic.'[30]

Note, however, that in this political vocabulary the notion of democracy has no positive connotation: it does not refer to equality of rights but to irresponsible politics which is influenced by mostly uneducated masses. Aristocratic politics started to mean for them moderate responsible government entrusted by those citizens who were able to comprehend the national cause ('the distinguished people') instead of the obsolete, privilege-based way of governing. However, this (elitist) model of the State did not result in decreasing class inequalities but preserved and occasionally deepened them.[31] It seems that the ruling liberals – as a result of their fears, early negative experiences and the complex political framework of the Dual Monarchy – perceived their room for manoeuvre in establishing the rule of law as narrower than it actually was. Their political creed prioritized the preservation and strengthening of the unity of the state and the supremacy of the Magyars in a multi-ethnic country.

The radical opposition party was not persistent in advocating democratic principles and freedoms, either. It became divided already in the years following the settlement. Dániel Irányi and his circle remained in a minority: they supported civil marriage, and persistently demanded freedom of religion, abolition of the death penalty, and tighter institutional control over the government. Irányi most resented the fact that even Kossuth himself denied his support for this agenda, claiming that the radical opposition's task was not to contribute to the stabilization of the regime with parliamentary motions and bills that would help to make it better. Instead of doing politics based on principle — which proved to be divisive among the members of the opposition — they should constantly call into question the legitimacy of the regime and in a day-by-day political struggle they should morally discredit it. This was the only way to gain enough popularity and to take over government.[32]

Kossuth referred to parallels in the English and Hungarian legal and political traditions when warning against the codification of constitutional institutions and freedoms that developed organically. Out of tactical consideration, he deemed that the maintenance of an unregulated framework provided the opposition with more room for manoeuvre in the political system of 1867 than the codification of certain principles would ever give:

> the English parliament and the Hungarian parliamentary institutions could have developed due to the fact that their responsibility had never been codified and drafted [...] The counties could have emerged as bastions of constitutional life without having their responsibilities codified. Where there is a 'tabula rasa', there 'charters' are inevitable. But codified freedom will be exceeded by life and will lead to civil war, as it did in America, while the organically developing body evolves as life does, it fits to life's necessities. Therefore you should beware of codification. Stick with elastic principles.[33]

For Irányi, the notion of democracy was used as a legal principle (meaning extension of freedom rights and humanistic politics), as and likewise for Deák, though he wanted to establish the norms of the rule of law faster and in a more radical way. Unlike Kossuth, he thought that his reform agenda could be carried out through the democratization of the political system of 1867. In the texts of Kossuth, democracy signifies a form of government, and its meaning is strongly intertwined with republicanism and the ideas of independence and self-governance: 'Democracy has the future. And democracy means self-governance, the governance of the people through the people. This is only possible within a republic.'[34] Kossuth claimed that the future of the country could only be secured by escaping the nets of the settlement; the formulation of a genuine democracy — which he also favoured — should take place afterwards.

The government and its opposition lost interest in the 1848/9 heritage of constitutional reforms for different reasons; the initial momentum was spent. Liberal principles mostly adjusted to the daily realities of politics. The freedom of citizens was extended definitely and generally only with a few Acts after 1867. The laws that were passed later gave rights to designated groups of people only occasionally and in a very limited way.

Hungarian law was not on the side of the citizen, quite the opposite: it secured more freedom for the state and protection against its own citizens' disorder. In case of a legal dispute, the offended citizen had to prove his right against the state by detailed references to the law. In Western Europe, the state was allowed to act only within the boundaries proclaimed by the law, while on the eastern side of the Rhine only a few protective Acts limited the omnipotence of the state. But nor did the state's scope for action have an identical extent everywhere in this region: the liberals in the Austrian part of the Habsburg Empire strove for the legal protection of individual liberty, and conclusively established the *Rechtsstaat* in the aftermath of the settlement.[35] At the same time, in Hungary the political elite increasingly subscribed to empowering the state further, both in order to maintain the leading position of Magyars[36] and to make up for weak social self-activity. The Hungarian governments regulated questions affecting fundamental rights at best in decrees that could be amended at any time, and thus it was the logic of virtually uncontrolled power that was able to mould the country's legal system and political culture.[37]

A prominent pro-government journalist and theoretician, Gusztáv Beksics, rushed to comfort those worrying about the ideas of freedom. In his book he presented disadvantages as advantages; moreover, he managed to depict the Hungarian situation as if it were the best of all possible worlds:

> both the English and the Magyar are retrospective people. They always cast their eyes over their backs in the course of constitutional struggles and fights for freedom. They never approached law, justice and freedom as principles. They never produced constitutional theories as the French did [...] This kind of morale is ill-suited for rapid development, instilling and fulfilling democratic aspirations. Indeed, England has not become a modern state yet and Hungary had just become [in 1848] one.[38]

Later on, he asks the question which is central to the topic of this chapter: 'To conclude, it is due to review our democratic transformation in 1848 and since, and we should ask, to what extent has it corresponded to the democratic requirements?'[39]

For Beksics the answer can only be positive. The state was established as a result of the decades-long reform struggles of successive political generations, which is a 'true royal democracy'. However, the Hungarian model has 'a different character compared to other democracies', because the protection of Magyar supremacy pervades public opinion and politics, but 'even so, besides racial politics, Hungary secured her place with great struggle among the most liberal and democratic nations. Therefore the future of liberalism and democracy cannot be doubted in Hungary.'[40] Both his assessment and his prediction proved to be erroneous. Most of the liberal ideas either adjusted to the compromises of practical government, or disappeared from political discourse. Gradually, instead of extending constitutional institutions and following European norms, being locked up in national myths became the rule.[41]

In summary, this chapter aimed to examine the constitutional discourse and lawmaking after the regime change in 1867, adopting Bruce Ackerman's theory of the constitutional moment. It tried to explore the democratic traditions in the political thought of Hungarian liberals, and it demonstrated their decline in Hungarian political life, which was shown to have been due to many unfounded fears as well as a number of practical and tactical reasons. The next chapter will analyse the same period in the history of Hungary from another aspect: it will examine the workings of the ancient unwritten constitutionalism with its values and myths in Hungarian politics. These studies combine to illustrate the complex characteristics of the political culture of Hungary in the long nineteenth century.

Notes

1. From *Vasárnapi Ujság*, 21 January 1866. p. 29.
2. For more detail, see László Katus, *Hungary in the Dual Monarchy 1867–1914* (New York, 2008), pp. 1–47.
3. The most important constitutional texts and political works were translated into Hungarian in a few years after the settlement. See e.g. *Alkotmányok gyűjteménye*, 2 vols (Pest, 1867); *A francia büntető törvénykönyv* (Sopron, 1867);

John Stuart Mill, *A képviseleti kormány* (translated by Ferencz Jánosi) (Pest, 1867); John Stuart Mill, *A szabadságról* (translated by Béni Kállay) (Pest, 1867); Édouard R. Laboulaye, *Az állam és határai* (translated by Antal Molnár) (Kolozsvár, 1869); Reginald Palgrave, *Képek az angol alsóház történetéből és működéséből* (translated by Lajos Csernátony) (Pest, 1870); Johann K. Bluntschli, *A politikai pártok* (translated by Géza Ballagi) (Pest, 1872), etc.
4. Kálmán Györgyi, 'Die Rolle Mittermaiers bei der Ausarbeitung des Strafgesetzentwurfes vom Jahre 1843', in B. Mezey (ed.), *Strafrectsgeschichte an der Grenze des nächsten Jahrtausendes* (Budapest, 2003), pp. 39–53.
5. Béla Mester, 'Mill magyarországi recepciója és a 19. század magyar politikai gondolkodása', in B. Mester and L. Perecz (eds), *Közelítések a magyar filozófia történetéhez. Magyarország és a modernitás* (Budapest, 2004), pp. 351–91.
6. Gusztáv Beksics, *Az egyéni szabadság Európában és Magyarországon* (Budapest, 1879), 'Előszó'.
7. The so-called December Constitution signed by Francis Joseph on 21 December 1867 includes six fundamental laws. One of them codified the civil liberties in Cisleithania: Fundamental Law on the General Rights of Citizens (*Staatsgrundgesetz über die allgemeinen Rechte der Staatsbürger*). See Wilhelm Brauneder, 'Die Entstehung der Verfassung 1867 (Dezemberverfassung)', in H. Rumpler and P. Urbanitsch (eds), *Die Habsburgermonarchie 1848–1918*, vol. VII (Vienna, 2000), pp. 174–87.
8. Beksics, *Az egyéni szabadság*, p. 46.
9. László Kun, *A magyar igazságügyi kormányzat. Horváth Boldizsártól Pauler Tivadarig* (Budapest, 1880), p. 5.
10. Gyula Schvarcz, *Államintézményeink és a kor igényei* (Budapest, 1879), pp. 498–9.
11. Melchior Lónyay, *Über Ungarns Finanzwesen* (Pressburg, 1874), pp. 6–7.
12. István Diószegi, *Bismarck und Andrássy. Ungarn in der deutschen Machtpolitik in der 2. Hälfte des 19. Jahrhunderts* (Budapest, 1999), pp. 52–62.
13. Although the records of this meeting are in the Hungarian National Archives, State Archives (Magyar Nemzeti Levéltár, Országos Levéltára, hereafter MNL OL), Section K, 27, they do not mention this agenda item, because it is 'accustomed by the Hungarian Ministers' Council that the most important issues are discussed off the record'. The debate can be retraced based on the diary of Menyhért Lónyay, School of Slavonic and East European Studies (SSEES) Library, University College London (UCL), Kónyi–Lónyay Collection, KON/3.
14. Katus, *Hungary in the Dual Monarchy*, pp. 105–20.
15. Salamon Gajzágó's letter to Károly Torma, Pest, 19 November 1869. Országos Széchényi Könyvtár Levelestár [Letter Collection, National Széchényi Library, Budapest. Hungary].
16. Imre Csatskó, *Magyar büntetőtörvénykönyv* [Hungarian Penal Code]. Manuscript. Magyar Tudományos Akadémia Könyvtárának Kézirattára (MTAK Kt.) [Manuscript Collection of the Library of the Hungarian Academy of Sciences, hereafter HAS] Jogtan Ált. 2. 93–4; Csatskó's letter to the Library of HAS, 25 March 1872. MTAK Kt. RAL 283/1872.

17. Lónyay's diary, 25 March 1869. SSEES Library, UCL, Kónyi–Lónyay Collection, KON/3.
18. Tibor Király, 'Das Strafgesetzbuch von 1878'. Der Csemegi-Kodex', in G. Máthé and W. Ogris (eds), *Die Entwicklung der Österreichisch–Ungarischen Strafrechtskodifikation im XIX–XX. Jahrhundert* (Budapest, 1996), pp. 221–36; Barna Mezey, 'Strafrechtskodifikation in Ungarn im Jahre 1878', in *Strafrectsgeschichte an der Grenze*, pp. 151–77.
19. MNL OL K. 27, Records of the cabinet meeting held on 5 September 1869.
20. MNL OL K. 27, Records of the cabinet meeting held on 12, July 1871.
21. MNL OL K. 27, Records of the cabinet meeting held on 7 December 1872.
22. See the interpretation of an oppositional newspaper: *A Hon*, 5 November 1872.
23. See Károly Eötvös and Nándor Szederkényi, two opposition MPs' critiques, 27 February 1881 in *Az 1878. évi október 19-ére hirdetett országgyűlés képviseőházának irományai*, vol. 22. No. 967 (Budapest, 1881), pp. 280–2.
24. Csaba Csapó, *A Magyar királyi csendőrség története, 1881–1914* (Pécs, 1999), pp. 20–51, 107–18.
25. *Rendőri Lapok* [Police Journal] assessed Law XXXIII of 1896, which curtailed the means of the authorities: 'It is a good, a fine law, but Hungary is too young for that. It is not cut out for us, at least, it does not correspond to the current situation.' Quotes: Nora Kollár (ed.), *A fővárosi rendőrség története* (Budapest, 1995), vol. 1, p. 343.
26. Ferenc Deák's speech on 25 February 1861, see Manó Kónyi (ed.), *Deák Ferenc beszédei*, vol. 2 (Budapest, 1897), p. 348.
27. Menyhért Lónyay's letter to Albert Lónyay, 13 November 1860. Quotes: András Cieger, *Lónyay Menyhért, 1822–1884* (Budapest, 2008), p. 97.
28. The largest taxpayers would automatically (without election) be members of the general assemblies of the municipalities: this was called *virilism* at the time. By introducing virilism, the governing party wished to create a new and strong middle class, which could be the engine of bourgeois transformation. However, the opposition thought that virilism was a privilege that could help a narrow, wealthy group gain decisive influence in controlling public affairs, creating a new feudal system. Virilism was incorporated into the Hungarian legal system by Law XLII of 1870.
29. Lónyay's diary, 20 and 23 August 1866. SSEES Library, UCL, Kónyi–Lónyay Collection, KON/1.
30. Mary Elizabeth Stevens's letter to her family, 24 May 1868, in K. Armstrong (ed.), *Letters from Hungary 1864 to 1869. Written by Mary Elizabeth Stevens to her Mother and Sister* (London, 1999), p. 173.
31. For the interpretation of the notion 'democracy' in the nineteenth century, see Otto Brunner, Werner Conze and Reinhart Koselleck (eds), *Geschichtliche Grundbegriffe. Historisches Lexikon zur politisch-sozialen Sprache in Deutschland*, vol. 1 (Stuttgart, 1972), pp. 821–99.
32. Lajos Kossuth's letter to Dániel Irányi, 9 December 1873. MNL OL R 90. I.5451.

33. Lajos Kossuth's letter to Dániel Irányi, 17 February 1870. MNL OL R 75.
34. Lajos Kossuth's letter to José María Orense, 6 December 1868, in F. Kossuth (ed.), *Kossuth Lajos iratai* [Documents of Lajos Kossuth], vol. 7 (Budapest, 1900), p. 428; György Miru, 'From liberalism to democracy: Key concepts in Lajos Kossuth's political thought', *East Central Europe / L'Europe du Centre Est* xli/1 (2014), pp. 1–31.
35. Karel Maly, 'Der österreichisch–ungarische Ausgleich und die allgemeinen Rechte der Staatsbürger in der 2. Hälfte des 19. Jahrhunderts', in G. Máthé and W. Ogris (eds), *Die Habsburgermonarchie auf dem Wege zum Rechtsstaat?* (Budapest and Vienna, 2010), pp. 121–64.
36. Marius Turda, *The Idea of National Superiority in Central Europe, 1880–1918* (Lewiston, NY, 2004), pp. 67–142.
37. For details see László Péter, 'The autocratic principle of the law and civil rights in nineteenth-century Hungary', in Miklós Lojkó (ed.), *Hungary's Long Nineteenth Century: Constitutional and Democratic Traditions in a European Perspective. Collected Studies of László Péter* (Leiden and Boston, MA, 2012), pp. 281–304.
38. Gusztáv Beksics, *A democratia Magyarországon* (Budapest, 1881), pp. 1–2.
39. Ibid., p. 67.
40. Ibid., p. 73.
41. László Péter, 'The Holy Crown of Hungary, visible and invisible', in Lojkó, *Hungary's Long Nineteenth Century*, pp. 15–112; András Cieger, 'National identity and constitutional patriotism in the context of modern Hungarian history', *Hungarian Historical Review* v/1 (2016), pp. 131–7.

CHAPTER 7

THE USE AND ABUSE OF FLEXIBILITY: HUNGARY'S HISTORICAL CONSTITUTION, 1867–1919

Thomas Lorman

In 1909, Count Albert Apponyi, one of Hungary's most prominent politicians and minister of education from 1906, contributed an ebullient account of his country's constitution, which he had penned seven years earlier, to a volume entitled *Hungary Today*. This book, edited by the British Liberal MP Percy Alden, was intended to familiarize an English-language audience with the various successes that Hungary had achieved in the decades following the settlement (*Ausgleich*) of 1867 which had transformed the Habsburg Empire into a 'dual' (Austro-Hungarian) monarchy. According to Apponyi, Hungary's ability to flourish in the decades after 1867 was the direct result of a 'political genius unequalled – dare I say it – on the Continent of Europe' and, he continued, 'the greatest conception of that genius, her Constitution'.[1]

Apponyi's fellow minister Gyula Andrássy was equally effusive about Hungary's constitutional development which, he insisted, could be traced back to 'the freedom of the nomad era', and whose 'unbroken continuity' had preserved 'the hegemony of the nation until this day'.[2] When it came, however, to actually describing the contents of Hungary's constitution, both of these experienced politicians found themselves on shakier ground. Apponyi himself conceded that there was 'no legislative instrument which one may designate the "Hungarian Constitution"', instead it was made up, he explained, of 'numerous constitutional laws of all periods – some still in force though very ancient, others fallen into desuetude though comparatively recent'.[3] To the obvious question of why only certain laws were 'still in force' Apponyi provided no answer.

Attempts to identify the precise contents of Hungary's constitution still occur, but they arguably miss the point.[4] Both Apponyi and Andrássy's enthusiasm for Hungary's historical constitution, along with an inability to clearly identify its contents, was no accident. In common with almost the entirety of Hungary's governing class in the last decades of the Habsburg Empire, both men were aware that it was precisely the murky character of their country's unwritten constitution, with its contents ill-defined and open to debate, which made it such a vital tool in shaping Hungary's relationship with both its ruler, the emperor, and its citizens. In fact, what Hungarian legal theorists termed the 'flexibility' (*rugalmasság*) of Hungary's unwritten constitution made possible many of Hungary's achievements in the five decades after 1867, but also helped provoke the turmoil that engulfed the country in 1918–19.

The Benefits of Autonomy

Hungary's successes in the period between 1867 and 1918 were certainly substantial. Both Francis Joseph, who reigned until 1916, and the last Habsburg emperor Charles IV, who resigned in 1918, underwent a separate coronation in Hungary's capital Budapest, while Hungary was granted the prestige of being included in the formal name of the empire, now renamed the 'Austro-Hungarian Monarchy'. She possessed her own cabinet government, headed by the prime minister, her own parliament, her own government ministries, and her own military force (*honvédség*) that operated in tandem with the common army. Her own courts operated on the basis of her own legal structures, and her counties and cities possessed their own forms of self-governance. Moreover, as C.A. Macartney astutely recognized, other factors gave Hungary a prestige that no other land in the empire possessed, namely her 'size, her strategic importance, her inaccessibility, and the resolution of her noble class, [which] had enabled her to maintain successfully the principle that she constituted an entirely separate body politic'.[5]

The autonomy that Hungary enjoyed after 1867 also brought practical benefits. László Kontler has, for example, highlighted the growth of foreign trade, which averaged around 3 per cent per annum, as a key contributor to the similar average growth in gross domestic product, which was somewhere between 2.4 and 3.7 per cent per annum, and which steadily transformed the country from an agrarian backwater into a fairly dynamic economy. As even Marxist historians recognized, prudent budgeting also helped end the dependence on foreign loans and laid the basis for sustained economic growth.[6] The modernization of the country's infrastructure was also both cause and consequence of this transformation. The railway system expanded tenfold in the five decades after 1867, and the telegraph service grew to 170,000 kilometres by 1914 by which time there were at least 20,000 telephones in the capital, Budapest, alone.[7]

The growth of education and culture was equally impressive. Already by the turn of the century 3,000 new schools had been opened since 1867, while the proportion of school attendees had increased from 50 to 81 per cent. Four new universities were also opened in the five decades after the 1867 settlement, the last of which, the University of Debrecen, formally began enrolling students at the very end of World War I. The expansion of education in turn triggered an explosion in the production of newspapers, journals, books and other reading materials. Many towns across the country were reconstructed, beautified and expanded, driven by a population that surged into the urban areas, while Budapest was transformed into one of Europe's great metropolises, replete with avenues that rivalled Paris, a parliament that rivalled Westminster, 'art galleries, museums and libraries [that] could compare with those of any European state of comparable size', and continental Europe's first underground railroad.[8]

Reasons for Dissatisfaction

Nevertheless, public opinion in other parts of the empire bridled at the behaviour of Hungary's political class and the emperor even drew up a secret plan to invade the country in order to bring her politicians to heel. Also, a growing number of foreign observers concluded that the Hungarian political class had abused the autonomy that it had been granted by the 1867 settlement.[9] At the same time, the internal dissatisfaction which would rip the country apart in 1918 was fomented by an electoral system that remained essentially unreformed and exclusionary, while much of the population remained mired in poverty, and more than half the population claimed to have a mother tongue other than Hungarian. These 'minorities' could point to the manifest ways in which they were discriminated against by the authorities, while their own cultural 'revivals', which gathered pace after 1867, inspired the growth of a range of nationalist movements that chafed against 'Magyar chauvinism'. The various branches of the socialist movement also grew in strength throughout the period and denounced the entire structure of government, including the legal system, as one that was rigged in favour of the privileged classes.

Some Hungarian nationalists were also sharply critical of the post-1867 political system, which, they argued, was the result of a 'compromise' or even a 'betrayal'. They were particularly incensed that the legislation passed by the revolutionary Hungarian government in 1849 remained stricken from the official record, including the dethronement of the House of Habsburg and Hungary's formal declaration of independence. For these nationalists, the 1867 settlement, and by extension the entire political system that governed the country for the next five decades, was unconstitutional and, therefore, invalid.[10]

The Post-1867 Constitution Framework

Even so, as the writings of Apponyi and Andrássy at the beginning of this chapter clearly indicate, much of Hungary's political class was enthusiastic about the 1867 settlement, and the legal inheritance that provided them with the opportunity to reconstruct the country. Although there were demands as early as the 1790s for Hungary to draw up a 'comprehensive written settlement' of its distinct legal status within the Habsburg Empire, most Hungarian politicians had by that point discovered that the country's combination of statutory and customary law provided a sufficient basis for the claim that Hungary already had a constitution.[11]

Unlike many of the provinces of the Habsburg Empire, Hungary possessed, for example, a crown of its own, which had only passed to the House of Habsburg after the death of the last Hungarian king in 1526. This crown was imbued with a 'doctrine' that conferred on its wearer certain rights and certain responsibilities, which could be equated with the checks and balances that Montesquieu had ascribed to a well-constructed constitution. In addition, Hungary possessed a parliament of its own, whose existence could be traced back to the medieval period. Its centuries of deliberations had produced a large body of statutory law, which was updated annually in the series *Corpus Juris Hungarici* – clear evidence that Hungary possessed a statutory law of its own.

Moreover, Hungary possessed its own system of local administration (specifically the county assemblies), its own series of courts, and its own juridical traditions, encapsulated by the great work of Stephen Werbőczy, the *Tripartitum* (1517), which had laid out in detail the rights of Hungary's nobility. It also possessed a long tradition of myth-making, which dated constitutional precedents as far back as the conquest of the country by the Hungarians in the ninth century. Descriptions of the Hungarian constitution published both before and after World War I frequently included, for example, the famous pagan 'blood oath', which had supposedly bound together the 'seven leaders' of the Magyars, who had led the conquering Hungarians westwards into the Carpathian Basin.[12]

One specific reason why Hungary's political class embraced the discovery that their country possessed a constitution of its own was that it repeatedly provided them with an opportunity to enhance Hungary's position within the Habsburg Empire. They realized that Hungary's historical constitution was a useful stick with which to beat back attempts, both real and imagined, by various Habsburg emperors to impose a centralized system of government on their diverse and inefficient possessions, most notably during the reign of Joseph II in 1780–90, and during the first years of Francis Joseph's reign in 1848–60. Both monarchs, in these years, refused to convene the Hungarian Diet, refused to undergo a separate coronation ceremony in Hungary, and sought to impose direct rule on the rebellious Hungarian nobility.

The widespread conviction of Hungary's more sober politicians and jurists, as László Péter has explained, was that Hungary's historical constitution was the appropriate instrument to reconcile the competing interests of the Hungarian Holy Crown held since 1526 by the House of Habsburg, and the interests of the nation (*ország*), usually represented by the nobility, embodied by men like Apponyi and Andrássy, who thanks to a narrow franchise, a generous dose of self-serving corruption and the politicization of the bureaucracy, were able to preserve their grip on parliament and insist that they were the legitimate representatives of the Hungarian nation. The 1867 settlement, which granted Hungary home rule, was therefore regarded by its defenders, who governed Hungary almost without interruption from 1867 to 1918, as a quintessential expression of the unwritten constitution's ability to secure for the Hungarians a level of autonomy which was accorded to no other people in the Monarchy.[13]

Nevertheless, even those who defended the 1867 settlement regarded it as only one step, albeit a necessary one, in Hungary's constitutional development. Moreover, as C.A Macartney perceptively highlighted, many Hungarian politicians regarded the settlement 'as unduly unfavourable to Hungary in detail; nearly all of them, in any case, looked on the decennial revision of its economic and financial clauses as an opportunity to press for every advantage which they could secure for their country at the expense of Austria'.[14] In addition, fresh debates broke out intermittently over a whole series of questions that the settlement did not or could not address. It was this protracted legal wrangling that persuaded one of Hungary's prime ministers, Dezső Bánffy, to insist that 'our constitutional life' only began in 1867.[15]

Initially, Hungarian jurists and politicians felt compelled to defend the ill-defined nature of this new constitutional 'life'. They were aware that the 1867 settlement rested on a legal fiction that ignored all of the legislation which had been imposed on Hungary by the revolutionary government in 1849, and by the emperor's ministers between 1850 and 1860. For example, Tivadar Pauler, a prominent historian and legal theorist, argued that there was no need for an obvious legal precedent for any constitutional development, as 'the law develops out of the nation in the manner of a plant, whose roots rest in the conviction of the people and evolve through customary practice.' Ferenc Deák, one of the architects of the settlement, argued in similar terms that the constitutional changes of the settlement were justified because they had 'emerged from the life of the nation' and it was perfectly normal that the constitution 'went through periodic changes in form and in substance [...] in response to the needs of the nation and the requirements of the age'.[16]

Exploiting Ambiguities

By the end of the century, however, the adaptability of the constitution had shifted from a defensive justification to a reason for its exaltation. Árpád Ferenczy, one of Hungary's foremost legal scholars at the beginning of the twentieth century, for example, offered a particularly sharp critique of what he called 'documentary constitutions' (*okiratalkotmány*), which he asserted 'very often are an cumbersome impediment [*nehézkesség*] to the development of the life of the state, cause rigidity and artificial paralysis, [and] exclude that flexibility which derives from the real needs, and not merely theoretical argumentation, which characterizes a historical constitution'.[17] The benefits of this flexibility for Hungary's political class rapidly became obvious for it allowed them to demand new concessions, cut deals with the emperor in Vienna and reconstruct the country.

A particularly revealing area of wrangling between Crown and *nation* concerned whether Hungary had a right to have her own army. Precedent suggested yes. The medieval kingdom of Hungary had possessed a sizeable army, and the feats of arms of the Hungarian revolutionaries in 1848/9 were embedded in the popular imagination. Practicality suggested no. As Archduke Albrecht, inspector general of the army from 1869 to 1895, explained, 'in no other country is unity, uniformity and the dynastic soldierly spirit as all-important [...] because only the dynasty and the army can hold the monarchy together.'[18] As Gunther Rothenberg has, however, noted, the 1867 settlement used 'deliberately obscure' language when it declared that 'all matters relating to the command and the internal administration of the entire army, and therefore of the Hungarian army as an integral part of the entire military establishment, are recognized as being reserved to His Majesty.'[19]

As a result, Hungarian politicians demanded, and were granted, the establishment of a separate Hungarian Home Guard (*Honvédség*) that coexisted with the regular unified army, and then spent the following five decades demanding more patriotic uniforms for their soldiers, more advanced weaponry for their regiments, and the use of Hungarian alongside German as a 'language of command' in the joint army. The need for Hungary to contribute a share of the funds allocated to the military budget, and approve the increases in funding necessary to modernize the empire's armed forces, gave Hungarian politicians a lever with which they endeavoured to extract concessions from Vienna, and the wrangling continued until the empire eventually collapsed in 1918.

Another example of how Hungarian politicians exploited the flexibility of their historical constitution to affirm the rights of the nation and diminish the rights of the Crown, while simultaneously avoiding outright rebellion, came with the aptly named 'constitutional crisis' of 1905 during which Hungarian conservatives had their ideas on the constitution, in László Péter's words, 'transformed'.[20] The crisis was provoked when the governing Liberal Party lost its majority in the 1905 elections. For the first time since 1867 critics of the settlement obtained a (slim) majority in parliament and immediately refused to authorize Hungary's contribution to the funding of the common army. Traditionally, Francis Joseph had always appointed a cabinet that was assured of parliament's support, but he now used the Crown's formal authority to appoint as prime minister a retired general, Géza Fejérváry, who had no meaningful support on the parliamentary benches but was, nevertheless, willing to drive through an electoral reform bill if a majority proved unwilling to support his ministry.

In response, conservative parliamentarians who had previously venerated the balance that the unwritten constitution had achieved between the rights of the Crown and the rights of the nation now insisted that parliament should stand supreme and could reject any minister appointed by the Crown. The Fejérváry government was accused of being 'unconstitutional', and at one point the army had to enter parliament to force its dissolution and fresh elections.[21] These elections permitted, however, 'constitutional innovation'. The anti-Habsburg parties that emerged with a majority in the 1906 elections promptly made a deal with the Emperor which permitted them to form a government while simultaneously accepting his right to nominate a pliant figure as prime minister, the ever-reliable Sándor Wekerle. Talk of electoral reform was quietly dropped while the new government also handed over the required contribution to the funding of the joint army.[22]

The enthusiasm that Hungarian legal scholars and politicians displayed for Hungary's constitution was not, however, merely due to its political elite's ability to reshape relations with Vienna. Revealingly, even after World War I and the break-up of the Habsburg Empire, writers on the Hungarian constitution praised its flexibility which allowed for 'extraordinary measures in extraordinary times'.[23] Writing almost 40 years after Ferenczy, another of Hungary's foremost legal historians, Ferenc Eckhart, argued that the fundamental problem with 'paper constitutions' was that, as he put it, they 'emerge and disappear according to the fashion of the time'. This flaw became, however, a virtue for Eckhart when applied to the precise contents of Hungary's unwritten constitution. Indeed, it was the capacity of Hungary's unwritten constitution to legitimate successive governments' efforts to transform the country that made it attractive. For Hungary's governing class the constitution's great value was not only that its 'principle' and 'ideal' constrained the Crown but that its flexibility empowered the nation, more precisely the leadership of the nation, and legitimized the effort to create what László Kontler has called 'a mirage of greatness'.[24]

The enthusiasm of Ferenczy and Eckhart for the constitution's flexibility can also be explained by the fact that the discovery that Hungary possessed a constitution enabled Hungarians to regard themselves as distinct from the many other peoples who inhabited the eastern 'backwater' of the multi-ethnic Habsburg Empire. They were instead, at least in terms of legal development, the equals of the great powers of Western Europe, such as France and Britain, and were able to distinguish themselves from both the 'despotic' Eastern powers such as the Ottoman Empire and Russia, which possessed no formal 'checks and balances' on the power of their own rulers, and the other 'lesser' peoples of the Monarchy who supposedly did not possess their own separate legal traditions.

For example, one feature of Hungary's unwritten constitution that appealed to Hungary's governing class was its similarity to Britain's own unwritten version.[25] Hungary was in the German cultural orbit, and much of its political system was modelled on the centralized French model, but Hungarian conservatives also lauded Britain's ability to curb the powers of the Crown, preserve the influence of the nobility and avoid revolutionary excesses. It was, therefore, appealing to share a legal framework, supposedly grounded in an unwritten constitution, with 'Foggy England', and use that to bolster Hungary's prestige in Britain. As late as 1939, the Hungarian minister for justice, András Tasnádi Nagy, swatted away concerns that Hungary was sliding towards totalitarianism when he insisted to his English readership that Hungary is 'the only nation whose own historical constitution is worthy of being mentioned by the side of theirs', supporting his argument with supposed parallels between Hungary's Golden Bull of 1222 and England's Magna Carta of 1215.[26] Even one of Hungary's sharpest critics, R.W. Seton-Watson, accepted these spurious parallels when he bemoaned the various abuses he documented as 'far from being worthy of a country whose constitutional charter dates from the thirteenth century'.[27]

The Growing Power of the State

The method that Hungarian politicians used after 1867 to ensure that their country began to live up to this exalted rhetoric was to adopt a distinctly Central European version of liberalism that stressed the state's leading role in the modernization of the country through its ability to harmonize the customs of the historical constitution with contemporary circumstances and practical necessity. On the one hand, as László Péter has noted, 'impressively large areas of law were brought under statutory control in property, contract, commerce, credit and in industrial laws' as 'codification became the new canon.' At the same time, crucial areas such as Church–State relations and freedom of speech and association, and the status of cultural organizations and political parties was left essentially to the government's discretion.[28]

An early example of this tendency came in 1861 with the drafting of a new civil code that would replace the Austrian civil code which had been imposed by the emperor after the defeat of the 1848/9 revolution and was regarded by Hungarian politicians as an alien law.[29] Hastily drafted by some 60 former judges and lawyers, the 'Provisional Judicial Regulations' (*Ideiglenes Törvénykezési Szabályok*) were, as Martyn Rady has noted, an awkward 'settlement between older Hungarian foundations and new legal outlooks' that was 'full of contradictions and inconsistencies'. As the name suggests, the Provisional Judicial Regulations were only intended to be a temporary measure, but because they gave the government the ability to exploit their flaws and flesh out their implications with a thicket of decrees, the regulations remained in force all the way up to 1959 when the Communist dictatorship finally enacted an entirely new civil code.[30]

In a similar fashion, the government also exploited the failure to clarify through statute the precise powers of local government to impose its authority through its own directly appointed representatives. As C.A. Macartney has explained, following the opposition parties' success in 1891 in blocking 'another extremely comprehensive Bill for defining the powers of the Jurisdictions' the government had to 'content itself with the enunciation of the general principle that administration in the Counties was a general duty'. As a result it was the sheriff (*főispán*) of each county, directly appointed by the minister of the interior, who oversaw local government in the countryside and generally ensured that little was ever done to challenge the supremacy of the government in Budapest.[31]

The immense amount of statutory law passed by parliament in the decades between 1867 and 1914, which resulted in almost 2,000 new bills receiving parliamentary assent, invariably assured that it was sloppily drafted and concerned with general principles, that again, as Rady persuasively argues, permitted the government to 'make up for deficiencies' with wave after wave of decrees that were invariably grounded in the principle that where the law was silent, the government was free to act as it pleased.[32]

Successive governments also benefited from the domination of parliament by the narrow swathe of the population that was always likely to endorse their particular version of liberalism. The former Upper House of the Diet was converted into the Upper House of the new parliament, with much the same membership, and thus continued to be dominated by generally pliant aristocrats and obedient prelates. The Lower House of parliament was elected, but the franchise was again explicitly based on previous custom rather than contemporary European practice. The vote was therefore granted to all those who had possessed the right to participate in the county assemblies prior to 1848, while a range of property, income and educational qualifications excluded three-quarters of the adult male population. Thus, the political supremacy of the nobility was preserved even after the entire population had been theoretically granted membership in the Hungarian 'political nation'. Moreover, continued use of the open ballot and the blatant politicization of the administration were justified by reference to long-standing customs. Determined opponents of the government could still win seats in parliament, and an electoral earthquake in 1906 briefly handed power to critics of the 1867 settlement, but, on the whole, the electoral system served the government well. Substantial electoral reforms were demanded, promised and even passed into law (in 1917) but were never actually put into practice until after Hungary imploded in 1918–19.[33]

Conversely, the historical constitution offered no guarantee against even established conventions being disregarded when the government believed that this was in the national interest. For example, a determination to overcome sectarian divisions within the country and curb the overweening influence of the Catholic Church persuaded the government to force through, in 1894, the abolition of centuries of customary law pertaining to marriage, divorce, the religious upbringing of children and the recording of all births, deaths and marriages. All of this had previously been overseen by local clergymen who had, it was alleged, abused this privilege to act in an unsystematic manner that affirmed their own sectarian interests and discriminated against citizens of denominations other than their own. From the government's perspective this was intolerable for, as Paul Hanebrink has explained, much of Hungary's political class assumed that 'in a multi-ethnic and multi-confessional state like Hungary, only the state and its laws could guarantee the survival of a cohesive and productive society' and this required 'the supremacy of civil law over religious faith'.[34] Confronted by this logic, even the threat of a veto by the Emperor proved incapable of preserving customary law, as the government held fresh elections, meddled with the composition of parliament, and defied the Emperor's right of veto, in order to enact its reform.[35]

As the political class's confidence increased, even statutory law could be, on occasion, disregarded. For example, the so-called Nationalities Law of 1868 was a relatively generous measure that assured the non-Magyar minorities a range of rights including the ability to use their native languages when interacting with officialdom. Admittedly, the law was again sloppily drafted. It claimed, for example, that the only nation in Hungary was the 'indivisible unitary Magyar nation' (*Magyar nemzet*) to which all the various minorities, or 'nationalities' (*nemzetiségek*) as the law termed them, belonged. It did not, however, explain what the distinction between a nation and a nationality actually was. As a result, historians have repeatedly come to entirely contradictory conclusions about the law's intentions. It has, for example, been lauded as 'one of the most enlightened measures of its kind ever adopted' and lambasted as a quintessential expression of Magyar chauvinism.[36]

In reality, as the idea of assimilating Hungary's minorities into the 'Magyar nation' appeared more feasible, the provisions of the nationalities law were either never actually enacted or were even deliberately contravened by the government. When confronted about these shenanigans in parliament, however, Prime Minister István Tisza admitted that the Nationalities Law was 'impossible to enact' because it was 'idealistic'. One of his predecessors, Prime Minister Dezső Bánffy, made much the same point when he argued that the 1868 law on the nationalities 'cannot be implemented [...] not least because in the thirty-six years since the law was enacted, our public life has gone through so many changes that the implementation of the letter of the law is impossible'.[37]

As a result, the treatment of the minorities largely depended on the instincts of the central government and the attitude of local officials. Andrássy, as minister of the interior in 1906–9, could declare, in one of his more bombastic outbursts, that 'I will not tolerate the political organization of the nationalities. I consider them to be in violation of our fundamental laws.'[38] Nevertheless, even political parties which represented the minorities continued to contest elections and secure seats in parliament while legal scholars debated their legality.[39] As for the cultural organizations established by the minorities, some were never permitted to actually open, the Slovak *Matica Slovenska* were first permitted (in 1867) and then disbanded (in 1875), while its Serbian equivalent flourished without significant impediment.[40] It was the flexibility of Hungary's constitution that, again, permitted the Hungarian political class to deal with the minorities on a case-by-case basis while persevering with its programme of assimilation.

Delegitimization and Destruction, 1918–19

It should, however, be unsurprising that the willingness of the political class to exploit the flexibilities inherent in Hungary's ambiguous constitution was regarded by its opponents as naked self-interest that was neither moral nor legal. One of Hungary's better legal theorists, Győző Concha, may have 'forgotten' about the exact provisions of the nationalities law when pressed on why they were not being applied, but representatives of Hungary's minorities and foreign critics were acutely aware of the discrepancy between the formal rights of the minorities and their arbitrary maltreatment by the authorities.⁴¹ For example, the self-appointed Slovak National Council, which assembled on 30 October 1918, and made the crucial decision to break away from Hungary and join the new Czechoslovak Republic, specifically accused the Hungarian government of 'defying existing laws' and dismissed Hungary's historical constitution as a 'medieval feudal system' that had 'destroyed our people economically and exploited them'.⁴² While the bitterness engendered by the loss of World War I played a role in causing this final estrangement, as did the anger caused by an electoral system that permitted the minorities only token representation in parliament, the conviction that Hungary's historical constitution had been transformed into an instrument of Magyar chauvinism also persuaded Croat, Romanian, Serb and Slovak nationalists in Hungary to exploit the chaos that engulfed the country at the end of World War I to join neighbouring states.

The parties of the left, including the Hungarian Social Democratic Party and its various offshoots, such as the government of Mihály Károlyi, 'the Red Count', which seized power on 31 October 1918 and the Bolsheviks headed by Béla Kun who took power in March 1919, also concluded that the existing constitution only served the interests of the 'exploitative classes'. Oszkár Jászi, one of the ideologues of the nationalist government that seized power in Hungary on 31 October 1918 and proclaimed the country to be an independent republic 16 days later, described the legal system that had developed after 1867 as 'sham constitutionalism' that 'could be maintained only by a corrupt and restricted electoral system, by open ballot, and by terroristic procedures in the administrative and military machine'.⁴³ The revolutionary Hungarian government in which Jászi served initially swore an oath to uphold 'the constitution', with the ceremony overseen by a Habsburg archduke acting as vice-regent of the last emperor, but it then proceeded to sever all ties with the Habsburg Empire and accept the dissolution of parliament with unfulfilled promises of new elections and a massive expansion of the franchise. Women were also theoretically granted the right to vote, without restriction, for the first time, although men and women would not enjoy equal voting rights in practice until after World War II.⁴⁴

As the head of the government, Károlyi explained in a telegram distributed throughout the country and pompously addressed 'to all the civilized nations' immediately after he assumed power, 'it was the institutions of the [1867] settlement which rendered the democratic development of the Hungarian nation impossible, it was the spirit of this settlement which permanently poisoned relations between the Hungarian nation and other nations [but now] every last root of this settlement has been ripped out [...] and every institution of the past, every person of the past, and the entire spirit of the past has been severed.' The reality was, however, more prosaic. Károlyi was appointed president, his government relied on rule by decree, which it renamed 'the law of the people' (*néptörvény*), and the bulk of the existing legislation remained in force while the government argued, dithered and rapidly collapsed.[45]

The Bolshevik party, which aligned with the Social Democrats to seize power on 21 March 1919, had even less tolerance for constitutional traditions than its progressive predecessors. Convinced that they were part of a worldwide revolution, they sought to emulate the Soviet Union's model of governance, with real authority wielded by 'people's commissars', empowered by a nationwide 'federation of councils', who poured out a torrent of patchily enacted decrees to realize, as Bryan Cartledge succinctly puts it, 'the complete Leninist agenda of expropriation, nationalization, regimentation and terror'.[46] The Bolsheviks' first decree imposed martial law upon the entire country, while the entire court system and the Provisional Judicial Regulations of 1861 were replaced by revolutionary tribunals a mere four days later. The legal revolution reached a crescendo on 23 June 1919 with the enactment of the 'Constitution of the Hungarian Socialist Federal Republic of Councils'.[47] Clearly inspired by the Soviet Union's first constitution, promulgated in 1918, which, as Aryeh Unger has emphasized, placed the structure of the state 'on the mass assemblies of the soviets (councils) which had sprung up in town and country since the February revolution', the Hungarian Bolshevik version was an equally laborious document which devoted most of its clauses to demarcating the precise functions of the various levels of officialdom.[48] The revolutionary character of this constitution was underscored by its opening declaration that 'in the Republic of Councils the proletariat has taken into its hands every institution, every law and every authority.' Among its 89 clauses there was only one concession to previous practices when it stated, in article 39, that 'in general, in the question of whether a locality is a village or a town, until further instruction the old bureaucratic arrangements will provide direction.'[49]

The arrival of the Romanian army into Budapest on 1 November 1919 put an end to Hungary's constitutional experimentation. By that point Hungary had lost two-thirds of its population and three-quarters of its territory. Its economy was a shambles, its prestige abroad eviscerated, its experiments in socialist and Bolshevik government thoroughly delegitimized, and the most politically active part of its citizenry appeared consumed by the search for scapegoats and a nostalgia for 'the world of yesterday'. Unsurprisingly, therefore, the new counter-revolutionary governments encountered little resistance when they turned back the constitutional clock. Law I of 1920, the first piece of legislation passed by the reconstituted parliament, declared all legislation that had been passed in the period after 16 November 1919 to be null and void, although this legislation could remain temporarily in force at the discretion of the appropriate ministry.[50] From then until the occupation of Hungary by the German army in 1944, the country was once again run by a political class that valued the flexibility provided by that collection of laws, decrees, customs and myths which continued to be described as Hungary's historical constitution.

Further Reading

Gerő, András, *Emperor Francis Joseph, King of the Hungarians* (New York, 2001).
Janos, Andrew C., *The Politics of Backwardness in Hungary, 1825–1945* (Princeton, NJ, 1982).
Katus, László, *Hungary in the Dual Monarchy, 1867–1914* (New York, 2008).
Lojkó, Miklós (ed.), *László Péter, Hungary's Long Nineteenth Century. Constitutional and Democratic Traditions in a European Perspective: Collected Studies by László Péter* (Leiden and Boston, MA, 2012).
Macartney, C.A., *The Habsburg Empire, 1790–1918* (London, 1968).
Ormos, Mária and Béla Király (eds), *Hungary. Governments and Politics, 1848–2000* (Boulder, CO, 2001).
Péter, László, 'Die Verfassungsentwicklung in Ungarn', in H. Rumpler and P. Urbanitsch (eds), *Die Habsburgermonarchie 1848–1918*, vol. VII (Vienna, 2000).
Vermes, Gábor, *István Tisza: The Liberal Vision and Conservative Statecraft of a Magyar Nationalist* (New York, 1985).

The Use and Abuse of Flexibility

Notes

1. Albert Apponyi, 'The constitution of Hungary', in P. Alden (ed.), *Hungary of To-day* (London, 1909), pp. 112–13.
2. Quoted in Paul Lendvai, *The Hungarians. A Thousand Years of Victory in Defeat* (Princeton, NJ, 2004), p. 307.
3. Apponyi, 'The constitution of Hungary', p. 113.
4. See, for example, the exhaustive effort by Zsolt Zétényi, *A történeti alkotmány. Magyarország ősi alkotmánya* (Budapest, 2010).
5. C.A. Macartney, *The Habsburg Empire, 1790–1918* (London, 1968), p. 31.
6. László Katus, 'Magyarország gazdasági fejlődése', in P. Hanák and F. Mucsi (eds), *Magyarország története, 1890–1918* (Budapest, 1978), p. 274.
7. László Kontler, *A History of Hungary* (Basingstoke, 2002), pp. 285–314.
8. Macartney, *The Habsburg Empire*, pp. 706–7; Kontler, *A History of Hungary*, pp. 285–314.
9. See, for example, the pessimistic description of Francis Joseph's relations with the Hungarians in András Gerő, *Emperor Francis Joseph, King of the Hungarians* (New York, 2001), pp. 186–91.
10. Peter Sugar, 'An underrated event: The Hungarian constitutional crisis of 1905–6', in P. Sugar (ed.), *Nationality and Society in the Habsburg and Ottoman Empire* (Aldershot, 1997), p. 283.
11. Martyn Rady, *Customary Law in Hungary: Courts, Texts and the Tripartitum* (Oxford, 2015), p. 216; Miklós Lojkó (ed.), László Péter, *Hungary's Long Nineteenth Century: Constitutional and Democratic Traditions in European Perspective: Studies by László Péter* (Leiden and Boston, MA, 2012), p. 66.
12. See, for example, Jenő Csuday, *A magyar alkotmány történeti fejlődése* (Budapest, 1922), pp. 27–8.
13. Péter, in Lojkó, *Hungary's Long Nineteenth Century*, pp. 56–77.
14. Macartney, *The Habsburg Empire*, p. 694.
15. Dezső Bánffy, *Magyar nemzetiségi politika* (Budapest, 1902), pp. 16, 69.
16. Rady, *Customary Law in Hungary*, p. 225; Zétényi, *A történeti alkotmány*, p. 54.
17. Árpád Ferenczy, *A politika rendszere* (Budapest, 1909), p. 190.
18. Quoted in Gunther Rothenberg, 'Toward a national Hungarian army: The military compromise of 1868 and its consequences', *Slavic Review* xxxi/4 (1972), p. 806.
19. Ibid., p. 807.
20. László Péter, 'The aristocracy, the gentry and their parliamentary tradition in nineteenth-century Hungary', *The Slavonic and East European Review* 1992/1, pp. 106–9.
21. Sugar, 'An underrated event', pp. 285–92.
22. Péter, 'The aristocracy, the gentry and their parliamentary tradition', pp. 106–9.
23. Ferenc Eckhart, 'A magyar alkotmány', in *Magyar Szemle* 1944/3, pp. 119–21.
24. See, in particular, Kontler, *A History of Hungary*, pp. 279–81.
25. Csuday, *A magyar alkotmány történeti fejlődése*, pp. 15–16.

26. Andrew Tasnádi Nagy, 'A thousand years of the Hungarian constitution', *The Hungarian Quarterly* 1939/5, p. 10.
27. R.W. Seton-Watson, *Corruption and Reform in Hungary: A Study of Electoral Practice* (London, 1911), p. 26.
28. László Péter, 'The principle of consuetedo in Hungarian law', in M. Rady (ed.), *Custom and Law in Central Europe* (Cambridge, 2003), p. 107.
29. Ibid., p. 106.
30. Rady, *Customary Law in Hungary*, pp. 224–9.
31. Macartney, *The Habsburg Empire*, pp. 696–7; see also the useful review of Hungary's administrative system in Piroska Balogh, 'The Kalman Tisza Epoch', in M. Ormos and B. Király (eds), *Hungary. Governments and Politics, 1848–2000* (Boulder, CO, 2001), pp. 80–3.
32. Rady, *Customary Law in Hungary*, p. 235; see also *Corpus Juris Hungarici, 1867–1914*.
33. László Péter, 'Die Verfassungsentwicklung in Ungarn', in *Die Habsburgermonarchie 1848–1918*, vol. VII (Vienna, 2000), pp. 340–6. See also Zsuzsanna Boros and Dániel Szabó, *Parlamentarizmus Magyarországon 1867–1944* (Budapest, 1999), pp. 124–35, and Ferenc Pölöskei, *A szabadelvű párt fényei és árnya, 1875–1906* (Budapest, 2010).
34. Paul Hanebrink, 'Christianity, nation, state: The case of Christian Hungary', in B. Berglunk and B. Porter-Szűcs (eds), *Christianity and Modernity in Eastern Europe* (Budapest and New York, 2010), pp. 65–7.
35. On the government's tactics in parliament see Katalin Ibolya Koncz, 'A polgári házasságról szóló törvényjavaslat vitája a képviselőház előtt', in *Publicationes Universitatis Miskolcinensis Sectio Juridica et Politica, Tomus XXXI* (2013), and for its more unorthodox methods in favour of the bill, see Macartney, *The Habsburg Empire*, pp. 698–9.
36. Samuel Cambel et al. (eds), *Dejiny slovenska*, 6 vols (Bratislava, 1985), p. 272; László Katus, *Hungary in the Dual Monarchy, 1867–1914* (Highland Lakes, TX, 2008), p. 102.
37. Banffy, *Magyar nemzetiségi politika*, p. 30.
38. László Szarka, *Szlovák nemzeti fejlődés. Magyar nemzetiségi politika, 1867–1918* (Bratislava, 2005), p. 57.
39. Károly Kmety, 'Közjogünk és a nemzetségi pártok', *Jogtudományi Közlöny*, 6 March 1914; Guido Gundisch, 'Nemzetiségi pártszervezetek közjogi szempontból', *Jogtudományi Közlemények*, 3 April 1914.
40. See Michal Potemra, 'Otázky verejnej správy Uhorska v politike Slovenskej Národnej Strány v rokoch 1901–1918', in *Historické Stúdie* xxvi (1982), p. 98, and Polányi, *A szlovák társadalom és polgári nemzet mozgalom a századfordulón 1895–1905* (Budapest, 1987), pp. 95–6.
41. Hugh and Christopher Seton-Watson, *The Making of a New Europe* (London, 1981), p. 49.
42. Joseph Mikuš, *Slovakia. A Political and Constitutional History (with Documents)* (Bratislava, 1995), p. 161.

THE USE AND ABUSE OF FLEXIBILITY   159

43. Oszkár Jászi, *The Dissolution of the Habsburg Monarchy* (Chicago, 1961), p. 112.
44. Bryan Cartledge, *The Will to Survive: A History of Hungary* (London, 2006), pp. 303–5.
45. Péter Kiss (ed.), *Magyar kormányprogramok 1867–2002*, vol. 1, pp. 440–1. For a good overview of the situation in Hungary in the immediate aftermath of World War I, see John Swanson, *The Remnants of the Habsburg Monarchy: The Shaping of Modern Austria and Hungary, 1918–1922* (Boulder, CO, 2001), pp. 123–58.
46. Cartledge, *The Will to Survive*, p. 308.
47. A provisional version of this constitution had already been enacted on 2 April, 1919. See Andor Csizmadia (ed.), *Magyar állam-és jogtörténet* (Budapest, 1972), pp. 592–3 and András Siklós, *Magyarország 1918/1919* (Budapest, 1978), pp. 267–75.
48. Aryeh Unger, *Constitutional Development in the USSR: A Guide to the Soviet Constitutions* (London, 1981), p. 14. See also Antal Tamás, *A hundred years of public law in Hungary, 1890–1990: studies on the modern hungarian constitution and legal history* (Novi Sad, 2012), pp. 109–15 and p. 163.
49. *Népszava*, 28 June 1919.
50. *Magyar Törvénytár. 1920. évi törvénycikkek* (Budapest, 1921), p. 7.

CHAPTER 8

LAW I OF 1920 AND THE HISTORICAL CONSTITUTION[1]

István Szabó

Prologue

At the end of World War I, revolution swept across Hungary and, as in the other two defeated states (Germany and Austria), plans were made to summon a new constitution-making national assembly. This brought to an end an almost 400-year-long period of Hungarian history. This chapter explores how the creation of an independent Hungarian state broke with the historical constitution, and also details the challenges that politicians faced in attempting to seek constitutional continuity. The aforementioned break was initiated by the destruction of the 1867 settlement, which had been the final reformulation of the rights that the House of Habsburg enjoyed since it had ascended to the Hungarian throne in 1526. According to this settlement, the clasp that held Hungary and the empire together was the person of the emperor. However, the resignation of Charles I of Austria (Charles IV of Hungary) on 13 November 1918 meant that this connection had been severed. Hungary had once again become an independent state, and it was hoped that elections would pave the way for a new constitutional framework.

Preparations for these new elections were, however, complicated by support from the victorious powers for the territorial dismantlement of Hungary. The final list of electoral districts, which was completed by 1 March 1919, included all the territories that had belonged to the

Hungarian state before 1918 – with the exception of Croatia, which had enjoyed autonomy since 1868.[2] Thus, even though the elections were to be held on 13 April 1919,[3] the victorious powers did not agree with this arrangement. At the same time, the government of Mihály Károlyi,[4] which had taken power on 31 October 1918, was not willing to continue resisting the growing territorial demands of Hungary's minorities, and on 21 March 1919 it handed over power to the Bolsheviks. In this way, the development of Hungary deviated from the other two defeated Central European powers. Whereas in Germany and Austria a newly elected national assembly drafted a new constitution, in Hungary an international military intervention was launched against the Bolsheviks, with the result that by August 1919 the entire country was under military occupation. Following the collapse of the Hungarian Soviet Republic on 1 August, 1919, and the short-lived 'trades union' government led by Gyula Peidl, which held power for precisely one week, István Friedrich[5] formed a government having received authorization from Charles IV's former representative in Hungary, Crown Prince József Habsburg.[6] The victorious powers, however, regarded Friedrich with suspicion as a result of his loyalty to the House of Habsburg, and compelled him, at the end of November, to hand over the premiership to Károly Huszár.[7] This was one of the most peculiar changes of government in Hungarian history, as a sitting prime minister – under his own authority – handed over power to a political rival. From that point onwards, the Huszár government oversaw all matters of governance until the election of Miklós Horthy as Regent in March 1920.

These developments had a profound impact on the political atmosphere in Hungary. After protracted debates with the victorious powers, the new parliamentary elections held in 1920, along with further elections held after additional territory was regained following the Treaty of Trianon,[8] demonstrated that a majority of the electorate rejected the ambitions of the revolutionaries who had first seized power in October 1918.

The newly elected National Assembly, which convened at the beginning of 1920, used the first law it enacted to formally invalidate all the legislation enacted between November 1918 and August 1919.[9] With this law, the constitutional arrangements which had governed Hungary previous to October 1918 appeared to have been restored.

In reality, this was only a partial restoration, for reasons which will be explored in the remainder of this chapter.

There were, in fact, several areas in which continuity with the pre-1918 constitutional order was not restored. As is demonstrated in the other contributions to this book, each period in the development of the Hungarian constitution cannot be characterized by simplistic claims about continuities and ruptures with the historical constitution. The idea of unchanging permanence is, in and of itself, a problematic idea, particularly as the historical constitution had constantly changed over time to the point that one can only conceive of an unchanging permanence within a given period. The type of government that emerged as a result of the legal system grounded in Law I of 1920 was, however, wedded not only to the general idea of the historical constitution but specifically to the structures of the state as it had existed between 1867 and 1918. The other two defeated powers in the region changed from monarchies into republics, and on 16 November 1918 Hungary also proclaimed itself to be a People's Republic, but the National Assembly that was elected at the beginning of 1920 decided to restore the monarchy. The public mood essentially demanded this, and from this followed the close ties to the legal system that had developed before 1918. On closer inspection, however, this depiction becomes more complicated. Hungary did, indeed, remain a monarchy but many of the ties (between the pre-1918 and the post-1920 monarchic type of government) were broken.

The dilemma of how to combine the need for both continuity and change was a central feature of the historical constitution and was also evident in the deliberations of the National Assembly that convened at the beginning of 1920. Although there was broad agreement that legal continuity with the historical constitution should be restored, there was no consensus over the extent to which the new political system should be connected to the legal system that had existed between 1867 and 1918. In the specialist literature that has concentrated on this dilemma, a distinction has been drawn between the idea of 'formal' (or formally enacted) continuity (*alaki folytonosság*) and 'substantive' (or *de facto*) continuity (*anyagi folytonosság*), and this chapter will now focus on the parliamentary debates that preceded the passing of Law I of 1920 in which the clash between these two rival concepts of legal continuity was evident.

Naturally, the question of whether Hungary should be a republic or a monarchy was also bound up with the question of how much of the historical constitution could and should be preserved, which explains why the National Assembly ultimately decided to restore the monarchy. This will be discussed in the second part of the chapter, while the third part will examine those areas of previously settled law which were disregarded after 1918. In summary, the most plausible way to measure the constitutional position of interwar Hungary is to compare and contrast it to the legal framework that governed the state between 1867 and 1918 in order to highlight both the continuities and the discontinuities.

The Concepts of a Continuity of Form and of Substance

As noted above, the National Assembly in 1920 sought to restore the historical constitution even though a complete restoration of the legal framework that had governed Hungary between 1867 and 1918 was impossible. Although there were members of parliament who favoured a complete restoration, there was no consensus in support of such a policy. The clash between those who favoured the complete restoration of the historical constitution and those who rejected this ideal was crystallized by the dispute between the 'legitimists' who favoured the hereditary principle of royal succession, and thus believed that only the last Habsburg emperor and King of Hungary, Charles IV, could be the legitimate ruler of the country, and the 'free-electors', who believed that the National Assembly had the right to select whomever it wished to be the next king of Hungary. In reality, however, both sides sought to avoid open conflict, and Law I of 1920 was, as will be demonstrated, carefully drafted so that the views of both sides were included in the relevant articles.

It was, however, an open question whether it was possible to restore the historical constitution while simultaneously breaking with the principle of legal continuity. In 1848 the Diet had voted for the principle of popular representation and had thereby transformed its own composition. The National Assembly, established in 1920, had its roots, however, in the 'revolutionary' legal system that had emerged in the immediate aftermath of World War I. Thus, this question could only be solved by redefining the principle of legal continuity. The original concept of genuine legal continuity, known as 'formal' (*alaki*) legal continuity, was therefore supplemented by the new concept of substantive (*anyagi*) legal continuity. Formal legal continuity could only have been preserved if, as in 1848, the constitutional reforms had been approved by the existing parliament and were endorsed by the king or his legitimate successor. In contrast, proponents of substantive legal continuity were concerned only with the restoration of the various institutions of the ancient regime and were unconcerned with whether the new order had, according to the old constitutional customs, been lawfully established.

The precise dividing line between the legitimists and the free-electors was not merely theoretical. Both camps agreed that the franchise needed to be extended, although there was some debate about the extent of this expansion, but the two sides were a long way from reaching a consensus about who should occupy the Hungarian throne. The removal of the Habsburgs could only be carried out by breaking with the principle of formal legal continuity, and this heightened the conflict between the two camps. Although those who supported the restoration of the Habsburgs, and by extension the principle of formal legal continuity, were uncertain even about the legality of the National Assembly, they did not voice their concerns in public. They did, however, cling to the principle that the need for legal continuity should determine who had the right to occupy the throne.

With respect to the various political parties that were represented in the National Assembly, it is fairly clear that the Party of Christian National Unification (*Keresztény Nemzeti Egyesülés Pártja*, hereafter KNEP), which obtained 71 of the National Assembly's initial 207 mandates, and represented urban, conservative opinion, favoured formal legal continuity, while the Christian National Smallholders' and Agrarian Labourers' Party (*Keresztény Országos Kisgazda és Földműves Párt*, hereafter Smallholder Party), which obtained 77 mandates, represented 'progressive' rural interests and favoured the more pragmatic concept of substantive legal continuity.[10] Both parties had, however, entered government and thus this was a debate that took place within the governing coalition. As both of these parties had obtained a meaningful role in the government led by Károly Huszár that had been formed at the end of November 1919, the conflict between the two was already evident when the cabinet began discussing the drafting of new legislation that eventually resulted in Law I of 1920. A furious debate broke out in the cabinet over whether the text of the law should include the text of the so-called 'Eckartsau declaration' in which Charles IV had submitted his resignation on 13 November 1918, as this would affect the possibility that he could one day reclaim his throne as the legitimists desired. Members of the KNEP such as Defence Minister István Friedrich and Interior Minister Ödön Beniczky openly clashed with Agriculture Minister Gyula Rubinek, who was one of the leaders of the Smallholder Party.[11]

One of the key figures involved in the drafting of Law I of 1920, Béla Turi, who also served as spokesman of the parliamentary committee on public law (*közjogi bizottság előadója*), accepted as established fact that legal continuity had been formally broken. Without the collaboration of the monarch the historical constitution could not be restored and, as the exercise of royal power had ended almost two years earlier, formal legal continuity was, therefore, impossible.[12] At the same time it was an open question whether the new legal system established by the National Assembly was temporary or permanent. In other words, the political situation in 1920 theoretically permitted either the restoration of legal continuity or the creation of an entirely new constitutional framework.

Those MPs who favoured the principle of substantive legal continuity dominated the parliamentary debate over the draft of Law I of 1920. Only Gyula Andrássy,[13] who was a well-known ally of the Habsburgs, spoke out in favour of the principle of formal legal continuity: his view was that any break with the traditions of the past would cause legal uncertainty and result in serious problems.[14] István Nagyatádi Szabó, one of the Smallholder Party's ministers, reflecting on Andrássy's speech, recognized the importance of the historical constitution, but he emphasized that it had continued to be shaped by the enduring inheritance of the pre-1848 feudal system, and thus required significant reform.[15] His thoughts on this matter were shaped, for example, by concerns about the composition of the Upper House of the old parliament, which had always consisted, prior to its dissolution in 1918, of unelected aristocrats and the leaders of Hungary's various religious denominations.[16] Another representative of the Smallholder Party, Rezső Rupert, directed his criticism not at the legacy of the pre-1848 feudal system but at the 1867 settlement. Specifically, Rupert argued that legal continuity should be traced back to Hungary's declaration of independence in 1849 rather than the 1867 settlement.[17] This meant, in particular, the re-authorization of the dethronement of the Habsburgs which had been proclaimed in February 1849 in Debrecen. In turn, Ottokár Prohászka, the bishop of Székesfehérvár and one of the leading intellectuals in the KNEP, directed his irony at those of his Smallholder Party opponents who claimed that they believed in the principle of formal legal continuity but only in connection with that period of Hungarian history which they personally admired.[18]

The Debate over the Future Form of Government in Hungary

The Reasons for the Restoration of the Monarchy

As noted above, a broad consensus emerged among the MPs elected to the new National Assembly, as regards the restoration of the monarchy, which was supported by every meaningful group of MPs. This is curious, for the anti-Habsburg members of the National Assembly could conveniently have chosen to propose that Hungary remain a republic as this would effectively have prevented Charles IV reclaiming the Hungarian throne. If, however, the monarchy was restored then a debate was always likely to ensue over whether with the dissolution of the Austro-Hungarian Monarchy Charles IV had automatically lost his legal right to the throne. Later it will be discussed precisely how this debate erupted. For now, it should only be noted that those who opposed the restoration of the House of Habsburg to the Hungarian throne nevertheless agreed that Hungary should again become a monarchy. They merely demanded that future monarchs should be determined by elections rather than the hereditary principle. The first legal scholarship on this dispute defended this free-elector position. At the beginning of January 1920, before the new National Assembly had even been convened, Károly Kmety published an article which argued that although Hungary's future form of government had not yet been determined, Hungary could prevent a Habsburg restoration without having to remain a republic, if it first worked out the principles by which a restored monarchy would be organized.[19]

Why precisely did those who came to power in 1920 cling to the idea that Hungary should be a monarchy? It was, of course, entirely understandable that those who favoured the restoration of the Habsburgs were simply awaiting the appropriate moment when Charles IV could reclaim his throne. The free-electors, however, did not propose any alternative person as a candidate to assume the throne. Their belief in an elected monarch was, therefore, purely theoretical, and could not be proposed as a practical course of action. One of their real aims was to use the restoration of the monarchy to mark a complete break with the preceding revolutionary period, but their primary concern was the territorial dismantlement of the country. The overarching ambition of all politicians in this period was to restore the territorial integrity of the country, which had been broken up by the Treaty of Trianon, and it was hoped that this could be realized by affirming the principle of continuity with the pre-1918 period. Thus, even the free-electors supported the proposal that Law I of 1920 should restore the monarchy.

The importance of territorial revision as a motive for the restoration of the monarchy is underscored by the fact that the victorious powers would have preferred that Hungary become a republic. In April 1919 the future prime minister István Bethlen even promised the victorious powers that, if they would assist in removing the Bolsheviks from power, Hungary would base its future legal development on the type of government that had emerged in November 1918, namely that it was willing to restore the so-called People's Republic.[20] Prime Minister Huszár also noted during the cabinet debate on the possible restoration of the constitution that the victorious powers had been promised that a referendum would determine Hungary's future type of government.[21] As three of the five victorious great powers (the United Kingdom, Italy and Japan) were actually monarchies, their demand that Hungary should become a republic was not inspired by a particular approach to constitutional law. Instead, these powers sought to ensure that the legal basis for a future revision of the Treaty of Trianon would be pre-emptively blocked by an enforced rupture with the pre-1918 legal system, and this rupture required the dethronement of the Habsburgs. In response, the National Assembly, including those who were anti-Habsburg, supported the restoration of a monarchy. We shall now show how the various steps towards the restoration of the monarchy were guided by this cautious opposition to the ambition of the victorious powers.

Steps towards the Promulgation of the Monarchy

The government of Gyula Peidl formally referred to itself as the Government of the Hungarian People's Republic (*Magyar Népköztársaság Kormánya*), and thus retained the form of government which had been established with the proclamation of the republic on 16 November 1918. The government of István Friedrich, which then seized power in a *coup d'état* on 7 August 1919, claimed, however, that its legitimacy was ensured by the formal authorization of Crown Prince József, the *homio regius* in Hungary. The Friedrich government, therefore, bound itself to the constitutional framework that had existed prior to 31 October 1918. In doing so it implicitly invalidated the period when Hungary had been a republic but, paradoxically, still preserved the republican type of government.[22] At the conclusion of the Friedrich government's first cabinet meeting, the assembled ministers issued a proclamation which stated that 'it is declared that Hungary's official name is the Republic of Hungary, presided over by Crown Prince József, who serves as the Regent.'[23] We should note that this declaration transformed the People's Republic into a mere republic.

In the day-to-day work of the Friedrich government the term 'republic' was, for practical purposes, used to describe the state. Letters that arrived at the Prime Minister's office were formally addressed to the 'Premier of the Hungarian Republic',[24] and this convention remained in force until March 1920. A further example of the use of the term 'republic' to refer to the state can be found in the legislation promulgated by the government, such as decree 4038/1919, which was issued by the prime minister's office and published in the *Budapesti Közlöny* on 20 August 1919. This decree stated that 'the courts will, prior to the complete restoration of the constitution, issue judgements in the name of the Hungarian republic.'[25]

The cabinet was certainly hesitant, up until the end of 1919, to formally restore continuity with the form of government that had existed up until 1918. At the cabinet meeting held on 4 December 1919 a debate was held regarding a proposal by the Hungarian Monarchist Party (*Magyar Királyság Pártja*) which called for the Holy Crown to be reincorporated into Hungary's coat of arms, and for the name of all public institutions to be prefaced by the term 'state' (*állami*) rather than 'republican' (*köztársasági*). The cabinet concluded, however, that for general political reasons this proposal was not desirable.[26] This was the case even though the proposal did not call for the restoration of the monarchy but simply for the state to be described in a neutral manner. It was, therefore, in this cautious spirit that the newly elected National Assembly began its work which continued to be characterized by uncertainty, or to put it more precisely, by an avoidance of any clear declaration on the form of government that existed at this time in Hungary. The influential parliamentarian Béla Turi spoke at the plenary session of the National Assembly about the distinctive features of the monarchic type of government,[27] and expressed his support for these principles on the grounds that they had been incorporated in the draft text of the law. He did not, however, declare which form of government he personally favoured.

The debates in the National Assembly on Law I of 1920 did reveal sharp differences of opinion between the 'free-electors', who dominated the Smallholder Party, and the so-called 'legitimists' who comprised most of the KNEP's fraction. For example, the law listed the rights of the Regent, but this provoked considerable debate over its precise wording because of its relevance to the question of whether the monarchy should be hereditary or elective. Thus, the wording in the original draft of the bill, which declared that 'the Regent [...] will act in accordance with the law as regards the question of the election of the new head of state,' was amended to remove the word 'election'. In its place the new version stated that 'the Regent [...] will act in accordance with the law as regards the question of the person to be appointed as head of state.'[28] The deletion of the term 'election' was the result of a compromise solution between the free-electors and the legitimists.

Similarly, debate erupted between the two camps over the precise wording of that part of the bill which described Charles IV's abdication, as this also had a direct bearing on the question of who should occupy the throne in future. It should be noted here that apart from the debate over the Eckartsau declaration, and the precise wording of the preamble, the final draft of the bill left open the question of whether the powers of the Crown remained in force as this would have had a substantial bearing on the debate over the form of government. As a result of the peculiarities of the historical constitution, the solution to the question of which form of government was appropriate for Hungary can be traced to one of the footnotes to the prologue of Law I of 1920. The monarchy, as a type of government, had not been established by specific legislation but had its roots in customary law. The legal principle was, however, that if legislation deviated from customary law, then the former would take precedence. If, however, the legislation that had superseded customary law was invalidated, then earlier customary law did not need a separate piece of legislation to regain its authority. Thus, Law I of 1920, by invalidating the 'People's Decree' that had brought about the republic, automatically brought the monarchy back to life. The lawmakers did not dare, however, to publicly proclaim the restoration of the monarchy, and even after the promulgation of Law I of 1920 on 28 February, and the election of Horthy as Regent on 1 March 1920, Hungary continued to be officially described as a republic. For example, the official stamps of the prime minister's office continued to mark all correspondence with the designation 'The Prime Minister's Office of the Hungarian Republic'.[29]

It is also interesting to witness the series of changes that took place in the preparation of the state's official stamps and the government's seals. In this respect Károly Huszár, as prime minister-designate, dispatched a letter to the newly elected Regent in early March 1920 that turned the determination of the state's coat of arms into a decisive question.[30] The convention had been that the coat of arms was not determined by parliamentary legislation but by the decree of the head of state. Thus the Regent had the right to decide on the design of the new coat of arms. The Prime Minister identified several points of uncertainty which required clarification. First, it was unclear when the different coats of arms should be used; specifically, when the 'middle' and the 'small' coat of arms should be used. The second point of uncertainty Huszár identified, which was crucial to the debate over the future form of the Hungarian government, was whether the Holy Crown should be included on the coat of arms. The People's Republic had, in November 1918, removed the Holy Crown from the coat of arms,[31] as it had been regarded as a symbol of the monarchical form of government. As previously noted, in response to a proposal from the Hungarian Monarchist Party,[32] the Friedrich government had earlier decided, at the end of 1919, to postpone any decision about the reincorporation of the Holy Crown onto the coat of arms owing to uncertainty over Hungary's future form of government. Huszár's proposal that the Holy Crown should be reincorporated into the coat of arms, and the official seal, was unambiguous but the reasoning was still cautious. It referred to the wording in Law I of 1920 which proclaimed the restoration of 'the form of government that had been Hungary's up to now'. The law did not, however, declare what this form of government actually was, and therefore Huszár's proposal added a further justification for reincorporating the Holy Crown into the coat of arms, namely that it was not only a symbol of royal power but also a symbol of the power of the state.

The first line of reasoning referred to the form of government that could conform to the use of the Holy Crown and this had to be, whether explicitly or implicitly, a monarchy. The second line of reasoning, in contrast, derived from the view that the Holy Crown could be reincorporated on the coat of arms even if the type of government was not a monarchy. This is underscored by the fact that, by 13 March 1920, when the proposal was put forward for the reform of the coat of arms, the government had still avoided adopting a public position as regards the form of government that would be appropriate for Hungary.

The formation of a new government under Sándor Simonyi-Semadam broke the deadlock and opened the way to an eventual solution. The new head of the government declared, at the first cabinet meeting following the formation of his government on 15 March 1920, that Hungary was not a republic but a monarchy, and he considered the question to be sufficiently important that it should be immediately addressed by a government decree.[33] The following day the Minister of Justice presented his proposal,[34] which formed the basis for the promulgation on 18 March of the decree of the prime minister's office, number 2394/1920, 'Concerning the naming of all state authorities, offices and institutions, and the use of the Holy Crown on the official coat of arms'. This legal regulation was, in essence, a decree that both explained and enacted Law I of 1920. It specifically declared that

> Law I of 1920 [...] did not alter Hungary's 1,000-year-old form of government [...] it invalidated those revolutionary acts that conflicted with the constitution with which they had sought to annihilate the institution of the monarchy [...] Thus, in this regard, for as long as the legislature has not determined otherwise, Hungary's type of government will remain a monarchy.

The government decree therefore dispelled the uncertainties that had plagued the debate about Hungary's form of government. It was this decree that restored the monarchy in Hungary.

To conclude this section on the new form of state it is worth pausing for a moment to again reflect on the symbolism of the Holy Crown. In redesigning the state's coat of arms the precise form of the state, which at this time was no longer a kingdom, had only limited influence on the design. Huszár's final conclusion was that the Holy Crown could still be incorporated into the Hungarian coat of arms; however, the presiding Prime Minister, in connection with the use of the state coat of arms on government stamps, raised a further question:[35] should the escutcheon display a medium-sized coat of arms (which included the coats of arms of all of the lands of the Holy Crown), or be permanently reduced in size? Initially he clearly advocated the latter solution. He referred to the fact that the use of symbols designating the entirety of Hungary's historical territories could potentially irritate the victorious powers before the peace negotiations had even begun. However, he then immediately added that the representation of the attached territories no longer under Hungarian control on the middle-sized coat of arms was first and foremost in the interests of Hungary's lost minorities, as this would reinforce their claims to autonomy in the successor states; in any respect, Huszár saw no obvious advantage to redesigning the escutcheon.

In truth the small coat of arms with the Holy Crown attached was itself a representation of territorial integrity superior to any representation of annexed territories on the escutcheon. Furthermore, because the Holy Crown also symbolized legal continuity, its inclusion in the state coat of arms could thus play multiple symbolic roles. Thus, the debate about the coat of arms mirrored the larger debate about whether Hungary could restore its historical constitution.

The Points of Separation with the Arrangement of the State between 1867 and 1918

The Debate over the Restoration of the House of Habsburg to the Throne

The principle of legal continuity could have been fully realized had Charles IV been restored to the throne. It was, however, noted earlier in this chapter that the National Assembly was sharply divided on this

LAW I OF 1920 AND THE HISTORICAL CONSTITUTION 173

matter. Indeed, the distinction between formal and substantive legal continuity manifested itself at cabinet meetings, in sharp debates which broke out there about each piece of legislation which related to the question of whether Charles IV could reclaim his throne. His restoration was also opposed by the victorious powers, so in practice it could not have been realized in 1920 even if the National Assembly had reached a consensus on the matter. Thus, both sides supported the election of the Regent, but as the restoration of the House of Habsburg remained a future possibility, the debate did not die down.

The debates in the cabinet over the wording of Law I of 1920 as it related to the question of formal or substantive legal continuity have already been referred to, particularly the focus on the text of the Eckartsau declaration,[36] which had particular significance as the resignation of the king was only binding if it was endorsed by the parliament. This old customary law had, following the 1867 settlement, been strengthened by codification,[37] and thus its validity could not be disputed by the free-electors. The old parliament had, however, dissolved itself in November 1918 without endorsing Charles IV's resignation.

The language in the first draft of the bill was clear on the matter, when it stated that 'the National Assembly recognizes and formally sanctions the following declaration by Charles IV.'[38] Had such language been included in the final draft of the law then it would have been clear that the National Assembly had accepted and validated his resignation. The situation remained, however, complicated because the King's resignation had also not received the necessary ministerial counter-signature and was, therefore, doubly invalid. Parliamentary authorization of an invalid abdication would only have created further chaos. The final draft of the bill thus removed all references to the Eckartsau declaration, and merely included it in the advisory text that was distributed along with the law to the various ministers.[39]

Charles IV's resignation in November 1918 should not, in any case, have been endowed with such importance, as this had not meant the abdication of the Habsburg dynasty but merely that one ruler had resigned to be replaced by the next in line to the throne. The free-electors deduced, however, that with the collapse of the Austro-Hungarian Monarchy, the Pragmatic Sanction of 1723, which had legitimized the House of Habsburg's claim to the Hungarian throne, had lost its authority. Thus, *ipso facto*, without any other specific legislation, the automatic right of the Habsburgs to inherit the throne had been abolished.[40] This was a debatable claim, but if the laws pertaining to royal inheritance were indeed no longer valid, then Crown Prince Ottó von Habsburg's automatic right to succeed to the throne after his father was called into question. On the other hand, Charles IV was the legally crowned king of Hungary, and even if the laws pertaining to the Habsburgs' royal inheritance were invalid, this had no bearing on his right to rule, merely on the right of his potential successor. Legal scholars have subsequently referred to this as 'actual' versus 'virtual' rights, that is, rights in existence versus rights that may be obtained later. The debate over the continuing validity of the Pragmatic Sanction provoked doubts among the free-electors, but if the text of the Eckartsau declaration had been included in the final text of Law I of 1920 then the same doubts would have been provoked with regard to the actual rights of the king. This was the essence of the debate about the inclusion or exclusion of the Eckartsau declaration into the final text of the law.

It should not, therefore, be surprising that a fierce debate broke out between the two camps in parliament over the precise phrasing of the law when it described Charles IV's earlier resignation. That the resignation had occurred was an acknowledged fact which even the legitimists were unwilling to challenge but they also knew that the description of the resignation could determine whether the House of Habsburg in general, and Charles IV in particular, had a rightful claim to the throne. The precise wording of the description of the resignation was, therefore, rewritten several times. The draft of the bill which was first presented to the National Assembly contained the following declaration: 'the exercise of royal power has, since 13 November 1918, been halted.'[41] The relevant committee in the National Assembly which dealt with public law declared, however, that that use of the term 'halted' (*szünetelés*) would, from a legal perspective, imply that royal power had been interrupted (rather than voluntarily ended), and therefore proposed that the word should be excluded from the bill, which in the revised version simply stated that 'royal power has, since 13 November 1918 not been exercised.'[42] This revision of the text caused, however, new problems. The phrase 'has not been exercised' could be understood to imply that a legal right existed (for the king to rule) which was merely not being currently exercised. According to this interpretation the exercise of royal power was temporarily interrupted and could be restored at any time.

Concerned about the legitimist implications of the proposed text, István J. Kovács, a Smallholder Party MP, put forward an amendment to the bill, which would have included in the preamble to Law I of 1920 the following text: 'Charles IV, on 13 November 1918, abdicated from all participation in state matters and from then on has remained estranged from the country.'[43] This alternative text once again placed the stress on the abdication of the ruler and was firmly resisted by the legitimists. In response, Béla Turi declared that he favoured a wording which declared 'the exercise of royal power, on 13 November 1918 has ceased (*megszűnt*).' This was accepted by Kovács who promptly withdrew his own proposal.[44] The difference between the phrases 'has not been exercised' and 'has ceased' was significant, but in the end it was the latter phrase that was included in the text of the law.

The question of whether the House of Habsburg should be restored remained, as a result of Law I of 1920, intractable, and for the entire period unresolvable. With hindsight, it is clear that the passage of time favoured those who opposed a Habsburg restoration, as Charles IV's death in 1922 made clear. The refining of the rules relating to the election of the Regent in 1937,[45] which declared that when the regency was vacated a new Regent would be elected, also made the likelihood of anyone ascending to the throne more and more unlikely.

The National Assembly (Parliament) and the Principle of Legal Continuity

Equally challenging was the determination of the actual legal standing of the National Assembly. The duration of the parliament which was elected in 1910 was extended in 1915 until six months had elapsed following the signing of a future peace treaty.[46] As the new National Assembly convened at the beginning of 1920, before a peace treaty had been signed, theoretically the mandate of the former parliament remained in effect and the National Assembly was illegitimate. Although the Lower House had agreed to dissolve itself on 16 November 1918, this action was invalid according to Hungarian law as the decision to dissolve parliament was exclusively the right of the Crown. The invalidity of the dissolution was indeed recognized in the formal explanation that accompanied the draft of Law I of 1920 which was circulated to government ministers.[47] The fact that a significant number of the former parliament's MPs now resided in territories occupied by Hungary's neighbours, and the fact that the old electoral law was too narrow, were compelling but had no bearing on the legality of the dissolution of the old parliament and the election of a new national assembly. This was particularly the case as those who accepted the validity of the pre-revolutionary legal system could not therefore challenge the legality of the former parliament (and its right to extend its duration until a peace treaty had been signed).

This problem also could not be ignored by the members of the National Assembly. The reconvening of the old parliament was evidently impossible, not least because this would have placed a question mark over the legitimacy of the new National Assembly. After all, would MPs have campaigned for election and accepted their appointment as MPs if they genuinely believed that the mandate of the former parliament was still in force? Gyula Andrássy clearly expressed this conundrum when he declared that any decision about the constitutionality of the National Assembly should have been expressed when the candidates first put themselves forward for election.[48] Thus, no proposal was put forward to reconvene the old parliament, and with the passage of six months after the signing of the Treaty of Trianon (on 4 June 1920) its theoretical right to remain in session was also terminated. Genuine legal continuity would have come closer to being restored if the elections to the National Assembly had taken place according to Law XVII of 1918, which enacted the last reform of the franchise to occur in the period between 1867 and 1918. The National Assembly was not, however, elected on this basis,[49] which once again placed a question mark over its legitimacy. As Béla Turi explained to his fellow parliamentarians, the application of the old legislation determining the size of the franchise would have been in vain, as only the king could call a new election and only he could convene a new parliament.[50]

Thus, in the case of parliament, restoring genuine legal continuity was actually more difficult than solving the question of the king. The latter was a precondition for the former, as in practice the exercise of royal power had to be restored for the question of the legitimacy of the National Assembly to be resolved. With the passage of time, those who desired genuine legal continuity gradually gave up the possibility of this taking place. They spoke of the future restoration of the House of

Habsburg but they did not propose holding fresh elections on the basis of the franchise introduced in 1918. The establishment of a reformed Upper House in 1926 represented another step towards the restoration of legal continuity, but only a Lower House elected according to the old franchise and an Upper House constituted as it had been before 1918 could have fulfilled the conditions for genuine legal continuity.

The debate in the National Assembly in 1925/6 over the restoration of a reformed Upper House is of interest because it involves ideas of legal continuity that had not been expressed in 1920. József Illés Viski, one of the leading legal historians of this period and also a member of the National Assembly, called attention to the fact that genuine legal continuity had been broken with the settlement of 1867, which validated Francis Joseph's right to inherit the Hungarian throne. In reality, Viski argued, the parliament which had accepted the resignation of Ferdinand V in 1848 and approved Francis Joseph's right to the throne had been summoned by Francis Joseph himself, even though, according to Hungarian law, he only had the right to assume the throne after the resignation of his predecessor had been accepted by parliament. As Ferdinand V was still alive, only he had the right to summon parliament to accept his resignation.[51]

Conclusion

Every period in the development of the Hungarian constitution varies in its relationship to the historical constitution. The National Assembly which was elected in 1920 as a result of the restoration of constitutionality was eager to ground its various political institutions in the traditions of the historical constitution, but at the same time, with regard to a number of substantial issues, it was not able to preserve legal continuity with the preceding period (1867–1918). This led to the idea of substantive legal continuity which represented the continuation of the historical constitution even though genuine, or as it was termed formal, legal continuity could not be maintained. The development of the concept of substantive legal continuity is relevant to later periods of Hungarian history because it shows that there is a possibility to restore the historical constitution even if genuine legal continuity is impossible. Genuine legal continuity may have been possible for a short period in 1920, but in 1990 or at the beginning of the twenty-first century it was impossible. Once, however, the distinction between these two kinds of continuity has been accepted, it becomes apparent that although the opportunity for a restoration of the historical constitution may intensify or diminish in specific periods it can never be permanently prevented.

With the passage of time, the restoration of genuine legal continuity became increasingly difficult. Even in 1920 it is doubtful that this could have occurred in its totality. Simply restoring the old institutions of the state was challenging enough, but even after this had been achieved, a question would have remained about what should be done with the laws that were passed in the period that was now deemed illegal. In the prologue, it was noted that Law I of 1920 invalidated all legislation passed during the revolutions that took place between November 1918 and March 1920 but this could not be achieved in its entirety as the revolutionary period had lasted for one and a half years. The government obtained, therefore, the authority to retain in force any of the legislation that had been placed on the statute books in the preceding revolutionary period and it exploited this authority. Thus, it would have been difficult to carry out a complete restoration even if there had been a unified desire to do so among all influential shades of political opinion. As the lawmakers who debated this restoration were bitterly divided amongst themselves, the chance of such a restoration occurring was reduced even further.

As demonstrated by József Illés Viski's comments regarding the restoration of the reformed Upper House, policies enacted on the basis of a historical constitution that stretched back over centuries invariably caused problems. In reality, the 1867 settlement dented the principle of legal continuity and that was by no means an isolated case. The passage of time, however, repaired the damage. It should not, therefore, be the case that earlier dents in Hungary's legal continuity prevent the restoration of the historical constitution on the erroneous grounds that such dents were, and still are, irreparable.

As there was insufficient desire in the National Assembly to attempt the complete restoration of genuine legal continuity, it is impossible to decide to what degree it could have been achieved. However, the extent to which the restoration took place is of great significance. The discussion here has focused on two aspects of state administration: the question of the restoration of the lawful Hungarian king, Charles IV, on the one hand, and the establishment of a new national assembly on the other – and in both of these cases legal continuity was clearly broken. However, if the workings of the institutions of jurisprudence in this same period are scrutinized, it becomes clear that legal continuity was in fact preserved in an entirely unbroken fashion. The same judges, in the same institutions, continued to pass judgement as they had done up until 1918.

In later periods of Hungary's constitutional development, varying assessments of the constitutional arrangements of the interwar period, which were defined by Law I of 1920, are evident. Law I of 1946, for example, declared that earlier efforts to dethrone the House of Habsburg were at the core of Hungary's constitutional tradition (such as the abolition of the exercise of royal power in November 1918, the dethronement of the House of Habsburg that had been proclaimed in Debrecen in 1849 and Ónod in 1707) but made no mention of developments between 1920 and 1944.[52] In contrast, the new Fundamental Law that was passed into law on 1 January 2012 describes the occupation of the country by Nazi Germany as the moment when legal continuity was ruptured and thus includes the entire interwar period prior to that point as part of Hungary's constitutional tradition. This, however, is a viewpoint grounded in the belief in substantive continuity as there was no genuine legal continuity with the pre-World War I era, merely an emotional attraction. The Fundamental Law also used language similar to Law I of 1920 when it invalidated the legislation produced by an earlier revolution it described as the result of illegal power.

It may be asked why then the National Assembly did not draft a new written constitution. This question would have been dismissed by contemporaries on the grounds that as the country already had a constitution, there was no compelling reason to draw up a new version. Such questions derive from the broad assumption nowadays that there is a qualitative difference between historical and codified constitutions and that the latter form of constitution is superior. This opinion was not shared either by earlier legal scholars or politicians who regarded historical constitutions as stable, and written constitutions as unstable.

As József Illés Viski argued,

> the growth of historical constitutions [*történelmi alkotmányok*] including our own [...] has meant a legal continuity characterized

by evolution and not cataclysmic revolutionary transformations [...] legal continuity is a concept that in historical constitutions is evident, but it is never the case in the so-called written or codified constitutions; as from time to time change occurs not as the result of the influence of natural forces but takes place artificially.[53]

In a similar fashion, one of the most influential politicians of the period, Pál Teleki,[54] declared that 'our constitution is unwritten – it is the culmination of all the laws and customs which have passed into the blood of the nation, from which time can take something, but not the actions of any person, any national assembly, or any generation.'[55]

Translated by Thomas Lorman

Notes

1. The present chapter has been produced under the aegis of the Hungarian Ministry of Justice, within the framework of the programme entitled 'The Elevation of the Standards of Legal Education'.
2. People's Law XXV, 1919.
3. Decree of the Prime Minister's Office, 1995/1919.
4. Count Mihály Károlyi (1875–1955), descendant of an ancient aristocratic family, an opponent of the 1867 settlement, and a leading figure of the 1918 revolution. Prime Minister from 31 October 1918 to 11 January 1919 and then President of the Republic until the extreme left seized power on 21 March 1919.
5. István Friedrich (1883–1951), Prime Minister from 7 August to 24 November 1919. A supporter of Mihály Károlyi before 1918, then served as a junior minister in the Defence Ministry. He opposed the Republic of Councils and during his premiership sought to restore legal continuity with the pre-1918 legal order.
6. Crown Prince Joseph of Habsburg–Lorraine (1872–1962) was appointed as King Charles IV's personal representative ('homo regius') in Hungary on 26 October 1918. After the collapse of the Republic of Councils he returned to politics and briefly served as Regent but resigned from this position on 23 August 1919.
7. Károly Huszár (1882–1941) served as Minister of Religion and Education in the government of István Friedrich and Prime Minister from 24 November 1919 until 15 March 1920.
8. Elections to the National Assembly could not be held in the 93,000 square kilometres of what remained of Hungary in 1919 as this territory was temporarily occupied by Romania (east of the Tisza) or, as in the case of Baranya county, was under Serb occupation. In contrast, elections could still take place

LAW I OF 1920 AND THE HISTORICAL CONSTITUTION   181

in the almost 70,000 square kilometres of territory, the Burgenland, which was later handed over to Austria but, at this point, still remained under Hungarian control.
9. Law I of 1920, article 9: '(1) All forms of people's laws, decrees or otherwise named edicts issued by the organs of the so-called people's republic and republic of councils are invalidated. In the same way the edicts and resolutions of the so-called national councils and their organs are invalidated (2) Those so-called people's decrees and people's laws are annulled from the National Compendium of Laws into which they had been registered.'
10. See John Swanson, *The Remnants of the Habsburg Monarchy: The Shaping of Modern Austria and Hungary, 1918–1922* (New York, 2001), p. 194.
11. Hungarian National Archive, Section-K, Cabinet meeting of 13 February 1920, p. 27. The exact quote reads 'Hadügyminiszter úr szerint is az eredeti fogalmazás és az eckartsaui levélnek a becikkelyezése valóságos detronizálást jelentene. Földművelésügyi miniszter úr: Igenis én detronizálni akarok! Belügyminiszter úr: Én életem végéig be akarom tartani eskümet!'
12. *Képviselőházi Napló* (hereafter KN), 1920, vol. I, p. 54. The exact quote reads 'A királyi hatalom gyakorlásának megszűnése mellett minden kísérletezés a Főrendiháznak, vagy a régi Országgyűlésnek összehívásával éppúgy hiányt hagyott volna maga után a formai jogfolytonosság szempontjából [...] mert törvényalkotás, sőt a nemzetre való appellálás sem történhetik királyiaktus nélkül a formai alkotmány szerint.'
13. Gyula Andrássy the Younger (1860–1929) supported the 1867 settlement; 1895–1896 and 1906–1910 minister; after 1920 one of the most prominent legitimist politicians. Son of Gyula Andrássy (1823–1890), Prime Minister of Hungary and Francis Joseph's Foreign Minister.
14. KN, 1920, vol. I, p. 72. The exact quote reads, 'Mert nekem alapmeggyőződésem, hogy a létező jognak felrúgása veszélyezteti a jogrendet állandóan; ez nemcsak egy törvénynek és egy jogszabálynak a megpendítését jelenti, hanem így az egész jogrend bizonytalanná válik.'
15. Ibid., p. 82. The exact quote reads, 'Gróf Andrássy Gyula például hivatkozik régi alkotmányunkra és arra kéri a Nemzetgyűlést, hogy azt a régi alkotmányt ne forgassuk ki eredetiségéből, mert az veszélyt rejt a jövőre. Én, mint a nép egyszerű fia, a magam álláspontja szerint azt mondhatom, hogy én azt a régi alkotmányt nem tekintem olyannak, amely mindenben megfelelt volna a nemzet érdekeinek, mert az egyoldalú alkotmány volt, amelyben csak nemesek és főurak voltak, de a nép egyáltalában nem volt benne [...] Természetesen régibb időkről, 1848 előtti időkről beszélek, mert előbb is volt Magyarországon alkotmány, nemcsak 1848 után. Vitatkozhatunk abban a tekintetben is, hogy mi ennek a régi alkotmánynak sem teljes megdöntését akarjuk, hanem kiépítését a mostani kornak és viszonyoknak megfelelő formában.'
16. The Upper House of Parliament consisted, prior to 1918, of three dominant groups: the senior aristocrats, who made up 65 per cent of the membership; notable religious and secular figures, who made up 20 per cent of the

membership; and those who had been personally appointed by the Crown, who made up 15 per cent of the membership. The smallholders did not want to exclude the senior aristocracy from the Upper House but they did want to drastically reduce their numbers.

17. KN, 1920, vol. I, p. 58. The exact quote reads, 'Volt egy szomorú [...] 1867-es időszak, amikor ez a nemzet elnemzetietlenedett, amikor ennek a nemzetnek keresztény erkölcsei is megfogyatkoztak [...], amikor minden olcsó és eladó volt. [...] Ez a javaslat dekretálja a nemzetnek azt a függetlenségét, szabadságát, amit 1849-ben az ő tragikus bukásával fel kellett adnia.'
18. Ibid., pp. 63–4. The exact quote reads, 'Az aggályos jogtisztelet minket nem nagyon zavar. [...] Lehetnek kényszerhelyzetek, lehetnek nagy szükségességek, lehetnek úttalan utak, amelyekbe éppen a jog kerget minket bele a summum jus summa injuria alapján [...] Azok a túlzó legalisták olyan Jónás próféták [...] akik a betűk lombja alá meghúzzák magukat, ez jólesik nekik és nem törődnek azzal, hogy a nagy város, a nagy civitas [...] a civitas Hungariae tönkremegy.'
19. Károly Kmety, 'A királyválasztás joga', *Magyar Jogi Szemle* 1920/1, p. 7.
20. József Ruszoly, 'Az első nemzetgyűlési választások előzményeihez', in Ruszoly József, *Alkotmánytörténeti tanulmányok 1* (Szeged, 1991), pp. 221–38.
21. MNL, OL K, 27, Records of the cabinet meeting held on 13 February 1920, p. 33.
22. Ruszoly, 'Az első nemzetgyűlési választások előzményeihez', p. 225.
23. MNL, OL, K-27, Records of the cabinet meeting held on 8 August 1919.
24. MNL, OL, K-26–1920-III-4674.
25. Decree of the Prime Minister's Office, 4038/1919.
26. MNL K, 27. 1919, Records of the cabinet meeting held on 4 December 1919.
27. KN, 1920, vol. I, p. 53.
28. Ibid., p. 29.
29. MNL, OL, K, 26, III/1443 (2160/1920).
30. MNL, OL, K-26–1920-III-2134.
31. Decree of the Prime Minister's Office, 5746/1918.
32. MNL, OL, K, 27, Records of the cabinet meeting held on 4 December 1919.
33. MNL, OL, K, 27, Records of the cabinet meeting held on 15 March 1920.
34. MNL, OL, K, 27, Records of the cabinet meeting held on 16 March 1920.
35. MNL, OL, K-26–1920-III-2134.
36. MNL, OL, K, 27, Records of the cabinet meeting held on 13 February 1920.
37. Law III of 1867.
38. MNL, OL, K-27, Records of the cabinet meeting held on 13 February 1920.
39. KN, 1920, vol. I, p. 14.
40. Károly Kmety, 'Véleményem a királykérdésben', *Jogtudományi Közlöny 1921/1; 1921/2*, p. 11; Móric Tomcsányi, *Magyarország közjoga* (Budapest, 1932), p. 318.
41. KN, 1920, Vol. I, p. 3.
42. Ibid., p. 29.
43. Ibid., p. 34.

LAW I OF 1920 AND THE HISTORICAL CONSTITUTION 183

44. Ibid., p. 58.
45. Law XIX of 1937, Articles 3–5.
46. Law IV of 1915.
47. KN, 1920, vol. I, p. 10. The exact quote is 'Ami különösen a képviselőház említett határozatát illeti, annak törvény ellenessége kétségtelen, mert alkotmányunk értelmében az országgyűlést törvényben megszabott tartamának eltelte előtt csak a király oszlathatja föl.'
48. Ibid., p. 82. The exact quote is 'Nem könnyen határoztam el magam, hogy erre az álláspontra helyezkedjem, hogy magam fellépjek a Nemzetgyűlésben. [...] De nem térhettem ki, el kellett fogadnom azt az utat, amelyre a kormány tért, mert ez az egyetlen járható, az egyetlen lehető út.'
49. In the autumn of 1919 the government by decree enacted the new franchise which was used to elect the National Assembly (Decree of the Prime Minister's Office, number 5985/1919). The extension of the franchise which had been passed by the previous parliament did not introduce female suffrage and tightly restricted the number of males who could vote. From a political perspective it was not, therefore, appropriate.
50. KN, 1920, vol. I, p. 54.
51. KN, 1922, vol. XLV, p. 301.
52. 'Magyarországon 1918. november 13-án megszűnt a királyi hatalom gyakorlása. A nemzet visszanyerte önrendelkezési jogát. Négyszáz esztendős harc, az ónodi gyűlés, az 1849-es debreceni határozat, két forradalom kísérlete és az ezt követő elnyomatás után a magyar nép újra szabadon határozhat államformájáról' (Law I of 1946, Preamble – see primary source no. 12 in the Appendix to this volume).
53. KN, 1922, vol. XLV, p. 300.
54. Count Pál Teleki (1879–1941) served as the Foreign Minister of the counter-revolutionary government formed in Szeged and was Prime Minister 1920–1 and 1939–41.
55. Teleki Pál, *Válogatott politikai írások*, edited by Ablonczy Balázs (Budapest, 2000), p. 443.

CHAPTER 9

LAW I OF 1946 AND LAW XX OF 1949: CONTINUITY OR DISCONTINUITY IN TRADITIONAL HUNGARIAN CONSTITUTIONALISM?

Balázs Fekete

The constitutional evolution of Hungary in the aftermath of World War II (in 1945–9) has continuously attracted the intense attention of historians and legal scholars. In general, their pieces either provide a predominantly descriptive analysis of the era's major legal acts[1] or familiarize the readers with the course of subsequent political events.[2] Contrary to this descriptive reading, this chapter tries to offer an analysis of a different quality as it will focus on the two major legal acts of this period – Law I of 1946 on the State Form of Hungary and Law XX of 1949 on the Constitution of the Hungarian People's Republic – from the perspective of the modern Hungarian constitutional tradition which is grounded in the idea of historical constitutionalism.[3] Further, as Stalinist principles were the primary inspiration for Law XX of 1949, the concept of external legal assistance will also be discussed. It is hoped, therefore, that new insights may be revealed through this approach and these may enrich our knowledge of Hungarian constitutional history. In sum, the evolution of legal and constitutional ideas in postwar Hungary is the main topic of this chapter. Consequently, its scholarly scope is necessarily restricted as compared to a general historical outlook. History, as a socio-political background, will be referred to as the context of the constitutional changes studied, but the main aim of the chapter will remain the discussion and analysis of the constitutional development in its own right.[4]

Thesis and Overview

The main thesis of this chapter is a relatively simple point. Centuries-long Hungarian constitutional traditions were broken by Law XX of 1949, and not by Law I of 1946 as is conventionally stated in the literature.[5] Undoubtedly, Law I of 1946 is a key point in twentieth-century Hungarian constitutional history as it transformed the former monarchical constitutional framework into a modern republican one. As its title – on the state form of Hungary – suggests, it set forth that the post-World War II state-form of Hungary would be a republic with a president, a new autonomous political actor in the Hungarian public scene. Nevertheless, the usual understanding of this constitutional act is oversimplified as it does not take into account the embeddedness of Law I of 1946 in the tradition of historical constitutionalism. Therefore, it was Law XX of 1949, which introduced the first codified constitution in the modern history of Hungary,[6] that marked the real break with the past. This constitution relied on the application of Stalinist principles – and thereby imported a vision of constitutionalism that had no roots in Hungarian constitutional traditions and explicitly denied any connection to the former historical constitutional tradition.

In order to explain this thesis, this chapter will first outline the historical context of the birth of Law I of 1946, and then the major provisions of this Act. Following on from this descriptive introduction, the problem of how this Act may be interpreted in the light of traditional Hungarian constitutionalism will be discussed, and at that point the chapter will invoke the findings of László Péter on the nature of the 'ancient' or 'historical' Hungarian constitution. As a next step the chapter will argue for a more 'empathic and realistic' reading of Law I of 1946, namely, it will argue for taking into account its strong ties with the substance of historical constitutionalism. The next section will briefly point out how the political climate of the country changed after 1947 and how the Hungarian Workers' Party emerged as a new and omnipotent power centre. Thereafter, Law XX of 1949, the very first codified constitution of the country, will be analysed, and the role and impact of Soviet legal assistance will be highlighted. Finally, a concluding section will present the main lessons of this inquiry into these two episodes of constitution-making in the first years after World War II.

A Constitutional Moment? The Years 1945 and 1946

It can be argued that the years 1945 and 1946 in Hungary are to be defined as a constitutional moment in the same sense that the American scholar Bruce Ackerman used this term.[7] Through an in-depth study of modern US political and constitutional history Ackerman pointed out that there are specific historical moments in the 'life' of a country, which he termed 'constitutional moments'. During these periods, fundamental questions concerning the organization and the interests of the political community are discussed. The distinction between 'normal politics' and 'higher lawmaking' is based on this insight.[8] Ideally, a constitutional moment begins with the formulation of the need for political reform, obtains the broad support of the public and concludes with legal codification. Naturally, the codification phase is preceded by political discussions and debates as well as the search for a proper legal vocabulary to express the reformist vision.[9] Obviously, constitutional moments do not necessarily succeed; failure is also a possible outcome of these political disturbances.

The end of World War II and the fall of both the political regime presided over by Miklós Horthy, who served as Regent of Hungary between 1919 and 1944, and the short-lived national socialist dictatorship presided over by Ferenc Szálasi during the final months of World War II, created the opportunity for a thorough reconstruction of Hungary. In fact, the country lost a considerable portion of its population due to the war, the Holocaust, the relocation of the *Volksdeutsche* to Germany and deportations to the Soviet Union. In addition, the country's industrial capacity and public facilities were seriously damaged by the war.[10] However, contrary to all these unpromising circumstances, a vivid discussion had started on the socio-political future of the country almost immediately after the arrival of the Soviet Red Army. And the argument that Hungary needed a Western-style re-establishment of the country's political and constitutional system could freely be formulated and promoted, too. Although, naturally, there was no chance of a swift consensus as there was a wide range of proposals regarding Hungary's future political development, politicians and public intellectuals all agreed on one question: the 'heritage' of the past had to be overstepped.[11]

It should not be forgotten that the international context also looked to be very favourable and supportive for this open and lively future-oriented political discussion from a general perspective.[12] The Declaration on Liberated Europe that was formulated by the victorious Allied Powers specifically prompted the people of Europe 'to create democratic institutions of their own choice' and called for free elections to be held in all liberated countries. Such language implied that the Hungarian people would be consulted about their future development. The first postwar general elections were held on 4 November 1945 and the centrist and middle-class oriented Party of Independent Smallholders (FKGP) obtained a clear majority of the votes and seats in the newly elected parliament.[13] However, due to diplomatic pressure from the Stalinist Soviet Union, whose military and intelligence services now operated throughout the country, a coalition government was formed in which almost all parties in the parliament participated including Social Democrats and Communists. This coalition government, led by centrist and Western-oriented political forces, had to establish a new constitutional order[14] under the constant political pressure of those politicians who were obedient to the interests of the Soviet Union.

Law I of 1946: An Overview

Law I of 1946 is certainly not among the longest bills in Hungarian constitutional history: its length is only 1,430 words.[15] In addition, its codification was surprisingly rapid. It was discussed by the Public Law and Constitutional Law Committee (Közjogi és Alkotmányjogi Bizottság) of the parliament and the plenary session of the parliament during January 1946,[16] and it was promulgated on 20 February 1946.[17] As for its structure, it was composed of a short preamble and 19 articles. In sum, the provisions of the Act are to be grouped around three major points.

Codification of Human Rights and Fundamental Constitutional Principles

The Act enumerated the citizens' fundamental freedoms and rights for the first time in the modern history of Hungary. That is, an explicit 'bill of rights' was prepared to precede the detailed constitutional law provisions. These were as follows:

(i) personal freedom;
(ii) the right to have a life free from repression, fear and deprivation;
(iii) freedom of thought and opinion;
(iv) the free exercise of religion;
(v) freedom of assembly and association;
(vi) the right to property;
(vii) the right to personal security;
(viii) the right to work and to a worthy existence
(ix) the right to culture
(x) the right of participation in public life (on both a national and a local level).

Although the historical constitution had also incorporated some of these rights and freedoms, it had done so in a fuzzy and incoherent way.[18] Thus, this 'bill of rights' can be regarded as a major development in the history of Hungarian constitutionalism as it ensured that the country conformed to general Western standards. Interestingly, and surprisingly, all these freedoms and rights were mentioned in the preamble of the Act.

That is, their legal status was not as obvious since the normative power of preambles is an evergreen question of constitutional theory. The post-World War II practice of constitutional courts, on both sides of the Atlantic, diverges when the normativity of constitutional preambles is at stake. One may argue that a preamble to a constitution is nothing more than a simple declaration, while its normative relevance may also be argued convincingly in a different constitutional context. That is, a consensual understanding of this problem has not come up thus far in Western constitutionalism.[19]

Further, the Act also declared the principles of due process and non-discrimination as foundations of the entire legal order. However, again, this was stated in the preamble, so the earlier disclaimer on the questionable legal status also applies here. Lastly, the republic as the state form of Hungary was also solemnly declared by the Act.[20]

All in all, it should be noted that most of the by now elementary constitutional principles (fundamental rights, due process and non-discrimination) are only a part of the preamble. This structural position of this 'bill of rights' might have given rise to doubts on their real legal status and relevance before the courts. However, once the legal culture of the country was transformed in 1949 this question lost its practical importance. That being said, Hungarian courts simply had no time – in historical terms – to discuss the consequences of the problem that all fundamental freedoms were part of the text of the preamble, but not included in the corpus of the Act.

The Status of the President of the Republic

As a main point, the Act established the institution of the president of the republic in Hungarian public law. The president was to be elected by two-thirds of the members in the National Assembly.[21] The main privileges of the president were as follows.

(i) The promulgation of all Acts of the National Assembly and a soft veto right in the legislative process. The president had the right to send back a legislative proposition for discussion once during the process, but the second version submitted back to the president upon a second reading had to be promulgated.[22]
(ii) Postponement of the sessions of the National Assembly without any justification once parliament had convened.[23]
(iii) The right to dissolve the National Assembly if it was requested by the government or by two-fifths of its members.[24]
(iv) Representation of Hungary in international relations.[25] However, any executive acts related to war (such as declarations of war, peacemaking, the use of force) could only be made on the basis of prior authorization by the National Assembly.[26]
(v) The power to grant pardons and a general power to grant exemptions from specific legal provisions that could impede the rights of the citizen.[27]
(vi) The appointment and removal of the prime minister and all other

ministers, albeit in consultation with the prime minister and always with respect to the principle of majoritarian rule.[28]

(vii) The appointment of high State functionaries and judges based on the relevant ministers' proposals.[29]

It can immediately be observed that the position of the president was certainly not merely symbolic.[30] He was intended to have a strong position in his dealings with the National Assembly, even though the exercise of any of his executive powers required a counter-signature.[31] Furthermore, the National Assembly was also under scrutiny by the president as he had considerable privileges that allowed him to promulgate acts and even dissolve the assembly. In sum, this balanced solution provided a constitutional framework in the new Hungarian republic which authorized the president to occupy a relevant place among the main constitutional powers.

Lastly, the Act incorporated an explicit declaration about the invalidity of all constitutional provisions related to the earlier state-form of monarchy and the position of the former Regent.[32] At this point – by giving such an explicit declaration – the Act obviously broke with the former monarchical tradition, which is regarded as one of the cornerstones of the centuries-old Hungarian constitutional tradition. However, the Act did not contain any provision that would have explicitly declared the denial of the historical constitutional tradition as such. So, the main question is whether the invalidity of monarchical components of the former tradition would imply the political and legislative intent to discredit and disrupt the entirety of the historical constitution.

General Assessment

Undoubtedly, Law I of 1946 transformed the constitutional setting of the Hungarian political scene in qualitative terms. With the 'bill of rights' in the preamble, it apparently linked it to the human-rights-centred Western tradition,[33] while by eliminating the monarchical tradition in such a symbolic way it also modernized it in accordance with a modern republican spirit. Moreover, the new republic even tried to ensure the respect of human rights by the instruments of penal law. Law X of 1946 set forth that disrespect by any state bureaucrat of the human rights included in the preamble of Law I of 1946 must be regarded as a criminal offence and if established, it might be sanctioned with a maximum term of five years' imprisonment.[34] However, with the recognition of all these developments, the question remains whether this modernizing turn in constitutionalism is equal to the end of Hungarian historical constitutionalism as such.

Law I of 1946 in the Light of Former Constitutional Traditions

The above-discussed features of Law I of 1946 may easily convince the reader of its modern and innovative nature with respect to the Hungarian constitutional tradition. Article 19 on the invalidation of all the provisions related to monarchy may certainly strengthen this view and may suggest that this Act is the starting point of a completely new era. However, if one applies László Péter's theses on the nature of 'ancient constitutionalism', this clear-cut and simple-looking interpretation may also be questioned from various directions.

As a first step, László Péter's main points have to be summarized. First, he claimed that one of the main features of Hungarian historical constitutionalism was the lack of a codified constitution, meaning that there was no single document containing all the relevant constitutional norms, provisions and conventions. Thus, the boundaries of both the constitution and constitutional law were imprecise and were subject to harsh controversies among the various political actors participating in public life.[35] Secondly, also an essential point, the real basis for the everyday functioning of the various constitutional institutions was a set of customs and conventions recognized by all the constitutional actors. That is, the political life of the country was organized by unwritten but broadly accepted customs. Therefore, the political actors considered these as general guidelines for their activity; specific legislative acts with a constitutional relevance were always regarded as exceptions to the general rule. Thirdly, constitutional law – in its broadest sense – contained privileges and obligations, and their major subjects were the parliament representing the country in its entirety (*ország*) and the Crown.[36]

In sum, the substance of the so-called 'ancient constitution' was composed of the rights and obligations of the nation, and the rights and obligations of the king. The constitutional system had a strikingly dualistic nature based on the relationships of the *ország* (the country) and the Crown. Furthermore, due to this bifurcated structure, the Hungarian constitution was always interpreted differently by the representatives of the country and the representatives of the Crown, and they were often in conflict, for example over the crucial question of whether the source of the Crown's powers derived from free election or the hereditary principle.[37]

Moreover, Péter also argued that the Hungarian constitutional tradition as it was conceived under the umbrella term of 'ancient constitution' at the beginning of the nineteenth century, had not disappeared from the public mind and constitutional scholarship of the end of the nineteenth century, but had instead incorporated certain modern concepts mostly due to the German intellectual influence (*Staatslehre*).[38] That is, even though the conceptual basis of constitutional thinking was certainly renewed in an intellectual and conceptual sense, its basic tenets and structure remained rather solid.

Why is the nature of nineteenth-century historical constitutionalism vital when assessing an Act from the mid-twentieth century that had a pronounced republican character? Although the contents of the Act and its spirit seem to be very modern in a Western constitutional sense, the *travaux préparatoires* (with special regard to the explanatory notes of the prime minister) also indicate that this Act had a much stronger connection to the former constitutional tradition than can be assumed at its first reading. There were, for example, numerous references to the historical constitution in the explanatory notes of this republican Act. That is, one can easily find arguments based on a clear historical – or traditional – understanding of constitutionalism in the preparatory notes, and this phenomenon cannot easily be explained if one regards the Act as the end of historical constitutionalism.

Let us have a closer look at these references. First, these notes and explanations argue that the Hungarian constitution never recognized the absolute nature of the king's power, and that these powers were always transferred by the nation to the king; that is, they had a limited scope by their very nature.[39] In other words, limiting sovereign political power through public law had been a constitutive component of the Hungarian tradition for a longer while.

Secondly, they also point out that the system of the Hungarian constitution was based on the idea of an elected and constitutionally limited monarchy. In the eyes of the legislator of 1946 this fact, again, could be regarded as a precursor of the republican tradition. That is, the concept of monarchy was a paramount component of the traditional constitutional setting but certainly not an imperative one without which this tradition could not exist.

Thirdly, the notes give a detailed explanation that popular participation in the exercise of parliamentary powers had been widening during the previous two centuries. At the end, it had become one of the constitutional traditions, and this centuries-long process resulted in the establishment of the first democratic republic, in which legislative powers are exclusively exercised by the parliament.[40] That is, Law I of 1946 was seen as a 'natural' or – to use a more proper term in the context of historical constitutionalism – 'organic' development of the historical broadening of democratic participation in Hungarian constitutionalism.

Fourthly, the explanations remind the readers that the republican idea is not irreconcilable with Hungarian traditions; moreover, it is not even contrary to the 'properly understood organic legal evolution', and it is also in harmony with the will of the parliament. In other words, a monarchical form of government was not considered as the final phase of this organic constitutional development, but instead should be understood as a stage of development that ultimately led to the creation of a republic.

Lastly, the notes emphasized the fact that this Act was not a simple copy of a specific foreign model but was instead tailored to the 'specific claims of our country'.[41] The notes thereby echoed the idea of original and *sui generis* Hungarian constitutional development widely shared by most of the constitutional lawyers. Again, this remark proved that contemporaries regarded this Act as part of the historical tradition.[42]

In conclusion, this modern and innovative Act was legitimized by robust historical arguments, which implied that the new republic and the creation of the office of the president were not a problem for the requirements of the constitutional traditions. This official argumentation challenges the current scholarly consensus which celebrates the Act as a symbolic break with earlier traditions. If this had been the case in 1946, clearly the prime minister would not have sought to provide legitimacy for the Act by excessive references to constitutional traditions.

Besides this strong historical and traditionalist argumentation there were other – structural – components in the Act that may remind us of the heritage of the concept 'historical constitution'. First, it is not too difficult to discover the impact of the former dualistic tradition on the details of the provisions on the president. The president is entitled to all privileges necessary for the exercise of his powers, and the parliament's powers are to a certain extent constrained. Again, the parliament has its own – much broader – reserved scope of actions (cf. *reservata* in the former construction), too, which cannot be interfered with by the president. Surprisingly, however, this Act establishing basic power relationships in the newborn Hungarian republic – therefore called by many contemporaries the 'small constitution' – contains only one single reference to the judiciary, while the status of the third branch of powers is not discussed in detail at all. That is, this setting of the division of powers within the State which focused on only two prominent actors may also remind us of the idea of power-balancing between the two major political actors (the king and the country, later nation) of the monarchical era that was one of the key points of nineteenth-century constitutionalism, as argued by László Péter.

Moreover, there is one explicit reference to the historical constitution in the explanation when the provision on the election of the president by the parliament is explained. When justifying this provision the explanatory note *expressis verbis* invokes the historical constitution in the argumentation. It argues that 'our constitution does not know the institution of referendum,'[43] therefore the election of the president has to be assigned to the parliament, the sole representative of the will of the people. This remark was not only of conceptual relevance but it also had a role to play in the political discourse around the new state-form. Cardinal Mindszenty, who considered himself the last legitimate representative of the Hungarian monarchy as the prince primate (the archbishop of Esztergom), passionately argued against the 'constitutional reforms' at the end of 1945. In addition, he proposed to hold a referendum on the introduction of the republic.[44] Thus, this remark may also be considered as a counter-argument against the political claims of the prince primate.

Towards a More 'Empathic and Realistic' Reading of Law I of 1946

The above interpretation requires a reassessment of this Act. Clearly, Law I of 1946 should be regarded as a much more organic constitutional development than it has hitherto been interpreted as by recent Hungarian legal scholarship. Though this Act introduces a qualitatively new model of the state-form for the country – as compared to the former monarchical pattern – it does so by invoking either the spirit or some components of the constitutional tradition. That is, the Act did not disrupt the former constitutional tradition in its entirety. It certainly set aside the monarchical component, but it also preserved some elements on a more abstract level (for example, the dualistic nature of power sharing, the lack of a single constitutional document, and the demand of historical legitimation).

In sum, the spirit of Law I of 1946 – in the sense of Montesquieu's understanding of the term *l'espirit* – was that of a modern, Western-styled democratic political system centred around both the parliament and a president. This novel setting was in conformity, by and large, with the structural features of the centuries-old Hungarian constitutional tradition, except its monarchical component. That is, it proved that modernism in a public law sense and organic constitutional development were not irreconcilable with each other in post-World War II Hungary. However, the dramatic change in post-World War II geopolitics that began in 1947 and resulted in the complete submission of Central Europe to Soviet influence did not allow history to test the functioning of the new constitutional order partially inspired by the spirit of tradition.[45]

From the second half of 1946 the political life of the country started to deviate from the original intentions of centrist coalition government step by step. At the end of March 1946 the parliament enacted Law VII of 1946 devoted to the protection of democracy and the republic by criminal law provisions.[46] Originally, this Act was intended to protect the new constitutional order; however, as the police and state security services were under Communist rule, it became an efficient tool in the hands of the Communist Party to dismantle its centrist and Western-minded competitors. For instance, Béla Kovács, general secretary of the Independent Smallholders Party, a widely known and popular opponent of growing Communist influence, was arrested on the basis of this Act in the last week of February 1947. This event made it obvious that the new constitutional framework created by Law I of 1946 would not be able to function properly, and the manifestly growing – Soviet-backed – Communist political power would simply disregard it in practice. In addition to this apparent undemocratic political pressure, the transformation of the economy had also started with the nationalization of the banks in November 1947,[47] which predicted the future weakening of the private-property-based free market system, and it had almost totally been realized by 1948.[48] All in all, the gradual narrowing of the room for democratic politics became a reality under swiftly growing Communist pressure from 1947 onwards, and it also gravely challenged the freshly established constitutional order and rule of law in the country.

The story of the first and second presidents of Hungary also illustrates this democratic and constitutional backlash process. The first president, Zoltán Tildy, one of the leading personalities of the centrist Independent Smallholders Party, only spent two years in office, as he had to resign when a strongly biased lawsuit was started against his son-in-law. From 1 August 1948 to 20 August 1949 a Stalinist representative of the Hungarian Workers' Party, Árpád Szakasits, was elected president of the republic and he also became the first president of the Presidential Council (A Népköztársaság Elnöki Tanácsa) established by the newly codified Stalinist constitution in the autumn of 1949. His appointment to these positions in 1948 suggested that his high position was nothing more than a device by which the Soviet-backed Communists could demolish the political-constitutional system of the country.[49]

The Emergence of the Hungarian Workers' Party as a Political Power Centre

The resignation of Zoltán Tildy as president of the republic, under external pressure from his Communist opponents, also illustrated that the political climate of the country had already begun to change drastically in the aftermath of the passing of Law I of 1946. In 1947, the Communist Party and its allies won the general election, although the fairness and legality of this vote were put into question by the extent of the fraud and intimidation that marred the voting.[50] The new coalition government was dominated by the Communists who, in mid-1948, forced the already domesticated Social Democratic Party to unite with the Communist Party. As a result, the Hungarian Workers' Party was founded in order to impose a Stalinist vision of socialism upon Hungary under the leadership of Mátyás Rákosi. Finally, a new general election was held in May 1949 in which, contrary to the earlier multi-party traditions, there was only one list of candidates, all of whom had been approved by the government. This list, the so-called Hungarian Popular Front of Independence (*Magyar Függetlenségi Népfront*), formally united the representatives of the previously competing political parties but, in practice, it meant that the Communist politicians were able to control the composition of the new parliament in an exclusive way.[51] Needless to say, irrespective of their formal party membership, solely Communist-friendly politicians took up their seats in the parliament due to this change in the spring of 1949.

Obviously, this dramatic transformation of the country's political regime, highlighted by the transition from a multi-party system to the formation of a Soviet-minded one-party regime, must have been reflected in the constitutional setting, too. Naturally, neither the presidential system based on Law I of 1946, nor the former constitutional traditions were able to prevent the establishment of the new totalitarian regime. Instead, the creation of a Communist dictatorship paved the way for a new codified constitution which totally disrupted constitutional tradition. This disruption should not only be understood in the formal sense that a qualitatively new form of constitution appeared in the history of Hungarian constitutionalism, but also in a substantive sense, as the new constitution embodied pure Stalinist socio-political principles.

Law XX of 1949: An Overview

The idea of a new and codified constitution and the creation of an entirely new legal framework had already been mooted during the summer of 1948 when the Hungarian Workers' Party accepted a programme declaration, that is, a broad guideline for future activities, in which the necessity of constitution-making was emphasized.[52] In February 1949, a proclamation of the Hungarian Popular Front of Independence (Magyar Függetlenségi Népfront) also stressed the importance of a new constitution to replace the former traditions.[53]

As a consequence, following the first general election to take place under the one-party system and the comprehensive dominance of the Hungarian Popular Front of Independence, a Preparatory Committee (Előkészítő Bizottság) was formed by the Council of Ministers to work out the text of this new constitution. This committee was led by Mátyás Rákosi, the all-powerful leader of the Hungarian Workers' Party. Experts on Hungarian constitutional history agree that two members, Imre Szabó and János Beér – devoted Communist lawyers at that time, who became leading personalities of Hungarian Socialist legal scholarship later – had the real impact on the final text.[54] The draft had been prepared by the beginning of August 1949, and was followed by a 'general social discussion' of the draft from 5 to 10 August. According to the reports of the official media, the population generally backed the text, although some points raised by these 'consultations' were supposedly incorporated into the final text. On 17 August the revised draft was submitted to parliament, where a two-day session was held after the bill was formally proposed by Rákosi. Finally, the proposal was unanimously supported by the members of the parliament and the new constitution came into force on the day of its proclamation, on 20 August 1949.[55]

Needless to say, the spirit and general attitude of this new constitution qualitatively differed from former constitutional traditions, though the text was surprisingly neutral and technical. Apart from some references to the power of the working class[56] and the establishment of socialism as a new social order,[57] the text does not reveal too much about the political intent of the regime.

However, contemporary public law commentaries were open about the revolutionary nature of the new constitution. János Beér, who had undertaken a substantial share of the preparatory work as an expert on constitutional law and edited both the first commentary on the constitution[58] and the first socialist manual of constitutional law,[59] prepared a six-point list of the novelties of the constitution, which he compared to the previous constitutional setting. First, as a preliminary point, he argued that the new constitution was not concerned with declaring various legal ambitions but instead a summary of the Hungarian achievements on the road of socialist development. Secondly, all its provisions originated from the doctrines of Marxism–Leninism, which it faithfully reflected. Thirdly, a main goal of the constitution was to create a social order that would be beneficial to the working class. Fourthly, he claimed that the new constitution rejected the idea of nationalism and a 'dominant nation', and instead endorsed proletarian internationalism, which was mirrored in the relevant provisions, such as those regarding the rights of Hungary's ethnic minorities.[60] Fifthly, the idea of 'real democracy' had inspired the constitution, and its provisions were intended to make the people free to rely on their democratic rights in public life without restrictions. Finally, the constitution codified fundamental rights through precise and detailed provisions which ensured that they would be respected.[61] In summary, the new constitution sought to incorporate the principles of Marxism–Leninism to the maximum extent possible.[62] Thereby it aimed at transforming the traditional, settled, constitutional and political framework that had emerged in a more-or-less organic way, and had developed both a Western European character and some national peculiarities.

The Constitution of the Hungarian People's Republic contained 71 articles and a three-sentence preamble explaining the 'Rákosist' narrative of the recent past. These 71 paragraphs were divided into 11 chapters. Chapter I on the Hungarian People's Republic had a predominantly ideological character as it declared the political dominance of the working class and also stressed the political alliance between the workers and the so-called 'working' peasantry.[63] In addition, it set forth that the final source of political power is the 'working people',[64] that is, a Marxist interpretation of the concept of popular sovereignty was echoed here. The last chapter, chapter XI, contained certain functional closing provisions, i.e. the date of entry into force and the need for additional, subsidiary legislation.[65]

The majority of the other nine chapters dealt with the organization of the society and the new Communist state. Chapter II explained the new social principles that determine the functioning of a Socialist society. The next five chapters, chapters III to VII, provided a detailed description of the main state bodies, that is, the formal structure of state administration was presented in this part.

According to chapter III, state power was represented by the parliament, which was vested with full legislative power,[66] while some limited – mostly international – executive competences were exercised by the so-called Presidential Council.[67] This was a collective organ, with a president, two vice-presidents, a secretary and 17 additional members.[68]

The head of the administration was the so-called Council of Ministers (Minisztertanács), as was explained in chapter IV. In fact, this council was the focus of executive powers as it was responsible for the execution of legislative Acts and also had a general power to control the work of ministries.[69] Further, this organ had the competence to issue general decrees that were, in fact, considered as the most important legal sources besides laws.[70] Local administration was based on the concept of local councils[71] – soviets in Soviet state law – and these were organized into greater units (i.e. county councils, sub-county (*járási*) councils and city councils).[72] Chapters VI and VII set forth the basic rules for the structure of the judiciary and the body of public prosecutors. In sum, the backbone of the Socialist administration was prepared by the constitution, while the real functioning of the various State organs was animated by specific laws, lower-level decrees and political practice.

In addition, chapter IX set forth the basic rules of election; however, the one-party nature of the political system was not mentioned at all. Symbolic questions were incorporated in chapter X, which described the coat of arms, the flag and the capital of the new-born People's Republic.

The most interesting part of the new constitution, in legal terms, was chapter VIII, which enumerated citizens' rights and obligations. As mentioned earlier, Law I of 1946 was the first piece of modern Hungarian legislation that contained a 'bill of rights'-like component. Likewise, the 1949 constitution contained a specific chapter superficially devoted to upholding basic human rights. This chapter, however, listed citizens' rights and obligations, that is, it did not speak about human rights in general – as was the case in 1946 – but instead endowed all citizens with specific rights that were contingent on their citizenship. By doing so, the new constitution emphasized the crucial role of the State in guaranteeing these rights, underscoring that the new Communist regime was the ultimate guarantor of these rights and freedoms.

In theory, the constitution provided quite an impressive list of basic rights: the right to work, the right to health, the right to education, equality before the law, the prohibition of any discrimination, the equality of men and women, religious freedom and freedom of conscience, the freedom of association, personal freedom, and the right to privacy.[73] Nevertheless, Article 58 (1) placed a serious curb on the universality of these rights. It stated that 'the Hungarian People's Republic guarantees these freedoms for all workers who live on its territory.' In a socio-political system where victory in the class struggle was one of the prominent goals, the preamble explicitly condemned 'the masters and defenders of the old order',[74] and implied that all those who were not allied to the Socialist revolution were excluded from the exercise of the aforementioned rights.

Moreover, supporting the formation of the people's democracy and military service were mentioned as the obligations of every citizen.[75] Indeed, in spite of the anti-clerical and aggressively secular character of the new regime, military service was described in the constitution as a 'holy duty for all citizens' to stress its preeminent importance.[76]

General Assessment

The enactment of Law XX of 1949 was the real turning point in modern Hungarian constitutional history. It was designed to reinforce the Stalinist transformation of the country, and was clearly inspired by classic Marxist–Leninist principles and the example of the Soviet Union's own constitution. Obviously, former constitutional traditions could have no influence on subsequent legal developments as they were the product of a 'bourgeois' understanding of law, politics and society that had been defeated in the new 'people's republic' (*Népköztársaság*). That is, the explicit disregard of the former traditions and the intent to break with these[77] were natural consequences of the new dominant Marxist–Leninist view.[78]

Thus, the constitution-makers of the summer of 1949 found a completely new source of inspiration for their work.[79] This was the impact of Soviet legal assistance.[80] As János Beér, again, explains, the presence of Soviet troops on the territory of Hungary proved to be a revolutionary factor as it weakened reactionary activities an
d defended the country from imperialist intervention. Thus, the material basis of the socio-political transformation was created. In an ideological sense, the teaching of Stalin – considered to be a 'true friend of Hungarians' – was the most important source of inspiration and motivation. That is, the ideological background for the transformation was also imported from the Soviet Union. More explicitly, to stress the role of the Soviet Union in the establishment of the Socialist regime, the preamble to the constitution began by lauding the 'armed forces of

the great Soviet Union' and mentioning the 'generous support of the Soviet Union' provided for the country in the post-World War II years.[81]

However, besides these rather broad political and intellectual influences, the new constitution was also drafted with specific legal assistance from the Soviet Union. Beér argued that the Soviet constitution of 1936, often termed a Stalinist constitution, was the absolute ideal for the Hungarian constitution-makers. In fact, he described its principles as 'the common treasure of all progressive people'. That is, Soviet legal culture and its influence was a key element in the birth of the new Hungarian constitution. This was even declared by the first commentary as it pointed out that 'the Soviet constitution and the Soviet legal order were an inexhaustible source of lessons for our people's democracy.'[82]

The structural similarities of the 1949 Hungarian constitution and the 1936 Soviet constitution are apparent. The chapters of the Hungarian constitution largely followed the pattern of the 1936 Soviet constitution although the Soviet chapters dealing with the federal organization of state power (for instance, chapter IV on the highest organ of state authority in the Union of Republics) had no counterparts in the Hungarian text. Another example is discussed chapter VIII in the 1949 Hungarian constitution that was nothing more than a word-for-word recitation of the relevant Soviet chapter. In fact, Hungarian constitution-makers generally did no more than incorporate the relevant Soviet articles into the corpus of the constitution, albeit with slightly different wording. Strikingly, the Hungarian constitution was, in places, more restrictive than the Soviet Union's 1936 constitution which had, for example, extended the various rights that it listed to all citizens of the USSR, while the Hungarian version extended these basic rights only to the 'working people'.[83]

In sum, the members of the preparatory committee not only subscribed to the teaching of Marxism−Leninism but also actively sought to copy the Soviet Union's legal framework and constitutional traditions. Needless to say, this 'Eastern turn' in constitutional thinking led to a complete disregard for former Hungarian constitutional traditions and, stemming from the conception of A.J. Vyshinsky, the leading personality of the Stalinist Soviet Union's legal academia, endorsed a socialist normativist[84] and, therefore, ahistorical understanding of both constitutionalism and constitutional law.

The Afterlife of Law XX of 1949

Needless to say, this constitution was nothing more than a so-called 'façade constitution'. These 'façade constitutions' usually have the appearance of conventional constitutions, which was certainly the case of Law XX of 1949; nevertheless, in practice, they are unable to guarantee the limitation of the arbitrary use of state powers. That is, although they may set up a formal hierarchy of institutions and various legal sources, they can be considered as 'dead letters' from the aspect of basic constitutional guarantees (*garantiste* function).[85]

This feature of 'façade constitutions' was promptly illustrated by the waves of so-called 'judicial terror' which occurred between 1950 and 1953. The political elite of this era – dominated by the oligarchic group of Mátyás Rákosi, Ernő Gerő and Mihály Farkas – proclaimed that the judiciary should 'strive to serve the class struggle' and the various judicial bodies as well as the police and intelligence services all made a considerable effort to meet this standard. As a consequence of this politically motivated attitude, one in three Hungarian families was involved in these fake political processes and trials.[86] In addition to this repression of society in general, based on vague and ambiguous legal provisions,[87] the judiciary was also used as a prominent instrument against possible political opponents and internal party rivals. See, for example, the trials of László Rajk et al. (1949) and Imre Geiger et al. (1950); László Sólyom et al. (1950); Árpád Szakasits et al. (1950); József Grősz et al. (1951); János Kádár et al. (1951); and Gábor Péter et al. (1953).[88]

A broad gap existed, therefore, between the provisions of the constitution and the totalitarian reality of the emerging 'popular democracy' in the 1950s. However, the development of world politics during the period of détente or 'mutual coexistence' from the second half of the 1960s, as well as the 'softening' of the Socialist bloc after the death of Stalin in 1953 and the Hungarian revolution of 1956, besides many other socio-political impacts, led to a reform of the constitution. This reform, enacted in 1972,[89] tried to harmonize the constitutional setting with the requirements of the New Economic Mechanism integrating some elements of market economy into the system of economic planning,[90] and also consolidated some parts of the constitution in a less

Socialist normativist spirit.[91] Symbolically, as regards basic rights, it extended the scope of these provisions to the 'citizens' of the Hungarian People's Republic in general[92] in place of the earlier, essentially Rákosist, category of 'workers'.

Conclusion

The chief argument of the above discussion is that the enactment of Law I of 1946 cannot be regarded as the closure of historical constitutionalism. In reality, this Act could also be regarded as an attempt to revitalize the traditional constitutional setting in the light of modern Western constitutionalism. The ideas of human rights and republicanism had considerable influence. Furthermore, the historical experiences of the working of a 'monarchy without a monarch' constitutional setting during the interwar period led to the elimination of the monarchical component from traditional constitutionalism. However, this did not result in the abandonment of the historical constitutional traditions as such, as was clear from the preparatory notes made by the Prime Minister. Law XX of 1946 demonstrated, therefore, that a modern interpretation of constitutionalism and organic constitutional development were not regarded as irreconcilable by Hungary's politicians in 1946.

Therefore, the real disruption of the traditional Hungarian constitutional culture actually occurred with the enactment of Law XX of 1949. It must be emphasized that this in turn would have been impossible without the military, political and ideological support of the Soviet Union. This new constitution was a near-complete copy of both the letter and the spirit of the Soviet Union's 1936 constitution. Its central objective was to legalize the Hungarian Communist Party's complete takeover of State powers and the introduction of a new, Soviet-styled socio-political model. This newly codified constitution, because of the copy-and-paste approach, had no relation to earlier 'bourgeois' constitutionalism. As a result, a new approach, which regarded the law as an instrument of socio-political transformation rather than a guarantee of individual freedoms,[93] was imposed on a country whose constitutional order had hitherto been based on a unique and rather developed historical constitutionalism considerably inspired by the classic Western liberal model.[94]

Notes

1. See, for example: Attila Horváth, '"A köztársaság az egyetlen lehetséges államforma." Az 1946. évi I. törvény megalkotása, a köztársaság kikiáltása', *Acta Humana* v/1 (2017), pp. 7–20; Zoltán Péteri, 'Constitution-making in Hungary', *Acta Juridica Hungarica* xxvi/3–4 (1994), pp. 152–3; Gizella Föglein, *Államforma és államfői jogkör Magyarországon (1944–1949)* (Budapest, 1993), pp. 60–122; József Ruszoly, 'A "Magyarország államformájáról" szóló 1946: 1. tc. létrejötte és előzményei', *Jogtörténeti Szemle* iv/2 (1992), pp. 16–28.
2. See, for example: László Kontler, *Millennium in Central Europe. A History of Hungary* (Budapest, 1999), pp. 391–404; István Vida, 'Sovietization and the nation's response', in M. Ormos and B.K. Király (eds), *Hungary. Governments and Politics. 1848–2000* (New York, 2001), pp. 275–313; György Gyarmati, 'From "tentative democracy" to communist rule', in I. Gy. Tóth (ed.), *A Concise History of Hungary* (Budapest, 2005), pp. 551–70; Bryan Cartledge, *The Will to Survive. A History of Hungary* (London, 2006), pp. 434–48.
3. For a general discussion in English see Sir Paul Vinogradoff, 'A constitutional history of Hungary', *Law Quarterly Review*, 21 October 1905, pp. 426–31, and Péteri, 'Constitution-making in Hungary', pp. 150–2.
4. In addition, this chapter subscribes to the intellectual tradition (where 'tradition' is used as applied by Michael Oakeshott referring to patterns being inherent in human activities, cf. Michael Oakeshott, 'Rational Conduct', in M. Oakeshott, *Rationalism in Politics* (London, 1962), p. 105) coined by István Bibó, Jenő Szűcs and László Péter – see for example István Bibó, 'A kelet-európai kisállamok nyomorúsága', in Bibó István, *Válogatott tanulmányok. 1945–1949* (Budapest, 1986), pp. 185–265 (shedding light on the role of political hysteria as a major driving force in the political cultures of Central Europe); Jenő Szűcs, *Vázlat Európa három történti régiójáról* (Budapest, 1983) (arguing that the politico-cultural setting of Central Europe, including Hungary, gravitates towards the West (*mundus occidentalis*), but the actual attachment of Central Europe to either the West or the East has always been dependent on external historical tendencies of European politics); and László Péter, 'Autokrácia Kelet-Európában', in P. László (ed.), *Az Elbától keletre* (Budapest, 1998), pp. 37–59 (submitting that autocracy has always been a dominant political tradition in Eastern Europe during modernity and it seriously deformed the understanding of politics in the region). A common point for Bibó, Szűcs and Péter was that they attempted to conceptualize Hungarian history by locating it within a broader regional context, namely the region of Central Europe. Therefore, their work had a broader vision, which challenged the conventional, nation-focused approach that has traditionally dominated Hungarian public opinion. Hopefully, this chapter may also be capable of offering some new conclusions when analysing and interpreting these two major Acts in their unique constitutional context: Hungarian historical constitutionalism.
5. Cf. Barna Mezey (ed.), *Magyar alkotmánytörténet* (Budapest, 1996), pp. 252–3; Ruszoly, 'A "Magyarország államformájáról" szóló 1946: 1. tc.'. In addition,

this position is also advocated implicitly by Föglein when arguing that this Act established a new 'public law basis' for the Hungarian state – see Föglein *Államforma és államfői jogkör Magyarországon (1944–1949)*, p. 92.

6. One may argue that the very first codified constitution in the history of Hungary was the constitution of the Hungarian Soviet Republic (*A Magyarországi Szocialista Szovjet Köztársaság Alkotmánya*) promulgated on 28 June 1919. However, this constitution was in force until 1 August 1919, when the government of the Hungarian Soviet Republic resigned and left the country. That is, in fact, it was in force a little bit longer than one month. In addition, at this period, the existence of the country as such was in question as the final borders were still unsettled. In sum, it cannot convincingly be argued that this 'document' is to be considered as a real constitution that had an impact on the country's socio-political life.

7. Bruce Ackerman, *We the People, Volume 1: Foundations* (Cambridge and London, 1993).

8. Ibid., p. 267.

9. Ibid., pp. 266–7.

10. Mária Schmidt, '"Most majd mindent úgy csinálnak, mint az oroszoknál." A kommunizmus kiépülése Magyarországon', in L. Lőrincz (ed.), *Egyezzünk ki a múlttal! Műhelybeszélgetések történelmi mítoszainkról, tévhiteinkről* (Budapest, 2010), pp. 91–2.

11. In László Kontler's words, 'Among different geo-political circumstances, the astonishing dilapidation, the near-tabula rasa that remained after the war, could have even proved advantageous for the future of the country [...] This was indeed how the history of Hungary, as well as that of the other countries of Central Europe, seemed to start anew: with free elections and an experiment with multi-party democracy in order to develop a form of government and policies suitable to their peoples' (Kontler, *Millennium in Central Europe*, p. 388).

12. The question whether the Allied Powers really wanted to support the democratization of Central Europe in the post-World War II period is hotly debated among Hungarian historians. For example, Mária Schmidt argues that the fate of Central Europe was already decided at Yalta. Others, for example, János Rainer M., submit that Soviet intentions for the region were not as obvious in 1945 or 1946 as they may seem to be retrospectively, and argue that the fall of the postwar transitory democratic regime occurred mainly because of the lack of political independence. Cf. M. Schmidt, '"Most majd mindent úgy csinálnak, mint az oroszoknál"' and János Rainer M., 'Demokrácia volt-e Magyarországon 1945 után? A "koalíciós korszak" és a Rákosi-korszak átmenetének kérdése', in L. Lőrincz (ed.), *Egyezzünk ki a múlttal! Műhelybeszélgetések történelmi mítoszainkról, tévhiteinkről* (Budapest, 2010), pp. 85–90.

13. For details, see Vida, 'Sovietization and the nation's response', pp. 283–92.

14. In the words of a contemporary observer: 'On February 1, Zoltan Tildy took the oath as President of the Republic [...]. It seemed natural to my mind to

associate [with] such an occasion [...] the hope that the vicissitudes of the Hungarian people were ending and that destiny was bringing them at last to the haven of law, civil rights and representative government.' H.F. Arthur Schoenfeld, 'Soviet imperialism in Hungary', *Foreign Affairs* xxvi/3 (1948), p. 560.
15. In contrast, Law XX of 1949 (the Communist constitution) consisted of 3,403 words.
16. For the details see Föglein, *Államforma és államfői jogkör Magyarországon (1944–1949)*, pp. 67–86; Ruszoly, 'A "Magyarország államformájáról" szóló 1946: 1. tc.', pp. 24–8.
17. For the details of this codification process and the historical context see Gábor Schweitzer, 'The proclamation of the Hungarian Republic in 1946', *Przeglad Prawa Konstytucynego* xl/6 (2017), pp. 115–25.
18. For an overview see Zoltán Péteri, 'Tradíciók és emberi jogok Magyarországon. Összehasonlító szempontok az emberi jogok eszméjének magyarországi térhódításában', in Z. Péteri (ed.), *Jogösszehasonlítás. Történeti, rendszertani és módszertani problémák* (Budapest, 2010), pp. 205–19, and Andor Csizmadia, 'Törekvések az emberi jogok biztosítására és büntetőjogi védelmükre a reformkori Magyarországon', *Jogtudományi Közlöny* xxx/12 (1975), pp. 681–9. Also see András Cieger's Chapter 6 in this volume.
19. For an overview of this problem see Liav Orgad, 'The preamble in constitutional interpretation', *International Journal of Constitutional Law* viii/4 (2010), pp. 714–38.
20. Law I of 1946, Art. 2 (1).
21. Ibid., Art. 4 (2).
22. Ibid., Art. 9.
23. Ibid., Art. 10 (1).
24. Ibid., Art. 10 (2).
25. Ibid., Art. 11.
26. Ibid., Art. 11 (2).
27. Ibid., Art. 12.
28. Ibid., Art. 13 (2).
29. Ibid., Art. 14.
30. Cf. József Ruszoly, 'A Magyar Köztársaság alapvetése. A "Magyarország államformájáról" szóló 1946: I tc. keletkezéstörténetéről', *Hitel* xix/8 (2006), p. 54. (Ruszoly argues that the functions of the president of the republic were not limited to representation, but he only had a secondary power position with respect to the parliament.)
31. Ibid., Art. 13 (1).
32. Ibid., Art. 19.
33. István Kukorelli, 'Az 1946. évi I. törvény közjogtörténeti jelentősége és az alkotmányos jogfolytonosság', *Acta Humana* v/1 (2017), p. 24.
34. See Law X of 1946 on the more actual protection of basic human rights. It must also be added that the provisions of this Act were never applied even though it was in force until 1987.

35. László Péter, 'Ország és királya a hatvanhetes kiegyezésben', in L. Péter (ed.), *Az Elbától keletre* (Budapest, 1998), p. 225. For a substantially different account of Hungarian historical constitutionalism see Zoltán Szente, 'A historizáló alkotmányozás problémái – a történeti alkotmány és a Szent Korona az új Alaptörvényben', *Közjogi Szemle* iv/3 (2011), pp. 1–13.
36. Ibid.
37. Ibid., p. 227.
38. Ibid., pp. 222–3.
39. Explanatory notes by the Prime Minister attached to Law I of 1946. The text of these notes is available electronically at http://www.rev.hu/sulinet45/szerviz/dokument/torvenycikk1.htm (accessed 3 March 2018).
40. Ibid.
41. Ibid.
42. For the analysis of this discourse see Gábor Schweitzer, 'A "magyar királyi köztársaságtól" a magyar köztársaságig. Az 1946. évi I. törvénycikk visszhangja a korabeli közjogi irodalomban', *Acta Humana* v/1 (2017), pp. 27–38. (Schweitzer points out that most of the contemporary experts on constitutional law wanted to integrate this Act into the frame of the historical constitution even though they all accepted that the monarchical component of the tradition was set aside by the Act.)
43. Explanatory notes by the Prime Minister attached to Law I of 1946.
44. See the letters of Cardinal Mindszenty to the Prime Minister (31 December 1945 and 1 February 1946). Available electronically at http://regnumportal.hu/regnum2/node/177 (accessed 3 March 2018).
45. On the emergence of the 'Russian shadow' over Central Europe see Piotr S. Wandycz, *The Price of Freedom. A History of East Central Europe from the Middle Ages to the Present* (London and New York, 2001), pp. 213–26.
46. Law VII of 1946 on the Criminal Law Protection of Democratic Political Order and the Republic.
47. Law XXX of 1947 on the Nationalization of the Hungarian-Owned Shares of the Hungarian National Bank and Banks Functioning as Public Companies Belonging to Kúria I of the Bank Centre.
48. Law XXV of 1948 on the Nationalization of Factories with more than 100 Employees.
49. For a detailed description of this process, see Schoenfeld, 'Soviet imperialism', pp. 557–66.
50. For details, see Vida, 'Sovietization and the nation's response', pp. 305–8.
51. Ibid., pp. 313–15.
52. János Beér (ed.), *Magyar alkotmányjog* (Budapest, 1951), p. 111.
53. Ibid., p. 112.
54. Mezey (ed.), *Magyar alkotmánytörténet*, p. 388.
55. Law XX of 1949 Art. 70.
56. For example: Law XX of 1949 Art 3.
57. For example: Law XX of 1949 Preamble.

58. János Beér and Szabó Imre (eds), *A Magyar Népköztársaság Alkotmánya. Az 1949: XX. törvény és magyarázata* (Budapest, 1949).
59. János Beér (ed.), *Magyar alkotmányjog*.
60. See Law XX of 1949 Art. 49 (2)–(3).
61. Ibid., Art. 120.
62. For a critical discussion of Socialist legal concepts and scholarship see Attila Horváth, 'A szocialista állam- és jogtudomány', in A. Jakab and A. Menyhárd (eds), *A jog tudománya* (Budapest, 2015), pp. 543–76.
63. Ibid., Arts. 2–3.
64. Cf. ibid., Art. 2 (2).
65. Cf. ibid., Art. 70.
66. Ibid., Art. 14 (1).
67. Ibid., Art. 20.
68. Ibid., Art. 19 (1).
69. Ibid., Art. 25 (1).
70. Ibid., Art. 25 (2).
71. Ibid., Arts. 31–3.
72. Ibid., Art. 30.
73. Ibid., from Art. 45 to 56.
74. Ibid., Preamble.
75. Ibid., Arts. 60–1.
76. Ibid., Art. 61 (1).
77. This was explicitly pointed out by Rákosi when presenting the draft during the plenary session of the parliament on 17 August 1949. 'The Hungarian people have had no constitution thus far. What was generally called as this, was a compilation of various customs and legislative acts.' *Országgyűlési napló* (1949), vol. I, p. 168.
78. Cf. Zoltán Péteri's conclusion on the impact of Law XX of 1949 with respect to traditional constitutionalism: 'Consequently, Hungary's constitution of 1949 made a radical break with the past in both substantive and formal aspects: on the one hand, it destroyed the earlier organization of the state burdened with feudal elements and, on the other, it dismissed finally the idea of "historical constitutionalism".' Péteri, 'Constitution-making in Hungary', p. 155.
79. For a comparative survey of the emergence of Stalinist constitutions in Central and Eastern Europe see Marek Debicki, 'Eastern European constitutionalism. Theory and practice', *Manitoba Law Journal* iv/1 (1970), pp. 113–34.
80. For an in-depth study of Soviet legal assistance during the early years of Socialism in Central Europe see Iván Halász, 'The institutional framework and the methods of implementation of Soviet legal ideas in Czechoslovakia and Hungary during Stalinism', *Journal on European History of Law* vi/2 (2015), pp. 29–37.
81. See Law XX of 1949 Preamble.
82. János Beér and Imre Szabó (eds), *A Magyar Népköztársaság Alkotmánya*, p. 18.

83. Articles 118–28 of the 1936 Constitution of the USSR always used the term 'Citizens of the USSR' when defining the subject of the various basic rights. For example: Article 118. 'Citizens of the USSR have the right to work, that is, are guaranteed the right to employment and payment for their work in accordance with its quantity and quality.' Source: *1936 Constitution of the USSR*. Available at https://www.departments.bucknell.edu/russian/const/1936toc.html (accessed 3 March 2018).
84. On Socialist Normativism see Péter Szilágyi, 'Szabó Imre szocialista normativizmusa. Ideológiakritikai adalékok', *Világosság* xlv/4 (2004), pp. 23–33.
85. For a detailed discussion see Giovanni Sartori, 'Constitutionalism: A preliminary discussion', *The American Political Science Review* lvi/4 (1962), pp. 861–2.
86. For more data see Tibor Zinner, 'Minden bírósági ügy az osztályharc egyik epizódja', *Jogtörténeti Szemle* viii/3 (2006), p. 13.
87. The two main instruments of this repression were Decree Law XXIV of 1950 on the criminal law protection of social ownership (even making capital punishment possible to use for these crimes) and Decree Law IV of 1950 on the criminal law protection of economic planning.
88. Tibor Zinner, 'A legjelentősebb "bűnper"-ek 1956 ősze előtt', *Jogtörténeti Szemle* viii/3 (2006), pp. 67–9.
89. See Law I of 1972 on the modification of Law XX of 1949 and the text in force of the Constitution of the Hungarian People's Republic. For an analysis and discussion see István Kovács, 'A quarter of a century on the path of popular democratic constitutional development (1949–1974)', *Acta Iuridica Academia Scientiarum Hungaricae* xvii/1–2 (1975), pp. 1–46.
90. For instance, Art. 9 of Law I of 1972 set forth that 'state enterprises and economic organizations, when serving the general interests of the society, make their economic activities autonomously based on the methods and responsibility defined by other acts'.
91. For instance, chapter VII on the basic rights and duties of the citizens started with a general declaration on the importance of human rights. (Art. 54 (1) of Law I of 1972 declared that 'the Hungarian People's Republic respects human rights'.)
92. See Arts. 54–68 of Law I of 1972.
93. For a general summary on the peculiarities of Socialist law, see András Sajó and Mónika Ganczer, 'Socialist law', in J.D. Wright (ed.), *International Encyclopedia of the Social and Behavioral Sciences* (Oxford, 2015), pp. 844–8.
94. I am very grateful to my colleagues and friends Zoltán Szente and Gábor Schweitzer, experts on modern Hungarian constitutional history, who spared the time to discuss my thesis and provided me with insightful comments and criticism. Furthermore, I learnt a lot from the editorial comments of Thomas Lorman and Ferenc Hörcher. Without their contribution I could not have developed my arguments in this way.

CHAPTER 10

IS A REVIVAL POSSIBLE?: THEORETICAL REFLECTIONS ON THE HISTORICAL CONSTITUTION

Kálmán Pócza

Introduction

In 1989/90 the Hungarian political elite opted not to adopt a new constitution which would have demarcated the old Communist political system from the new democratic one in both practical and symbolic terms. Instead, negotiations between representatives of the democratic opposition and the Communist leaders led to a series of amendments being made to the 1949 Communist constitution.[1] Although the new amendments changed the substance of the constitution almost completely, several factors weakened the formal and empirical legitimacy of this revised constitution. Some critics condemned the absence of democratic legitimacy, as the constitutional amendments had been enacted by the last Communist parliament whose members had been selected by a rigged election. Other critics complained that these amendments were a poor substitute for an entirely new constitution that would otherwise have been drafted by legitimate representatives of the people.[2] Certainly, the short preamble of the 1989 constitution underpins the argument that those who dismantled the communist system in 1989/90 regarded these constitutional amendments as merely provisional, and only valid 'until the country's new Constitution is adopted'.³ The idea that the 1989 constitution was temporary, however, faded over time, particularly because of the failure of new political parties to enact a new constitution.⁴ In turn, the 1989 constitution gained a certain kind of empirical legitimacy, as the most important political actors accepted it to have established rules by which politics had to be conducted.

The possible adoption of a new constitution returned to the forefront of political disputation during the election campaigns of 2010. Hungary had been savaged by the 2008 financial and economic crisis, and right-wing opposition leader Viktor Orbán, who was widely touted to become the country's next prime minister, suggested that if his party obtained a landslide victory then it would enact a new constitution. This constitution would, he asserted, complete the unfinished task of regime change, which had begun in 1989, and help solve the economic and social problems that afflicted the country.⁵ During the election campaign, however, no drafts of a new constitution were circulated, and the constitution-making process did not produce a new constitutional text until 2011, when it was adopted by a two-thirds right-wing majority in the Hungarian parliament. The legitimacy of the new constitution was subsequently challenged by the opposition parties, who refused to participate in the drafting of the constitution, and who encouraged popular demonstrations against the new Fundamental Law.⁶ One of the main objections of these left-wing and liberal parties concerned one of the new document's most interesting moves, namely the claim to revive continuity with the historical constitution of Hungary. This was denounced as an anachronistic reference to an ancient, undemocratic tradition that had legitimized and empowered a semi-authoritarian regime during the interwar period, and that had also allegedly paved the way for the horrors that afflicted Hungary during World War II.⁷

Certainly, the new Fundamental Law of Hungary denied that Hungary's constitution was simply the product of one single constitutional moment, or that it consisted of only *one* written document. Instead, it implicitly and explicitly indicated that the text of the Fundamental Law was *only one part* of the Hungarian constitution. In fact, the text of the Fundamental Law explicitly referred to the historical constitution of Hungary, which it described as an integral part of the present-day Hungarian constitution. In the legal scholarship, however, these references continued to arouse intense debate, or were simply ignored as being irrelevant to constitutional interpretation.[8] In what follows, I will first outline the main objections raised by legal scholars against the revival of the idea of the historical constitution. Secondly, I will provide some refutations of these arguments. Since both theoretical and empirical objections have been presented in the legal scholarship to date, I will attempt to provide both theoretical and empirical counter-arguments. Having said that, the arguments put forward in this chapter will place more emphasis on theoretical forms of counter-argumentation, and suggest some of the possible directions for empirical research that may be conducted in the near future.

It should be noted that this chapter deliberately focuses on theoretical questions generated by references to the historical constitution in the new Fundamental Law. While a more general assessment of the political controversies surrounding the new constitution and the party-political context would be valuable, the main topic of this chapter has been narrowed down to presenting theoretical arguments and counter-arguments concerning the possibility of the revival of the historical constitution. This has been done with an eye on present-day Hungarian political campaigns. Nevertheless, readers will find several articles, edited volumes or monographs which deal with recent political developments in Hungary.[9]

The Historical Constitution in the New Fundamental Law

Given that there is a published document called the 'Fundamental Law of Hungary', and given that the empirical legitimacy of this document has increased since its adoption in 2011, it might appear that everybody is clear about *what exactly comprises* the Hungarian constitution. The reader might expect a lack of debate over *what* the constitution is or about *who* has been authorized to interpret this constitution definitively. The reader might also expect that the one and only point of discussion is *how* the new Fundamental Law should be interpreted.[10]

Nevertheless, rigorous readers of the Fundamental Law may be surprised that this is not the case, at least as far as the above expectations are concerned. The confusion does not only derive from the empirical fact that there are still some opposition and civil society groups who challenge the legitimacy of the new Fundamental Law. Rather, confusion also stems from a close reading of the text which, as with all written constitutions, should both *theoretically* and *practically* preclude all uncertainty concerning the precise identity of the constitution. Written constitutions, which are usually the products of a constitutional moment, are normatively expected to settle all issues about the identity of the constitution, i.e. they should provide clear answers to the question 'what is the constitution?'.

In a highly paradoxical manner, however, the new Fundamental Law denies that Hungary's constitution is simply a product of a constitutional moment and that it consists merely of a written document. It implicitly presupposes that the text of the law is *only one part* of the Hungarian constitution: this is why it is called a 'Fundamental Law', and not a constitution. Apart from the Fundamental Law there are other legal regulations that are also specifically considered to be part of the Hungarian constitution. Indeed, according to the text of the new Fundamental Law, Hungary's constitution consists of the Fundamental Law *and* the historical constitution. The text of the Fundamental Law thus explicitly refers to *other parts* of the Hungarian constitution that exist outside of the text. It thus explicitly blurs the demarcation line between the new charter and the various manifestations of the Hungarian (written and unwritten) constitutional tradition, usually referred to as the 'historical constitution'.

This paradoxical relationship between the final written text, which should serve as *the* ultimate reference point for current constitutional debates, and the very phrasing of the text that loosens its own finality (i.e. the open-ended references to an indeterminate subject, the so-called 'historical constitution') is certainly one of the most perplexing conundrums of present-day Hungarian constitutionalism. This conundrum is intensified by the fact that the new Fundamental Law also explicitly refers to uncodified elements of the historical constitution.

The first mentions of the term 'historical constitution' occur in the preamble (National Avowal) to the new Fundamental Law:

> We honour the achievements of our historical constitution and we honour the Holy Crown, which embodies the constitutional continuity of Hungary's statehood and the unity of the nation (National Avowal)

We do not recognize the suspension of our historical constitution due to foreign occupations. We declare that no statutory limitation applies to the inhuman crimes committed against the Hungarian nation and its citizens under the national socialist and communist dictatorship. (National Avowal)

The provisions of the Fundamental Law shall be interpreted in accordance with their purposes, with the National Avowal contained therein, and with the achievements of our historical constitution. (Article R para 3)

Several renowned legal scholars have, however, proposed that these references should be ignored and that the focus should be solely on the written text of the Fundamental Law.[11] Indeed, there are very few positive evaluations of the above stipulations in the existing legal scholarship.[12] This is, in part, because there is confusion regarding the exact definition of the 'historical constitution'. Since there is no agreement over which parliamentary acts and/or unwritten constitutional norms constitute the historical constitution, let alone over their precise meanings or significance, legal scholars have almost unequivocally rejected the idea of the revival of the historical constitution.

Reasons for Rejecting the Idea of the Historical Constitution

Generally speaking, there are four reasons why legal scholars (and some of the judges of Hungary's Constitutional Court) have rejected the idea of reviving the historical constitution. As suggested above, there are two *theoretical* and two *empirical* arguments.

Formal Indeterminacy

Starting with the *formal indeterminacy* objection, several scholars argue that references to the historical constitution cause serious problems of interpretation because its contents are not unambiguous.[13] Since there is no formal or informal consensus among legal scholars (or historians) on which parliamentary acts or unwritten constitutional norms should be included in the historical constitution, its exact contents cannot be determined. Indeed, some scholars include legal acts or unwritten norms in the corpus of the historical constitution that others exclude. Whereas codified constitutions have authors, who determine the scope of the constitution in a constitutional moment, historical or uncodified constitutions emerge out of a much more complex process of selection. According to this argument, the formal indeterminacy of historical constitutions means that they are poor instruments for the reduction of incalculability, which is one of the most important functions of a legal system.

Material Indeterminacy
The new Fundamental Law of Hungary refers, however, not simply to the historical constitution, but to the *achievements* of the historical constitution. This might suggest that there is a clear criterion for facilitating the selection/demarcation process. Only those legal Acts and unwritten norms should be considered as part of the historical constitution which deserved to be preserved. 'Achievement' means in this sense that the legal Acts adopted in previous historical periods are compatible with our modern political and moral principles. They might even reinforce such modern principles or, to put it differently, exist as precursors to our contemporary principles, which nevertheless express these achievements in a more nuanced manner.[14] Legal scholars challenging the idea of a historical constitution on this point argue that even if there were agreement about the contents of the historical constitution (see the formal indeterminacy argument), its achievements would still be debatable. This would lead once again to endless disputes on what should, and what should not, be considered an achievement.[15] This is why this kind of objection to the idea of the historical constitution may be referred to as the issue of *material indeterminacy*. Even if there was a corpus of legal acts accepted by almost everyone, i.e. even if the body of the historical constitution could be formally determined, the problem of how to define what outcomes count as *achievements* would still arise.

Incompatibility
These *theoretical* objections aside, it may still be argued that there are other serious problems concerning the achievements of the historical constitution. As certain scholars claim, even if it were possible to determine the contents of the historical constitution and to separate its achievements from its retrograde elements, they would not be *applicable*

to the social and political circumstances of the twenty-first century, since they often reflect the social and political contingencies of earlier periods. These achievements may thus simply be incompatible with the political and social conditions of the twenty-first century. Some have gone even further and argued that earlier ideas, such as the doctrine of the sovereignty of the Holy Crown, explicitly *contradict* modern political principles.[16] Although this idea should certainly be considered as part of the historical constitution, and while it might be accepted as an achievement of the historical constitution, several scholars have argued that an application of this doctrine today would clearly contradict the modern idea of popular sovereignty. This is because the sovereignty of the Holy Crown and the sovereignty of the people are assumed to be incompatible ideas, and because popular sovereignty is likewise assumed to be superior to the sovereignty of the Holy Crown.[17] This *argument of incompatibility* is particularly popular among legal scholars.

Disruption

The fourth stream of objection is perhaps the most sympathetic towards the idea of the historical constitution. Proponents of such protestations are, however, at least as strongly convinced that the resurrection of historical constitutionalism is impossible. They argue that a tradition or a social practice which became extinct after World War II cannot be revived. Traditions exist as long as they are practised. Once they have been abandoned, they cease to exist and cannot be revived artificially. Customs cannot be revived without social practices. According to this view, the idea of a historical constitution might be relevant from *only* one perspective, and that is the perspective of the so-called *invisible constitution*. Here the term 'invisible constitution' is understood to refer to a body of judicial decisions, in particular, to the systematic interpretations of the 1989/90 constitution by the Hungarian Constitutional Court (HCC) after 1990.[18] This idea of gradual development by judicial interpretation is consistent with the idea of a gradually developing historical constitution, and as such, this is the only way that references to the historical constitution might be consistently understood. More explicitly, because 40 years of communism disrupted the constitutional traditions of Hungary so extensively, the one and only way that historical constitutionalism might be meaningfully understood is through attempts to identify the invisible constitution as shaped by the successive decisions of the HCC after 1989.

Four Assumptions

In examining the above objections, four assumptions may be detected that underpin and determine these critical positions. In order to outline my counter-arguments, it is of utmost importance to highlight these implicit or explicit assumptions, which are fundamental to the objections listed above. As for the first objection (*formal indeterminacy*), this argument assumes that there is a sharp and clear-cut difference between a historical/uncodified constitution, on the one hand, and a codified constitution, on the other. Secondly, the *material indeterminacy* objection assumes that codified constitutions are not only radically different, but that they are clearly *superior* to uncodified/historical constitutions, as they decrease indeterminacy and increase calculability in constitutional disputes.[19] Today it is an almost universally accepted tenet of constitutional law that the first and most important function of codified constitutions is to generate calculability through unambiguity and the rule of law. And it is also widely accepted that codified constitutions are superior in this regard because they decrease indeterminacy. Thirdly the *incompatibility argument* presupposes (but does not prove) that the notion and idea of the historical constitution is incompatible with modern political and social phenomena. Finally, the *disruption thesis* insists that all relevant constitutional customs were extinguished during the Communist regime, and that there are no relevant constitutional customs or conventions which could be revived after the fall of communism in 1989/90.

Counter-Arguments

These assumptions are, however, either entirely or at least partially untenable. The counter-arguments are as follows. First, I argue that there is *no sharp difference* between written/codified constitutions and unwritten constitutional conventions: there are not radically different kinds of constitution, but instead, only one kind of constitution. Since there is perhaps a difference in degree but certainly not in *genus*, my second counter-argument is that products of constitutional moments (written constitutions) are *not superior* to the unwritten (i.e. slowly developed) constitutional norms of historical constitutions. Written constitutional norms do not avoid ambiguity or fundamental political conflict (constitutional crisis situations) any more than unwritten ones. Indeed, it is precisely unwritten constitutional conventions and norms that prevent us from backsliding to situations where fundamental political issues are radically challenged. Thirdly, I will argue that it is not impossible to adapt old principles to modern circumstances, even if this adaptation may require some innovation and creative interpretation. Finally, I will try to explore some of the unwritten norms that determined the behaviour of the political actors after the regime change of 1989/90, and map out whether they might have had some connections to the Hungarian political traditions that predated 1990 or even 1944. No one would deny, in spite of over 40 years of Fascist and Communist dictatorship, that there were at least *some* long-standing political and constitutional traditions that influenced political actors or Hungarian citizens during (and directly after) the regime change of 1990. I will, therefore, argue that insufficient research has been carried out on the unwritten constitutional conventions that were (re-)established after 1990, as well as on their roots in long-standing traditions and conventions.

To further present this line of argumentation, however, first the answers to two questions must be sought: what is a constitution, and what was the historical constitution? The discussion of these issues is indispensable to the plausibility of the counter-arguments which will refute each of the principal objections to the revival of the historical constitution.

What is a Constitution?

In order to be able to underpin my claims, I must first clarify what constitutions consist of. From a completely legalist or *formal perspective* (modern) constitutions are *codified* documents that *constitute* and at the same time *constrain* state power in order to coordinate social interactions. Additionally, constitutions are often thought to be more entrenched than ordinary law, i.e. they belong to a class of higher laws, which are more difficult to change than ordinary laws.[20] These higher laws influence social interactions through the interpretations of experts (constitutional lawyers), who act as the 'mouth of the constitution'. The role of constitutional lawyers is, therefore, confined to making explicit what is inherent in the text of the constitution. Today, quite a few scholars would stop at this stage of definition, regarding it as unsophisticated legal positivism that is no longer dominant among legal scholars.[21]

More *dynamic definitions* of the term 'constitution' accept that constitutional provisions and the concepts they contain are highly abstract and that, consequently, there is always a need to interpret constitutional concepts in order to make them more specific in the case of their application. Most members of the legal profession are convinced that interpretation should be carried out by institutions exclusively authorized to perform this task.[22] Moreover, it is also widely held that these institutions (usually constitutional courts) should perform their interpretative work on the basis of legal doctrines. This means that legal scholars are ready to transcend legal positivism, so long as two requirements are met: *First*, there must be a written document to rely on, as it precludes disputes about the contents of the constitution. *Secondly*, they are eager to determine which player on the political/legal field is *exclusively* authorized to have the last say in disputes over constitutional questions.[23] This is claimed because disputes over *who* has the exclusive competence to decide constitutional disputes must also be absent. According to the classic phrasing of Chief Justice Hughes, 'we are under a Constitution, but the *Constitution is what the judges say it is*, and the judiciary is the safeguard of our liberty and of our property under the Constitution.'[24] Legal scholarship is now dominated by these presuppositions: a constitution consists of a written document along with an authorized interpretation by the judiciary.[25]

According to this approach, historical constitutions are primitive and backward phenomena since they fail to answer the question of *what* a constitution consists of and *who* has the exclusive authority or competence to interpret the constitution.[26] There are some countries which are presumed to be able to coordinate the social interactions of modern complex societies without having either a written constitution or a clearly predetermined authority on constitutional interpretation, but this is a very rare phenomenon. Indeed, it is only Great Britain which is thought to be able to rely on a historical constitution and on unwritten constitutional conventions when settling political conflicts. Thus, this rare exception only reinforces the assumption that the combination of written constitutions and bodies exclusively authorized to settle constitutional conflicts represents a higher level of social development.

But is this dynamic approach to constitutions plausible? Recent theoretical literature and literature on the US constitution argue that beyond the text of the US constitution there is (and always must be) an unwritten US constitution which has been shaped *partly* by judicial decisions and *partly* by unwritten constitutional conventions.[27] This literature deals with the social phenomena, namely customs and conventions, which dominate American constitutional practice. A range of authors have recognized that beyond the written text *and* its judicial interpretation there are informal and unwritten customs which fill the gaps where the text of the constitution and judgements interpreting it are silent. Most of the time these conventions work quite well, effectively coordinating the behaviours of political actors without serious conflict. On other occasions they face serious challenges. The most important thing is, however, that they determine the behaviour of political actors in a special way; since unwritten conventions interpret or fill in the gaps of the constitution in a way that all the members of a political community expect, they do not generate conflict and consequently do not require the interference of the judiciary which, according to the dynamic legalistic view, is authorized to formally settle constitutional conflicts. Obviously, conflicts may arise if there is a disagreement about fundamental political issues. But most of the time unwritten constitutional conventions determine the political process up until the moment when parties disagree on the interpretation of the constitution. This means that issues that are only partly or ambiguously regulated in constitutions are invariably clarified by old conventions predating the written constitution, or by political actors who initiate new conventions if they have the necessary support to do so. Since the basic characteristic of conventions is that they are deliberately accepted by political actors (they are not imposed by an external actor like the court), they pass unrecognized by careless observers.

Though emerging social practices or unwritten constitutional customs often escape attention, this does not mean that they should be neglected. Indeed, for a more comprehensive understanding of a constitution it is necessary to revise and expand the phrase formulated by Chief Justice Hughes: a constitution is what the judges say it is *and/or* what the relevant social practice/unwritten convention suggests it is. According to this definition, a written constitution consists of a text usually formulated in a constitutional moment, the interpretations of judges, *and* several social practices and conventions which fill the gaps of the text without generating conflicts among political actors.[28]

What was the Historical Constitution?

By accepting this definition of the term 'constitution', let us turn to the question of what the main elements of historical constitutions are. Three elements of historical constitutions have been, hitherto, identified. First, they include (special) written laws or other legal regulations (such as secondary legislation) which are generally accepted as highly important from the perspective of the political community, but which are not codified in one written constitution. Secondly, they include highly important judicial decisions. Thirdly, they include unwritten constitutional conventions or customs that determine political processes (without having anything to do with the judiciary).[29]

Certainly, the question emerges whether all of these elements are required in order to be able to talk about a historical constitution. In practice, historical constitutions always include all three elements, namely some written legal regulations, important judicial decisions and unwritten conventions rooted in a more or less distant past.[30] This last element is crucial in differentiating historical constitutions from the unwritten social practices (customs) connected to the constitution. At the same time, it is of utmost importance that the continuity of these social practices (customs) is not a requirement, since social practices and unwritten customs might be neglected and then rediscovered or (re)invented. The key point is that these unwritten customs have a broadly accepted origin in the past. According to the following argumentation, the revival of a historical constitution with all of its three elements is not impossible in spite of the discontinuity which characterizes the Hungarian historical constitution.

Apart from the difference in the status of the various laws in codified constitutions (based on the principle of a hierarchy of laws) and historical constitutions (in which all laws are equal), the main elements of the written and historical constitutions actually correspond with each other, namely that both types of constitution amalgamate written laws, judicial decisions and unwritten constitutional conventions.[31] There is, therefore, as Murphy has noted, a continuity between historically emerging customs and written laws.[32]

Is there a *Differentia Specifica*?

Even if important elements of codified and uncodified constitutions actually correspond, there might be differences in the relationship of these elements to each other. One line of argumentation stresses that in the case of codified constitutions *written* constitutional regulations (in fact, by means of *judicial interpretation*) always prevail over and override unwritten constitutional conventions. This is because while written (constitutional) laws are always expected to be enforced, unwritten constitutional conventions can be jettisoned.

There is a wide variety of literature (primarily focused on the British context) regarding the differences or similarities between (written constitutional) law and (unwritten constitutional) convention.[33] One group of scholars of customary law convincingly argue, however, that there is no sharp difference between written laws and unwritten conventions, even from the perspective of enforcement. Nevertheless, it should be admitted that there might be a difference in degree.[34] This literature stresses that there are (constitutional) laws which are not enforced at all, and, in turn, that there might be also unwritten conventions which are enforced (either by the judiciary or by public pressure). If the alleged *differentia specifica* (actual enforcement of laws) cannot conform to actual practice, because some unwritten constitutional conventions will be enforced, while some parts of the written constitutions will not, then the drawing of a sharp distinction between written laws and unwritten conventions is untenable.

The Constitution: An Interplay between Written Norms, Judicial Interpretations and Unwritten Norms

Legal scholars always stress that, in case of conflict, written constitutional regulations (must) always prevail over unwritten constitutional norms. Considering the literature on unwritten constitutional norms, this approach is, however, defective because it focuses on only one type of interplay (namely a conflictual one) between law and convention, and even then it overlooks the fact that written laws *do not always* prevail over unwritten conventions in the case of conflict. The predominant view of legal scholars is that there are only two possible interactions between law and convention. Unwritten laws either exist *in harmony* with written laws, thus mutually reinforcing each other, or they are *overridden* by written laws. At first glance, this approach seems to be convincing. But the relationship between written and unwritten constitutional norms is not as simple as this dominant view suggests. There are at least four other possible interactions between these two kinds of norm.[35]

Incorporation by Void Filling

First, unwritten conventions might *fill a void* or regulate something that the written constitution is silent about. This phenomenon was, for example, evident in the US prior to 1951, when a constitutional amendment was ratified that explicitly forbade a third term for a president who had already been twice elected. The two-term limit was, however, a constitutional reality long before this amendment explicitly forbade a third term. Before 1951 there were no regulations at all concerning the term limit, but constitutional practice had filled this gap. While the unwritten custom of electing presidents for only two terms had prevailed before, in 1940 it was jettisoned, and Roosevelt was elected for a third term. It is also true that after his death the unwritten custom had been restored and even codified in 1951. But void-filling is not unknown even in the Hungarian context: the 1989 constitution and the cardinal law on the Hungarian Constitutional Court (HCC) declared that all procedural regulations which were not included either in the constitution or in the law that established the HCC should be clarified by subsequent regulations. Nevertheless, this did not occur until 2001, more than a decade after its establishment. Until that point, there was no official document which clarified how the HCC should act after receiving a petition.[36] Although the general principles of the constitution and the Law on the HCC remained in force, these were defective. For more than a decade, *unwritten* conventions had to determine the practice of an institution which was considered to be the crown jewel of any *written* constitution.

Incorporation by Refinement

Secondly, there is the possibility that unwritten conventions *refine* some of the terms, concepts or regulations of a written constitution. Although the nomination of constitutional judges was quite clearly regulated by the 1989 constitution and the Law on the HCC's establishment in 1989, the manner in which judges have been nominated and elected has been repeatedly refined. Informal (and often secret) meetings of influential politicians became a key element in the nomination and election processes which were, from early on, guided by the custom of always putting forward at least two nominees. This meant, in practice, that vacancies were filled only if there were two, or occasionally four, vacancies, thus ensuirng that the rival right- and left-wing political parties were evenly represented on the HCC. This practice continued as a constitutional convention until 2010, when the right-wing parties changed the nomination rules (and with that disregarded this custom) and elected judges (formally legally) without the consent of the left-wing parties. Of course, this latter event cannot be evaluated as incorporation by refinement, it is simply a break with a convention.

Repudiation by Void Creation

Thirdly, unwritten conventions might repudiate some written constitutional norms by simply neglecting them. The concept of *desuetudo* is very well known in the British constitutional tradition, where several prerogatives of the British monarch are still incorporated in written laws but have not been employed for decades and, in some cases, even for centuries. The term *Sozialstaatsprinzip* (principle of the welfare state) in the German Basic Law is another example of void creation. Although it has been retained in the constitution, the German Federal Constitutional Court has never referred to this principle of the German constitution.[37] The concept of *desuetudo* also played a significant role in the history of Hungarian constitutional law,[38] and there are examples from recent political practices, too: although the new Fundamental Law explicitly prescribed that the HCC must interpret the Fundamental Law in accordance with the achievements of the historical constitution, it has mostly ignored this obligation and has rarely referred to the historical constitution in its decisions.

Repudiation by Substitution

Although void creation can be free of controversy and challenge, the regulations of a written constitution can also be repudiated by explicitly *contradicting* them. Perhaps the most well-known contradiction between the written constitution and actual practice is the existence of the Japanese army, which was explicitly prohibited by Article 9 of the Japanese constitution. It is well known that the Japanese constitution was influenced by American advisors who, during the drafting of a constitution for Japan in 1947, sought to avoid the recurrence of armed conflict. Nevertheless, political practice, legitimized by the interpretation provided by the Japanese Constitutional Court, disregarded this constitutional regulation.[39] Likewise, in Hungary, the coronation oath of Hungarian monarchs contained a clause which repeated from time to time the abrogation of the Hungarian nobility's right of resistance (*ius resistendi*). This 'abrogation clause' was incorporated into the coronation oath as late as 1916, although this right was *explicitly* abrogated from the *Corpus Juris Hungarici* in 1687.[40]

According to this short overview of the possible forms of interplay between written and unwritten constitutional norms it is far from certain that written laws always prevail over unwritten norms, even though that is still the predominant view in legal scholarship. Taking into account the variety of possible interactions between written norms and unwritten conventions and bearing in mind the recent literature on constitutional change (which focuses on *informal* constitutional amendments or transformations without explicit alterations to the texts of constitutions), it is clear that uncodified constitutions have to rely on unwritten norms, but it is also clear that written constitutions are also extended, refined, changed or even repudiated in accordance with unwritten norms.[41]

If all constitutions are properly understood as the interplay between written norms, their judicial interpretations *and* unwritten norms, one cannot argue that there is a sharp difference between written and unwritten constitutions. This is so because unwritten conventions and customs form a substantial part of all written constitutions. There might be a *difference in degree* over the extent to which unwritten conventions effectively influence the behaviour of the political actors, but written and unwritten norms invariably form both codified and historical constitutions.

According to this view, a constitution, written or unwritten, consists of (1) written text(s); (2) its judicial interpretation; *and* (3) unwritten conventions or social norms which either *bolster*, *amend* or even *contradict* written law. The 'living constitution', i.e. the actual political order, might emerge from the interplay of these three factors. The importance of each factor depends on the political context, but one cannot argue *a priori* (theoretically) that written constitutions are more likely to decrease indeterminacy and thus coordinate social interactions more effectively. By showing that there is a difference only *in degree* between written and unwritten constitutions, and that written constitutions are not by definition superior to unwritten ones, the discussion arrives at the most fundamental question of this chapter: which of the three elements of a constitution is *the* decisive element?

Having enumerated the possible aspects of interplay between written and unwritten norms, this chapter has demonstrated that conventions extend or even repudiate written constitutional norms from time to time. Consequently, unwritten norms (depending on the context and practice) might be at least as important as written norms. Bearing this in mind, the argument that the historical constitution might *theoretically* play an important role in Hungarian constitutional practice, even today, can be substantiated.

Empirical Counter-Arguments

This chapter is not able to develop the empirical counter-arguments that would also refute claims that references to the historical constitution in Hungary's current Fundamental Law are inappropriate. It is, however, useful to clarify the framework around which these empirical arguments might be built up.

Incompatibility

Even if one is willing to accept that there is no categorical difference between written and unwritten constitutions, and that written constitutions are not necessarily superior to unwritten ones, two further objections may be raised to any attempt to restore the historical constitution in Hungary. Both problems are *empirical* rather than *theoretical*. The first *empirical* objection against the possibility of the revival concerns the incompatibility with modern social conditions of the concepts of the historical constitution.

As mentioned above, one illustration of this objection concerns the doctrine of the Holy Crown, which is supposed to be incompatible with the principle of popular sovereignty. Although the issue of the relationship between the doctrine of the Holy Crown and popular sovereignty will not be discussed in detail here, it should be noted that, as some scholars have argued, reducing the concept of the historical constitution to the doctrine of the Holy Crown is an unacceptable oversimplification. The concept of the historical constitution is far more multilayered than that, and it has several connotations which are independent of the notion of the Holy Crown. They are also clearly compatible with modern political and social conditions, such as the 1848 April Laws or even Law I of 1946 on the state form of Hungary.[42] Restricting the concept of the historical constitution to the doctrine of the Holy Crown deprives the idea of the historical constitution of its rich historical content. This is not only unfair, but also historically inaccurate for a phenomenon which has survived radical social and political turbulence, and has given the development of Hungarian law a special flavour. Undoubtedly, a creative interpretation of, and an innovative approach to, the quite elastic principles of the historical constitution is necessary to be able to fit the concept of the historical constitution to modern social conditions. But this is not inconceivable: the historical constitution survived various forms of social order from medieval times to the mid-twentieth century, and it performed well in coordinating social interactions.[43] Thus, as demonstrated above, one cannot – and therefore should not – exclude *a priori* that there are possible interpretations of old principles that are compatible with modern circumstances.

Disruption

To show that the revival of the historical constitution is not impossible, one must also deal with the objection that the constitutional traditions of Hungary have been irrevocably and permanently severed. At first glance the disruption thesis seems to stand on rather swampy ground, since the historical constitution endured for several centuries in spite of the fact that earlier periods of Hungarian history were also afflicted by radical disruptions and turning-points. Revolts, revolutions and radical changes of regime have always characterized Hungarian history from the early modern period onwards. Nevertheless, the historical constitution was able to endure as the central reference point in political debates up until the end of World War II. The historical constitution was, indeed, shaped by this traumatic continuity of discontinuities – at least until the constitution formulated by a totalitarian Soviet regime in the Communist period.

It is also obvious that the 40-year-long Communist regime had a fundamental impact on the constitutional traditions which had been so vivid until World War II. The resistance of the legal profession towards the revival of the historical constitution shows not only that the cultivation of the Hungarian constitutional tradition has been abandoned, but also that there is no inclination in most of the present generation of lawyers to resuscitate this tradition. This hostility to the historical constitution among much of the legal profession is underpinned by the objection that references to the historical constitution have been almost completely absent from legal discourse since the transition to democracy in Hungary. Thus, there is no *empirical* evidence of a continuing constitutional tradition, as the historical constitution's chain of tradition has been ruptured. Broken traditions are lost traditions, since continuity is a precondition for the existence of a tradition. The absence of *empirical* evidence also supposedly makes it *impossible* to resuscitate the historical constitution.[44]

Our *empirical* counter-argument denies, however, that discontinuity precludes the reinstatement of a lost tradition. Traditions can be, and have been, reinvented several times in Hungarian history. Just to mention the most relevant case, even the Hungarian historical constitution was formed by a series of creative interpretations. It happened several times that Hungary's constitutional tradition disappeared but was then reinvented due to various (mainly instrumental) factors. The most obvious examples of this kind of *intermittent* formation of tradition include not only the centrepiece of the Hungarian historical constitution, i.e. the Golden Bull,[45] but even the concept and tradition of the Holy Crown.[46]

To find the first indication of an attempt to link the lost tradition of Hungarian constitutionalism (i.e. the historical constitution) with the present constitutional narratives, one has to turn to the speeches of the prime minister of Hungary elected to office in 1990 following the collapse of communism. In one of his first speeches in parliament, József Antall referred several times to the continuity of Hungarian constitutional tradition, especially to parliamentary tradition. In his view, the building of the Hungarian parliament represents 'the continuity of Hungarian constitutionalism' (*a magyar közjogi folytonosság háza*).[47] References to Hungarian constitutional tradition, which served to establish the continuity between the distant past and the present, were in general the most important characteristics of the political narrative of the first prime minister after 1990.[48]

Although the restoration or reinvention of a constitutional tradition has been a widely ignored or at least neglected phenomenon in international scholarly research, the indications are that this phenomenon has recently become more topical.[49] The willingness of the Baltic states, especially Latvia, to restore their pre-Communist constitutions and constitutional traditions provides a clear example that constitutional traditions can be reinvigorated even after decades of Soviet occupation.[50] Another example of reinvented constitutional identity, which presupposes that a former traditional identity has been lost, concerns the case of unenumerated rights in the constitution of the US. This tradition has been reinvented by constitutional interpretation, as one of the leading academics of jurisprudence put it in his recent book.[51]

Conclusion

Both *theoretical* arguments and (still sporadic) *empirical* indications show that the revival of the historical constitution is not *impossible* as such. Whether it is also *desirable* remains a question to be answered in another book.

Indeed, even those who are inclined to accept the theoretical and empirical counter-arguments presented in this chapter will still have to grapple with the question of whether the revival of the historical constitution is not only possible but also *desirable*. The crucial point is whether, beyond the principle of legal certainty, there are other competing principles which should be considered as equally important and decisive in the constitution-making processes as well as in constitutional adjudication. Since a restoration of the historical constitution would only be possible by opening up the text of the written constitution, this would certainly lead to growing legal uncertainty. Although the arguments presented above have shown that formal and material indeterminacy is not an exclusive characteristic of historical constitutions, and that there is a difference – which is gradual and certainly not categorical – between the two types of constitution, it is undeniable that codified constitutions provide less breathing space for legal uncertainty. Consequently, anyone rejecting the importance of the principle of legal certainty must put forward at least one alternative principle that has primacy.

Notes

1. The 1949 constitution was amended several times in the 1950s and 1960s, and it was once again redacted into a unitary form in 1972.
2. András Körösényi, Csaba Tóth and Gábor Török, *The Hungarian Political System* (Budapest, 2009), p. 34.
3. 'In order to facilitate a peaceful political transition to a constitutional state, establish a multi-party system, parliamentary democracy and a social market economy, the Parliament of the Republic of Hungary hereby establishes the following text as the Constitution of the Republic of Hungary, until the country's new Constitution is adopted' (Law XX of 1949. The Constitution of the Republic of Hungary as modified in 1989).
4. Between 1994 and 1997 a coalition of the post-communist Hungarian Socialist Party and the liberal Hungarian Free Democrats had a constitutional majority, and a process to make a new constitution was launched, but in the end the parties, mainly due to the conflict within the governing coalition, could not adopt a new constitution. See Andrew Arato and Zoltán Miklósi, 'Constitution making and transitional politics in Hungary', in L.E. Miller (ed.), *Framing the State in Times of Transition* (Washington DC, 2010), p. 370.
5. Viktor Orbán, *Nem lesz árnyékkormány!, Beszéd a Magyar Polgári Együttműködés Egyesület Új államépítés, új irány, új feladatok című konferenciáján Kecskeméten 2009. november 8-án* [There won't be a shadow cabinet! Speech at the conference 'New State-building, New Direction, New Tasks', organized by the Hungarian Civil Cooperation Association, on 8 November 2009]. Available at http://2010-2015.miniszterelnok.hu/beszed/nem_lesz_arnyekkormany (accessed 3 March 3, 2018). Also: Viktor Orbán, *Újjá kell építeni Magyarországot, évértékelő beszéd, 2010. február 5.* [We should rebuild Hungary! Speech on the State of Hungary on 5 February 2010]. Available at http://2010-2015.miniszterelnok.hu/beszed/ujja_kell_epiteni_magyarorszagot (accessed 3 March 2018).
6. The secession of two left-wing parties from the constitution-making process was implicated by the amendment of the 'old' 1989 constitution by the right-wing constitutional majority in the summer of 2010. This amendment cut the competences of the Constitutional Court. For the process, see Pál Sonnevend, András Jakab and Lóránt Csink, 'The constitution as an instrument of everyday politics: The basic law of Hungary', in A. von Bogdany and P. Sonnevend (eds), *Constitutional Crisis in the European Constitutional Area. Theory, Law and Politics in Hungary and Romania* (Oxford and Portland, OR, 2015), p. 44.
7. See for example the opinion of the Hungarian Socialist Party on the draft constitution of 21 March 2011, available at http://mszp.hu/nyomtatas/312 (accessed 3 March 2018).
8. While the doctrine of the Holy Crown and the idea of the historical constitution had been elaborated by the end of the nineteenth century by legal scholars, legal scholarship was reserved if not hostile to the idea of the historical constitution after the 1990 democratic transition. See László Péter, 'The Holy Crown of

Hungary, visible and invisible', in Miklós Lojkó (ed.), László Péter, *Hungary's Long Nineteenth Century: Constitutional and Democratic Traditions in European Perspective: Studies by László Péter* (Leiden and Boston, MA, 2012), p. 109.

9. For a general assessment of the second Orbán government, see John O'Sullivan and Kálmán Pócza (eds), *The Second Term of Viktor Orbán. Beyond Prejudice and Enthusiasm* (London, 2015). As for the third term of Viktor Orbán from highly divergent perspectives, see Bálint Magyar (ed.), *Post-Communist Mafia State. The Case of Hungary* (Budapest, 2016); Frank Furedi, *Populism and the European Culture Wars: The Conflict of Values between Hungary and the EU* (London and New York, 2017); András László Pap, *Democratic Decline in Hungary. Law and Society in an Illiberal Democracy* (London, 2018).

10. André Brodocz, 'Verfassunggebung in konsolidierten Demokratien und Postkonfliktgesellschaften. Perspektiven einer Theorie der Deutungsmacht', in E. Bos and K. Pócza (eds), *Verfassunggebung in konsolidierten Demokratien: Neubeginn oder Verfall eines politischen Systems?* (Baden-Baden, 2014), p. 45.

11. As illustrative examples in English see Miklós Bánkuti, Gábor Halmai and Kim Lane Scheppele, 'Hungary's illiberal turn: Disabling the constitution', *Journal of Democracy* xxiii/3 (2012), pp. 138–46; Sándor Radnóti, 'A sacred symbol in a secular country: The Holy Crown', in G.A. Tóth, *Constitution for a Disunited Nation: On Hungary's 2011 Fundamental Law* (Budapest and New York, 2012), pp. 85–110; Kim Lane Scheppele, 'The unconstitutional constitution', *New York Times*, 2 January 2012; István Császár and Balázs Majtényi, 'Hungary: The historic constitution as the place of memory', in M. Suksi, K. Agapiou-Josephides, J-P. Lehners and M. Nowak (eds), *First Fundamental Rights Documents in Europe* (Cambridge, 2015), pp. 57–69; Gábor Halmai, 'The Hungarian constitutional court and constitutional identity', Verfassungsblog, 10 January 2017 (available at http://verfassungsblog.de/the-hungarian-constitutional-court-and-constitutional-identity/ (accessed 3 March 2018). In Hungarian: Zoltán Szente, 'A historizáló alkotmányozás problémái – a történeti alkotmány és a Szent Korona az új Alaptörvényben', *Közjogi Szemle* iv/3 (2011), pp. 1–13; Zoltán Szente, 'Az Alaptörvény és az alkotmányos változások szakmai és tudományos reflexiói 2010 után', *Fundamentum* xix/2–3 (2015), pp. 62–70; Imre Vörös, 'A történeti alkotmány az Alkotmánybíróság gyakorlatában', *Közjogi Szemle* ix/4 (2016), pp. 44–57.

12. From the perspective of political philosophy but not from a legal perspective in English, see Ferenc Hörcher, 'The national avowal', in L. Csink et al. (eds), *The Basic Law of Hungary. A First Commentary* (Dublin, 2012); Ferenc Hörcher, 'Communal values in the new Hungarian fundamental law: The Habermas–Ratzinger debate and the use of the humanities in constitutional interpretation', in E. Bos and K. Pócza (eds), *Verfassunggebung in konsolidierten Demokratien: Neubeginn oder Verfall eines politischen Systems?* (Baden-Baden, 2014), pp. 346–64. From the perspective of legal scholars in Hungarian, see Ádám Rixer, *A történeti alkotmány helye mai jogunkban* (Budapest, 2012); Péter Smuk, 'Nemzetfogalom és történeti narratíva az Alaptörvényben', in G. Kecskés (ed.),

Is A Revival Possible? 233

Doktori Műhelytanulmányok. Széchenyi Egyetem Állam- és Jogtudományi Doktori Iskola (Győr, 2013), pp. 259–303; András Milánkovich and Boldizsár Szentgáli-Tóth, 'Díszítő elem, vagy új értelmezési távlatok? A magyar közjog történeti dimenziói az Alaptörvény tükrében', *Közjogi Szemle* vii/4 (2014), pp. 65–74; Zsuzsanna Szakály, 'A történeti alkotmány és az alkotmányos identitás az Alaptörvényben', *Pro Publico Bono* ii/2 (2015), pp. 24–38. András Zs. Varga, 'Történeti alkotmányunk vívmányai az Alaptörvény kógens rendelkezésében', *Iustum Aequum Salutare* xii/4 (2016), pp. 83–9.
13. Vörös, 'A történeti alkotmány', p. 45.
14. This means that by using the idea of achievements, legal scholars could exclude norms which do not pass our present-day standards.
15. Ibid., p. 46.
16. The doctrine of the Holy Crown refers to the crown of the first Christian king of Hungary, which was sent by the Pope to the inauguration of King Stephen I. This original crown was later lost, but even the crown known today as the Holy Crown dates from as early as the twelfth century according to historians. This holy object has had a highly adventurous 'life'; nevertheless, it has been preserved and transmitted through centuries. From the thirteenth century onwards, the inauguration and coronation of any Hungarian king was only valid and accepted by the Hungarian public if the archbishop of Esztergom put that very crown on the head of the new king. In contrast to other famous crowns, like the British one for example, the Hungarian crown has remained one and the same masterpiece from the twelfth century to date. The fact that this historical object has been preserved for long centuries has certainly contributed to the formation and emergence of a doctrine attached to this piece of historical heritage. The doctrine of the Holy Crown refers to a simple idea of the Hungarian public law: sovereignty does not belong to the king or the people of Hungary, but to the Holy Crown. This idea excludes the absolute sovereignty of both the Hungarian king and the people, since it is only the Holy Crown that is absolutely sovereign. It is the ultimate source of legitimacy for the kings and the state. In this sense the Holy Crown, that very historical object, becomes a symbol of Hungarian statehood, too, which is also explicitly reflected in the new Fundamental Law: 'We honour the Holy Crown, which embodies the constitutional continuity of Hungary's statehood and the unity of the nation' (National Avowal). For the doctrine of the Holy Crown, see Péter, 'The Holy Crown', pp. 15–111.
17. Szente, 'A historizáló alkotmányozás problémái', pp. 3–4.
18. The idea of an 'invisible constitution' originates from the first president of the Hungarian Constitutional Court, László Sólyom. Sólyom argued that the coherent adjudicational practice, i.e. the systematic dogmatic contained in the decisions of the Hungarian Constitutional Court, serves as the basis of the so-called 'invisible constitution'. The invisible constitution is visible in the written text of the decisions of the HCC but formally is not part of the written constitution. For the invisible constitution, see László Sólyom and Georg

Brunner, *Constitutional Judiciary in a New Democracy. The Hungarian Constitutional Court* (Ann Arbor, MI, 2000).
19. Renáta Uitz, *Constitutions, Court and History* (Budapest, 2005), pp. 2–14.
20. Stephen Holmes, 'Constitutions and constitutionalism', in M. Rosenfeld and A. Sajó (eds), *The Oxford Handbook of Comparative Constitutional Law* (Oxford, 2012), p. 189. Dieter Grimm, 'Types of constitutions', in M. Rosenfeld and A. Sajó (eds), *The Oxford Handbook of Comparative Constitutional Law* (Oxford, 2012), p. 103.
21. On legal positivism see Mario Jori, 'Legal positivism', in E. Craig (ed.), *Routledge Encyclopedia of Philosophy* (London, 2005), p. 550.
22. Before the global spread of constitutional review (and in some countries even today), the organs which were authorized to authentically interpret the text of the constitution were not of judicial character but were the ordinary or specific legislative bodies. With a few exceptions (like the Nordic countries in Europe), today this task is attributed to constitutional courts in almost all the democratic systems.
23. John Gardner, 'Can there be a written constitution?', *Oxford Studies in Philosophy of Law* clxii/1 (2011), p. 11.
24. Speech before the Chamber of Commerce, Elmira, New York (3 May 1907); published in *Addresses and Papers of Charles Evans Hughes, Governor of New York, 1906–1908* (1908), p. 139.
25. Andrew M. Siegel, 'Constitutional theory, constitutional culture', *Journal of Constitutional Law* xviii/4 (2016).
26. Brodocz, 'Verfassunggebung in konsolidierten Demokratien', p. 45.
27. In the theoretical literature see Mark Tushnet, 'Constitution', in M. Rosenfeld and A. Sajó (eds), *The Oxford Handbook of Comparative Constitutional Law* (Oxford, 2012), p. 222; Gardner, 'Can there be a written constitution?', pp. 23, 35. In the literature on the unwritten US constitution, see Akhil Reed Amar, *America's Unwritten Constitution. The Precedents and Principles We Live By* (New York, 2012); Akhil Reed Amar, 'American constitutionalism – written, unwritten, and living', *Harvard Law Review Forum* cxxvi/195 (2013); Keith E. Whittington, 'The status of unwritten constitutional conventions in the United States', *University of Illinois Law Review* 2013/5, pp. 1847–70; Stephen E. Sachs, 'The "unwritten constitution" and unwritten law', *Illinois Law Review*, 2013/5, pp. 1797–1846; Jason Mazzone, 'Federalism unwritten', *Illinois Law Review*, 2013/5, pp. 1871–1934. Lawrence B. Solumn, 'Originalism and the unwritten constitution', *Illinois Law Review*, 2013/5, pp. 1935–84; Michael W. McConnell, 'Ways to think about unenumerated rights', *Illinois Law Review*, 2013/5, pp. 1985–98.
28. Gardner, 'Can there be a written constitution?', p. 11.
29. Rady refers to two different meanings of customary law in Hungary, depending on the level of the courts which determined its content. While in the case law of the primary courts customary law reflected the prevalent social practices, at the Curia or courts of appeals customary law rather meant the case law or precedents

of the courts of appeal. See M. Rady, *Customary Law in Hungary. Courts, Texts and the Tripartitum* (Oxford, 2015).

30. Here unwritten is understood in a highly strict sense: it excludes, besides written legal documents adopted by the legislator or any executive body, any kind of written documents including judicial decisions. Consequently, unwritten customary law is contrasted in this respect to both legislative–executive acts *and* judicial decisions. It is a living custom. See James B. Murphy, *The Philosophy of Customary Law* (Oxford, 2014).

31. In this respect, it is irrelevant how constitutional law and constitutions are enacted (specific supermajorities) since unwritten constitutional conventions or customs, being highly important conventions of the community, prevail only if a wide range (even wider than specific supermajorities in the case of written constitutional norms) of political actors *deliberately* accept their directives *in fact*. One could even argue that effective constitutional conventions or customs are approved by an even *broader agreement* than *qualified majorities*, which are the usual requirements for constitutional laws. For this point, see Tushnet, 'Constitution', p. 223.

32. Murphy, *The Philosophy of Customary Law*, p. 120.

33. Amanda Perreau-Saussin and James B. Murphy (eds), *The Nature of Customary Law. Legal, Historical and Philosophical Perspectives* (Cambridge, 2007); Nicholas Barber, *The Constitutional State* (Oxford, 2010); Murphy, *The Philosophy of Customary Law*.

34. Barber, *The Constitutional State*, p. 89.

35. The following list is based on Richard Albert, 'How unwritten constitutional norms change written constitutions', *Dublin University Law Journal* xxxviii/2 (2015), pp. 2–26, and Nicholas W. Barber and Adrian Vermeule, 'The exceptional role of courts in constitutional order', *Notre Dame Law Review* xcii/2 (2016), pp. 817–58.

36. Árpád Erdei, 'Az alkotmánybírósági eljárás', in B. Bitskey (ed.), *Tíz éves az Alkotmánybíróság* (Budapest, 2000), pp. 181–90.

37. Adrian Vermeule, 'The atrophy of constitutional powers', *Oxford Journal of Legal Studies* xxxii/3 (2012), pp. 421–44.

38. For the term 'desuetudo' in Hungarian constitutional history, see László Péter, '*Ius resistendi* in Hungary', in Miklós Lojkó (ed.), *Hungary's Long Nineteenth Century: Constitutional and Democratic Traditions in European Perspective: Studies by László Péter* (Leiden and Boston, MA, 2012), p. 122, and László Péter, 'The primacy of consuetudo in Hungarian law', in M. Rady (ed.), *Custom and Law in Central Europe* (Cambridge, 2003), p. 104. On 'desuetudo' more generally, see Richard Albert, 'Constitutional amendment by constitutional desuetudo', *American Journal of Comparative Law* lxii/2 (2014), pp. 641–86.

39. David S. Law, 'The myth of imposed constitution', in D.J. Galligan and M. Versteeg (eds), *Social and Political Foundations of Constitutions* (Cambridge, 2013), pp. 239–69.

40. Péter, *Ius resistendi*, p. 122.

41. Xenophon Contiades (ed.), *Engineering Constitutional Change. A Comparative Perspective on Europe, Canada and the USA* (London and New York, 2013).
42. For the latter, see Chapter 9 in this volume.
43. András Jakab, *Az új Alaptörvény keletkezése és gyakorlati következményei* (Budapest, 2011), p. 199.
44. As a very early reflection on the question of disruption see Péter Paczolay, 'A történeti alkotmány és a konzervatív jogi gondolkodás', in L. Tőkéczki (ed.), *Magyar konzervativizmus, hagyomány és jelenkor* (Budapest, 1994), p. 34. Péter Paczolay served as the president of the Hungarian Constitutional Court from 2008 to 2015, and expressed his reservations about the revival of the historical constitution even during and after the constitution-making process of 2011. For that see P. Paczolay, 'Alkotmány és történelem', speech at the conference of the Association of Hungarian History Teachers, 8 October 2011. Available at http://tte.hu/paczolay-peter-alkotmany-es-toertenelem/ (accessed 3 March 2018).
45. Márton Zászkaliczky, 'Eszmetörténeti szempontok a történeti alkotmányosság közép- és kora újkori magyarországi történetéhez', *Közjogi Szemle* 2015/3, pp. 14–25.
46. Kees Teszelszky, *Az ismeretlen korona* (Pannonhalma, 2009).
47. Speech of J. Antal of 22 May 1990. For a general assessment of his approach to Hungarian history, see Zoltán Gábor Szűcs, '"A közjogi folytonosság házában": A nemzeti történelem Antall József felfogásában', *2000: Irodalmi és Társadalmi Havilap* xvii/1 (2005), pp. 44–53.
48. Zoltán Gábor Szűcs, *Az antalli pillanat: A nemzeti történelem szerepe a magyar politikai diskurzusban, 1989–1993* (Budapest, 2010).
49. William Partlett, 'Restoration constitution-making', *Vienna Journal on International Constitutional Law* ix/4 (2015), pp. 514–47.
50. On the restoration of the former Latvian constitution see Sigita Urdze, 'Latvia', in A. Fruhstorfer and M. Hein (eds), *Constitutional Politics in Central and Eastern Europe* (Wiesbaden, 2017), pp. 413–15.
51. Michael Rosenfeld, *The Identity of the Constitutional Subject: Selfhood, Citizenship, Culture, and Community* (London and New York, 2010), pp. 73–126.

CHAPTER 11

EPILOGUE: ON THE FUTURE(S) OF THE HISTORICAL CONSTITUTION

Ferenc Hörcher and Kálmán Pócza

Preliminary Considerations

By surveying the different connotations of the term 'historical constitution' in Hungarian political thought and practice, this book provides a general overview of an issue which is still topical in present-day Hungarian political debate. Each chapter of the book examines what exactly was meant by politicians and theoreticians in different historical periods when they referred to the idea of a historical constitution in their speeches and writings, or when they reformulated its legal framework according to their own particular political interests. This history of the idea and practice of the historical constitution will prove useful, therefore, to readers engaged in the history of political thought, constitutional history or, more generally, those simply interested in the constitutional development of a Central European country.

Some clarifications concerning the present-day relevance of the idea of a historical constitution have been made in the Introduction and in the previous chapter. However, as a collective endeavour of scholars who work in different disciplinary backgrounds in both the British and the Hungarian academic communities, this book also needs to assess the prospects of the present constitutional rearrangements. Although having provided details of the historical development and theoretical reflections upon some of the key issues in Hungary's constitutional history, it is not the purpose of this book to provide a comprehensive overview of the constitutional history of Hungary. Rather, its focus falls upon one specific aspect of Hungarian constitutionalism: the dynamic changes that occurred within what came to be called the 'historical constitution'.

Beyond these considerations, however, readers may find themselves pondering some further questions. One might question the general utility of this attempt. Setting aside the question of whether the 'historical' narrative will prevail or simply disappear in the Hungarian political arena, one might be interested in whether and to what extent the revival of the idea of a historical constitution might be useful or beneficial in both Hungarian and European political and constitutional thought (and practice). Also, one might wonder what kind of *normative* arguments and counter-arguments might underpin or delegitimize the *desirability* of this revival and its ideological background. Let us briefly examine each of these issues separately.

The Utility of the Revival

If one accepts the premise that the Hungarian political community exhibits certain features symptomatic of a post-traumatic society, the question is whether, and if so, how, the search for a traditional constitutional framework, one that was violently disrupted by German and Soviet totalitarian invaders, might play a positive role in repairing political injuries and healing the 'wounds' of public mentality. One can hardly doubt that a historically traumatized society, one that is itself not innocent of atrocities, needs to reflect on its own recent past. Moreover, it can be argued that it needs to find its way back to the point when its constitutional tradition was broken if it wants to rebuild its broken sense of communal identity. It is in this context that the revival of the historical constitution might be seen to fit into a more general narrative of community-building, one that is intended to recreate emotional ties among community members by offering them a chance to engage with a common historical heritage.

Of course, these claims lead to the further question of whether the introduction of 'historical' constitutionalism is indeed a tool that is conducive to the reconstruction of a 'lost' Hungarian political community. Historical narratives may well strengthen the emotional ties among members of the political community. But they can have the opposite effect, too. According to László Péter: 'The Holy Crown tradition is conducive to social and national cohesion. It undoubtedly has been for many people; at the same time, however, it has been culturally divisive, too [...] the doctrine creates social conflict as well as healing it.'[1] While right-wing voters tend to back the historicization of politics in Hungary, and politically less committed voters might also support a search for historical 'justice' and the reconstruction of the political community's identity, opponents of the Orbán government have sharply criticized attempts to revive historical constitutionalism as an anachronistic, partisan effort on the part of the governing party. Indeed, it can be regarded as an effort to turn the public gaze towards a nostalgic past and away from the challenges of the moment and prospects of the future. Thus, just as historical reminiscences, including references to the historical constitution in the Fundamental Law, can be seen as peaceful, if one-sided, efforts to re-establish the political community which was destroyed by the German and Russian occupation, so too can they be seen as obstacles to that very same end.[2] Counter-narratives that strongly criticize the historical narrative of the right-wing government or indeed the conduciveness of any historical narratives to the cause of community building are highly prominent in the Hungarian political arena, as well as in scholarly disputes.[3] Thus, for the time being, it is difficult to estimate whether community-building through the use of historical narratives (including references to the historical constitution) will be successful or not at the national level.

The Desirability of the Revival

Beyond the question of utility there is a further issue which should be addressed here. While the feasibility of the historicization of politics remains open to debate, and requires a descriptive answer, the problem of whether the revival of the historical constitution might be desirable or not proves to be a normative one. This problem is more serious as several political commentators and movements argue that even if 'historical' constitutionalism may serve certain utilitarian ends, there is no need for this revival.

This challenge of desirability brings us back to methodological questions. Because there is no place for normative argumentation in historical reconstructions of the past, the question of the desirability of the revival of the historical constitution comprises a problem that could not be tackled in a scholarly manner in the chapters of this book. In this epilogue, we, too, wish to remain close to the general tenor of this book, and avoid the thorny set of issues that are related to the question of normativity. Nevertheless, the question of whether or not the revival of the historical constitution is desirable for this political community is something that needs to be addressed, at least in an epilogue, and thus we feel we cannot entirely avoid confronting the normative question.

As argued in the previous chapter, one of the most significant challenges to the revival of the historical constitution is the concern that this would increase legal uncertainty. Missing dogmatics, differences between the legal formulations of different epochs, and an uncertain corpus of relevant legal norms might increase the leeway available to political agents to (re)formulate abstract categories according to their particular interests, at the same time undercutting the legitimacy of politicians who are prepared to embrace the idea for less partisan, although still undoubtedly 'political', ends. Furthermore, the above-mentioned obstacles might hamper the successful work of the judges of the constitutional court, who are otherwise entitled to phrase and determine the exact meaning of the basic rules of the political community in particular legal disputes. From these perspectives, increasing uncertainty is reflected both in the formal question of what exactly the historical constitution consists in, and in the substantive question of how the historical constitution should be interpreted in a legal environment of codified law books.

But before addressing these issues, we must first determine, *in abstracto*, how legal certainty emerges and, secondly, whether providing legal certainty is really the most important function of a constitution, or whether there are further, competing constitutional priorities.

How does Legal Certainty Emerge?

First, one should detect which factors contribute decisively to the creation of legal certainty: is it the text of a constitution, or the practices of a constitutional body (for example the Constitutional Court), or perhaps the more-or-less uniform, or at least coordinated, interpretation of the text by the community of legal scholars, lawyers and politicians in general (i.e. the constitutional culture of a given political community)? Here, we argue that the legal–constitutional culture of those involved in constitutional interpretation, and the institutional mechanisms of law enforcement, are the decisive factor. This is due in part to the abstract level of constitutional language, and also to the high number of problematic cases in constitutional adjudication.[4] When the external boundaries of the semantic fields of written constitutional regulations are vague or ambiguous, the ways in which practitioners of constitutional interpretation rely on each other's work and on institutional dialogue to resolve disputed cases is of decisive importance. In other words: be it a codified constitution or an unwritten/historical one, it is not the dead words of the text of the law that will determine the exact meaning of the constitution, but the internal dynamics of those participating in its interpretation. This means that in constitutional deliberation – perhaps even more so than in other branches of the law – the know-how or tacit knowledge of the judges and the legal community becomes more relevant than the know-what or explicit contents of the texts.[5] There is no strict syllogistic procedure that can be applied as a 'magic formula', which leads from the facts of the case, the text of the legal norm, and the interpretation of their relationship, straight to the actual judgement. For this reason, the internal exchanges of those participating in constitutional debates and constitutional interpretation are of crucial importance, as decisions will ultimately result from the practical wisdom, experience and traditions of these practitioners. In other words, it is within the internal dynamics of the legal profession that legal certainty is worked out, and it cannot be safeguarded simply by an *a priori* assumption that constitutions need to take the form of charters.

To verify the above claim, let us examine whether the adjudicative practices of a constitutional court can alone engender legal certainty. If the bulk of the court's decisions do not meet the expectations of the legal and political community, legal uncertainty might emerge as a result of the contradictory interpretations of the constitution by the court, on the one hand, and the professional and lay community, on the other. Consequently, the common horizon of expectations of the legal and political community is certainly more decisive in this process of securing legal certainty than any written formula or court decision.

What the constitution consists of heavily depends on the common sense of the legal profession and the political community. In sum, what is decisive is not the written document or the practice of constitutional courts alone which provide and maintain legal certainty, but the norms and expectations of the legal and political community.[6]

Functions of a Constitution

However, even if we accept that the common horizon of expectations is the decisive element in guaranteeing legal certainty, there are further problems. One should realize, for example, that positions arguing the undesirability of the revival of the genre of the historical constitution are based on an implicit unfounded presumption. The point of departure of these critical positions is the assumption that the dominant (or even exclusive) function of modern constitutions is to establish power, defend the individual rights of citizens and secure legal certainty and calculability.[7] Certainly, it is true that modern constitutions both constitute and constrain political power at the same time. Furthermore, they will only endure if they can provide legal certainty. But is that all? Or do constitutions have any further important functions?

According to the literature on constitutional theory, constitutions can assume functions in addition to those mentioned above. No doubt, on one level, constitutions reflect the power struggle and power relations of the daily politics of the moment of the constitution-making process, and in more fortunate cases, they can also express the fundamental values of the political community.[8] Certainly, creative interpretation can help to reshape it when the power structure of the community is dramatically changed. But constitutions also possess a symbolic dimension, beyond creating and constraining political power. They have to sum up various social and political practices, relevant interpretations of the nation's past, constitutional myths, memorial days, and political debates over the correct form of social order. They are thus symbolic expressions of the debates on divergent visions of the long-term political and social order.[9] They can serve as symbolic tools for social integration, as the example of the early or the post-Civil War US constitution or the constitution of the German Federal Republic after World War II demonstrates. Constitutions may acquire a totemic or symbolic importance, and therefore contribute to social cohesion. It is, however, not necessary for the constitution to serve as a tool of social integration, as there may be different means of completing this integrative function. In France, for example, it is not the constitution which serves as a dew point of the integration process, but the idea of the nation and its *gloire*. In Germany, for many years following the Bismarck era, it was the abstract concept of the State which served as a focal point of social integration.[10] With some theoretical reservations, we could argue that in Hungary the idea of the historical constitution and the Holy Crown were the central *loci* of this imaginative process of creating a community out of the multitude of different social and religious groups.[11]

A constitutional practice based on this extended meaning of the term generates emotional ties that act to promote the process of social integration, even if the concepts of political order symbolized by constitutions vary heavily over time and/or within one and the same political community in a given period.[12] Constitutions necessarily contain highly general and often stylistically elevated abstract terms and phrases, and as a consequence they cannot help but to induce different interpretations or visions of political order. Surely, social cohesion will rarely be created by judicial interpretation. Social cohesion and community building needs more emotion and less rigid legal logic and juridical rationality.[13] Here politics is once again at the forefront: a political community cannot be governed in the long run without construing a sense of community that appeals to the emotional dispositions of its members and their groups. And for this reason, the most important functions of constitutions will never be exhausted by constituting or constraining political power and maintaining legal certainty — even if constraining power and providing legal certainty is an unquestionable function of them according to the principle of the rule of law. But like it or not, it seems inevitable that modern constitutions stand at the focal point of social integration processes that presuppose some kind of emotional engagement. Whether constitutions can fulfil this function in an appropriate manner might be evaluated on an individual basis, and unfortunately only retrospectively. Whether the new Fundamental Law of Hungary and its supposed return to the historical constitution will achieve these goals at any time in the future remains an open (political and practical) question to be answered in the decades to come. But it is undeniable that constitutions, including the Fundamental Law of Hungary, play a highly important role that extends well beyond the formal functions of the constitution mentioned above.

Final Considerations

The questions posed in this Epilogue, of course, are further connected to those direct political criticisms of the constitutional practice of the present government which are not directly connected to the historical constitution, and therefore could not be addressed here. But there is no doubt that the assessment of the present political situation in Hungary will be a key to one's assessment of the (un)reasonability of introducing this idea into the text of the basic law.[14] In fact, this is necessarily so according to the rules of the game we call symbolic politics. On the other hand, the historical overview provided in this book has hopefully also helped to clarify the issues around which the political debate is evolving, and this epilogue tried to identify the possible non-political rationale of this hotly debated constitutional rearrangement.

With these reservations let us conclude by expressing the hope that we provided arguments which help to find answers to the well-defined questions we posed. If that is granted, the normative question whether it is desirable to revive the idea of the historical constitution could be transformed into another one: since constitutions might have several functions, the question is whether the integrative function of the Hungarian constitution would be furthered or blocked by the revival of the historical constitution. To answer this transformed question, those who are proponents of the revival process must prove that the restoration of the historical constitution will be able to promote the social integration of the political community. Those who do not accept that a revival might have such beneficial effects are expected to give reasons why they think the integrative function is not furthered by the new constitutional arrangement. In addition, irrespective of whether or not the integrative function will be fulfilled, there remains a further question: at what price, with what risks, and how effectively this integrative function would occur. These are, however, questions that will only be answered by the mid- and long-term fate of Hungary's historical constitution.

Notes

1. László Péter, 'The Holy Crown of Hungary, visible and invisible', in Miklós Lojkó (ed.), László Péter, *Hungary's Long Nineteenth Century: Constitutional and Democratic Traditions in European Perspective: Studies by László Péter* (Leiden and Boston, MA, 2012), p. 109.

2. A recent overview of the relationship between the historical constitution and the Fundamental Law is András Zs. Varga, 'Történeti alkotmányunk vívmányai az Alaptörvény kógens rendelkezéseiben', *Iustum Aequum Salutare* xii/4 (2016), pp. 83–9.
3. István Császár and Balázs Majtényi, 'Hungary: The historic constitution as the place of memory', in M. Suksi, K. Agapiou-Josephides, J-P. Lehners and M. Nowak (eds), *First Fundamental Rights Documents in Europe* (Cambridge, 2015), pp. 57–69; Gábor Halmai, 'The Hungarian constitutional court and constitutional identity', *Verfassungsblog*, 10 January 2017, available at http://verfassungsblog.de/the-hungarian-constitutional-court-and-constitutional-identity/ (accessed 3 March 2018). In Hungarian: Zoltán Szente, 'A historizáló alkotmányozás problémái – a történeti alkotmány és a Szent Korona az új Alaptörvényben', *Közjogi Szemle* iv/3 (2011), pp. 1–13.
4. In order to assess the problems of constitutional culture in this region, the present writers organized an international conference, entitled 'Constitutional Culture in Western and Central Europe', at Pázmány Péter Catholic University in Budapest, in November 2013. For the executive summary of the conference plan, see https://btk.ppke.hu/uploads/articles/220225/file/coCu6-jav_logo.pdf (accessed 3 March 2018). For a recent overview of the normative relevance of constitutional culture, see Andrew M. Siegel, 'Constitutional Theory, Constitutional Culture', Seattle University School of Law Research Paper. Available at http://scholarship.law.upenn.edu/cgi/viewcontent.cgi?article=1600&context=jcl (accessed 3 March 2018).
5. For different ways of presenting the distinction between know-how and know-what, see the relevant works of Michael Oakeshott, Michael Polányi and Gilbert Ryle.
6. Let us take the example of Britain: this is a country which runs along the lines of an unwritten constitution, and few would claim that its constitutional life is disabled by the legal uncertainty caused by the traditional nature of its constitution. It is true that there, too, we find critics who would like to see the introduction of a written, codified constitution; and in fact, recent political efforts, including the introduction of radical institutional changes, have eroded much of the unwritten nature of the British constitution.
7. Legal certainty was a key concept for the first president of the Constitutional Court of Hungary, László Sólyom, who regarded it as even more important than a more substantial notion of justice. With respect to the first constitutional court, one should take into account the fact that it had the historical mission to safeguard the legality of the regime transition of 1989/90, and establish the rule of law in the country. However, the simplifying assumption that the defence of individual rights is the primary aim of the constitution is widespread among constitutional lawyers these days. In turn, political scientists, theorists and philosophers note that this important function is not an exclusive one. On this point in a US context see Ioannis G. Dimitrakopoulos, *Individual Rights and Liberties under the U.S. Constitution. The Case Law of the U.S. Supreme Court* (Leiden and Boston, MA, 2007).

8. On various functions of constitutions see Denis J. Galligan and Mila Versteeg, 'Theoretical perspectives on the social and political foundations of constitutions', in D. J. Galligan and M. Versteeg (eds), *Social and Political Foundations of Constitutions* (Cambridge, 2013), pp. 3–50.
9. For the thesis that constitutions have a highly important symbolic dimension and have, consequently, an integrative function, see Hans Vorländer, 'Constitutions as symbolic orders', in P. Blokker and C. Thornhill (eds), *Sociological Constitutionalism* (Cambridge, 2017), pp. 209–40. See also the analysis of the Fundamental Law of Hungary from the perspective of communal values in Ferenc Hörcher, 'Communal values in the new Hungarian Fundamental Law: The Habermas–Ratzinger debate and the use of the humanities in constitutional interpretation', in E. Bos and K. Pócza (eds), *Verfassunggebung in konsolidierten Demokratien: Neubeginn oder Verfall eines Systems?* (Baden-Baden, 2014), pp. 346–64.
10. Hans Vorländer, 'Integration durch Verfassung? Die symbolische Bedeutung der Verfassung im politischen Integrationsprozess', in H. Vorländer (ed.), *Integration durch Verfassung* (Wiesbaden, 2002), p. 24.
11. Certainly, the idea and the meanings of the term 'Holy Crown' changed over time; nevertheless, with varying and frequently contested connotations, the Holy Crown served for several hundred years as the focal point of Hungarian political discourse. For the various meanings of the concept of the Holy Crown in Hungary see Ferenc Eckhart, *A szentkorona-eszme története* (Budapest, 1941).
12. André Brodocz, *Die symbolische Dimension der Verfassung* (Wiesbaden, 2003), p. 228.
13. Chris Thornhill, *A Sociology of Constitutions* (Cambridge, 2011), pp. 1–20.
14. For readers interested in Hungarian politics after 2010 see: John O'Sullivan and Kálmán Pócza (eds), *The Second Term of Viktor Orbán. Beyond Prejudice and Enthusiasm* (London, 2015).

PRIMARY SOURCES ON HUNGARIAN CONSTITUTIONAL HISTORY

APPENDIX I
THE GOLDEN BULL OF 1222[1]

[NB: the numbering of the articles is a seventeenth-century innovation.]

In the name of the Holy Trinity and Indivisible Unity. Andrew, by grace of God, King of Hungary, Dalmatia, Croatia, Rama, Serbia, Galicia and Lodomeria. In perpetuity.

Since the liberties established by the king, St Stephen, in favour of the nobles of our realm as well as of other persons have been much diminished by the might of certain kings, some of whom took vengeance out of personal spite, others of whom paid heed to the false counsel of wicked and self-seeking men, these same nobles have repeatedly importuned our Serenity and that of their kings, our predecessors, with numerous pleas and entreaties for the reform of our kingdom.

We therefore desiring to fulfil their petition in all respects, as we should, especially because this situation has often led to no small bitterness between them and us, which it befits to avoid so that the royal dignity be preserved, which can be achieved by none better than they, do grant both to them and to other men of our kingdom the liberty given by the holy king, and we usefully ordain as follows what further pertains to the reformation of the state of our kingdom:

(1) That we are bound to celebrate the feast of St Stephen annually in Székesfehérvár unless we be beset by some urgent matter or prevented by illness. And if we cannot be present, the Palatine will definitely be there for us, and shall hear cases in our place, and all the servientes who wish shall freely gather there.

(2) It is further our wish that neither we nor our successors should at any time seize or cause the ruin of any serviens for the benefit of some mighty man, unless they be first summoned and duly sentenced by judicial process.

(3) Again, we shall gather neither the *collecta* nor the freemen's pennies on the estates of servientes, nor shall we exact hospitality in their houses or villages unless invited. We shall not gather the *collecta* at all from the people attached to their churches.

(4) Should a serviens die without a son, his daughter shall receive a quarter of his possessions, but he may dispose of the rest as he chooses. And if prevented by death, he shall not have been able to make arrangement, those kinsmen closer to him shall obtain them. If he has no kin at all, the king will obtain them.

(5) The lords of the counties shall not judge the estates of servientes, except in case of coinage and tithes. The lords of the counties shall judge no one at all except the people of their castle. Thieves and robbers shall be judged by royal judges, but only in the presence of the lord.

(6) Again, people united in a sworn association shall not be able to accuse thieves, as they have been accustomed to do.

(7) If the king, however, wishes to lead an army outside the kingdom, the servientes shall not be obliged to accompany him unless at his own expense and after his return he shall not take the fine of campaign from them. Should, however, an army descend on the kingdom from abroad, all are obliged to go, without exception. Also, if we lead an army outside the kingdom, all those who have counties or receive money from us are bound to accompany us.

(8) The Palatine shall judge impartially all the men of our kingdom, but cases involving nobles, which lead to the loss of the head or the loss of possessions shall not be concluded without the

king's knowledge. He shall not have deputies, except the one at his own court.

(9) Our lord of the court, may judge everyone for as long as he resides in court, and shall have the right to conclude cases anywhere that have been started there, but when he stays on his estate he shall not be able to send out his bailiff or cite parties to law.

(10) If any retainer, having an honour, dies on campaign, his son or kinsman shall be granted a similar honour; and if a serviens dies in the same way, his son shall be given as the king deems fit.

(11) If foreigners, namely good men, come to the kingdom, they shall not be raised to dignities without the consent of the kingdom.

(12) The wives of those who die either by sentence of death or by falling in duel or by any other cause shall not be cheated out of their dower.

(13) Retainers may follow the court or travel anywhere only inasmuch as the poor are not oppressed or despoiled by them.

(14) If any lord does not honourably conduct himself according to the character of his county [office] or ruins the people of his castle, he shall upon conviction be dishonourably deprived of his office before the whole kingdom and return what has been taken.

(15) Grooms, houndsmen and falconers shall not dare to descend upon the villages of servientes.

(16) We shall not bestow in perpetuity whole counties or any other dignities as estates or possessions.

(17) No one shall at any time, moreover, be deprived of possessions obtained by proper service.

(18) Again, servientes who have received permission from us can freely go to our son, or from the older to the younger, without their possessions being destroyed. We shall not receive anyone whom our son has condemned by proper judgement or whose case has been opened before him until it be concluded in his court, and our son shall do likewise.

(19) Castle warriors shall be maintained in the liberty established by the holy king. Similarly, foreign guests of whatever nation shall be maintained in the liberty originally granted them.

(20) The tithe shall not be paid in silver but, as the earth brings it forth, rendered in wine and grain, and should the bishops object, we will not support them.

(21) The bishops shall not give over to our horses the tithe on the estates of servientes, nor shall their people be obliged to convey these tithes to royal estates.
(22) Our pigs shall not be pastured in the forests or meadows of the servientes against their will.
(23) Our new coins shall be valid for a year, from Easter to Easter, and pennies shall be the same as they were under King Béla.
(24) Ishmaelites and Jews shall not be made lords of the chamber of the mint, of salt and of toll [or] nobles of the kingdom.
(25) Salt shall not be stored in the centre of the kingdom, except in Szalacs and Szeged, and in the borderlands.
(26) Possessions shall not be granted outside the kingdom; if some have been granted or sold, they shall be returned to the people of the kingdom for redemption.
(27) The sable tax shall be rendered in the manner established by King Koloman.
(28) If someone has been condemned by judicial process, no man of might may protect him.
(29) Lords shall enjoy only the rights of their county office; the rest that pertains to the king, namely the bucket tax, tolls, the ox tax and two-thirds of castle dues, the king shall obtain.
(30) Again, none other than these four retainers – the Palatine, the ban, and the lords of the court of the king and queen – shall hold two offices.
(31) And in order that this grant and ordinance of ours shall be valid in our time as well as in that of our successors for ever more, we have ordered that seven identical letters be drawn up and confirmed with our golden seal, so that one copy be sent to the lord pope that he may have it copied in his register, a second copy in the keeping of the Hospital, a third in the keeping of the Temple, a fourth with the king, a fifth with the chapter of Esztergom, a sixth with that of Kalocsa, and the seventh shall be reserved for the incumbent Palatine, so that he, having this text always in his sight, shall not depart in any way from the aforesaid, nor shall he permit the king, the nobles or anyone else to depart from it, so that they may rejoice in their liberty and on this account remain always faithful to us and our successors and not deny the obedience due to the royal crown.

Appendix I

We have also decreed that if we or any of our successors should at any time seek to go against this settlement, both the bishops and the retainers and the nobles of the kingdom, in common or singularly, now and in future, have by this authority for ever more the freedom to resist and speak against us and our successors, without the taint of infidelity.

Given by the hand of Cletus, chancellor of our court and dean of the church of Eger, in the year of the Incarnation of the Word 1222, when the venerable John is Archbishop of Esztergom, the venerable Ugrin the Archbishop of Kalocsa, Desiderius the Bishop of Csanád, Robert of Veszprém, Thomas of Eger, Stephen of Zagreb, Alexander of Várad, Bartholomew of Pécs, Cosmas of Győr and Briccius of Vác, in the seventeenth year of our reign.

Note

1. Re-translated, with the kind permission of Charles Schlacks, from the text published in János M. Bak et al. (eds), *Decreta Regni Mediaevalis Hungariae – The Laws of the Medieval Kingdom of Hungary 1000–1301* (Idyllwild, CA, 1999), pp. 32–5.

APPENDIX II

THE RÁKOS DECLARATION (1505)[1]

We Thomas, cardinal of St Martin ai Monti of the Holy Roman Church, and Gregory of Frankopan, archbishops of Esztergom and of the canonically united Kalocsa and Bács, and Sigismund Thurzó bishop of Transylvania, George bishop of Oradea, royal chancellor, Francis bishop of Győr, Nicholas Csáki bishop of Csanád, Nicholas Báthori bishop of Vác, Stephen bishop of Nitra, and John Ország bishop-elect of Srem, and Bartholomew prior of Vrana and count of Dubica; item Emeric Perényi, perpetual count of Abaújvár, Palatine and Judge of the Cumans, Count Peter count of Sväty Júr and Pezinok, judge royal and voivode of Transylvania [followed by 29 named barons and principal office-holders, and a further 24 lesser office-holders]; item Stephen Keserű of Gibarth and Ladislas of Sveti Petar of Vukovar County; Francis Herczeg of Szekcső, Stephen Istvánffy of Kisasszonyfalva, John Bika of Teremhegy, George Orbonász of Caraşova and Leonard Dacsó de Őr of Baranya County [followed by a further 69 persons listed by county], all the aforesaid nobles, lords and magnates of the same kingdom gathered at our present Diet and general assembly on the Field of Rákos, ordered by our lord, King Wladislas, for the feast day just passed of the Blessed Archangel Michael, do commend to all by these presents the following. Since nothing on earth is more pleasing to God or commensurate with human nature than a common fatherland where all men may gather, it is proper to have most ample and diligent discussion and to expend every effort, endeavour and care, and indeed every thought and purpose, on the welfare and security of the fatherland and its people, so that it be safe and sound, and to defend it both now and in the perilous times ahead with precision and vigilance, and thus ward off the dangers which may easily befall it on account of the carelessness and sloth of its guardians, so that it may reside in safety and tranquillity and be fast on every side. We, therefore, being always mindful of the grievous and almost complete waste and want of this renowned kingdom of Hungary, wishing in the manner of the best gentlemen of the realm and as lovers and guardians of our fatherland responsibly to discuss its desolation and the urgent threat to it, have held many diets, rendering there great and unimaginable effort, labour and expense. And some matters were on these occasions improved and made right on account of these endeavours and efforts, but we ascertained one in particular that has overwhelmingly reduced this kingdom of ours to ruin and exhaustion, and to shameful desolation and disfigurement in all its parts. It is that this kingdom has on very many occasions been ruled by alien and foreign lords and kings. Whichever way we look at those times, it is easily apparent that this kingdom never suffered greater damage, danger and desolation than when it was held and governed by a foreign rulership not of its language. For these foreign rulers pursued their private affairs, and before they came to learn the manners and customs of this Scythian people (which just as it originally took this kingdom with the greatest shedding of its blood and the enormous death of its kinsmen, is still accustomed to defend itself with weapons of iron), always inclined more to idle ease than to arms. It is a fact that Bosnia, Serbia, Halych, Volodymyr, Bulgaria and Dalmatia, and many other fortified places, were lost to this kingdom by their neglect, to such an extent that, with the extremities lopped off, we are astonished that the attacks of the enemy have not reached the centre. We judge losses to have been far fewer when this Hungarian people, drawn by the sweetness of the native soil, chose for themselves a suitable king not from among foreign nations but from their own people. For brevity's sake, we omit the deeds and splendid accomplishments of the most serene Andrew II, namely the father of King Béla IV, and of Louis and Matthias and of other godlike kings of Hungary (by which they made the Scythian people not only resplendent and magnificent in name and reputation, but also spread and diffused its renown far and wide across the whole world and even to the heavens). None of these, who are known to have been raised to high kingly rank from the lineage of Hungary, incurred loss but they brought instead expansion and benefit to the kingdom; by contrast, those who were of a foreign nation have not only brought danger to this kingdom but also the greatest ignominy to this people, even to the extent that savage forces sometimes cruelly attack the innards of the kingdom. They wish on top of this that the greatest harm and supreme loss should befall us – that our current and most gracious lord, Lord Wladislas, king of Hungary and Bohemia, who has not only graciously governed and preserved us in all our grace and freedom but also renewed many of our liberties, should perish and die without male heirs, that we and this kingdom should remain in the greatest crisis and that some foreign prince should violently usurp the kingdom, reducing it to permanent servitude. Above all else, we are fully led by the reason that throughout the whole world there is no nation or people that does not choose its king and lord from its own people, blood and nation. Lest this kingdom, which is the bastion and shield of Christendom and which with great slaughter of its own has always defended Christendom, should seem humbler and more luckless than others, we have decided and in complete unanimity, both from the highest to the lowest and from the lowest to the highest, decreed and ordained that from now on whenever and however often this kingdom shall lack a prince and king, and there be no male heirs who by the law and custom of this kingdom are entitled to succeed, then we shall ever more choose as our king no one from foreign nations and their languages, but only a Hungarian who is fit and proper for the office of ruler, and we shall appoint him as our lord and king by equal vote and unanimous consent and will, and on the Field of Rákos and nowhere else, and elect, appoint and accept him. Since there are, however, several neighbouring princes and rulers, who strive daily to claim this kingdom for themselves, and who after the death of our aforementioned most serene king, should he die – God forfend! – without male heirs, or even in his own lifetime, may endeavour to assault or invade with arms this kingdom or its parts and appendages, and to subdue him and us by force of arms even, and lest in such a case this kingdom and its parts, and especially our kinsmen and friends on the frontier, are subdued by those who wish to occupy and take for themselves this kingdom without our unanimous election and our statute on this matter or in any other way, we have promised and sworn and do promise and swear in our persons and in the names of our succeeding heirs, all with the hand of obligation, we the prelates on the purity of our conscience, and we the barons, lords and nobles on our

Christian faith and on our honour and goodness that in such a case none shall desert the other, but each support one another with his entourage to uphold what has been prescribed above and the content of this statute of ours and, should there be the need, with as much might as he has to faithfully bring succour at all times, and, if necessary, the whole of this kingdom, and thus we, each and every one of us, are obliged to rise up to engage the enemy and to fight to the death for our fatherland. Nor, in the meantime, shall we conclude any treaty until and up to the point that we have secured our freedom from the enemy, freed with God's help this kingdom from attack or invasion, and returned it to a condition of peace. Should any of us presume to do contrary to the above then they shall be considered permanent traitors to the kingdom, whom neither the Royal Majesty then incumbent nor the entire kingdom may pardon, but they shall bear the yoke of perpetual servitude and servility without possibility of remission. Recorded in writing and confirmed by our seals (we the prelates and barons applying our seals with our true devices; we the aforesaid lords and nobles under the official seals of the aforementioned lords, Emeric Perényi, Count and Palatine, and Count Peter, Judge Royal and Voivode of Transylvania). Given on the aforesaid Field of Rákos, on the fifteenth day of our said general assembly. 1505.

Thirty-six impressed seals may still be counted below the text with additional impressions and spaces. No chancellery or notarial marks are discernible but there is a faint scribal monogram on the verso.

Note

1. Hungarian National Archives, State Archives (Magyar Nemzeti Levéltár, Országos Levéltára, hereafter MNL, OL), Section DL, 39335; the Latin text is also given in János M. Bak, *Königtum und Stände in Ungarn im 14.–16. Jahrhundert* (Wiesbaden, 1973), pp. 158–9; see also Henrik Marczali, *A magyar történet kútfőinek kézikönyve* (Budapest, 1901), pp. 317–20.

APPENDIX III

EXTRACTS FROM STEPHEN WERBŐCZY'S *TRIPARTITUM* (1517)[1]

Part One, Chapter 3

[6] But after the Hungarians came to recognize the truth and receive the Catholic faith, inspired by the grace of the Holy Spirit and through the efforts of our holy king, and they elected him their king and crowned him of their own free will, then the community, by the authority of the community, transferred to the jurisdiction of the holy crown of this realm and consequently to our prince and king, the right and full power of ennoblement, and therefore of donating estates that adorn the nobles and distinguish them from the non-nobles, together with supreme power and government. Hence now all nobility originates from him, and these two, by virtue of some mutual transfer and reciprocal bond between them, depend upon each other so closely that neither can be separated and detached from the other and neither can exist without the other.

[7] For the prince is elected only by the nobles, and nobles are created and adorned with the dignity of nobility only by the prince.

Part One, Chapter 9

The four privileged and chief liberties of noblemen

Although nobles possess a great number of liberties, as are set out in royal letters of privilege and statutes, the four which are regarded as the principal ones I have thought to list here.

Appendix III

(1) The first is that they cannot ever be arrested by anyone in their person at anyone's instance, complaint or request without being first cited or summoned and condemned by judicial process.

(2) This right, however, is extinguished in criminal deeds and cases, namely homicide, the burning of villages, theft, robbery, or banditry as well as violent adultery; in which cases any such person would lose the honour, title, and liberty of nobility. And, if possible, such a person can be freely detained even by a peasant hand at the place where the crime and wrong were committed and condemned according to his misdeeds and deservedly punished.

(3) However, if he flees the place of the wrong and evades the hands of his pursuers, afterwards he must not be condemned and punished unless by way of citation or summons and judicial process.

(4) The second liberty is that the nobles of the whole realm are subject to the power of no one other than the lawfully crowned prince (as explained above); even our prince himself may not, by virtue of his ordinary power, disturb any of them in his person or his belongings upon anyone's mere complaint and malevolent insinuation without legal proceedings and without the hearing the other part.

(5) The third is that they can freely use and enjoy as they will their legitimate [property] rights and all revenues within the boundaries of their estates at all times; they are held entirely exempt and free from any servile obligation, and from paying taxes and dues, tolls, customs, and the thirtieth. They need only to serve under arms in defence of the realm.

(6) The fourth (not to mention the others) and last one is that if any of our princes and kings would venture to act contrary to the liberties of the nobles stated and expressed in the general *decretum* of the most excellent prince our former lord King Andrew the Second, called 'of Jerusalem' (which decree every Hungarian king is wont to swear an oath to observe before the holy crown is placed on his head), then they have the perpetual liberty to resist and oppose without the taint of infidelity.

(7) By 'nobles' in this context you should understand in general all the lord prelates, barons, and the rest of the magnates, as well as the other lords of this realm, who (as explained above) are always protected by the prerogative of one and the same liberty.

Note

1. Re-translated, with the kind permission of Charles Schlacks, from the text published in János M. Bak et al. (eds), Stephen Werbőczy, *The Customary Law of the Renowned Kingdom of Hungary in Three Parts (The 'Tripartitum')* (*Decreta Regni Mediaevalis Hungariae*, Vol. 5) (Idyllwild, CA, and Budapest, 2005), pp. 50–1, 56–7.

APPENDIX IV

THE LAWS OF 1687[1]

Law I [The Coronation Oath]

We Joseph, by the Grace of God, king of Hungary etc., swear by the living God, by His most holy Mother the Virgin Mary, by all the saints: that we will keep the Churches of God, the prelates, barons, nobles, free cities, and all inhabitants of the country in their immunities and liberties, laws and privileges, and in their old, good and approved customs, as the king and the assembled Estates as the king and the assembled estates shall agree on the interpretation and application thereof; we will do justice to all, we will observe the decree of His Majesty Andrew of blessed memory (excepting and excluding Article 31 of that decree, from 'if we, etc.', to 'taint of infidelity'); we will not alienate nor diminish the frontiers of our kingdom of Hungary, nor of anything that belongs to it by whatever right or title, but rather increase and extend them so far as we are able; and we will do all else that we can justly do for the general good, honour and increase of all the estates and of all our kingdom of Hungary; so help us God and all the Saints.

Law II

[...] And in commemoration of these great and ever-memorable benefits [i.e. the liberation of the kingdom from Ottoman occupation], and in ever-visible token of their gratitude and humble devotion, the said estates of the realm of this kingdom of Hungary and of the territories attached thereto declare that in future they will for all time recognize as their legitimate lord and king none other than the male heir in primogeniture truly and lawfully begotten by this His Imperial and Royal Majesty (as already determined by Law V of 1547 and other laws relating thereto) and will therefore always, and whenever the occasion of such inauguration recurs, after reception of articles contained in the above-mentioned diploma, or royal assurance thereon, and oath taken in the form used by his predecessors, crown him in the assembled Diet within this kingdom of Hungary.

Note

1. The first English translation of these texts can be found in C.A. Macartney, *The Habsburg and Hohenzollern Dynasties in the Seventeenth and Eighteenth Centuries* (New York, 1970), pp. 85–6.

APPENDIX V

THE LAWS OF 1790/1[1]

A total of 74 laws were enacted at the Diet of 1790/1, many of which would not be considered to be of 'constitutional' standing in modern jurisprudence (for example, the royal oath refers to the pursuit of 'glory' and the 'aggrandizement' of the kingdom through conquest and the acquisition of dominion, while other laws deal with municipal issues, tax exemptions, and the naturalization of specifically named foreign nobles). Of prime constitutional importance, however, were Laws I and II. The first of these recorded how Leopold was to be crowned according to the hereditary laws of succession (Laws I and II of 1772/3), while the second stipulated that the Inaugural Diploma should retain the form of the by then 'traditional' diploma of 1711. Law III outlined how the inauguration and coronation of new rulers should take place within six months; this was designed to prevent any recurrence of Joseph's omission of the coronation oath. Law IV recorded the election of Archduke Alexander Leopold, the king's brother, as Palatine, who was to reside in Hungary and take command of the national armed forces, as stated in Law V. Law VI laid down that the Holy Crown was to be kept in Buda. Laws X and XII declared Hungary to be a free and independent kingdom, and also granted the nobility the shared right to enact, annul and interpret the laws. Law XIII stipulated that the Diet was to be held each three years in order to address both royal legislative proposals and the grievances of the nobility (later this Act was, of course, often ignored by Francis I). Law XIV affirmed that the Vice-Regal Council was the highest political organ in the country, and that Hungarians should make representations directly to the king if unlawful commands were issued to the country. Law XVI banned the introduction of 'foreign languages' (meaning German) in matters of government, while Law XVII declared that Hungarians would be appointed to the various ministries of state, and that they would be involved in decision making related to foreign affairs. Law XIX pronounced that no subsidies or contributions, whether in cash, kind or recruits, would be levied without the consent of the Diet. Law XXVI granted Protestants the right to practise their religion freely: they were free to build churches and schools without the oversight of the Catholic Church. However, matters pertaining to marriages and divorces were taken away from civil courts and handed over to ecclesiastical jurisdictions, where Catholics retained certain prerogatives. For example, mixed faith marriages could only be held before a Catholic priest, and lawsuits deriving from such marriages were brought before Catholic episcopal sees. Children born of such families were to be raised as Catholics if the father was Catholic; if the mother was Catholic, then the children would follow their parents' religion on the basis of gender. Conversion to Protestantism was to be reported to the king, and converts were required to undertake six weeks of religious education; if they still wished to convert afterwards then they were free to do so. Similarly to the above, Law XXVII affirmed the religious rights of the orthodox Greek or non-united church. Gambling was banned by Law XXXI. Law XXXV urged the nobility to treat their peasants fairly and ensure justice after the reinstatement of the manorial courts; otherwise it guaranteed peasants the right to move on 12 March of each year after settling debts to their lords and acquiring permission from the county's vice-lieutenant. The system of Maria Theresia's *Urbarium*, which regulated the upper limit of the peasantry's payments to the nobility, was left intact. Law XXXVIII granted Jews the right to relocate to all areas of Hungary from where they had been expelled (apart from mining towns). Law XLII banned the use of torture to exact confession, as physical punishment was restricted to criminal law. Finally, Law XLIII granted burghers and ignobles the right to appeal against court decisions, a privilege previously reserved for the nobility. While a detailed exploration or indeed exhaustive translation of these laws is beyond the scope of this book, what follows below is a brief sample of some of the above.

The Royal Oath Sworn by Leopold II upon his Coronation

We, Leopold II, supreme Roman Emperor chosen by God's grace, the Apostolic King of Germany, Hungary, Bohemia, Dalmatia, Croatia, Slavonia, etc., Archduke of Austria, etc., as the King of Hungary and its annexed lands as mentioned above, hereby swear to the living God, to his holy mother the Virgin Mary, and to all saints, that we shall preserve the Churches of God, the prince primate, knights of the banner, magnates and noble lords, the free cities, and kingdom-dwellers of all orders, in all their immunities and freedoms, rights, laws, privileges and in all their old good and accepted customs; we will administer justice to all; we will maintain the laws of the late Supreme King Andrew (except for and excluding the clause of Article 31 which begins: *Quodsi vero nos* etc., and continues up to the words: *in perpetuum facultatem*); we will not cede or sever the boundaries of our country, or indeed any of its parts that belong to it by right or title; indeed, we shall seek to enlarge and expand them insofar as it is possible, and do everything we justly can for the public good, glory, and aggrandizement of every order and all people of Hungary. May God and all his saints help us.

Article X of 1790/1

On the Independence of the Kingdom of Hungary and of the Parts Thereto Annexed

On the humble proposal of the Estates and Orders of the Realm, His most Sacred Majesty has deigned to recognize that although the Succession of the Female Line of the Austrian House – established in Hungary and the Parts thereto annexed by Laws I and II of 1723 – belongs according to the fixed Order of Succession, in indivisible and inseparable possession, to the same Prince to whom it belongs in the other kingdoms and hereditary domains situated inside or outside Germany; nevertheless, Hungary and the Parts thereto Annexed is a free Kingdom, and with regard to its entire lawful form of administration independent (including therein every branch of its Dicasteria [i.e. counties and municipalities]), that is, it is not subject to any other Kingdom or people, but possessed of its own Consistence and Constitution; therefore it must be ruled and governed by its hereditary and lawfully Crowned kings, consequently by His most Sacred Majesty too, and by his Successors, according to its own Laws and

Customs, and not after the example of other Provinces, as is stipulated by Law III of 1715 and Laws VIII and XI of 1741.

Article XII of 1790/1

On the Exercise of Legislative and Executive Power

That the Right to the enactment, abolition and interpretation of the laws in Hungary and her annexed Parts, without violation of law VIII of 1741, is jointly shared by the lawfully crowned Prince and the lawfully assembled Orders and Estates at the Diet, and that [this right] cannot be exercised with its [the Diet's] exclusion: His Sacred Majesty voluntarily acknowledges and gracefully declares that He shall uphold this right of the Orders as inviolate, and just as He has received it from his Divine Forebears, so too will He transmit this right to his August Successors unimpaired, thus assuring the Orders and Estates of the Realm that he shall never govern the Kingdom and its Annexed Parts through Edicts or so-called Patents, which in any case are never to be accepted by the Realm's Courts of Law; the issuing of Patents is reserved only for Matters whereby their Publication is the sole effective means of accomplishing a necessary end that is in any case concordant with the Law. Furthermore: The form of the judicatures as they have already been, or are to be, established by law, shall not be altered by Royal Authority; neither shall the execution of lawful sentences be obstructed by edict, nor shall their obstruction by others be permitted; nor shall the lawful sentences of the Law Courts be overruled, nor revised by the Crown, or indeed by any political office of government; instead, judges who are to be appointed without distinction of religion are to hold courts of law in accordance with the existing laws and accepted customs of the country, or [in accordance with] those [laws] that are to be adopted; executive power is to be exercised by Royal Authority in accordance with the laws.

Article XVI of 1790/91

That Public Affairs shall not be conducted in Foreign Languages and that the Hungarian Language shall be Conserved

His Holy Majesty assures the faithful Orders and Estates that no foreign language will be introduced for any matter; and in order that the native Hungarian language may spread and become more polished, a special teacher will be appointed to teach Hungarian language and composition in the gymnasiums, academies, and at the Hungarian university, so that those who do not know and wish to learn this language, and those who already know the language but who wish to perfect their knowledge, may gain the opportunity to fulfil their desires in accordance with the aforesaid goals; matters of government will for the time being be negotiated in Latin.

Translated by Philip Barker

Note

1. The first English translation of certain of these texts was provided in C.A. Macartney, *The Habsburg and Hohenzollern Dynasties in the Seventeenth and Eighteenth Centuries* (New York, 1970), pp. 141–6.

APPENDIX VI

ROBERT TOWNSON'S TRANSLATION OF LAW XXVI OF 1790/1[1]

In *Travels in Hungary, with a Short Account of Vienna in the Year 1793*, published in 1797, the English natural historian and mineralogist Robert Townson (1762–1827) provided an account of his journeys through Vienna, Hungary and the Tatra Mountains, accompanied by the Carpathian–German botanist Thomas Mauksch (1749–1832). Townson, sometimes residing with notable Hungarians such as Count Ferenc Széchényi (see notes above), eschewed stereotypical descriptions of the Hungarians as 'savages' by their Austrian neighbours, and set out to methodically describe both the natural peculiarities and socio-political structure of Hungary. In doing so, he commented upon what he saw as the Magyars' failings (such as the jealous retention of noble privilege and the widespread poverty of the peasantry), and their achievements, such as Law XXVI of 1790/1, 'On the Matter of Religion', which Townson lauded for its spirit of toleration. 'Where is there a nation in Europe, in which the seceding religions have the privileges they have here?' asked Townson, although he later tempered his admiration by suggesting that tolerance was largely secured by monarchical imposition: 'I am sorry to be obliged to detract something from this favourable account by observing, that the kings of Hungary, as first patrons of the Church, have great influence in religious matters.'[2] Even so, Townson felt the law remarkable enough to provide a translation for his contemporaries. This translation is provided below:

Appendix VI

'[...] in future, without respecting any new ordinances or privileges, all orders, barons, magnates, nobles, royal free towns; as likewise the market towns and villages, shall have the free exercise of their religion; with liberty of building churches, even with steeples and bells, and possessing schools and churchyards: and nobody, of whatever rank he may be, under any pretext, shall be in anywise hindered or impeded in the enjoyment of this privilege, by his majesty, or other landlords. The peasants, whether resident in market towns, villages, or royal domains, shall likewise, for the general good and public peace, not be prevented from enjoying the same advantages, either by his majesty, his ministers, or other landlords. For the confirming of which it is decreed, that henceforth all distinction of public and private worship shall cease; that private shall no longer exist; but that everywhere it shall be public; consequently it shall now be permitted to the protestants (as it will be fixed afterwards) to appoint ministers, build and repair churches, with or without steeples, parsonage houses and schools, everywhere; even in those places where hitherto there have been none; without further leave being granted; but with this proviso, that, as the government must be particularly attentive to the support of the *tax-bearing* subjects, where it is intended to introduce free religious worship, to build churches, chapels, or to appoint ministers, previously a mixed committee of the county, in the presence of the landlord, yet without the diocesan, shall be held, accurately to examine and to acquaint the county of the requisite expenses to be incurred; of the number and wealth of the people and settled inhabitants, and whether they are able to bear the requisite expenses; and when according to this examination it appears that the number of the people and the funds are sufficient, the landlord shall fix a spot of ground, where the church, parsonage house, and school may be built. But the catholic inhabitants are by no means bound to assist, either by money or labour. This is likewise to be observed towards the protestant landlords and people, when a catholic church is to be erected.

'But it is to be observed, that the introducing of religious worship, the building and repairing of the churches and parsonage houses, &c. always remain free and unrestrained to the protestant nobles and landlords.

'In consequence of this religious liberty, the protestants cannot under any pretext, under the penalty of pecuniary fines, whether they are artificers or people of rank, be compelled to be present at the holy mass, processions, or other religious ceremonies, notwithstanding corporation privileges.

'The protestants of both confessions must in religious matters depend on their own spiritual superiors alone; but that this subordination in spiritual matters may obtain its proper organization, his sacred majesty has resolved to establish that order, which meets with the general approbation of the clergy and laity of the protestant religion, as well concerning the appointment of superiors and directors, as the other regulations, without invading religious liberty; for which reason his majesty, in consequence of his right of supreme inspection, will hear the protestants, and likewise take care that a proper discipline, agreeable to the principles of their religion, shall be introduced: in the meantime it is decreed, that the church laws already existing, which are introduced by their directors, and which at present are followed, and likewise those which in future, according to the sense of this law, shall be introduced, shall not be altered by any *dicasterial* or royal ordinance. They shall not only be allowed to form consistories, but likewise to call synods; his majesty to appoint the place of their meeting: but his majesty must previously be informed of the number of the persons to be present, and the business to be considered, which shall likewise be determined by him; and likewise such a synod called by permission of his majesty, whether it be of the Lutherans or Calvinists, must admit to be present a deputy from his majesty, if he requires it, of whatever religion this deputy may be; who indeed cannot direct or preside, but only have the inspection. But the church laws or ordinances made in these synods, shall only be valid after the royal inspection and approbation; and his majesty, notwithstanding the mentioned liberties, has reserved to himself the executive power of supreme inspector, through the legal courts, as likewise the other royal prerogatives in the religious concerns of the protestants.

'The protestants can likewise retain their *trivial* and grammar schools where they are already existing; and can, with the royal consent, establish new ones, both inferior and superior; appoint or dismiss professors, rectors, subrectors, and school-masters; increase or diminish them; and in future elect local, superior, and general directors, or curates, of the schools from amongst themselves; likewise fix the method and order of study: but here likewise his majesty has reserved to himself, through the legal courts, the superintendance, so that the general management of the literary *police*, the determination of which the states have most humbly referred to his majesty, shall extend over this. The students shall be permitted to collect (money) for themselves, or for their ministers, and to frequent foreign academies, and enjoy all the *stipendia* destined for them. The protestants can freely print *symbolic* (catechistical), theological, and other religious books, under the care of those whom they have chosen for this purpose, and whose names have been transmitted to the royal lieutenancy; but with this condition, that they contain no derision, ill-natured or satirical remarks upon the catholic religion; upon the responsibility of the *censors*, who have permitted their impression. The three copies, as ordained by the law, must be transmitted to his majesty, through the royal lieutenancy.

'The church dues which the protestants have hitherto paid to the catholic parish priests, school-masters, or other such officers, either in money, productions, or labour, shall in future entirely cease, and after three months, reckoning from the publishing of this law, shall be no more anywhere demanded, except the protestants make use of them of their own accord; and in this case they must render the same as the catholics. How this deduction, from the incomes of the catholic parish priests, may be made good to them his majesty will condescend to hear the representations of the royal lieutenancy; but it is now made known, that he will never permit anything to be demanded from the *tax-bearing people*,[3] or the royal treasury, on account of these indemnifications.

'On the building or repairing of churches, parsonage-houses and schools, the protestants are not obliged to assist the catholics with labour, nor the catholics the protestants; therefore the former contracts of this nature are hereby declared invalid.

'The protestant ministers may visit the sick and imprisoned of their religion, with the requisite care and prudence, at all times and in all places; prepare them for death, accompany them to, and support them at, the place of execution; but may not make any harangues to the people. The catholic priests when they are called to the sick imprisoned, or to those sentenced to die, and observe the requisite care, can by no means be denied admittance.

'The public charges, offices, and honours, whether high or low, great or small, shall be given to natural-born Hungarians, who deserve well of their country, and possess the other requisite qualifications, without any respect to their religion.

'The protestants are freed from swearing by the usual legal oath, that is, *by the holy Virgin Mary, the saints and chosen of God.*

'The pious foundations and donations of the protestants which already exist, or which may in future be made for their churches, ministers, schools and students, hospitals, orphan-houses, or their poor, cannot be taken from them under any pretext, nor yet the care of them: but rather the unimpeded administration of them shall be intrusted to those from amongst them to whom it legally belongs; and those foundations, which perhaps may have been taken from them under the last government, shall be returned them without delay. The supreme royal inspection extends itself likewise over such foundations, to the end that the intent of the founders may be answered.

'All affairs of marriage of the protestants are left to the decision of their own consistories: nevertheless his majesty, out of his royal care, after having consulted the protestants, will take such measures that the organization of the consistories may secure the rights of the litigating parties; and at the same time the principles by which these are to judge mall be transmitted for his inspection and approbation. In the meantime, these lawsuits on marriage shall be tried in the civil courts according to the principles laid down of late years, that is, before the courts of justice, in the counties and districts where these exist; and before the magistrates in the royal free and mining towns; yet with the right of appealing, when the circumstances require it, to the royal court, and even to the *Septem-viral* court.

'It must be observed, that the sentence of divorce only possesses a civil effect, and the bishops cannot be bound to admit of the entire dissolution of the marriage bond; nor extend it to the catholics in cases where what is considered by the laws as a degree of consanguinity prohibited in marriage is by the principles of the protestants allowable. His majesty has, as it was done under the Emperor Joseph, allowed them once for all, to contract marriages in the third and fourth degree of consanguinity, without further dispensation.

'As by these laws the free exercise of religion and the maintenance of the churches, schools, &c. &c. of the protestants are provided for in the surest manner; it is likewise determined, for the further maintenance of peace and harmony between the catholics and protestants, that both parties shall remain in the possession of the churches, schools, &c. &c. which they now possess; the foundations of the catholics being in future applied to the benefit of the catholics, and those of the protestants for the use of the protestants; so that not only all recoveries on both sides shall be forbidden (except that the protestants are allowed to prove their claim to the Zirmay, Hrabowsky and Apaffy foundations), but likewise no such taking possession of churches, schools, &c. &c. can be permitted, and those who shall be guilty of such acts of violence shall be fined six hundred guldens (about sixty pounds), according to the intent of the fourteenth article of 1647.

'Since the changing from the catholic religion, to either of the protestant religions permitted by the constitution, is contrary to the principles of the catholic religion, such cases must be made known to his majesty, to prevent any rash steps. It is likewise prohibited, under severe punishments, to entice by any means a catholic to the protestant religion.

'It has been already made known, that these privileges of the protestants are only valid in the kingdom of Hungary; wherefore the kingdoms of Dalmatia, Croatia, and Sclavonia, are left in the further enjoyment of the laws of their country. The protestants therefore within the limits of these kingdoms are not permitted to possess immoveable property, nor to fill public or private offices: yet they have the liberty of maintaining, through the medium of the laws, their ancient rights; and when they by this means obtain their possessions, his majesty takes upon him to provide for their indemnification; and the few places in lower Sclavonia, which are partly Lutherans, partly Calvinists, shall continue in the enjoyment of free religious worship, as hitherto. Lastly, the protestants shall have, on account of commerce and manufactures, free liberty to hire dwellings; but not to acquire houses or landed property from nobles or citizens.

'Children that are, or shall be, born of a mixed marriage (and it is to be noticed that such marriages must always be performed by catholic priests, who are strictly forbid, under any pretence, to attempt to hinder them) shall all be of the religion of the father, if he be a catholic; but if the mother be a catholic, then the male children only are to follow the religion of the father.

'Law-suits on marriage, as well those which exist from the connection between the two religions, as likewise those which arise from the conversion of one sex from the protestant religion to the catholic, belong to the spiritual catholic jurisdiction, because in both cases it is concerning a true sacrament.

'The protestants of both confessions are bound externally to observe the feasts which are now celebrated by the catholics, but not internally, as in their own dwellings, where they are allowed to carry on all their usual professions, which do not disturb religious meditation; and it is by this ordered, that all landlords and masters of families, under the penalty of public prosecution, do not prevent their subjects and servants, whether they be catholics or protestants, from the observance of the festivals and ceremonies of their religion.'

Notes

1. Robert Townson, *Travels in Hungary, with a Short Account of Vienna in the Year 1793* (London, 1797), pp. 170–9.
2. Ibid., p. 179.
3. The reader should be informed that when a peasant through poverty or any other cause is obliged to leave his farm, which is a kind of copyhold estate, his landlord takes possession of it; which then being in the hands of a nobleman pays nothing to the government.

APPENDIX VII

THE 'APRIL LAWS' OF 1848[1]

What follows is a brief selection of the April Laws, which are commonly thought to have marked the transformation of the feudal Hungarian kingdom into a modern constitutional monarchy. The famous Law III stipulated that a Palatine-Vicegerent would exercise the prerogatives of the absent Habsburg emperor, and established an independent ministry, responsible to the Hungarian Diet in Budapest, that would oversee an independent civil administration, armed forces and judiciary. Law IV established an annual Diet in Budapest. Law V amended the old feudal system of representation and extended suffrage from roughly 2–3 per cent to 7 per cent of the population, enfranchising males over 20, qualified by restrictions according to property, income and education. Law VI ordered the incorporation of the Partium into the lands of the Crown, while Law VII decreed the union of Hungary and Transylvania. However, while all the former lands of the Holy Crown were to be included as part of the Hungarian State, Law V decreed that parliamentary representatives must speak Hungarian. Law VIII abolished noble tax exemption, and Law IX discontinued the *robot* (the labour owed by peasants to their landlords) and abolished the manorial courts, while providing state-financed compensation to landowners. Law XIII abolished the tithe, while Law XV abolished *avicitas*, the principle of the legal inalienability of the noble estates. Law XVIII affirmed the end of censorship and the liberty of the press, while full religious freedom was granted by Law XX. Laws XXI and XXII established the national colours, coat of arms, and a national guard. While these laws were constitutionally confirmed by Emperor Ferdinand I on 11 April

1848, Austria denied their validity after the defeat of the Hungarian Revolution in 1849, even if many Hungarians continued to insist on their legality.

Law III of 1848[2]

On the Formation of a Responsible Hungarian Ministry

ARTICLE 1. The person of His Majesty the King is sacred and inviolable.

ART. 2. In the absence of His Majesty the Palatine-Vicegerent shall, within the country and its annexed parts, while preserving the integrity of the relationship between the Crown and the empire, in conformity with the law and the constitution, exercise with full authority the executive power, and in this respect the person of the current Palatine, Imperial and Royal Archduke Stephen, is similarly inviolable.

ART. 3. In the absence of His Majesty the Palatine-Vicegerent shall exercise executive power in conformity with law, through the independent Hungarian ministry, and no ordinance, order, decision, or appointment shall have force unless it is countersigned by one of the ministers residing at Budapest.

ART. 4. Each member of the ministry shall be responsible for all of his official actions.

ART. 5. The official seat of the ministry is Budapest.

ART. 6. In all matters which have heretofore been within the power of the Royal Hungarian Chancellery, of the Royal Council of the Regency, and of the Royal Council of the Treasury, including therein mining, and especially in all civil, ecclesiastical, financial, and military affairs, and in general in all matters relating to national defence, His Majesty shall henceforth exercise the executive power exclusively through the Hungarian Ministry.

ART. 7. It shall be within the immediate power of His Majesty, in every case with the countersignature of the proper responsible Hungarian minister, to appoint archbishops, bishops, priors, and abbots as well as standard-bearers, to exercise executive clemency, to grant noble rank, titles, and orders.

ART. 8. His Majesty shall also only pass resolutions concerning the deployment of the Hungarian Army outside of the country's borders, and furthermore concerning appointments to military offices, with the countersignature of the minister who shall always be in attendance upon the person of His Majesty, in accordance with Article 13.

ART. 9. Those matters which were previously submitted to His Majesty by the government offices listed in Article 6, not including those matters described in articles 7 and 8, shall now be submitted by the ministry to the Palatine-Vicegerent for resolution in the absence of His Majesty from the country.

ART. 10. The ministry shall be composed of a Prime Minister and of eight other ministers, if the Prime Minister does not himself assume one of the portfolios.

ART. 11. The Prime Minister, in the absence of His Majesty from the country, shall be appointed by the Palatine-Vicegerent, with the approval of His Majesty.

ART. 12. In order to ensure that they meet highest the standard of approval, the Prime Minister shall submit proposals for the appointment of fellow ministers.

ART. 13. One of the ministers shall always be in attendance upon the person of His Majesty, and shall take part in all affairs which are common to Hungary and the hereditary provinces, and in such affairs he shall, under his responsibility, represent Hungary.

ART. 14. Besides the member in attendance upon the person of His Majesty for the affairs mentioned in Article 13, the ministry shall be divided into the following departments:

(a) Internal affairs.
(b) National finance.
(c) Public Works, transport, and shipping.[3]
(d) Agriculture, industry, and commerce.[4]
(e) Religion and public education.
(f) Justice and pardons; and
(g) National defence.

ART. 15. A separate minister shall be at the head of each department and of the official personnel thereof, which shall be under the direction of the respective chiefs of divisions.

ART. 16. The manner of conducting business within the departments shall be regulated by the ministry itself.

ART. 17. The Prime Minister of the Ministry shall preside over all ministerial committees in the absence of His Majesty or the Palatine-Vicegerent, and he may convene ministerial committees at any time he deems it necessary.

ART. 18. Each minister shall be responsible for the orders which he signs.

ART. 19. For the consideration of the public affairs of the country under the directorship of His Majesty, or the Palatine-Vicegerent, or the Prime Minister of the Ministry, a Council of State shall be established at Budapest, which shall be permanently organized by the next Diet.[5]

ART. 20. In addition, two councillors of state shall be assigned to the minister in attendance upon the person of His Majesty, along with the necessary staff of officers; such councillors are to be selected from among the active councillors of the Royal Hungarian Chancellery, and nominated upon the proposal of the relevant minister.

ART. 21. The affairs enumerated in Article 7 as reserved immediately to His Majesty shall be administered by the responsible Hungarian minister in attendance upon the person of His Majesty, together with the councillors of state and officers associated with him.

ART. 22. The other active councillors of the Royal Hungarian Chancellery shall be transferred to the Council of State mentioned in Article 19.

ART. 23. The Royal Hungarian Council of the Regency, and the Royal Council of the Treasury shall be divided among the respective departments of the ministry in pursuance of the provisions of Law 58 of 1791,[6] which shall also be taken into consideration in the organization of the Council of State.

ART. 24. Ranking members of the government offices described in Article 6 shall have seats in the Council of State designated by Article 19, and shall preside therein in the absence of His Majesty, the Palatine-Vicegerent, or the relevant Ministers.

ART. 25. All officers and employees of the government offices mentioned in Article 6, not only those who receive new appointments, but also those who cannot be given places in the above-mentioned departments of the ministry, shall retain their present salaries until other provision is made.

ART. 26. The legal powers of all local governing bodies of the country shall remain in full force.

ART. 27. The legally established courts shall preserve their legal independence and shall retain their present organization until further provided by law.

ART. 28. The ministers shall have seats in the two houses of the Diet and must be heard therein when they wish to speak.

ART. 29. Ministers shall be bound to attend in either house of the Diet when requested, and to give proper explanations.

ART. 30. Upon demand of either house of the Diet the ministers shall be bound to submit their official papers for examination by the house itself or by a committee appointed by the house.

ART. 31. Ministers shall have a vote in the Diet only in case they are legal members of the Table of Magnates or have been elected as representatives in the House of Representatives.

ART. 32. Ministers may be held responsible:

(a) For every act committed or order executed by them in their official capacity which violates the independence of the country, the guaranties of the constitution, the provisions of existing laws, personal liberty, or the inviolability of property.
(b) For misapplication or illegal use of money or other property intrusted to them.
(c) For failure to execute the laws or to maintain public peace and security, in so far as such neglect could have been avoided by the use of means placed at their disposal by the law.

ART. 33. The Lower House may impeach ministers by a majority vote.

ART. 34. Jurisdiction in such a case shall be vested in a court, chosen by means of a secret ballot by the Upper House from among its own members;

the procedure shall be public, and the penalty shall be fixed in proportion to the offence. Thirty-six members in all shall be elected, of whom twelve may be rejected by the impeachment commission of the Lower House, twelve by the ministers under impeachment. The court thus composed of twelve persons shall try the impeached ministers.

ART. 35. With respect to a convicted minister royal pardon may be granted only in case of a general amnesty.

ART. 36. For other criminal offences committed by ministers in an unofficial capacity, they shall be amenable to the ordinary laws.

ART. 37. The ministry is bound to submit to the Lower House for its examination and approval an annual statement of the income and needs of the country, and the account of the income administered by it during the past year.

ART. 38. The salary for Ministry officials, until defined by further decree, shall be established by the Palatine-Vicegerent.

Law IV of 1848

On the Annual Sessions of the Diet

ARTICLE 1. As the Diet will in future hold annual sessions at Pest, His Majesty shall annually assemble the Estates of the country, and whenever circumstances permit, during the winter months.

ART. 2. Hereafter the laws to be promulgated may also be approved by His Majesty during the course of the annual session.

ART. 3. Representatives shall be elected to a Diet to continue for three years, and for all three sessions of such a Diet.[7]

ART. 4. After 1848 the new election of representatives shall take place throughout the country at the expiration of each third year, within six weeks before the opening of the first annual session of the new Diet; members elected during the interval between general elections retain their seats in the next Diet only by means of a new election and so retain them for each of the three annual sessions of a Diet.

ART. 5. His Majesty shall have the right to prorogue or to adjourn the assembled annual session and even to dissolve the Diet before the expiration of three years, and in such a case to order a new election of representatives; but in the latter case His Majesty shall order the meeting of the new Diet in such a manner that it shall assemble within three months after the dissolution of the former Diet.

ART. 6. The annual session must not be adjourned, nor the Diet dissolved, before the ministry has submitted the final accounts for the previous year and the budget for the next year, and reached a decision concerning these matters.

ART. 7. His Majesty shall appoint the president and vice-president of the Table of Magnates from the members of that house; the secretaries shall be elected by the house from among its own members, by secret ballot.

ART. 8. As the Royal Table[8] henceforth ceases to be an integral part of the House of Representatives, this house shall elect from among its own members, by secret ballot, a president, two vice-presidents, and the secretaries. The presidents of the two houses shall be chosen for the entire legislative period of the Diet; the other officials shall be chosen annually in the first sitting; in such sitting the oldest member of the Diet shall preside.

ART. 9. The presidents of the two houses shall receive salaries from the public treasury, the amount of which shall be fixed in the first annual session of the new Diet.

ART. 10. The sittings of the two houses shall continue to be public. Each house shall make the regulations for the maintenance of the necessary peace and order in its deliberations, and of silence among those listening to its proceedings; each president respectively is charged with the strict enforcement of such rules.

ART. 11. In this regard it is hereby provisionally directed that the audience shall in no way disturb the deliberations.

ART. 12. Should the audience or one of the persons present disturb the deliberations and the first warning of the president be without effect, the president may upon the second occasion, referring to the present law, order the expulsion of the audience or of a member thereof and the closing of the galleries.

ART. 13. After this is done the deliberations shall be continued upon the same day or later, as the majority decides, but always publicly.

ART. 14. Peace and order shall be maintained by sergeants-at-arms, with the assistance of the national guard, if necessary.[9]

ART. 15. In addition to the regulations contained in the foregoing sections, each house shall, in its first annual session, immediately adopt an order of business, in which the manner and form of deliberating and of voting and in general the internal affairs of the house shall be regulated. The part of this order of business which relates particularly to the order of deliberating may be altered only at the end of the annual session, after the close of the consideration of bills.

Law V of 1848

Concerning the Election of Representatives on the Principle of the Representative System

[...]

ART. 2. All inhabitants of the country and its annexed parts, native or naturalized, who are at least 20 years of age, who are not subject to the authority of their parents, guardians, or seigneurs, and who have not been condemned for having committed a breach of faith, smuggling, robbery, murder, or arson, excepting women, but without prejudice against legally recognized religious differences, may vote [if they meet the following criteria]:

(a) Those who possess, in free royal cities or communities with established councils a house to the value of 300 silver forints, or who in other communities possess exclusively, or in common ownership with their spouse and offspring of minor age, according to the Urbarial system, [at least] $\frac{1}{4}$ of a [peasant] holding or a plot of similar size.

(b) Who, as craftsmen, merchants, or industrialists have residence due to their possession of a workshop, trading facility or factory, or if they are otherwise craftsmen who permanently work with at least one aide.

(c) Who, even if they do not fall into the above classes, are able to demonstrate a permanent and fixed income of 100 silver forints per annum from their own land holdings or capital acquisitions.

(d) Who, irrespective of their income, are scholars, surgeons, lawyers, engineers, academy artists, teachers, members of the Hungarian Academic Society, pharmacists, pastors, curates, municipal notaries

and school teachers, in those constituencies where they possess a permanent home.
(e) Who were previously town citizens, even if they do not conform to the points adumbrated above.

ART. 3. Those who are permissible [to stand] for election must be eligible to vote, must be over 24 years old, and must be able to meet the requirements of law that decree Hungarian as the sole language of legislation.
[...]

ART. 5. The House of Representatives shall consist, not including Transylvania, of 377 members, who shall enjoy equal voting rights, and who shall be elected in accordance with the apportionment made on the basis of population, territory, and economic conditions [...] Transylvania, if it wishes to participate [...] shall send 69 delegates.

Law VIII of 1848

On Equality in Regard to Taxation

All the inhabitants of Hungary and its dependencies are subject without distinction, equally and proportionately, to all public charges [...]

Law XVIII of 1848

On the Press

The previous censorship being abolished forever, and the freedom of the press having been re-established, the guaranty of this freedom shall be provisionally assured by the following stipulations:

ARTICLE 1. Every person can freely express and circulate his thoughts through the medium of the press [...]

Law XX of 1848

On the Matter of Religion

ART. 2. Absolute equality and reciprocity are established without distinction with regard to all the religious confessions that are legally recognized in this country [...]

Introduction, selection and translations of supplementary provisions by Philip Barker.

Notes

1. The following translations have been supplemented and adapted from the versions found in Walter F. Dodd (ed.), *Modern Constitutions – A Collection of the Fundamental Laws of Twenty-Two of the Most Important Countries of the World, with Historical and Bibliographical Notes*, Vol. 1 (Chicago, 1909), pp. 93–106, and Herbert F. Wright (ed.), *Constitutions of the States at War, 1914–1918* (Washington DC, 1919), pp. 28–34. Because these translations include later amended items of legislation and omit other items that were repealed, their texts have been updated, and translations of Law III Articles 2, 3, 8, 9, 11, 12, 14, 17, 19, 24, 38, Law IV Article 6, and Law V have been added to this appendix.
2. Articles 2, 9, 11 and 38 of this law were repealed and Articles 3, 17, 19 and 24 were modified by Law VII of 1867, which suspended the office of Palatine. Article 8 was also subsequently amended, as military affairs were in later years conducted by the joint Austro-Hungarian government.
3. As amended by Law XVIII of 1889, this became the Ministry of Commerce.
4. Similarly, according to Law XVIII of 1889, this became the Ministry of Agriculture.
5. The Council of State was never established, and thus Articles 19–24 never came into force.
6. This law provided that the attributions of the Regency Council be extended to Croatia–Slavonia, which consequently should have a fixed number of representatives therein.
7. Law I of 1886 extended the life of a Diet from three to five years.
8. The Supreme Court of Hungary, which before 1848 formed part of the House of Representatives, its president presiding in that body.
9. The national guard was replaced by the regular army as enacted by Laws XL and XLI of 1868 and VI of 1889.

APPENDIX VIII

LAW XII OF 1867[1]

On the relations of common interest between the lands of the Hungarian crown and the other lands under His Majesty's rule, and the method of treating them.

(i) His imperial and apostolic royal Majesty, having invested his other lands and provinces with constitutional rights, in the gracious speech from the throne with which he opened the present Diet.
(ii) Called upon the Diet, taking the Pragmatic Sanction as a mutually recognized legal basis, to provide ways of preserving unimpaired both Hungary's and its associated lands' constitutional and internal autonomy, which too was guaranteed by the Pragmatic Sanction, and the essential conditions of the empire's security and integrity and which would, at the same time, also guarantee the constitutional influence in the constitutional treatment of the said common matters between, on the one hand, the lands of the Hungarian crown, and on the other, the other lands and provinces of His Majesty.
(iii) The Diet welcomed with sincere pleasure this gracious decision by His imperial and apostolic royal Majesty, according to which in desiring to establish the system of constitutional government in the whole empire he would, thereby, wish to base the glory of his throne and the strength and power of the empire on the natural and thus the firmest foundation: the involvement of all his peoples in public affairs.

(iv) For this reason, the magnates and representatives of Hungary could not neglect to provide ways of rendering possible the maintenance in the future, substantially unimpaired, of the fundamental contract which laws I, II and III of 1723 had established between the majestic ruling house and Hungary, and which had secured, on the one hand, the indivisible and inseparable possession of the lands and provinces which, in the sense of laws I and II of 1723, belong to the imperial connection and, on the other hand, the autonomous legislative and governmental independence of Hungary.

(v) Consequently, it having become necessary to specify exactly and explicitly the relations of common interest existing between the lands of the Hungarian crown and the other lands under the rule of His Majesty, and to define precisely the mode of contract respecting the treatment of these common relations between the two constitutional representatives which are independent of each other, the Diet in this respect resolved the following:

Para 1

That connection which has legally come to exist between, on the one hand, the lands of the Hungarian crown and, on the other, the other lands and provinces of His Majesty rests on the Pragmatic Sanction as accepted by laws I, II and III of 1723.

Para 2

Inasmuch as this solemn fundamental contract established the right of cognatic succession of the House of Habsburg, it declared at the same time that those lands and provinces which, according to the established order of succession, come under one common ruler were to be possessed together, indivisibly and inseparably. By virtue of this categorically declared principle, the defence and maintenance of common security through joint effort is a common and mutual obligation which originates directly from the Pragmatic Sanction.

Para 3

However, side by side with this established obligation, the Pragmatic Sanction also expressly laid down the condition that Hungary's constitutional autonomy as regards public law and internal government be maintained unimpaired.

Para 4

With these two fundamental principles in view the Hungarian Diet defined those relations which are the common concern of Hungary and the other lands under the rule of the common monarch. And whereas, on the one hand, Hungary will always be prepared in the future, as it has been in the past, to fulfil all that the defence and the maintenance of common security through joint effort, in accordance with the Pragmatic Sanction, indispensably requires; on the other hand, [Hungary] cannot take upon itself obligations that extend beyond this aim and are not unavoidably necessary for their attainment.

Para 5

As regards Hungary, formerly, everything concerning the said relations was settled between the Hungarian Diet and the Hungarian king by mutual consent and no other land possessed influence in the disposition of these measures: for the Hungarian king, as absolute monarch of the other lands under his rule, disposed of their interests and duties with absolute authority. Now, however, in view of the gracious speech from the throne, the situation has changed substantially because His Majesty has 'invested his other lands with constitutional rights so that henceforth he cannot represent these with absolute authority and cannot ignore their constitutional influence'.

Para 6

The Diet regards these considerations as paramount in specifying the main principles which are fundamental in the definition of common relations. Its starting point in this respect is the Pragmatic Sanction, which has been designated by His Majesty and the Diet as the mutually recognized basis.

Para 7

According to the Pragmatic Sanction, although the ruler is common insofar as the crown of Hungary is vested in the same monarch who also rules in the other lands, this does not, however, make it necessary that the cost of maintaining the monarch's household be settled in common.

Such a common settlement is not required by the aim set out in the Pragmatic Sanction, while it is much more appropriate to the constitutional autonomy of Hungary and to the high monarchical authority of the Hungarian king that the Hungarian Diet should, at the proposal of the responsible Hungarian ministry, separately vote the costs of the royal Hungarian household. The vote and the delivering of the costs shall not, therefore, be regarded as common matters.

Para 8
The effective conduct of foreign affairs is one of the instruments of the common and joint defence which derives from the Pragmatic Sanction. The effectiveness of such conduct demands common treatment in respect of those foreign affairs which concern jointly all the lands under the rule of His Majesty. For this reason, the diplomatic and commercial representation of the empire abroad, and the measures that may arise as regards international treaties, shall be part of the tasks of the Common Minister for Foreign Affairs, [acting] in agreement with the ministries of both parties and with their consent. Each ministry shall inform its own legislature of the international treaties. Hungary, too, therefore considers these foreign affairs to be common, and is prepared to contribute to the costs of these, to be determined in common, according to the proportion which shall be fixed in accordance with the method described in paragraphs 18, 19, 20, 21 and 22 below.

Para 9
The other means of common defence is the army, and measures relating thereto – in short: military affairs.

Para 10
Bearing in mind all that has been stated above, especially under paragraph 5, the following principles are laid down with respect to the community of military affairs.

Para 11
By virtue of the constitutional monarchic rights of His Majesty in military affairs everything that concerns the unitary leadership, command and internal organization of the whole army, and thereby

Appendix VIII

also of the Hungarian army as a complementary part of the entire army, is recognized as being reserved to His Majesty.

Para 12
However the land reserves to itself the right, on the basis of the existing laws, both in the legislative and in the governmental sphere, to supplement the Hungarian army from time to time and to grant recruits, to determine the conditions of the grant and the period of service as well as the measures concerning the quartering and the provisioning of the soldiers.

Para 13
Furthermore the land declares that the system of defence concerning Hungary can be established or altered only with the consent of the Hungarian legislature. As, however, both such establishment and any subsequent alteration can be effectively carried out only on the basis of identical principles, the two ministries will, therefore, in every such case, after prior agreement between them, submit to the two legislatures proposals based on identical principles. In order to resolve any differences that may arise between the viewpoints of the legislatures, they will communicate with each other by means of deputations.

Para 14
With respect to such Hungarian civil relations, rights, and obligations of members of the Hungarian army as are not related to military service, it is the Hungarian legislature and the Hungarian government that shall have competence.

Para 15
All costs relating to defence are common insofar as the proportion contributed by Hungary is determined after prior negotiation through mutual bargaining, as stipulated in paragraphs 18, 19, 20, 21 and 22 below.

Para 16
Finance is recognized by the Hungarian Diet as common, insofar as there are expenses which cover the subjects that have been recognized as being in common. This, however, is to be understood in the sense that all

the costs required by the above-mentioned subjects shall be determined in common by the method laid down in the paragraphs below relating to [their] management. But with regard to the levying, collection and the transfer to the appropriate place of the proportion of the costs that, in accordance with the method described in paragraphs 18, 19, 20, 21 and 22 below, Hungary is to bear, the Diet of Hungary and its responsible ministry shall be competent as laid down by the paragraphs below relating to the management [of these sums].

Para 17

All other state expenditures of Hungary shall be determined by the Diet, by constitutional means, at the instance of the responsible ministry. The Hungarian ministry shall, with the exclusion of all foreign influence and on its own responsibility, levy, collect and administer these sums as all taxes in general.

Para 18

These are the subjects the common nature of which, as described above, is to be regarded as deriving from the Pragmatic Sanction. Should an agreement with regard to these be obtained with the consent of both parties the proportion according to which the lands of the Hungarian crown bear the burdens and costs of matters recognized as common by virtue of the Pragmatic Sanction, shall be determined in advance, through mutual bargaining.

Para 19

This bargaining and agreement shall take place in such a way that, on the one hand, the Diet of the lands of the Hungarian crown and, on the other, the Diet of the other lands of His Majesty shall each elect a deputation of equal size. The two deputations, in cooperation with the two respective responsible ministries, shall work out a proposal supported by detailed evidence concerning the above-mentioned proportion.

Para 20

Each ministry shall bring this proposal before its respective Diet where it shall be discussed in the normal way. Each Diet will through the respective ministry communicate its resolutions to the other, and the agreements reached by this method between the two parties shall be submitted for sanctioning by His Majesty.

Para 21
Should the two deputations fail to agree on the proposal the opinions of both parties shall be brought before both Diets. And in case the two Diets fail to agree, then the matter shall be settled by His Majesty on the basis of the data submitted.

Para 22
The agreement to be concluded concerning the proportion [of the costs] shall be valid only for a fixed period on the expiry of which bargaining shall once more take place in the said manner.

Para 23
With regard to the treatment of the subjects described above, any change in the arrangement heretofore existing in law does not, strictly speaking, derive from obligations laid down in the Pragmatic Sanction, but is made expedient by the changed circumstances described in paragraph 5 above. The Diet declares that it wishes to deal with the other lands of His Majesty *qua* constitutional peoples provided that the independence of both parties is preserved.

Para 24
This being the reason for and the purpose of this resolution concerning the common matters and the manner of their treatment, it is self-evident that the maintenance of the constitution of Hungary forms one of its fundamental conditions.

Para 25
The other fundamental condition is that full constitutionalism should be brought into effect in His Majesty's other lands and provinces because, as regards any common relations, Hungary can deal only with the constitutional representatives of those lands. And His Majesty himself wished to change the method of negotiations on the said matters heretofore used because he has invested his other lands also with constitutional rights, and in the treatment of common matters regards their constitutional influence as indispensable.

Para 26
Subject to these two fundamental conditions the treatment of the common matters would be as follows:

Para 27
One common ministry shall be created for those subjects which, being indeed in common, belong neither to the government of the lands of the Hungarian crown nor to the government of His Majesty's other lands. This ministry cannot administer, nor exercise influence over, matters beyond those in common which belong to the separate government of either part. Every member of this ministry shall be responsible for all those [matters] which belong to his remit, and the ministry as a whole shall be responsible for such official actions as it has jointly approved.

Para 28
With regard to such common matters as are not purely governmental, Hungary does not consider appropriate either a Reichsrat in its entirety or a common or central parliament, however called, and accepts none of these, but insists that as also [stated] in His Majesty's gracious speech from the throne, the common basis is the Pragmatic Sanction: on the one hand, the lands of the Hungarian crown [taken] together, and on the other hand, His Majesty's other lands and provinces [taken] together, should be regarded as two separate parties with completely equal rights. Consequently between the two parties full parity as regards the treatment of common matters is an indispensable condition.

Para 29
It follows from this principle of parity that the Hungarian Diet should for Hungary elect a committee (*delegatio*) of a fixed number chosen from both houses of the Diet. The other lands and provinces of His Majesty should likewise elect, in a constitutional manner, a committee of exactly the same number of members for their part. The numbers in these committees shall be determined with the consent of the two parties. This number cannot exceed sixty on either side.

Para 30
The said committees are to be elected for one year, that is for one session of the Diet only, and at the end of the year, that is at the

beginning of the next session, their competence ceases entirely. Their members are, however, eligible for re-election.

Para 31
Each committee separately shall freely choose from its own ranks, its chairman, notary, and any other officials it may require, and lays down its own standing orders.

Para 32
The committees shall always be convened on a date specified by His Majesty and at the place where His Majesty is staying at that time. The Hungarian legislature wishes, however, that the sessions be held alternately, one year in Pest, the following year in Vienna; or, should the Diet of His Majesty's other lands and His Majesty so wish, in one of the other capitals of those lands.

Para 33
Each committee holds separate sittings and decisions shall be taken by an absolute majority vote of all members of the committee. The majority decision is to be regarded as the resolution of the committee as a whole. Individual members may, in order to justify themselves [to their constituents], record a dissenting opinion in the minutes, but this shall not affect the validity of the resolution.

Para 34
The two committees may not hold joint sittings, but each communicates its opinions and resolutions to the other in writing and in case of a difference of opinion informs the other in writing. Each committee shall prepare its message in its own language attaching to it the authoritative translation thereof.

Para 35
If the two committees cannot come to an agreement through these written messages they shall hold a joint sitting but with the object of voting only. At this joint sitting the chairman of the two committees shall preside alternately. A resolution may be taken only if at least two-thirds of each of the two delegations are present. Resolutions are always taken by an absolute majority [vote]. As, however, the effective

application of the principle of parity in the interests of both sides is nowhere more important than in voting, should one or more members of either delegation be absent for any reason the delegation of the other party shall have to reduce its membership so that the delegations of both sides are entirely equal in numbers. The larger delegation shall reduce its numbers by lot. The minutes shall be taken by each side in its own language by the two notaries and shall be authenticated jointly.

Para 36
In the event of three unsuccessful exchanges of messages, each side has the right to suggest that a joint vote should be taken on the matter, in which case the chairmen of the two sides shall together determine the place, date and time of the sitting at which such a vote is to be taken, and each chairman invites the members of his own committee thereto.

Para 37
Only those subjects are within the competence of the said committees which, being joint, have been explicitly assigned by this resolution to the said committees. The committees cannot go in their actions beyond these [subjects] and cannot interfere in matters reserved to the Hungarian Diet and to the Hungarian government.

Para 38
The committee set up to discuss the common matters, having been freely elected by the Diet, represents the Diet vis-à-vis His Majesty's other lands in the matters and in the manner specified and outlined in this resolution. This committee cannot be bound by prior instructions.

Para 39
As regards procedure, it is laid down that any subject which, according to this resolution, lies within the remit of the said committees, shall be brought before each committee separately by the common ministry. Each committee shall have the right to put questions to the common ministry or, according to the department, to a respective member, and to request an answer and information. Likewise the common ministry shall have the right and, when called upon, the duty,

to appear before either committee to answer orally or in writing, and, if it can be done without damage, to give information, producing in addition the necessary documents.

Para 40

The most important annual task of the said committees shall be the settling of the common budget. This budget, which is limited solely to expenditures which, by [virtue of] this resolution, are designated as common, shall be prepared with the cooperation of both responsible ministries by the common ministry and shall then be passed on to each committee separately. The committees shall deliberate in accordance with the method described above, separately, and shall communicate their observations to each other in writing. Should there be points on which their views are not in agreement, these shall be decided by vote in joint sitting.

Para 41

The budget thus settled shall not be subject to further discussion by the individual lands and each is duty-bound to bear its share of the common budget, the proportion of which has been determined in advance (in accordance with paragraphs 18, 19, 20, 21, and 22 of this resolution). As, however, with regard to these common expenditures the determination of the levying, collecting and tax system in Hungary is part of the remit of the Hungarian Diet and Hungarian responsible ministry, the Hungarian ministry shall always include in the budget to be laid before the Hungarian Diet those sums which, according to the above-mentioned proportion, are to be borne by Hungary from the common budget already determined. But the amount under these heads cannot be further queried. The Hungarian responsible ministry, having collected the sum necessary for the common expenditures thus settled, shall transfer every month to the Common Minister of Finance, that part of the state revenues, collected in each month, which serves to cover the common expenditures according to the proportion in which the sum of the common expenditures stands to the sum of the land's expenditures. The Common Minister of Finance shall be responsible for spending the sums received on the designated purposes, it being understood that the administrator of the monies shall be strictly accountable.

Para 42

The auditing of these expenditures is likewise to be carried out by the said committees, which shall proceed in this regard, too, in the manner described above.

Para 43

A similar procedure shall be followed in respect of all other subjects which, as common matters, are within the remit of the said committees. These too shall be brought by the common ministry before each committee separately, shall be discussed by the committees separately and they shall communicate their observations to each other in writing. Should they not be able to agree in this way, then, as stated above, they shall decide at a joint sitting by vote. It is understood that their resolutions, in so far as they require approval by the monarch, should be submitted to His Majesty and if they are approved by His Majesty shall have binding force. His Majesty shall, however, inform each Diet of these resolutions, thus approved by the monarch, through its respective separate responsible ministry. Those resolutions which have been taken in the delegations in the manner described above, and which have been sanctioned by His Majesty, after they have been communicated to the Hungarian Diet, can be implemented in Hungary by His Majesty only through the Hungarian responsible ministry. And likewise, all those expenditures which, by the resolution of the committee taken in this manner and sanctioned, are to be borne by Hungary, shall be levied and collected by the Hungarian responsible ministry, together with the Hungarian budget, as passed by the Diet.

Para 44

Apart from those [subjects] which the common responsible ministry submits to the committees of the common matters (*delegatio*) each of these committees has the right to initiate but only in relation to subjects which, as common subjects, are strictly within the remit of the said committees, according to this resolution. Each committee may make such proposals and may communicate them in writing to the other committee. And a proposal thus initiated is to be discussed in the same way as has already been described concerning the other subjects within the remit of the committees.

Para 45

The sittings of the committees shall normally be public. The exceptions in this respect shall be laid down by the standing orders. A resolution can, however, be taken only in open session.

Para 46

Should His Majesty dissolve either Diet the delegation of the dissolved Diet shall also cease [to exist] and the new Diet shall elect a new committee (*delegatio*).

Para 47

The members of the committees can never be called to account for statements made in the course of the discussion of matters designated as common in this resolution. Moreover neither can they, until the termination of their mandate, be arrested nor proceeded against, either on a charge that may lead to arrest or because of a crime or offence, unless caught *in flagrante delicto*, without the prior authorization of the respective Diet or, should that not be in session, of the committee of which they are members. When the respective Diet is not in session, the respective committee shall likewise decide whether any member caught *in flagrante delicto* [should] be kept in custody or released. Furthermore, the standing orders shall provide for measures to prevent any disorder that might occur in the course of the sittings.

Para 48

Should any member of either committee, in the interim, decease or be deprived of his liberty through lawful judgement or likewise, if he were to resign his position for good reason, the position thus vacated is to be filled forthwith by the respective Diet. In order to facilitate this, the Diet, when electing the committees, shall also elect, in addition to the required number, reserve members, determining, at the same time, the order in which reserve members are to be called upon to fill the vacated position by the chairman of the respective committee.

Para 49

In case of resignation the respective Diet or, when it is not in session, the respective committee shall decide on the adequacy of the grounds of resignation and on the acceptance of the resignation.

Para 50

Concerning the responsibility of the common ministry and the form it is to take: both committees shall have the right, when they deem necessary because of the infringement of constitutional[ly enacted] laws, to move the impeachment of the common ministry, or any individual member thereof, and also to inform the other committee of this motion in writing. If both committees pass the motion of impeachment or, because of disagreement between them, such a motion is passed by a majority in the voting sitting, as aforesaid, this decision is to be regarded as being legally binding forthwith.

Para 51

The tribunal for the trial thus decided upon shall be composed as follows: each committee shall separately propose twenty-four members, not from among its own ranks but from citizens of independent standing and learned in the law, from the lands it represents. Each committee shall have the right to reject up to twelve of the twenty-four members, proposed by the other, without giving reason. The defendants, too, shall have the right, jointly and collectively, to demand the rejection of up to twelve members, only in such a way, however, that the number of the judges selected by each committee shall remain equal. The members thus remaining shall form the tribunal.

Para 52

In addition to the common subjects described above which, deriving from the Pragmatic Sanction, are regarded as [the subjects] to be treated as common, there are further public matters of great importance, the common character of which does not derive from the Pragmatic Sanction, but which it may, nevertheless, be more expedient to deal with by common consent than by keeping them strictly separate, partly out of political considerations, and partly out of the coincidence of the interests of the two parties.

Para 53

Concerning the state debts: such debts as have been incurred without the lawful consent of the land cannot in the strictly legal sense burden Hungary by virtue of its constitutional position.

Appendix VIII

Para 54

This Diet has already declared, however, that 'if true constitutionalism will in fact be restored as soon as possible in our land and in His Majesty's other lands it is prepared to do what it is permitted to do and what it can do without injury to the autonomy and the constitutional rights of the land, over and above its legal obligations, on the basis of equity, out of political considerations so that the well-being of His Majesty's other lands and with it that of Hungary should not collapse under the heavy burden of the policies that the absolutist system has built up and the damaging consequences of the hard times of the past should be averted'.

Para 55

Out of these considerations, and solely on this basis, the land is prepared to shoulder a part of the burden of the state debt, and to this end, by prior consultation, enter into bargaining, with His Majesty's other lands as one free nation with another.

Para 56

As regards the future, credits shall be in common whenever both Hungary and His Majesty's other lands, in the light of circumstances and their own interests, consider it to be expedient to obtain a new loan jointly and in commmon. With such loans, all that relates to the making of the contract and the use and repayment of the monies borrowed shall be dealt with in common. But the initial decision on whether a particular loan should be taken out in common shall, as regards Hungary, in every case be made by the Hungarian Diet.

Para 57

Moreover, through this resolution, the land also solemnly declares that in view of that fundamental principle of true constitutionalism according to which debts cannot be imposed on the land without its consent, Hungary shall not in the future [as it has not in the past] recognize as binding upon itself any state debt whatever for which the land's lawful and express consent has not been obtained.

Para 58

Nor does the community of commercial matters derive from the Pragmatic Sanction in terms of which the lands of the Hungarian crown, as lands legally separate from the monarch's other lands, could act through their own responsible government and legislature, and could regulate their commerce by [means of] tariff boundaries.

Para 59

As, however, there exist many and important matters of reciprocal interest between Hungary and His Majesty's other lands, the Diet is prepared in commercial matters to conclude, from time to time, customs and commercial alliances between the lands of the Hungarian crown, on the one hand, and His Majesty's other lands, on the other.

Para 60

This alliance would determine which matters pertain to commerce, and would establish the mode of management of all commercial matters.

Para 61

The alliance would be concluded through mutual bargaining in the way that similar negotiations take place between two lands legally independent of each other. The responsible ministries of the two parties shall prepare the detailed proposal concerning the alliance by common consent, and each shall submit it to its own Diet and the agreements of the two Diets shall be submitted to His Majesty for sanctioning.

Para 62

Likewise, at the same time as the proportion of common expenses will be determined according to paragraphs 18, 19, 20, 21 and 22 above, the customs and commercial alliance between the lands of the Hungarian crown on the one hand and His Majesty's other lands on the other is to be concluded in accordance with paragraphs 59 and 61 above, in which [*sc.* the alliance] it shall at the same time be declared that the validity of commercial treaties with other countries hitherto shall be extended to include Hungary.

Para 63

On this occasion, likewise through bargaining, according to paragraphs 59 and 61 above, regulations could be established regarding the kinds of indirect taxes, their equitable apportionment and management which are closely connected with industrial production and which preclude the possibility of one legislature's or responsible government's measures in this respect bringing about the curtailment of income of the other party. The method can, at the same time, be established for the future whereby reforms, concerning these taxes, could be introduced by the two legislatures in concert.

Para 64
Further, it would be established by whom and in what manner the uniform management of all tariffs should be supervised and it would be stated that the excise should defray common expenditures; the total revenue from this shall therefore be deducted from the sum total of common expenses beforehand.

Para 65
Since the railway is an essential means of promoting commerce, at the same time as the customs and commercial alliance shall be concluded, it can be decided, in the sense of the bargaining to be established by paragraphs 59 to 61 above, which [projected] railway lines require common measures in the interests of both parties, and the extent of such measures. The respective ministry and Diet shall be exclusively responsible for all other railway lines running through its territory.

Para 66
The establishment of the monetary system (*Münzwesen*) and the money standard are closely related to commerce. It is therefore not only desirable but also necessary in the interests of both parties that both the monetary system and the money standard in the lands belonging to the customs alliance to be created should be the same. For the same reasons, when the customs and commercial alliance is concluded it shall also be necessary, in accordance with paragraphs 59 and 61, to provide for the monetary system and the money standard through bargaining. Should it subsequently prove necessary or expedient to alter these arrangements or to introduce a new monetary system and money standard, this shall be done with the mutual consent of the two ministries and the approval of the two Diets. It is self-evident that the monarchic rights of the Hungarian king in respect of minting and issuing money are to remain intact.

Para 67

At the same time as the quota is established and the customs alliance concluded the annual contribution to the state debt to be borne by Hungary shall be fixed through free bargaining, as stipulated in paragraphs 55 and 61.

Para 68

It is self-evident that if and in so far as the bargaining over the subjects listed in paragraphs 58 to 67 prove unsuccessful, the land reserves its right to take independent lawful action and all its rights in this regard also remain unimpaired.

Para 69

The method and proportion according to which the associated lands are to participate in the committee (*delegatio*) to be sent out, by virtue of this resolution, on behalf of the lands of the Hungarian crown, shall be determined later.

This agreement, as described above, having been sanctioned by royal approval, is hereby enacted as law.

Those provisions of this law which concern the method of the management of the common matters shall come into force only after the lands of His Majesty, not belonging to the Hungarian crown, have also, for their part, constitutionally agreed to their substance.

We, therefore, having graciously heard and accepted the humble petition of the aforesaid Followers, the Magnates and the representatives of the land, have ordered the articulation of the laws, submitted to Our Majesty in the manner described above, into this letter of ours word for word, and having declared them jointly and severally right, pleasing and acceptable, we have, on the 12th day of June of this year, and this day as stated below, given to them our royal agreement and consent, and by virtue of our royal authority approved, confirmed and sanctioned them, assuring the Magnates and the Representatives of the land, our Followers, that everything contained in the above articulated laws shall be kept by Ourselves, and also by our other followers, as accepted, approved and confirmed by our royal signature in accordance with the power and authority of this letter of ours.

Appendix VIII

Countersigned by our truly beloved follower, the honourable and esteemed Count Andrássy Gyula of Csíkszentkirály and Krasznahorka, our Hungarian Minister-president [and] dated in our imperial capital, Vienna, in Austria on the twenty-eighth day of July in the year of our Lord one thousand eight hundred and sixty-seven.

Ferencz József, m.p.
(place of seal)
Count Andrássy Gyula m.p.

Translated by Peter Sherwood

Note

1. From the text published in Dezső Markus (ed.), *Corpus Jurus Hungarici. Magyar Törvénytár. 1836–1868. évi törvények* (Budapest, 1896), pp. 333–44.

APPENDIX IX

THE DECLARATION OF THE FIRST HUNGARIAN REPUBLIC (NOVEMBER 1918)[1]

The National Council of Hungary in accordance with the will of the people has decided upon the following

PEOPLE'S RESOLUTION

Article I

Hungary is a people's republic free and independent of all other countries.

Article II

The constitution of the people's republic will be established by a constitutional national assembly, urgently convened on the basis of a new electoral law.

The Lower and Upper Houses of the Hungarian parliament are dissolved and abolished.

Article III

Until the constitutional national assembly has determined otherwise, state authority will be exercised by the people's government under the presidency of Mihály Károlyi, with the support of the executive committee of the Hungarian National Council.

Article IV

The people's government shall urgently draft people's laws:

(1) On a universal, secret, equal, direct franchise, also extending to women, for the National Assembly, county, and local elections;
(2) On the freedom of the press;
(3) On trial by jury;
(4) On the freedom of association and assembly;
(5) On the provision of land to the people working the land.

These laws must be urgently enacted and executed by the people's government.

Article V

The legal authority of all legislation conflicting with the above is abolished. All other legislation remains in force.

Budapest, on the 16th day of November 1918

Translated by Philip Barker and Thomas Lorman

Note

1. From the text published in Gyula Térfy (ed.), *Corpus Jurus Hungarici. Magyar Törvénytár. 1918. évi törvénycikkek és néptörvények* (Budapest, 1919, p. 203).

APPENDIX X

THE PREAMBLE TO THE CONSTITUTION OF THE HUNGARIAN SOCIALIST FEDERAL REPUBLIC OF COUNCILS (1919)[1]

The Fundamental Principles of the Constitution of the Hungarian Socialist Federal Republic of Councils.

1. In the Republic of Councils the proletariat has taken into its hands every freedom, right and power with the aim of ending the capitalist order and the rule of the bourgeoisie, and replacing it with socialist production and social order. The proletarian dictatorship is, however, merely an instrument to end every form of exploitation and every kind of class rule; it is the preparation of a social order that does not recognize classes, and in which the primary instrument of class rule, {namely} the power of the state, will come to an end.
2. The Republic of Councils is the republic of the workers, soldiers and agricultural workers' councils. The Republic of Councils provides no place for {capitalist} exploiters in any kind of council. In the councils of the workers, soldiers, and agricultural workers the working people make the laws, carry them to their conclusion, and pass judgement upon those who transgress them. The proletariat exercises all central and local power through the councils.

3. The Republic of Councils is a free federation of free peoples.
The foreign policy of the Republic of Councils, with the aid of the world revolution, wants to achieve peace for the world that belongs to the workers. It wants peace without occupation or military reparations on the basis of the right of self-determination for the workers. In place of the imperialism that provoked the world war, the Republic of Councils wants the consolidation and federation of the world proletariat, and an international republic of workers. Therefore, it opposes exploitative war, and the oppression and subjugation of all peoples. It rejects the methods of the class-state, especially those pertaining to secretive diplomacy.The rights and responsibilities of the workers in the Hungarian Socialist Federal Republic of Councils.
4. The Republic of Councils strives to pass all means of production into the ownership of the society of workers, in the interests of abolishing exploitation, and organizing and improving production. Thus it takes into common ownership every agricultural, industrial, mining and transport facility that exceeds the size of a small business.
5. The rule of financial capital is ended in the Republic of Councils as institutions of finance and insurance are taken into common ownership.
6. Only those who work have a place in the Republic of Councils. The Republic of Councils decrees the imposition of general compulsory work, but in contrast [sic] establishes the right to work. Those who are incapable of work, and all those who want to work, but for whom the state cannot provide work, will be supported by the state.
7. In the interest of guaranteeing the power of the working masses, and preventing the reestablishment of the power of the exploitative [class], the Republic of Councils will arm the workers and disarm the exploiters. The Red Army is the class army of the proletariat.
8. In the Republic of Councils the opinions of the workers can be freely expressed in writing and in speech, but the power of capital to degrade the press into an instrument for disseminating the capitalist mode of thought and obfuscating the proletariat's self-awareness is abolished. The dependence of the press upon capital is also abolished. The right to publish all forms of publication belongs to the workers, and the Republic of Councils will ensure that the ideals of socialism are freely spread throughout the entire country.
9. In the Republic of Councils the workers' right of association is absolute. Every proletarian has the right to freely attend meetings and arrange

demonstrations. With the smashing of bourgeoisie rule, every obstacle obstructing the workers' right of free association has been removed, and the Republic of Councils has not only granted the workers and the impoverished agricultural labourers the complete freedom of association and organization, but will also provide for them all forms of material and intellectual assistance in order to guarantee and augment their freedom of association.

10. The Republic of Councils has abolished the educational exclusivity of the bourgeoisie and opens the way for the workers to achieve genuine educational development. Therefore it guarantees free, and considerably more extensive education for workers and agricultural labourers.
11. The Republic of Councils defends the true freedom of conscience of the workers by completely separating the church from the state, and education from the church. Everyone can freely practise their religion. Both religious and anti-religious propaganda is freely permitted.
12. The Republic of Councils proclaims the idea of the unification of the world's proletariats, and therefore grants to every foreign proletarian those rights which the Hungarian proletarian enjoys, and empowers every local council to proclaim all foreign workers as naturalized Hungarians if they so request.
13. Every foreign revolutionary has the right of refuge in the Republic of Councils.
14. The Republic of Councils does not acknowledge racial or national differences. It does not tolerate the oppression of national minorities in any way or the imposition of limitations upon the use of their own languages. Everyone can freely speak in their mother tongue, and every authority is obligated to accept all submissions presented in the languages used in Hungary, and to hear out and converse with everyone in their native language.

Translated by Philip Barker and Thomas Lorman

Note

1. From the text first published in *Népszava*, 26 June 1919.

APPENDIX XI

THE PREAMBLE TO LAW I OF 1920[1]

On the restitution of constitutionalism and temporary measures concerning the practice of supreme state authority.

We remind all those concerned that the National Assembly of Hungary has enacted the following article of law:

The national assembly, as the exclusive legal representative of national sovereignty, declares that the practice of royal power was abolished on 13th day of the month of November in the year 1918. It further establishes that the indissoluble and inseparable consolidated possession of Hungary and its associated lands, alongside other kingdoms and countries, as represented in the former Austrian Imperial Council, has as a result of recent events been abolished.

The National Assembly reserves the right to establish the ramifications of all these facts in the time period following the armistice.

It further establishes that the Lower House of parliament, which was legally convened on the twenty-first day of June in the year 1910, declared itself to be dissolved with the resolution passed on the sixteenth day of the month of November in the year 1918; the Upper House, in the session held on that same day, acknowledged this resolution, and suspended its deliberations, leading to the cessation of the functioning of parliament. In result, the practice of supreme state authority within the orderly framework of the constitution, became impossible.

In accordance with the fundamental principles of our constitution, the temporary governments formed after the seventh day of August in the year 1919, turned to the nation to elect a national assembly that was charged to represent its will on the basis an electoral law that was extended to women, universal, secret, equal, direct, and compulsory.

In consequence, the election of representatives to the national assembly was held in every part of the country where enemy occupation did not render the election impossible; the elected parliamentary representatives, on the sixteenth day of February in the year 1920 in Budapest, in the confines of the parliament, gathered together to form a national assembly.

Translated by Philip Barker and Thomas Lorman

Note

1. From the text published in Gyula Térfy (ed.), *Corpus Juris Hungarici. Magyar Törvénytár. 1920. évi törvénycikkek* (Budapest, 1921), p. 3.

APPENDIX XII

THE PREAMBLE TO LAW I OF 1946[1]: ON THE FORM OF GOVERNMENT OF HUNGARY

In Hungary, on 13 November 1918, the exercise of royal power ended. The nation won back its right of self-government. After four hundred years of struggle, the Council of Ónod, the 1849 Debrecen resolution, two attempts at revolution and the persecution that followed, the Hungarian people can once again freely decide on their form of government. Elected by a universal, equal, direct and secret ballot, the National Assembly can, in the name of the people and with the confidence of the people, determine the form of government which best suits the will and interests of the nation: the Hungarian republic.

The Republic ensures for its citizens the natural and inalienable human rights, for the Hungarian people an orderly communal life and peaceful cooperation with other peoples. The natural and inalienable rights of citizens are in particular: personal freedom, a right to a life free from oppression, fear and want, the free expression of thought and opinion, the freedom to practise [one's own] religion, the right of cooperation and association, to property, to personal security, to work and the right to a dignified livelihood, to the right of free education, and the right of participation in the running of state and local government life.

These rights cannot be removed from a single citizen of the state without due legal procedure and the Hungarian state shall guarantee, uniformly and equally, these rights to every citizen, without any form of discrimination, within the framework of the democratic state order. For the realization of this goal, the National Assembly of Hungary has, before all else, enacted the following laws:

1. The exclusive source and possessor of state power is the Hungarian people. The Hungarian people shall exercise its legislative power via the National Assembly, which is elected by general, equal, direct and secret ballot.
2. (1) Hungary is a republic. (2) The head of the republic is the President. The President of the Republic shall be elected for a four year term by the National Assembly.
3. Every Hungarian citizen can be elected President of the Republic who has reached his thirty-fifth year and who possesses the electoral right of a member of the National Assembly.
4. (1) The election of the President of the Republic is preceded by nominations. The validation of a nomination requires at least fifty members of the National Assembly to propose this in writing. The nomination must be submitted to the President of the National Assembly before the vote takes place. Every member of the National Assembly can only nominate one candidate. For those who nominate more than one candidate, all of their nominations are invalid. (2) If only one candidate obtains the necessary nomination, then in the presence of at least two-thirds of the National Assembly's members the nominee can be elected by public acclamation. If necessary, the election is by secret ballot. If necessary, multiple rounds of voting can take place. On the basis of the first round of voting, the elected President of the Republic is the nominee who obtains the vote of at least two-thirds of all members of the National Assembly. (3) If on the occasion of the first round of voting no candidate wins this majority, a new vote must be held in accordance with the stipulations of paragraph 1. Similarly, a two-thirds majority vote of all members of the National Assembly is necessary for election [of a nominee] during a second round of voting. (4) If on the occasion of the second round of voting no nominee wins the desired majority, a third round of voting must be held. On this occasion, it is only possible to vote for the two candidates who won the most votes during the second round of voting. On the basis of the third round of voting the elected

President of the Republic is – irrespective of the number of participants in the vote – the nominee who wins the majority of the votes. (5) The electoral procedure must be completed in three consecutive days at most.

5. Nobody can be elected as President of the Republic on two consecutive occasions.
6. (1) The President of the Republic will swear an oath or solemn promise before the National Assembly. (2) The text of the oath is as follows: 'I [...] swear on the living God that I will be faithful to Hungary and its constitution. I will uphold its laws and legally binding customs and hold others to the same and perform my duties as the President of the Republic in agreement with the national assembly and for the benefit of the Hungarian people. So help me God.' (3) The words of the solemn promise are as follows: 'I [...] on my honour and conscience promise to be faithful to Hungary and its constitution. I will uphold its laws and legally binding customs and hold others to the same and perform my duties as the President of the Republic in agreement with the National Assembly and for the benefit of the Hungarian people.'
7. An official record must be made of the election of the President of the Republic, his oath, or his declaration of his solemn promise. This official record must be signed by the President of the Republic, and must be counter-signed by the Prime Minister. This official record must be published in the official gazette.
8. Following the oath or solemn promise of the newly elected President of the Republic, the institution of the National Supreme Council shall be dissolved.

Translated by Philip Barker and Thomas Lorman

Note

1. From the text published in the *Magyar Törvénytár. 1946. évi törvénycikkek* (Budapest, 1946).

APPENDIX XIII

THE CONSTITUTION OF THE HUNGARIAN PEOPLE'S REPUBLIC (1949):[1] CONSTITUTION OF THE HUNGARIAN PEOPLE'S REPUBLIC

Budapest 1949

The armed forces of the great Soviet Union liberated our country from the yoke of the German fascists, crushed the power of the great landowners and capitalists who were ever hostile to the people, and opened the road of democratic progress to our working people. Having acceded to power in hard struggles fought against the masters and defenders of the old order, the Hungarian working class, in alliance with the working peasantry and with the generous assistance of the Soviet Union, rebuilt our war-ravaged country. Led by the experiences of the socialist revolution of 1919 and supported by the Soviet Union, our people began to lay down the foundations of socialism and now our country is advancing towards socialism along the road of a people's democracy. The already realized achievements of this struggle and this constructive work, the fundamental changes effected in the economic and social structure of our country, are embodied in the Constitution of the Hungarian People's Republic, which also indicates the direction of our further advance.

Section One

Article 1

Hungary is a People's Republic.

Article 2

(1) The Hungarian People's Republic is a state of workers and working peasants.
(2) In the Hungarian People's Republic all power belongs to the working people. The workers of town and country exercise their power through their elected representatives who are responsible and accountable to the people.

Article 3

The Hungarian People's Republic defends the power and liberty of the Hungarian working people and the independence of the country; it opposes every form of the exploitation of man by man and organizes the forces of society for socialist construction. In the Hungarian People's Republic the close alliance of the workers and working peasantry is made a reality under the leadership of the working class.

Section Two

The Social Structure

Article 4

(1) In the Hungarian People's Republic the bulk of the means of production is owned, as public property, by the state, by public bodies or by co-operative organizations. Means of production may also be privately owned.
(2) In the Hungarian People's Republic the force directing the national economy is the state power of the people. The working people gradually dislodge the capitalist elements and consistently build up a socialist system of economy.

Article 5

The economic life of the Hungarian People's Republic is determined by a state national economic plan. Basing itself on the publicly owned enterprises, the state banking system and the agricultural machine stations, the state directs and controls the national economy with the object of expanding the forces of production, increasing the national wealth, raising to an ever higher level the material and cultural standards of the working people and strengthening the defences of the country.

Article 6

The land, its mineral resources, the forests, the waters, the natural sources of power, the mines, the large industrial enterprises, the means of communication such as railways, road, water and air transports, the banks, the postal, telegraph and telephone services, the wireless, the state-sponsored agricultural enterprises such as state farms, machine stations, irrigation works and the like, are the property of the state and of public bodies as trustees for the whole people. All foreign and all wholesale trade is carried on by state enterprises, all other trade is under state supervision.

Article 7

(1) The Hungarian People's Republic recognizes and guarantees the right of the working peasants to the land and regards it as its duty to assist the socialist development of agriculture by establishing state farms and machine stations and giving every support to productive co-operative societies based on voluntary association and joint work.

(2) The state recognizes and supports every genuine co-operative movement of the workers that is directed against exploitation.

Article 8

(1) The constitution recognizes and protects all property acquired by labour.

(2) Private property and private enterprise must not be such as to run counter to the public interest.

(3) The constitution guarantees the right of inheritance.

Article 9

(1) In the Hungarian People's Republic labour is the base of the social order.

(2) Every able-bodied citizen has the right, and the duty to work to the best of his ability and is bound in honour to do so.

(3) By their labour, by participation in work competitions, by tightening labour discipline and improving working methods, the workers serve the cause of socialist construction.

(4) The Hungarian People's Republic strives to apply in practice the socialist principle: 'From each according to his ability, to each according to his work.'

Section Three

The Highest Organs of State Authority
Article 10

(1) The highest organ of state authority in the Hungarian People's Republic is Parliament.
(2) Parliament exercises all the rights deriving from the sovereignty of the people and determines the organization, direction, and conditions of government.
(3) In accordance with this its competence Parliament:
    (a) creates legislation,
    (b) determines the state budget,
    (c) decides the national economic plan,
    (d) elects the Presidential Council of the People's Republic,
    (e) elects the Council of Ministers,
    (f) sets up and abolishes ministries and defines and changes the sphere of activity of the several ministries,
    (g) decides upon declaring war and concluding peace,
    (h) exercises the prerogative of amnesty.

Article 11

(1) Parliament is elected for a term of four years.
(2) Members of Parliament may not be arrested or prosecuted without the consent of Parliament, except when taken in the act.
(3) All political, economic or other activity or conduct detrimental to the interests of the workers is incompatible with the quality of a Member of Parliament.

Article 12

(1) Parliament meets in regular session not less than twice a year.
(2) Parliament must be convened at the written demand of one-third of its members or if the Presidential Council of the People's Republic so decides.

(3) Parliament elects a speaker, two deputy speakers and six recorders from among its own members.
(4) The sessions of Parliament are convened by the Presidential Council of the People's Republic.
(5) Parliament lays down its own rules of procedure and agenda.

Article 13

As a general rule, the sessions of Parliament are held in public. In exceptional cases Parliament may decide to hold a secret session.

Article 14

(1) The right of legislation is vested in Parliament.
(2) Legislation can be initiated by the Presidential Council of the People's Republic, by the Council of Ministers and by any member of Parliament.

Article 15

(1) Parliament can take valid decisions only if at least one half of its members are present.
(2) Parliament decides issues by a simple majority.
(3) Changes in the constitution require the votes of two-thirds of the members of Parliament.

Article 16

Acts passed by Parliament are signed by the President and Secretary of the Presidential Council of the People's Republic. New acts are promulgated by the President of the Presidential Council. Promulgation is effected by publication in the official gazette.

Article 17

(1) Parliament may at need appoint, out of its own members, a committee to investigate any matter.
(2) It is the duty of all public authorities, offices and institutions as well as of all citizens to put at the disposal of such parliamentary committees all the data required by the committee and also to give evidence before the committee if required to do so.

Article 18

(1) Parliament may pronounce its dissolution before the expiration of its term.
(2) In the event of war or other emergency Parliament can prolong its mandate for a stated length of time.
(3) In the event of war or other emergency the Presidential Council of the People's Republic can re-convene a Parliament that has already been dissolved. A Parliament thus convened can itself decide the duration of its mandate.
(4) In the event of dissolution a new Parliament must be elected within not more than three months from the day of dissolution.
(5) A newly elected Parliament must be convened by the Presidential Council of the People's Republic within one month of polling day.

Article 19

(1) At its first sitting Parliament elects from among its own members the Presidential Council of the People's Republic, consisting of a President, two Vice-Presidents, a secretary, and seventeen members.
(2) The Chairman of the Council of Ministers, its Deputy Chairmen and its members are ineligible for election to the Presidential Council of the People's Republic.

Article 20

(1) The competence of the Presidential Council of the People's Republic extends to:
  (a) issuing the writ for a general election;
  (b) convening Parliament;
  (c) initiating legislation;
  (d) holding a plebiscite on matters of national importance;
  (e) concluding international treaties on behalf of the Hungarian People's Republic;
  (f) appointing diplomatic representatives and receiving the letters of credence of foreign diplomatic representatives;
  (g) ratifying international treaties;
  (h) appointing the higher civil servants and the higher officers of the armed forces, in accordance with the provisions of the law;

(i) awarding the orders and titles instituted by Parliament and authorizing the acceptance of foreign orders and titles;
(j) exercising the prerogative of mercy;
(k) deciding issues specially submitted to its jurisdiction by an Act of Parliament.

(2) The Presidential Council of the People's Republic may annul or modify any by-law, regulation or measure introduced by central or local organs of government, if they infringe the constitution or are detrimental to the interests of the working people.
(3) The Presidential Council of the People's Republic may dissolve any local organ of government the activities of which infringe the constitution or are seriously detrimental to the interests of the working people.
(4) When Parliament is not in session, its functions are exercised by the Presidential Council of the People's Republic; that body cannot, however, change the constitution.
(5) The enactments of the Presidential Council of the People's Republic are legally binding decrees, which must, however, be submitted to Parliament at its next sitting.
(6) All decisions and measures taken by the Presidential Council of the People's Republic are signed by the President and the Secretary of that body and must be published in the official Gazette.

Article 21

(1) The term of office of the Presidential Council of the People's Republic expires when Parliament elects a new Presidential Council of the People's Republic.
(2) The Presidential Council of the People's Republic is responsible to Parliament and is under the obligation of rendering an account of its activities to Parliament.
(3) Parliament has the right to recall the Presidential Council of the People's Republic or any member of it.
(4) In order to make valid decisions, at least nine members of the Presidential Council of the People's Republic must be present, in addition to the President and Secretary.

(5) The Presidential Council of the People's Republic draws up its own rules of procedure, which require the approval of Parliament.

Section Four

The Highest Organs of State Administration
Article 22

The highest organ of state administration is the Council of Ministers of the Hungarian People's Republic.

Article 23

(1) The Council of Ministers consists of
 (a) the Chairman of the Council of Ministers;
 (b) the Deputy Chairman or Chairmen of the Council of Ministers;
 (c) the Minister or Ministers of State;
 (d) the Ministers heading the various ministries.
(2) The Council of Ministers or single members of it are elected to, or relieved of, office by Parliament on the recommendation of the Presidential Council of the People's Republic.
(3) Members of the Council of Ministers who are not members of Parliament may attend the sittings of Parliament and take part in its debates.

Article 24

The Ministries of the Hungarian People's Republic are:

the Ministry of Foreign Affairs;
the Ministry of Home Affairs;
the Ministry of National Defence;
the Ministry of Finance;
the Ministry of Justice;
the Ministry of Heavy Industry;
the Ministry of Light Industry;
the Ministry of Foreign Trade;
the Ministry of Home Trade;
the Ministry of Building;

the Ministry of Communications and Postal Services;
the Ministry of Adult Education;
the Ministry of Religion and Public Education;
the Ministry of Social Welfare.

Article 25

(1) The Council of Ministers:
   (a) directs the work of the ministries and of the other organs immediately subordinate to it;
   (b) ensures the enforcement of the laws and of the decrees issued by the Presidential Council of the People's Republic;
   (c) ensures the fulfilment of the economic plans;
   (d) deals with all the matters subject to its jurisdiction.
(2) In the execution of its duties the Council of Ministers may issue decrees which must not, however, infringe the law or the decrees issued by the Presidential Council of the People's Republic.
(3) Decrees issued by the Council of Ministers are signed by its Chairman. Such decrees must be published in the official gazette.
(4) The Council of Ministers is empowered to annul or modify any regulation, decision or measure of any central or local organ of government if such regulations, decisions or measures infringe the constitution or are detrimental to the interests of the working people.

Article 26

(1) The Chairman of the Council of Ministers presides over the meetings of the Council, provides for the execution of the orders and decisions of the Council and directs the work of the organs immediately subordinate to it.
(2) The Ministers direct the branches of state administration entrusted to them and the work of the organs immediately subordinate to them, in accordance with the laws and the decrees and decisions of the Council of Ministers.
(3) In the execution of their duties the Chairman of the Council of Ministers and the Ministers are empowered to issue decrees, which may not, however, infringe the laws of the People's Republic or the decrees made by the Presidential Council of the People's Republic

or its Council of Ministers. Such decrees must be published in the official gazette.

Article 27

(1) The Council of Ministers is responsible for its activities to Parliament and must render regular accounts of its work to that body.
(2) The Chairman of the Council or Ministers (or his Deputy) and its members are individually responsible for their actions and conduct. A special law regulates the implementation of this responsibility.
(3) Any member of Parliament may put to the Council of Ministers, its Chairman or members, questions relating to any matter within the competence of the persons named and such questions must be answered by them in the House of Parliament.

Article 28

(1) The Council of Ministers may take measures on any matter touching state administration either directly or through one of its members.
(2) The Council of Ministers is empowered to take under its own immediate control any branch of the state administration and can set up special organs for this purpose.

Section Five

The Local Organs of State Power
Article 29

(1) For purposes of administration the territory of the Hungarian People's Republic is divided up into counties, districts, towns and boroughs. Larger towns and cities may be subdivided into smaller administrative units.
(2) Changes in the territorial jurisdiction of the various local administrative organs can be made by the Council of Ministers.

Article 30

(1) The local organs of state administration are the county council, the district council, the town council, the borough council and the town precinct council.

(2) The members of the councils are elected by the voters in the area in question, for a term of four years in accordance with the principles established in connection with the election of members of Parliament.

(3) The members of the local councils can be recalled by their constituents in accordance with the law.

Article 31

(1) The local councils exercise their administrative functions in their area of jurisdiction in accordance with the constitutionally created laws, decrees and other enactments and within the limits defined by their superior organs.

(2) Local councils:
- (a) direct the economic, social and cultural activities in their area;
- (b) prepare the local economic plan and budget and supervise their fulfilment;
- (c) enforce the laws and the regulations made by superior organs;
- (d) direct and supervise the activities of the state administrative and executive organs subordinate to them;
- (e) ensure the maintenance of public order and the protection of public property;
- (f) protect the rights of the workers;
- (g) direct and supervise the activities of economic enterprises of a local character;
- (h) give support to the co-operative societies of the workers;
- (i) deal with all matters within their competence as defined by a valid enactment.

(3) Local councils can issue regulations within the area of their jurisdiction; but such regulations must not infringe the laws, decree-laws, or decrees issued by the Council of Ministers, the Ministers, or a superior council. The orders issued by local councils must be promulgated according to the local custom.

(4) Local councils can annul or modify the orders, decisions or measures of the councils subordinate to them, if such orders, decisions or measures infringe the constitution or a constitutionally created enactment.

Article 32

(1) The local councils exercise their functions in close contact with the population, ensure the active participation of the workers in the work of local government and encourage initiative and vigilance on their part.

(2) Local councils must give an account of their activities to their constituents not less than twice every year.

Article 33

(1) The executive and administrative organs of the local councils are the Executive Committees, which they elect from among their own members.

(2) The Executive Committee is presided over by a Chairman. Its business is conducted by a Secretary subordinate to the Chairman. The Chairman and his Deputy or Deputies, and the Secretary are elected by the Executive Committee from among its own members.

(3) The Executive Committees are directly responsible to the local councils and to the Executive Committees of the superior councils. In their activities they must comply with the directives of the organs of state administration.

(4) Local councils have the right to recall the Executive Committees as a whole or any of their members.

Article 34

The organs of state administration may set up special departmental organs outside the local councils. Such special organs receive their general directives from the higher organs of state administration but in their immediate local activities are subordinate to the local Executive Committee.

Article 35

Detailed regulations relating to the activities of the local councils and executive committees are the subject of a special Act of Parliament.

Section Six

The Judicature
Article 36

(1) In the Hungarian People's Republic justice is administered by the Supreme Court of the Hungarian People's Republic, by the high courts, the county courts, and the district courts.
(2) By provision of the law special courts may be set up to deal with specific groups of cases.

Article 37

The courts are composed of judges and lay members. The law can establish exceptions to this rule.

Article 38

The Supreme Court of the Hungarian People's Republic exercises the right of supervising in principle the judicial activities and practice of all other courts. For this purpose the Supreme Court can establish directives and take decisions on questions of principle, which are then binding for all courts.

Article 39

(1) In the Hungarian People's Republic all judicial offices are filled by election and the elected Judges may be recalled.
(2) The judges of the Supreme Court are elected for a period of five years, the judges of the county and district courts for a period of three years.
(3) The President and judges of the Supreme Court and the Presidents of the high courts are elected by Parliament.
(4) The judges are accountable to their electors in respect of their judicial activities.
(5) The election of the judges of the high courts, county courts and district courts is regulated by rules laid down in a special Act of Parliament.

Article 40

(1) The hearings before all courts of law are public unless otherwise prescribed by law.

(2) All those accused before the courts are guaranteed the right of defence during the judicial proceedings.

Article 41

(1) The Courts of the Hungarian People's Republic punish the enemies of the working people, protect and safeguard the state, the social and economic order and the institutions of the people's democracy and the rights of the workers and educate the working people in the observance of the rules governing the life of a socialist commonwealth.
(2) Judges are independent and subject only to the law.

Section Seven

The Public Prosecutor

Article 42

(1) The function of the Chief Public Prosecutor of the Hungarian People's Republic is to watch over the observance of the law.
(2) In the exercise of this function the Chief Public Prosecutor supervises the observance of the law by the ministries, the authorities, offices, institutions and other organs, by the local organs of the state executive and by citizens.
(3) The Chief Public Prosecutor sees to it that all actions detrimental to, or endangering, the social order, security or independence of the Hungarian People's Republic be consistently prosecuted.

Article 43

(1) The Chief Public Prosecutor of the Hungarian People's Republic is elected by Parliament for a period of six years. Parliament has the right to recall the Chief Public Prosecutor before the expiration of his term of office.
(2) The Chief Public Prosecutor is responsible and accountable to Parliament in respect of his official activities.
(3) Public prosecutors are appointed by the Chief Public Prosecutor.
(4) The machinery of the prosecution of offenders is under the general direction of the Chief Public Prosecutor's office.

Article 44
Public prosecutors proceed independently of the central and local administrative and executive organs of the state.

Section Eight

The Rights and Duties of Citizens

Article 45
(1) The Hungarian People's Republic guarantees for its citizens the right to work and the right to remuneration in accordance with the quantity and quality of the work done.
(2) This right is implemented by the Hungarian People's Republic by means of the planned development of the forces of production and by a manpower policy based on economic planning.

Article 46
(1) The Hungarian People's Republic ensures the right of rest and recreation for its citizens.
(2) This right is implemented by the Hungarian People's Republic by means of a legally determined working day, holidays with pay and the organization of the rest and recreation of the workers.

Article 47
(1) The Hungarian People's Republic protects the health of the workers and assists them in the event of sickness or disability.
(2) The Hungarian People's Republic implements this protection and assistance by means of a comprehensive social insurance scheme and the organization of medical services.

Article 48
(1) The Hungarian People's Republic ensures the right to education for every worker.
(2) The Hungarian People's Republic implements this right by means of an extension to all educational facilities, by means of a free and compulsory general schooling scheme, by the provision of secondary and higher schools, by educational facilities for adult workers and by financial aid to those receiving schooling of any kind.

Article 49

(1) The citizens of the Hungarian People's Republic are equal before the law and enjoy equal rights.
(2) Discrimination of any kind against any citizen on grounds of sex, religion, or nationality is a severely punishable offence.
(3) The Hungarian People's Republic ensures to all nationalities living within its borders the possibility of education in their native tongue and the possibility of developing their national culture.

Article 50

(1) In the Hungarian People's Republic women enjoy equal rights with men.
(2) The equal rights of women are implemented by the safeguarding of their working conditions on a par with those of men, maternity leave with pay in the event of pregnancy, increased legal protection of mother and child, and a system of maternity and child welfare institutions.

Article 51

The Hungarian People's Republic protects the institution of marriage and the family.

Article 52

The Hungarian People's Republic devotes special care to the education and development of the young and accords them special protection.

Article 53

The Hungarian People's Republic effectively supports all scientific work serving the cause of the working people, as well as the arts which depict the life and struggle of the people and proclaim the victory of the people. It gives every support to the emergence of intellectual workers faithful to the people.

Article 54

(1) The Hungarian People's Republic safeguards the liberty of conscience of all citizens and the freedom of religious worship.

(2) In order to ensure the liberty of conscience, the Hungarian People's Republic separates the Church from the State.

Article 55

(1) In accordance with the interests of the workers the Hungarian People's Republic ensures for its citizens freedom of speech, freedom of the press and freedom of assembly.
(2) In order to implement these freedoms, the state places at the disposal of the workers the material resources required.

Article 56

(1) In order to develop the social, economic and cultural activities of the workers, the Hungarian People's Republic constitutionally guarantees the right of organization.
(2) In fulfilling its tasks, the Hungarian People's Republic bases itself on the organizations of the class-conscious workers. In order to defend the people's democracy, promote participation in socialist construction, widen the scope of cultural and educational work, implement the rights of the people and develop international solidarity, the workers establish trade unions, democratic organizations of women and young people as well as other mass organizations and put into practice the close co-operation and democratic unity of the industrial, agricultural and intellectual workers. The leading force in such political and social activities is the working class, led by its advance guard and supported by the democratic unity of the whole people.

Article 57

The Hungarian People's Republic safeguards the freedom and inviolability of the person, the privacy of the home and the correspondence of its citizens.

Article 58

(1) The Hungarian People's Republic guarantees these rights and freedoms to all workers living within its borders.
(2) Foreign citizens, persecuted for their democratic attitude or their activities in the interests of the liberation of the peoples, enjoy the right of asylum in the Hungarian People's Republic.

Article 59

It is the fundamental duty of all citizens of the Hungarian People's Republic to defend the property of the people, consolidate social assets, increase the economic strength of the Hungarian People's Republic, raise the living standard and cultural level of the workers and strengthen the people's democratic system.

Article 60

Military service is the honourable duty of the citizens of the Hungarian People's Republic in accordance with the law on universal military service.

Article 61

(1) Defence of the home country is the sacred duty of all citizens of the Hungarian People's Republic.
(2) Treason, violation of the military oath, desertion to the enemy, espionage and every action detrimental to the military strength of the country – constituting a betrayal of the cause of the country and of the workers – is subject to the severest penalties of the law.

Section Nine

The Electoral System
Article 62

(1) Members of Parliament are elected by the citizens of the Hungarian People's Republic on the basis of universal, equal, and direct suffrage by secret ballot.
(2) The elected members are accountable to their constituents.
(3) The constituents have the right to recall their elected member of Parliament.

Article 63

(1) All citizens of the Hungarian People's Republic who are of age have the right to vote.
(2) Enemies of the working people and those who are unsound of mind are excluded from the suffrage by law.

Article 64

At elections every citizen entitled to vote has one vote and all votes are equal.

Article 65
All citizens who have the vote are eligible for election.

Article 66
Details of the election and recall of members of Parliament are laid down in a special Act of Parliament.

Section Ten

The Coat of Arms, the Flag and the Capital of the Hungarian People's Republic

Article 67
The coat of arms of the Hungarian People's Republic is:

A hammer and ear of wheat in a round blue field surrounded by a wreath of wheat; in the upper part of the field a five-pointed star radiating rays onto the field: below the field a band in the colours red, white, and green.

Article 68
The flag of the Hungarian People's Republic is of horizontal bands of red, white and green with the arms of the Hungarian People's Republic in the centre.

Article 69
The capital of the Hungarian People's Republic is the city of Budapest.

Section Eleven

Final Provisions

Article 70
(1) The constitution of the Hungarian People's Republic enters into force on the day of its promulgation. Its enforcement is the duty of the Council of Ministers.
(2) The Council of Ministers has the duty of submitting to Parliament the bills required for the implementation of the constitution.

Article 71
(1) The constitution is the fundamental law of the Hungarian People's Republic.

APPENDIX XIII 331

(2) The constitution as well as all constitutional enactments are obligatory for all organs of state power and all citizens alike.

Official translation of the Hungarian government, 1949

Note

1. From the official English translation published in Budapest in 1949.

APPENDIX XIV

EXCERPTS FROM THE CONSTITUTION OF THE REPUBLIC OF HUNGARY: (AS AMENDED BY ACT NO. XXXI. OF 1989)[1]

In furtherance of a peaceful transition to the rule of law seeking to establish a multi-party system, parliamentary democracy, and a social market economy the Parliament hereby adopts the following text of the Constitution to be in force until such time as a new Constitution of Hungary will have been enacted.

Chapter I

GENERAL PROVISIONS

Art. 1. Hungary shall be a republic.

Art. 2. (1) The Republic of Hungary shall be an independent, democratic state under the rule of law which shall enhance the values of both bourgeois democracy and democratic socialism.

(2) In the Republic of Hungary all power shall belong to the people, which shall exercise national sovereignty through its elected representatives as well as directly.

(3) No single social organization, state organ, or citizen shall be engaged in force activities directed towards capture or exercise of power

by force or exclusive possession thereof. It shall be a right and a duty of everyone to take action under the law against such designs.

Art. 3. (1) Subject to observance of the Constitution and the constitutional provisions, any party may be freely formed and may freely function in the Republic of Hungary.

(2) Parties shall cooperate in articulating and expressing the will of the people.

(3) Parties shall not directly exercise public power and accordingly no party shall direct any state organ. With view to separation of parties and public power, the posts and public offices not open to members or representatives of parties shall be specified by law.

Art. 4. Trade unions and other representative organizations shall defend and represent the interests of workers, members of cooperatives, and entrepreneurs.

Art. 5. The Republic of Hungary shall defend the liberty and power of the people, the independence and territorial integrity of the country, and its borders as defined by international agreements.

Art. 6. (1) The Republic of Hungary shall renounce war as a means of settlement of international disputes and shall refrain from the use or threat of force against the independence or territorial integrity of other states.

(2) The Republic of Hungary shall seek cooperation with all peoples and countries of the world.

(3) The Republic of Hungary shall have a sense of responsibility for the fate of Hungarians living beyond its borders and shall promote their cultivation of ties with Hungary.

Art. 7. (1) The legal system of the Republic of Hungary shall accept the generally recognized rules of international law and shall ensure harmony between obligations under international law and the municipal law.

(2) The legislative procedure shall be governed by a law of constitutional force.

Art. 8. (1) The Republic of Hungary shall recognize man's fundamental rights inviolable and inalienable, and it shall be a prime duty of the state to respect and protect those rights.

(2) Rules establishing fundamental rights and duties shall not be laid down except by laws of constitutional force.

(3) Exercise of fundamental rights shall be subject to no restrictions except those imposed by laws of constitutional [force] in the interest of protecting national security, the internal order, public safety, public health, public morals or the fundamental rights and freedoms of others.

(4) The fundamental rights set forth in Articles 54 to 56, Article 57 paragraphs (2) to (4), Article 60, Articles 66 to 69, and Article 70/E shall not be restricted or suspended even in a state of public emergency or siege or peril.

Art. 9. (1) Hungary's economy shall be a market economy profiting by the advantages of planning and according equal protection to public and private property on an equal footing.

(2) The Republic of Hungary shall, under the principle of neutrality to competition, be subject to no restrictions other than those established by a law of constitutional force.

Art. 10. (1) The property of the Hungarian State shall be national property.

(2) The scope of the State's exclusive ownership and exclusive economic activity shall be determined by a law of constitutional force.

Art. 11. State enterprises and economic organizations shall enjoy autonomy and bear responsibility as defined by law.

Art. 12. (1) The State shall support the cooperative movement based on voluntary association and shall recognize the autonomy of cooperatives.

(2) The State shall recognize the emergence and operation of producers' self-management and the property of self-governments.

Art. 13. Property shall not be expropriated save in exceptional cases in the public interest and in the manner defined by law, and expropriation shall be subject to full, unconditional, and prompt compensation.

Art. 14. The Constitution ensures the right of inheritance.

Art. 15. The Republic of Hungary shall protect the institutions of marriage and the family.

Art. 16. The Republic of Hungary shall devote a particular measure of care to youth's security of existence, education and training and shall protect their interests.

Art. 17. The Republic of Hungary shall provide for the needy by an extensive scheme of social measures.

Art. 18. The Republic of Hungary shall recognize and implement the right of everyone to a healthy environment.

[....]

Chapter XII

FUNDAMENTAL RIGHTS AND DUTIES

Art. 54. (1) Every human being in the Republic of Hungary shall have the inherent right to life and dignity, of which no one shall be arbitrarily deprived.

(2) No one shall be subjected to torture or to cruel, inhuman or degrading treatment or punishment and, in particular, no one shall be subjected without his consent to medical or scientific experimentation.

Art. 55. (1) Everyone in the Republic of Hungary shall have the right to liberty and security of person; no one shall be deprived of his liberty except on such grounds and in accordance with such procedures as are established by law.

(2) Anyone who has been the victim of unlawful arrest or detention shall have a right to compensation.

Art. 56. Everyone in the Republic of Hungary shall have legal capacity.

Art. 57. (1) All persons in the Republic of Hungary shall be equal before the courts, and in the determination of any criminal charge against him, or of his rights and obligations in a suit of law, everyone shall be entitled to a fair and public hearing by an independent and impartial tribunal established by law.

(2) No one shall be held guilty of any criminal offence until his criminal responsibility has been established by a final court judgement.

(3) Every person against whom a criminal proceeding has been instituted shall have the right to defend himself in every phase of the proceedings. The defense counsel shall not be held responsible on account of his opinion expressed in defending the accused.

(4) No one shall be held guilty of, and be punished for, any criminal offence on account of any act which did not constitute a criminal offence under Hungarian law at the time when it was committed.

(5) Everyone in the Republic of Hungary shall be entitled to the legal remedies defined by law against court judgements or decisions of administrative or other authorities infringing his rights or lawful interests.

Art. 58. (1) With the exception of cases defined by law, everyone lawfully within the territory of Hungary shall have the right to liberty of movement and freedom to choose his place of sojourn, including the right to leave the place of residence or the country.

(2) An alien lawfully in the territory of Hungary may be expelled from the country only in pursuance of a decision reached in accordance with law.

Art. 59. Everyone in the Republic of Hungary shall have the right to good reputation, the inviolability of the privacy of his home and correspondence, and the protection of his personal data.

Art. 60. (1) Everyone in the Republic of Hungary shall have the right to freedom of thought, conscience and religion.

(2) This right shall include freedom to have or to adopt a religion or belief of his choice, and freedom, either individually or in community with others and in public or private, to manifest, or not to manifest, his religion or belief in worship, observance, practice or teaching.

(3) The Church in the Republic of Hungary shall be separated from the State.

Art. 61. (1) Everyone in the Republic of Hungary shall have the right to freedom of expression and to receive and impart information of public interest.

(2) The Republic of Hungary shall recognize and protect the freedom of the press.

Art. 62. The Republic of Hungary shall recognize the right of peaceful assembly and the free exercise thereof.

Art. 63. (1) Everyone in the Republic of Hungary shall have the right, on the basis of the freedom of association, to form and join organizations for purposes not prohibited by the law.

(2) No armed organization shall be formed for political purposes on the basis of the freedom of association.

Art. 64. Everyone in the Republic of Hungary shall have the right, either individually or in community with others, to submit written appeals or petitions to the competent state organs.

Art. 65. (1) Subject to the conditions defined by law, the Republic of Hungary shall guarantee asylum for aliens who in their country, or for stateless persons who in their place of residence, are persecuted on racial, religious, national, linguistic, or political grounds.

(2) No person enjoying asylum shall be extradited to another State.

Art. 66. (1) The Republic of Hungary shall guarantee the equality of men and women in respect of all civil and political as well as economic, social and cultural rights.

(2) Mothers in the Republic of Hungary shall, under separate provisions of law, enjoy support and protection before and after childbirth.

(3) The protection of women and young persons in employment shall also be guaranteed by separate provisions of law.

Art. 67. (1) All children in the Republic of Hungary shall be entitled to such protection by the family, the state and society as is required for their appropriate bodily, intellectual, and moral development.

(2) Parents shall have the right to choose the type of education they wish to ensure for their children.

(3) The state responsibilities regarding the situation and protection of the family and youth shall be laid down in separate provisions of law.

Art. 68. (1) The national and linguistic minorities in the Republic of Hungary shall share in people's power, being constituent factors of the State.

(2) The Republic of Hungary shall accord protection to the national and linguistic minorities, ensuring their collective participation in public life, the cultivation of their culture, the use of their mother tongue, education in their mother tongue, and the right to use names in their own language.

Art. 69. (1) No one in the Republic of Hungary shall be arbitrarily deprived of his Hungarian citizenship and no Hungarian citizen shall be expelled from the territory of the Republic of Hungary.

(2) Any Hungarian citizen staying abroad may return to Hungary at any time.

(3) While legally abroad, every Hungarian citizen shall be entitled to protection by the Republic of Hungary.

Art. 70. (1) Every adult citizen of Hungary shall have the right to vote and to be elected at parliamentary and municipal elections, provided he is domiciled in Hungary.

(2) Whoever is placed under curatorship restrictive or exclusive of his disposing capacity, has been barred by a final court judgement from performing public functions, is serving a sentence of imprisonment, or has in criminal proceedings been validly subjected to compulsory medical treatment in an institute shall have no franchise.

(3) Under separate provisions of law, non-nationals permanently settled in Hungary shall also have the franchise at the election of local councilors.

(4) Every Hungarian citizen shall have the right to take part in the conduct of public affairs and to perform public functions appropriate to his ability, qualification and professional competence.

Art. 70/A (1) The Republic of Hungary shall guarantee for everyone in its territory all human and civil rights without distinction of any kind, such as race, colour, sex, language, religion, political or other opinion, national or social origin, property, birth or other status.

(2) Any discrimination in respect of para. (1) shall be an offence severely punishable by law.

(3) The Republic of Hungary shall promote the achievement of equality or rights also by measures aimed at eliminating inequality of opportunity.

Art. 70/B. (1) Everyone in the Republic of Hungary shall have the right to work and to the free choice of employment and profession.

(2) Everyone shall have the right to equal pay for equal work without distinction of any kind.

(3) Every worker shall be entitled to a remuneration appropriate to the quantity and quality of the work done.

(4) Everyone shall have the right to rest, leisure, and periodic holidays with pay.

Art. 70/C. (1) Everyone shall have the right to form, in association with others, or to join organizations for the protection of his economic and social interests.

(2) The right to strike may be exercised in conformity with the relevant laws.

Art. 70/D. (1) All persons living in the territory of the Republic of Hungary shall have the right to the highest attainable standard of physical and mental health.

(2) The Republic of Hungary shall implement this right by organizing labour safety, health-care institutions and medical services as well as by protecting the man-made and natural environment.

Art. 70/E. (1) The citizens of the Republic of Hungary shall have the right to social security and to a livelihood in the event of old age, sickness, disability, widowhood, orphanhood, and unemployment in circumstances beyond their control.

(2) The Republic of Hungary shall realize the right to social services through social insurance and a network of social welfare institutions.

Art. 70/F. (1) The Republic of Hungary shall recognize the right of everyone to education.

(2) The Republic of Hungary shall realize this right by extending and universalizing public education, by means of free and compulsory primary education, granting access to secondary and higher education for all in accordance with their abilities, and providing financial support for those receiving education.

Art. 70/G. (1) The Republic of Hungary shall respect and support the freedom of scientific and artistic life, academic freedom, and the freedom of teaching.

(2) Scientists shall have the exclusive right to decide on scientific truths and to determine the scientific value of research.

Art. 70/H. (1) The defense of the country shall be a duty of every citizen of the Republic of Hungary.

(2) On the basis of universal liability for national service, citizens shall render military service, armed or unarmed, or to take part in civil defense subject to the conditions defined by law.

Art. 70/I. Every citizen of the Republic of Hungary shall be liable for general taxation in accordance with his income and financial situation.

Art. 70/J. Parents or custodians in the Republic of Hungary shall provide for the education of their infant children.

Art. 70/K. Claims arising out of violation of fundamental rights may be enforced before, and complaints about state decisions concerning compliance with obligations may be lodged with, courts.

Note

1. Géza Kilényi-Vanda Lamm (eds.): *Democratic Changes in Hungary. Basic Legislations on a Peaceful Transition from Bolshevism to Democracy*, Public Law Research Center of the Hungarian Academy of Sciences, Budapest, 1990, 35–36; 50–53.

APPENDIX XV

THE FUNDAMENTAL LAW OF HUNGARY[1]

God Bless the Hungarians!

National Avowal

WE, THE MEMBERS OF THE HUNGARIAN NATION, at the beginning of the new millennium, with a sense of responsibility for every Hungarian, hereby proclaim the following:

We are proud that our King Saint Stephen built the Hungarian State on solid ground and made our country a part of Christian Europe one thousand years ago.

We are proud of our forebears who fought for the survival, freedom and independence of our country.

We are proud of the outstanding intellectual achievements of the Hungarian people.

We are proud that our people has over the centuries defended Europe in a series of struggles and enriched Europe's common values with its talent and diligence.

We recognize the role of Christianity in preserving nationhood. We value the various religious traditions of our country.

We promise to preserve the intellectual and spiritual unity of our nation torn apart in the storms of the last century.

We proclaim that the nationalities living with us form part of the Hungarian political community and are constituent parts of the State.

We commit to promoting and safeguarding our heritage, our unique language, Hungarian culture, the languages and cultures of nationalities living in Hungary, along with all man-made and natural assets of the Carpathian Basin. We bear responsibility for our descendants; therefore we shall protect the living conditions of future generations by making prudent use of our material, intellectual and natural resources.

We believe that our national culture is a rich contribution to the diversity of European unity.

We respect the freedom and culture of other nations, and shall strive to cooperate with every nation of the world.

We hold that human existence is based on human dignity.

We hold that individual freedom can only be complete in cooperation with others.

We hold that the family and the nation constitute the principal framework of our coexistence, and that our fundamental cohesive values are fidelity, faith and love.

We hold that the strength of community and the honour of each man are based on labour, an achievement of the human mind.

We hold that we have a general duty to help the vulnerable and the poor.

We hold that the common goal of citizens and the State is to achieve the highest possible measure of well-being, safety, order, justice and liberty.

We hold that democracy is only possible where the State serves its citizens and administers their affairs in an equitable manner, without prejudice or abuse.

We honour the achievements of our historical constitution and we honour the Holy Crown, which embodies the constitutional continuity of Hungary's statehood and the unity of the nation.

We do not recognize the suspension of our historical constitution due to foreign occupations. We deny any statute of limitations for the inhuman crimes committed against the Hungarian nation and its citizens under the national socialist and the communist dictatorship.

We do not recognize the communist constitution of 1949, since it was the basis for tyrannical rule; therefore we proclaim it to be invalid.

We agree with the Members of the first free National Assembly, which proclaimed as its first decision that our current liberty was born of our 1956 Revolution.

We date the restoration of our country's self-determination, lost on the nineteenth day of March 1944, from the second day of May 1990, when the first freely elected organ of popular representation was formed. We shall consider this date to be the beginning of our country's new democracy and constitutional order.

We hold that after the decades of the twentieth century which led to a state of moral decay, we have an abiding need for spiritual and intellectual renewal.

We trust in a jointly shaped future and the commitment of younger generations. We believe that our children and grandchildren will make Hungary great again with their talent, persistence and moral strength.

Our Fundamental Law shall be the basis of our legal order; it shall be an alliance among Hungarians of the past, present and future. It is a living framework which expresses the nation's will and the form in which we want to live.

We, the citizens of Hungary, are ready to found the order of our country upon the common endeavours of the nation.

[...]

Article R

(1) The Fundamental Law shall be the foundation of the legal system of Hungary.
(2) The Fundamental Law and legal regulations shall be binding on everyone.
(3) The provisions of the Fundamental Law shall be interpreted in accordance with their purposes, the National Avowal contained therein and the achievements of our historical constitution.

Official translation of the Hungarian government, 25 April 2011

Note

1. From the official English translation available at www.kormany.hu/download/e/ 02/00000/The%20New%20Fundamental%20Law%20of%20Hungary.pdf.

BIBLIOGRAPHY

Ablonczy, Balázs (ed.), *Teleki, Pál, Válogatott politikai írások* (Budapest, 2000).
Ackerman, Bruce, *We the People, Volume 1: Foundations* (Cambridge and London, 1993).
Albert, Richard, 'How unwritten constitutional norms change written constitutions', *Dublin University Law Journal* xxxviii/2 (2015).
Alden, Percy (ed.), *Hungary of To-day* (London, 1909).
A magyar anyáknak az országgyűlésére egybegyült ország nagyjai s magyar atyák elejébe terjesztett alázatos kérések (Pest, 1790).
Amar, Akhil Reed, *America's Unwritten Constitution. The Precedents and Principles We Live By* (New York, 2012).
——— 'American constitutionalism – written, unwritten, and living', *Harvard Law Review Forum* cxxvi/195 (2013).
Ammerer, G. et al. (eds), *Bündnispartner und Konkurrenten des Landesfürsten? Die Stände in der Habsburgermonarchie* (Vienna and Munich, 2007).
Arato, Andrew et al. (eds), *Opinion on the Fundamental Law of Hungary* (Budapest, 2011).
Armstrong, Katherine (ed.), *Letters from Hungary 1864 to 1869. Written by Mary Elizabeth Stevens to her Mother and Sister* (London, 1999).
Az 1848–1849. évi törvények. Available at https://1000ev.hu/index.php?a=2&k=3&f=5268 (accessed 3 March 2018).
Bak, János M., *Königtum und Stände in Ungarn im 14.–16. Jahrhundert* (Wiesbaden, 1973).
——— (ed.), *The Customary Law of the Renowned Kingdom of Hungary in Three Parts (The 'Tripartitum') – Decreta Regni Mediaevalis Hungariae*, vol. 5.
Ballagi, Géza, *A politikai irodalom Magyarországon 1825-ig* (Budapest, 1888).
Bánffy, Dezső, *Magyar nemzetiségi politika* (Budapest, 1902).
Bánkuti, Miklós, Gábor Halmai and Kim Lane Scheppele, 'Hungary's illiberal turn: Disabling the constitution', *Journal of Democracy* xxiii/3 (2012).
Banyó, Péter and Martyn Rady (eds), *The Laws of the Medieval Kingdom of Hungary – Decreta Regni Mediaevalis Hungariae*, vol. 4 (Idyllwild, CA, and Budapest, 2012).
Barany, George, *Stephen Széchenyi and the Awakening of Hungarian Nationalism, 1791–1841* (Princeton, NJ, 1968).

BIBLIOGRAPHY 345

Barber, Nicholas W., *The Constitutional State* (Oxford, 2010).
—— and Adrian Vermeule, 'The exceptional role of courts in constitutional order', *Notre Dame Law Review* xcii/2 (2016).
Barcsay, Ákos, *Herrschaftsantritt im Ungarn des 18. Jahrhunderts. Studien zur Verhältnis zwischen Krongewalt und Ständetum im Zeitalter des Absolutismus* (St Katharinen, 2002).
Bártfai Szabó, László, *A Sárvár-Felsővidéki gróf Széchenyi-család története*, vol. II (Budapest, 1911).
Bay, Ferenc (ed.), *1848–49 a korabeli napilapok tükrében* (Budapest, 1943).
Beales, Derek, *Joseph II against the World, 1780–1790* (Cambridge, 2009).
Beér, János (ed.), *Magyar alkotmányjog* (Budapest, 1951).
Beér, János and Imre Szabó (eds), *A Magyar Népköztársaság Alkotmánya. Az 1949: XX. törvény és magyarázata* (Budapest, 1949).
Beksics, Gusztáv, *Az egyéni szabadság Európában és Magyarországon* (Budapest, 1879).
—— *A democratia Magyarországon* (Budapest, 1881).
Beller, Steven, 'Including the middle: A response to R.J.W. Evans', *Central Europe* i/2 (2003).
Benda, Kálmán, *A magyar jakobinusok iratai*, 3 vols (Budapest, 1952).
—— (ed.), *Magyarország történeti kronológiája* (Budapest, 1982).
Benkő, Loránd, *A magyar nyelv történeti-etimológiai szótára*, 4 vols (Budapest, 1967–84).
Berend, Nora, *At the Gate of Christendom: Jews, Muslims and 'Pagans' in Medieval Hungary* (Cambridge, 2010).
Bérenger, Jean, *A History of the Habsburg Empire 1700–1918* (London, 1997).
—— and Károly Kecskeméti, *Országgyűlés és parlamenti élet Magyarországon 1608–1918* (Budapest, 2008).
Berglunk, Bruce and Brian Porter-Szűcs (eds), *Christianity and Modernity in Eastern Europe* (Budapest and New York, 2010).
Besenyei, Lajos, Géza Érszegi and Maurizio Pedrazza Gorlero (eds), *De Bulla Aurea Andreae Regis Hungariae MCCXXII* (Verona, 1999).
Bevir, M. (ed.), *Encyclopedia of Political Theory* (London, 2010).
Bibó, István, *Válogatott tanulmányok. 1945–1949* (Budapest, 1986).
Bireley, Robert, *Ferdinand II, Counter-Reformation Emperor, 1578–1637* (Cambridge, 2014).
Bíró, Ferenc, *A fiatal Bessenyei és íróbarátai* (Budapest, 1976).
Bitskey, Botond (ed.), *Tíz éves az Alkotmánybíróság* (Budapest, 2000).
Blokker, B. and C. Thornhill (eds), *Sociological Constitutionalism* (Cambridge, 2017).
Bogdany, A. and Sonnevend, P. (eds), *Constitutional Crisis in the European Constitutional Area. Theory, Law and Politics in Hungary and Romania* (Oxford and Portland, OR, 2015).
Bónis, György, *Hajnóczy József: 1750–1795* (Budapest, 1954).
Boros, Tamas, *Constitutional amendments in Hungary: The government's struggle against the constitutional court* (Budapest, 2013).
Bos, E. and K. Pócza (eds), *Verfassunggebung in konsolidierten Demokratien: Neubeginn oder Verfall eines politischen Systems?* (Baden-Baden, 2014).
Bozóki, András (ed.), *The Roundtable Talks of 1989. The Genesis of Hungarian Democracy. Analysis and Documents* (Budapest, 2002).
Brodocz, André, *Die symbolische Dimension der Verfassung* (Wiesbaden, 2003).

Brunner, Otto, Werner Conze and Reinhart Koselleck (eds), *Geschichtliche Grundbegriffe. Historisches Lexikon zur politisch-sozialen Sprache in Deutschland*, vol. 1 (Stuttgart, 1972).
Burgess, Glenn, *The Politics of the Ancient Constitution* (University Park, PA, 1993).
Cambel, Samuel et al. (eds), *Dejiny slovenska*, 6 vols (Bratislava, 1985).
Cartledge, Bryan, *The Will to Survive. A History of Hungary* (London, 2006).
Cieger, András, *Lónyay Menyhért, 1822–1884* (Budapest, 2008).
—— 'National identity and constitutional patriotism in the context of modern Hungarian history', *Hungarian Historical Review* v/1 (2016).
Concha, Győző, *A kilenczvenes évek reformeszméi és előzményeik. Irodalomtörténeti vázlat* (Budapest, 1885) (Reprint: 2005).
Contiades, Xenophon (ed.), *Engineering Constitutional Change. A Comparative Perspective on Europe, Canada and the USA* (London and New York, 2013).
Corpus Juris Hungarici (Budapest). Available electronically as *1000 év törvényei* at https://1000ev.hu/ (accessed 3 March 2018).
Csapó, Csaba, *A magyar királyi csendőrség története, 1881–1914* (Pécs, 1999).
Csatskó, Imre, 'Magyar büntetőtörvénykönyv'. Manuscript. Manuscript Collection of the Library of the Hungarian Academy of Sciences.
Csink, L. et al. (eds), *The Basic Law of Hungary. A First Commentary* (Dublin, 2012).
Csizmadia, Andor, 'Törekvések az emberi jogok biztosítására és büntetőjogi védelmükre a reformkori Magyarországon', *Jogtudományi Közlöny* xxx/12 (1975).
—— (ed.), *Magyar állam-és jogtörténet* (Budapest, 1972).
—— et al. (eds), *A magyarországi polgári államrendszerek* (Budapest, 1981).
Csorba, László and Ferenc Velkey, *Reform és forradalom, 1790–1849* (Debrecen, 1998).
Csuday, Jenő, *A magyar alkotmány történeti fejlődése* (Budapest, 1922).
Davis, Walter W., *Joseph II: An Imperial Reformer for the Austrian Netherlands* (Dordrecht, 1974).
Deák, Ágnes, 'Együttműködés vagy konkurencia. Az alsó-ausztriai, a csehországi és a magyarországi ellenzék összefogási kísérlete 1847–1848-ban', *Aestas* xiv/1–2 (1999). Available at http://epa.oszk.hu/00800/00861/00011/1h-02.html (accessed 3 March 2018).
Deák, Ferenc, *Adalék a magyar közjoghoz. Észrevételek Lustkandl Vencel munkájára: "Das ungarisch-österreichische Staatsrecht" a magyar közjog történelmének szempontjából* (Pest, 1865).
Deák, István, *The Lawful Revolution: Louis Kossuth and the Hungarians, 1848–1849* (New York, 1979).
—— *A törvényes forradalom. Kossuth Lajos és a magyarok 1848–49-ben*, translated by Éva Veressné Deák (Budapest, 1994).
Debicki, Marek, 'Eastern European constitutionalism. Theory and practice' *Manitoba Law Journal* iv/1 (1970).
Dickson, Peter, 'Monarchy and bureaucracy in late eighteenth century Austria', *The English Historical Review* cx (1995).
Dimitrakopoulos, Ioannis G., *Individual Rights and Liberties under the U.S. Constitution. The Case Law of the U.S. Supreme Court* (Leiden and Boston, MA, 2007).
Diószegi, István, *Bismarck und Andrássy. Ungarn in der deutschen Machtpolitik in der 2. Hälfte des 19. Jahrhunderts* (Budapest, 1999).

BIBLIOGRAPHY 347

Dobszay, T. et al. (eds), *Rendiség és parlamentarizmus Magyarországon. A kezdetektől 1918-ig* (Budapest, 2013).
Dodd, Walter F. (ed.), *Modern Constitutions – A Collection of the Fundamental Laws of Twenty-Two of the Most Important Countries of the World, with Historical and Bibliographical Notes*, vol. 1 (Chicago, 1909).
Eckhart, Ferenc, *A szentkorona-eszme története* (Budapest, 1941).
——— 'A magyar alkotmány', *Magyar Szemle* 1944/3.
Ember, Győző and Heckenast Gusztáv (eds), *Magyarország története, 1686–1790* (Budapest, 1989).
Engel, Pál, *The Kingdom of Hungary, 896–1526* (Budapest, 2006).
Erdődy, Gábor, '"Szabadságot mindenben és mindenkinek". A belga alkotmányos rendszer létrejötte és működése 1831–1848' (Budapest, 2006).
Evans, R.J.W., 'Central Europe, past and present', *Central Europe* i/2 (2003).
——— *Austria, Hungary and the Habsburgs. Essays on Central Europe, c. 1683–1867* (Oxford, 2006).
Ferenczy, Árpád, *A politika rendszere* (Budapest, 1909).
Föglein, Gizella, *Államforma és államfői jogkör Magyarországon (1944–1949)* (Budapest, 1993).
Fruhstorfer, A. and M. Hein (eds), *Constitutional Politics in Central and Eastern Europe* (Wiesbaden, 2017).
Furedi, Frank, *Populism and the European Culture Wars: The Conflict of Values between Hungary and the EU* (London and New York, 2017).
Galligan D.J. and D.J. Versteeg (eds), *Social and Political Foundations of Constitutions* (Cambridge, 2013).
Gángó, Gábor, '1848–1849 in Hungary', *Hungarian Studies* xv/1 (2001).
Gardner, John, 'Can there be a written constitution?', in L. Gree and B. Leiter (eds), *Oxford Studies in Philosophy of Law* (Oxford, 2011).
Gergely, András, *Egy nemzetet az emberiségnek. Tanulmányok a magyar reformkorról és 1848-ról* (Budapest, 1987).
——— (ed.) *19. századi magyar történelem 1790–1918* (Budapest, 1998).
Gerő, András, *Emperor Francis Joseph, King of the Hungarians* (New York, 2001).
Giesey, Ralph E., 'The juristic basis of dynastic right to the French throne', *Transactions of the American Philosophical Society*, N.S., 51 (1961).
Goldie, M. and R. Wokler (eds), *The Cambridge History of Eighteenth-Century Political Thought*, reprint edition (Cambridge, 2016).
Gragger, Robert, *Preussen, Weimar und die ungarische Königskrone* (Berlin and Leipzig, 1923).
Gundisch, Guido, 'Nemzetiségi pártszervezetek közjogi szempontból', *Jogtudományi Közlemények*, 3 April 1914.
Gyáni, Gábor, 'A történelmi esemény fogalma', *Magyar Tudomány* clxxii/11 (2011).
Gyurgyák, János, *Ezzé lett Magyar hazátok* (Budapest, 2013).
Halász, Iván, 'The institutional framework and the methods of implementation of Soviet legal ideas in Czechoslovakia and Hungary during Stalinism', *Journal on European History of Law* vi/2 (2015).
Halmai, Gábor, 'The reform of constitutional law in Hungary after the transition', *Legal Studies* xviii/2 (1998).
——— 'The Hungarian constitutional court and constitutional identity', Verfassungsblog, 10 January 2017. Available at http://verfassungsblog.de/

the-hungarian-constitutional-court-and-constitutional-identity/ (accessed 3 March 2018).

Hanák, Péter and Ferenc Mucsi (eds), *Magyarország története, 1890–1918* (Budapest, 1978).

Hanebrink, Paul, *In Defense of Christian Hungary: Religion, Nationalism and Antisemitism, 1890–1944* (Ithaca, NY, 2009).

Hegedüs, Dániel István, *A történeti magyar közjog jelenkori hagyatéka: a történeti alkotmány és a Szent Korona*, Studia Iuvenum Iurisperitorum, 8/2016.

Hóman, Bálint and Gyula Szekfű, *Magyar történet*, 5 vols (Budapest, 1935).

Hörcher, Ferenc, 'Töprengések a szavazófülkés forradalomról', *Kommentár* 2010/4.

—— 'Enlightened reform or national reform? The continuity debate about the Hungarian reform era and the example of the two Széchenyis (1790–1848)', *Hungarian Historical Review* v/1 (2016).

Horváth, Attila, 'A szocialista állam- és jogtudomány', in A. Jakab and A. Menyhárd (eds), *A jog tudománya* (Budapest, 2015).

—— '"A köztársaság az egyetlen lehetséges államforma." Az 1946. évi I. törvény megalkotása, a köztársaság kikiáltása', *Acta Humana* v/1 (2017).

Horváth, István, 'Balogh Péter', in *Nógrád Megyei Múzeumok Évkönyve* XX (Nógrád, 1995).

Hungarian Declaration of Independence, April 1849, published in Henry M. De Puy, *Kossuth and his Generals* (Buffalo, NY, 1852). Available at https://ecommons.cornell.edu/handle/1813/1446 (accessed 3 March 2018).

Jakab, András, *Az új Alaptörvény keletkezése és gyakorlati következményei* (Budapest, 2011).

—— (ed.), *Az alkotmány kommentárja*, vols I–III (Budapest, 2009).

Jászi, Oszkár, *The Dissolution of the Habsburg Monarchy* (Chicago, 1961).

Jori, Mario, 'Legal positivism', in E. Craig (ed.), *Routledge Encyclopedia of Philosophy* (London, 2005).

Judson, Pieter M., *Exclusive Revolutionaries. Liberal Politics, Social Experience, and National Identity in the Austrian Empire, 1848–1914* (Ann Arbor, MI, 1996).

Kann, Robert A. and Zdeněk V. David, *The Peoples of the Eastern Habsburg Lands, 1526–1918* (Seattle, WA, 1984).

Kassics, Ignác, *Enchiridion seu Extractus Benignarum Ordinationum Regiarum*, 3 vols (Pest, 1825).

Katus, László, *Hungary in the Dual Monarchy 1867–1914* (New York, 2008).

Kecskés, Gábor (ed.), *Doktori Műhelytanulmányok. Széchenyi Egyetem Állam- és Jogtudományi Doktori Iskola* (Győr, 2013).

Kemény, Zsigmond, *Forradalom után* (Pest, 1850).

—— *Még egy szó a forradalom után* (Pest, 1851).

Király, Béla K., *Hungary in the Late Eighteenth Century: The Decline of Enlightened Despotism* (New York, 1969).

Kiss, Anita, János Nagy and Adrienn Kapitány (eds), *Pest-Pilis-Solt vármegye országgyűlési követutasításai a 18. században* (Budapest, 2015).

Kiss, Péter (ed.), *Magyar kormányprogramok 1867–2002*, 2 vols (Budapest, 2004).

Klaniczay, Gábor et al. (eds), *Multiple Antiquities, Multiple Modernities: Ancient Histories in Nineteenth Century European Cultures* (Frankfurt, 2011).

Kmety, Károly, 'Közjogunk és a nemzetségi pártok', *Jogtudományi Közlöny*, 6 March 1914.

—— 'A királyválasztás joga', *Magyar Jogi Szemle* 1920/1.

——— 'Véleményem a királykérdésben', *Jogtudományi Közlöny* 1921/1.
Kollár, Nora (ed.), *A fővárosi rendőrség története*, vol. 1 (Budapest, 1995).
Koncz, Katalin Ibolya, 'A polgári házasságról szóló törvényjavaslat vitája a képviselőház előtt', *Publicationes Universitatis Miskolcinensis Sectio Juridica et Politica, Tomus XXXI* (2013).
Kontler, László, *Millennium in Central Europe. A History of Hungary* (Budapest, 1999).
——— *A History of Hungary* (Basingstoke, 2002).
Kónyi, Manó (ed.), *Deák Ferenc beszédei*, vol. 2 (Budapest, 1897).
Köpeczi, Béla, 'A francia és magyar felvilágosodás', *Irodalomtörténet* xiii (1986).
Körner, Axel, 'The European dimension in the ideas of 1848 and the nationalization of its memories', in A. Körner (ed.), *1848 – A European Revolution? International Ideas and National Memories of 1848* (Houndmills, 2000).
Körösényi, András, Csaba Tóth and Gábor Török, *The Hungarian Political System* (Budapest, 2009).
Kossuth, Ferenc (ed.), *Kossuth Lajos iratai*, vol. 7 (Budapest, 1900).
Kossuth Lajos Összes Munkái (KLÖM) XI. Available at www.arcanum.hu/hu/online-kiadvanyok/Kossuth-kossuth-lajos-osszes-munkai-1/kossuth-lajos-osszes-munkai-xi-CE85/kossuth-lajos-184849-ben-i-kossuth-lajos-az-utolso-rendi-orszaggyulesen-184748-CE8D/iii-harc-a-polgari-alkotmanyert-1848-marc-3marc-17-DB4A/144-pozsony-1848-marcius-3-kossuth-nagy-beszede-es-felirati-javaslata-az-orszaggyulesi-teendok-targyaban-DB4B/ (accessed 3 March 2018).
Kovachich, J.N., *Lectiones Variantes decretorum comitialium* (Pest, 1816).
Kovács, István, 'A quarter of a century on the path of popular democratic constitutional development (1949–1974)', *Acta Iuridica Academia Scientiarum Hungaricae* xvii/1–2 (1975).
Kujbusné Mecsei, Éva, 'Az 1790–91-es diétai történések a szabolcsi követjelentések tükrében', *Szabolcs-Szatmár-Beregi Levéltári Évkönyv* xii (1997).
Kukorelli, István, 'Az 1946. évi I. törvény közjogtörténeti jelentősége és az alkotmányos jogfolytonosság', *Acta Humana* v/1 (2017).
——— and Károly Tóth, *A rendszerváltozás államszervezeti kompromisszumai* (Lakitelek, 2016).
Kun, László, *A magyar igazságügyi kormányzat. Horváth Boldizsártól Pauler Tivadarig.* (Budapest, 1880).
Kurucz, György, 'Kényszer és szolgálat. Portrévázlat Festetics Györgyről', *Századok* cxl/6 (2006).
Lackó, Mihály, *Széchenyi és Kossuth vitája* (Budapest 1977).
Law, David S., 'The myth of imposed constitution', in D.J. Galligan and M. Versteeg (eds), *Social and Political Foundations of Constitutions* (Cambridge, 2013).
Lendvai, Paul, *The Hungarians. A Thousand Years of Victory in Defeat* (Princeton, NJ, 2004).
Lojkó, Miklós (ed.), László Péter, *Hungary's Long Nineteenth Century: Constitutional and Democratic Traditions in European Perspective: Studies by László Péter* (Leiden and Boston, MA, 2012).
Lónyay, Melchior, *Über Ungarns Finanzwesen* (Pressburg, 1874).
Lőrincz, László (ed.), *Egyezzünk ki a múlttal! Műhelybeszélgetések történelmi mítoszainkról, tévhiteinkről* (Budapest, 2010).
Lorman, Thomas, *Counter-Revolutionary Hungary, 1920–1925: István Bethlen and the Politics of Consolidation* (Boulder, CO, and New York, 2006).

Macartney, C.A., *Hungary* (London, 1934).
—— *Hungary. A Short History* (Edinburgh, 1962).
—— *The Habsburg Empire, 1790–1918* (London, 1968).
McConnell, Michael W., 'Ways to think about unenumerated rights', *Illinois Law Review* 2013/5.
McIlwain, Charles Howard, *Constitutionalism, Ancient and Modern* (Ithaca, NY, 1947).
Maddox, Graham, 'Constitution', in T. Ball et al. (eds), *Political Innovation and Conceptual Change* (Cambridge, 1989).
Magyar, Bálint (ed.), *Post-Communist Mafia State. The Case of Hungary* (Budapest, 2016).
Malory, Sir Thomas, *Le Morte d'Arthur*, edited by Stephen H.A. Shepherd (New York, 2004).
Mályusz, Elemér, *Sándor Lipót főherceg nádor iratai 1790–1795* (Budapest, 1926).
Marczali, Henrik, *Magyarország története a szatmári békétől a bécsi congressusig (1711–1815)* (Budapest, 1898). See also the revised version published in English entitled: *Hungary in the Eighteenth Century* (Cambridge University Press, 1910).
—— 'Alkotmánytervezetek 1790-ben', *Budapesti Szemle* cxxv (1906).
—— *Az 1790/1-diki országgyűlés*, 2 vols (Budapest, 1907).
Márki, Sándor, 'A koronaőrző nemesek naplója 1790-ből', *Századok* xv (1881).
Marx, Karl and Friedrich Engels, *Manifest der Kommunistischen Partei* (London, 1848).
Máthé, G. and W. Ogris (eds), *Die Entwicklung der Österreichisch–Ungarischen Strafrechtskodifikation im XIX–XX. Jahrhundert* (Budapest, 1996).
Maurice, C. Edmund, *The Revolutionary Movements of 1848–9 in Italy, Austria–Hungary, and Germany. With Some Examinations of the Previous Thirty-Three Years* (New York, 1969).
Mazzone, Jason, 'Federalism unwritten', *Illinois Law Review* 2013/5.
Melhárd, Gyula, *Somogyvármegye a rendi országgyűléseken I. 1661–1812* (Veszprém, 1906).
Mérei, Gyula and Károly Vörös (eds), *Magyarország története tíz kötetben, 1790–1848*, vol. 1 (Budapest, 1980).
Mester, B. and L. Perecz (eds), *Közelítések a magyar filozófia történetéhez. Magyarország és a modernitás* (Budapest, 2004).
Mezey, Barna, 'Jogalkotás a 16–19. századi Magyarországon', *Rubicon* vii/1–2 (1996).
—— *Strafrectsgeschichte an der Grenze des nächsten Jahrtausendes* (Budapest, 2003).
—— (ed.), *Magyar alkotmánytörténet* (Budapest, 1996).
Mikuš, Joseph, *Slovakia. A Political and Constitutional History (with documents)* (Bratislava, 1995).
Milánkovich, András and Boldizsár Szentgáli-Tóth, 'Díszítő elem, vagy új értelmezési távlatok? A magyar közjog történeti dimenziói az Alaptörvény tükrében' (Decorative element or new perspective of constitutional interpretation?), *Közjogi Szemle* vii/4 (2014).
Miller, L.E. (ed.), *Framing the State in Times of Transition* (Washington DC, 2010).
Miru, György, 'From liberalism to democracy: Key concepts in Lajos Kossuth's political thought', *East Central Europe / L'Europe du Centre Est* xli/1 (2014).
—— *Az alkotmányozás politikai nyelve 1848–49-ben* (Budapest, 2015).
Miskolczy, Ambrus, *Kazinczy Ferenc útja a nyelvújítástól a politikai megújulásig. I. Orpheus világában, avagy a magyar demokratikus politikai kultúra kezdetei* (Budapest, 2009).

BIBLIOGRAPHY

Mit kíván a magyar nemzet? Szabad, független, demokratikus Magyarországot (1989). A copy of the original leaflet is available at http://m.cdn.blog.hu/re/retropol/file/13-mitkivan1.jpg (accessed 3 March 2018).

Mohnhaupt, Heinz and Dieter Grimm, *Verfassung. Zur Geschichte des Begriffs von der Antike Bis zur Gegenwart: Zwei Studien* (Berlin, 1995).

Montesquieu, Charles de Secondat, *The Political Theory of Montesquieu*, selected and translated by Melvin Richter (Cambridge, 1977).

Murdock, Graeme, '"Freely elected in fear": Princely elections and political power in early modern Transylvania', *Journal of Early Modern History* vii (2003).

Murphy, James B., *The Philosophy of Customary Law* (Oxford, 2014).

Nagy, Balázs and Martyn Rady (eds), *Medieval Buda in Context* (Leiden and Boston, MA, 2016).

Naponként-való jegyzései az 1790dik eztendőben felséges IIdik Leopold tsászár, és magyar országi király által, szabad királyi várossába Budára, Szent Jakab havának 6dik napjára rendelt, 's Szent András havának 3dik napjára Posony királyi várossába általtétetett, 's ugyan ott, következő 1791dik esztendőben böjt-más havának 13dik napján béfejezett magyar ország gyűlésének; mellyek eredet-képen magyar nyelven írattattak, és az ország gyűlésének fő-vigyázása alatt, hitelesen deák nyelvre fordíttattak (Buda, 1791).

Nevers, Renée de, *Comrades, No More. The Seeds of Change in Eastern Europe* (Cambridge, 2003).

Oakes, Amy, *Divisionary War: Domestic Unrest and International Conflict* (Stanford, CA, 2012).

Oakeshott, Michael (ed.), *Rationalism in Politics* (London, 1962).

Orbán, Viktor, *Nem lesz árnyékkormány!, Beszéd a Magyar Polgári Együttműködés Egyesület Új állampítés, új irány, új feladatok című konferenciáján Kecskeméten 2009. november 8-án* (There won't be a shadow cabinet! Speech at the conference 'New State-Building, New Direction, New Tasks' organized by the Hungarian Civil Cooperation Association on 8 November 2009). Available at http://2010-2015.miniszterelnok.hu/beszed/nem_lesz_arnyekkormany (accessed 3 March 2018).

——— *Újjá kell építeni Magyarországot, évértékelő beszéd, 2010. február 5.* (We should rebuild Hungary! Speech on the state of Hungary on 5 February 2010). Available at http://2010-2015.miniszterelnok.hu/beszed/ujja_kell_epiteni_magyarorszagot (accessed 3 March 2018).

Orgad, Liav, 'The preamble in constitutional interpretation', *International Journal of Constitutional Law* viii/4 (2010).

Ormos, Mária and Béla Király (eds), *Hungary: Government and Politics 1848–2000* (New York, 2001).

O'Sullivan, John and Kálmán Pócza (eds), *The Second Term of Viktor Orbán. Beyond Prejudice and Enthusiasm* (London, 2015).

Paine, Thomas, *Paine: Political Writings*, edited by Bruce Kuklick (Cambridge, 1989).

Pajkossy, Gábor, *Magyarország története a 19. században. Szöveggyűjtemény* (Budapest, 2006).

Paksa, Rudolf, *Magyar Nemzeti-Szocialisták* (Budapest, 2013).

Pap, András László, *Democratic Decline in Hungary. Law and Society in an Illiberal Democracy* (London, 2018).

Partlett, William, 'Restoration constitution-making', *Vienna Journal on International Constitutional Law* ix/4 (2015).

Perreau-Saussin, Amanda and James B. Murphy (eds), *The Nature of Customary Law. Legal, Historical and Philosophical Perspectives* (Cambridge, 2007).

Péter, László, 'The aristocracy, the gentry and their parliamentary tradition in nineteenth-century Hungary', *The Slavonic and East European Review* 1992/1.

—— *Az Elbától keletre* (Budapest, 1998).

—— and Martyn Rady (eds), *Resistance, Rebellion and Revolution in Hungary and Central Europe: Commemorating 1956* (London, 2008).

Péteri, Zoltán, 'Constitution-making in Hungary', *Acta Juridica Hungarica* xxvi/3-4 (1994).

—— (ed.), *Jogösszehasonlítás. Történeti, rendszertani és módszertani problémák* (Budapest, 2010).

Petőfi, Sándor, *Összes prózai művei és levelezése* (Budapest, 1960).

Pilch, Martin, 'Rechtsgewohnheiten aus rechtshistorischer und rechtstheoretischer Perspective', *Rechtsgeschichte* xvii (2010).

Pocock, John G.A., *The Ancient Constitution and the Feudal Law* (Cambridge, 1987).

Polányi, Imre, *A szlovák társadalom és polgári nemzet mozgalom a századfordulón, 1895-1905* (Budapest, 1987).

Political diary of Menyhért Lónyay, School of Slavonic and East European Studies (SSEES) Library, University College of London, Kónyi-Lónyay Collection.

Pölöskei, Ferenc, *A szabadelvű párt fényei es árnya, 1875-1906* (Budapest, 2010).

Porkoláb, Tibor and Ágoston Nagy, '"Ősi ruhát, igét, szívet meg tartotok": A nemzeti viselet és a koronaőrző bandériumok a 18. század végi politikai diskurzusokban', in *Docendo Discimus* (Miskolc, 2013).

Potemra, Michal, 'Otázky verejnej správy Uhorska v politike Slovenskej Národnej Strány v rokoch 1901-1918', *Historické Stúdie* xxvi (1982).

Pray, Georgius, *Epistolae Procerum Regni Hungariae* (Bratislava, 1806).

Pruzsinszky, Sándor, *Ürményi József* (Budapest, 1990).

Radnóti, Sándor, 'A sacred symbol in a secular country: The Holy Crown', in G.A. Tóth (ed.), *Constitution for a Disunited Nation: On Hungary's 2011 Fundamental Law* (Budapest and New York, 2012).

Rady, Martyn, 'Judicial organization and decision making in old Hungary', *Slavonic and East European Review* cx (2012).

—— 'Hungary and the Golden Bull of 1222', *Banatica* xxiv/2 (2014).

—— *Customary Law in Hungary: Courts, Texts, and the Tripartitum* (Oxford, 2015).

—— (ed.), *Custom and Law in Central Europe* (Cambridge, 2003).

Reiszig, Ede, 'Somogy vármegye története', in D. Csánki (ed.), *Somogy vármegye* (Budapest, s.d. [1914]).

Rixer, Ádám, *A történeti alkotmány helye mai jogunkban* (Budapest, 2012).

Rosenfeld, Michael, *The Identity of the Constitutional Subject: Selfhood, Citizenship, Culture, and Community* (London and New York, 2010).

—— and Sajó An (eds), *The Oxford Handbook of Comparative Constitutional Law* (Oxford, 2012).

Rothenberg, Gunther, 'Toward a national Hungarian army: The military compromise of 1868 and its consequences', *Slavic Review* xxxi/4 (1972).

Rumpler, Helmut and Peter Urbanitsch (eds), *Die Habsburgermonarchie 1848-1918* (Vienna, 2000).

Ruszoly, József, 'Az első nemzetgyűlési választások előzményeihez', in J. Ruszoly (ed.), *Alkotmánytörténeti tanulmányok 1* (Szeged, 1991).

——— 'A "Magyarország államformájáról" szóló 1946: 1. tc. létrejötte és előzményei', *Jogtörténti Szemle* iv/2 (1992).
——— 'A Magyar Köztársaság alapvetése. A "Magyarország államformájáról" szóló 1946: I tc. keletkezéstörténetéről', *Hitel* xix/8 (2006).
Sachs, Stephen E., 'The "unwritten constitution" and unwritten law', *Illinois Law Review* 2013/5.
Sajó, András and Mónika Ganczer, 'Socialist law', in J.D. Wright (ed.), *International Encyclopedia of the Social and Behavioral Sciences* (Oxford, 2015).
Sakmyster, Thomas, *Hungary's Admiral on Horseback: Miklós Horthy, 1918–1944* (New York, 1994).
Sartori, Giovanni, 'Constitutionalism: A preliminary discussion', *The American Political Science Review* lvi/4 (1962).
Scheppele, Kim Lane, 'The unconstitutional constitution', *New York Times*, 2 January 2012.
Schlett, István, 'Elszalasztott lehetőség vagy zsákutca?', *Politikatudományi Szemle* v (1996).
Schoenfeld, H.F. Arthur, 'Soviet imperialism in Hungary', *Foreign Affairs* xxvi/3 (1948).
Schvarcz, Gyula, *Államintézményeink és a kor igényei* (Budapest, 1879).
Schweitzer, Gábor, 'A "magyar királyi köztársaságtól" a magyar köztársaságig. Az 1946. évi I. törvénycikk visszhangja a korabeli közjogi irodalomban', *Acta Humana* v/1 (2017).
——— 'The proclamation of the Hungarian Republic in 1946', *Przeglad Prawa Konstytucynego* xl/6 (2017).
Seton-Watson, Hugh and Christopher, *The Making of a New Europe* (London, 1981).
Seton-Watson, R.W., *Corruption and Reform in Hungary. A Study of Electoral Practice* (London, 1911).
——— 'The era of reform in Hungary', *The Slavonic and East European Review*, American Series 2 (1943).
Sheenan, James J., *German History, 1770–1866* (Oxford, 1989).
Siegel, Andrew M., 'Constitutional theory, constitutional culture', *Journal of Constitutional Law* xviii/4 (2016).
Siklós, András, *Magyarország 1918/1919* (Budapest, 1978).
Sinor, Denis, *History of Hungary* (Woking and London, 1959).
Solumn, Lawrence B., 'Originalism and the unwritten constitution', *Illinois Law Review* 2013/5.
Sólyom, László, *Az alkotmánybíráskodás kezdetei Magyarországon* (Budapest, 2001).
——— 'The role of constitutional courts in the transition to democracy, with special reference to Hungary', *International Sociology* xviii/1 (2003).
——— *Alkotmányértelmezés az új alkotmánybíróságok gyakorlatában* (Budapest, 2005).
——— and Georg Brunner, *Constitutional Judiciary in a New Democracy. The Hungarian Constitutional Court* (Ann Arbor, MI, 2000).
Spira Gy. and J. Szűcs (eds), *Nemzetiség a feudalizmus korában* (Budapest, 1972).
Sprujt, B.J., '"En bruit d'estre bonne luterien": Mary of Hungary (1505–58) and religious reform', *English Historical Review* cix (1994).
Strada, Ferenc, 'Izdenczy József, az Államtanács első magyar tagja', *A Gróf Klebelsberg Kunó Magyar Történetkutató Intézet Évkönyve* x (1940).
Stroup, Edsel Walter, *Hungary in Early 1848: The Constitutional Struggle against Absolutism in Contemporary Eyes*, Foreword by Steven Bela Vardy (State University

College at Buffalo, Program in East European and Slavic Studies Publication no. 11) (Buffalo, NY, 1977).

Sugar, Peter, *Nationality and Society in the Habsburg and Ottoman Empire* (Aldershot, 1997).

Suksi M., K. Agapiou-Josephides, J.-P. Lehners and M. Nowak (eds), *First Fundamental Rights Documents in Europe* (Cambridge, 2015).

Sulkunen, Irma, Nevala-Nurmi Seija-Leena and Markkola Pirjo (eds), *Suffrage, Gender and Citizenship* (Cambridge, 2009).

Swanson, John, *The Remnants of the Habsburg Monarchy: The Shaping of Modern Austria and Hungary, 1918–1922* (New York, 2001).

Szabad, György, 'Az önkényuralom kora (1849–1867)', in E. Kovács and L. Katus (eds), *Magyarország története, 1848–1890* (Budapest, 1979).

——— 'A kormány parlamenti felelősségének kérdése', in Gy. Szabad (ed.), *A magyar országgyűlés 1848/49-ben* (Budapest, 1998).

Szajbély, Mihály (ed.), *Mesterek, tanítványok. Ünnepi tanulmánykötet Csetri Lajos tiszteletére* (Budapest, 1999).

Szakály, Zsuzsanna, 'A történeti alkotmány és az alkotmányos identitás az Alaptörvényben' (Historical constitution and constitutional identity in the Fundamental Law), *Pro Publico Bono*, ii/2 (2015).

Szarka, László, *Szlovák nemzeti fejlődés. Magyar nemzetiségi politika, 1867–1918* (Bratislava, 2005).

Széchenyi, István, *A kelet népe* (Pest, 1841).

Szente, Zoltán, 'A historizáló alkotmányozás problémái – a történeti alkotmány és a Szent Korona az új Alaptörvényben', *Közjogi Szemle* iv/3 (2011).

——— 'Az Alaptörvény és az alkotmányos változások szakmai és tudományos reflexiói 2010 után', *Fundamentum* xix/2–3 (2015).

Szentpétery, Imre, *Scriptores rerum Hungaricarum*, vol. 1 (Budapest, 1937).

Szijártó, István M., 'A vármegye és a jómódú birtokos köznemesség a 18. században', *AETAS* xiii/2–3 (1998).

——— *A diéta: a magyar rendek és az országgyűlés, 1708–1792* (Budapest, 2005).

——— *Nemesi társadalom és politika. Tanulmányok a 18. századi magyar rendiségről* (Budapest, 2006).

——— *A 18. századi Magyarország rendi országgyűlése* (Budapest, 2016).

Szilágyi, Péter, 'Szabó Imre szocialista normativizmusa. Ideológiakritikai adalékok', *Világosság* xlv/4 (2004).

Szűcs, Jenő, *Vázlat Európa három történti régiójáról* (Budapest, 1983).

Szűcs, Zoltán Gábor, '"A közjogi folytonosság házában": A nemzeti történelem Antall József felfogásában', *2000: Irodalmi és Társadalmi Havilap* xvii/1 (2005).

——— *Az antalli pillanat: A nemzeti történelem szerepe a magyar politikai diskurzusban, 1989–1993* (Budapest, 2010).

Takáts, József, *A megfelelő ötvözet* (Budapest, 2014).

Tasnádi Nagy, Andrew, 'A Thousand Years of the Hungarian Constitution', *The Hungarian Quarterly* 1939/5.

Taxner, Ernő, 'Tudósítások a szent korona 1790-es diadalútjáról', *Magyar Szemle* xxi (2012).

Teszelszky, Kees, *Az ismeretlen korona* (Pannonhalma, 2009).

Thornhill, Chris, *A Sociology of Constitutions* (Cambridge, 2011).

Tőkéczki, László (ed.), *Magyar konzervativizmus, hagyomány és jelenkor* (Budapest, 1994).

Tomcsányi, Móric, *Magyarország közjoga* (Budapest, 1932).
Tóth, Gábor Attila (ed.), *Constitution for a Disunited Nation; On Hungary's Fundamental Law* (Budapest and New York, 2012).
Tóth, I. György (ed.), *A Concise History of Hungary* (Budapest, 2005).
Tóth, László, 'A magyarországi LMBT-mozgalmi színtér politikai aktivitásának alakulása, különös tekintettel a 2010-től kezdődő időszakra', *Replika*, 84/2013.
Townson, Robert, *Travels in Hungary, with a Short Account of Vienna in the Year 1793* (London, 1797).
Trencsényi, Balázs (ed.), *Whose Love of Which Country? Composite States, National Histories and Patriotic Discourses in Early Modern East Central Europe* (Leiden and Boston, MA, 2015).
Turda, Marius, *The Idea of National Superiority in Central Europe, 1880–1918* (Lewiston, NY, 2004).
Uitz, Renáta, *Constitutions, Court and History* (Budapest, 2005).
Unger, Aryeh, *Constitutional Development in the USSR. A Guide to the Soviet Constitutions* (London, 1981).
Varga, András Zs., 'Történeti alkotmányunk vívmányai az Alaptörvény kógens rendelkezésében', *Iustum Aequum Salutare* xii/4 (2016).
Vermeule, Adrian, 'The atrophy of constitutional powers', *Oxford Journal of Legal Studies* xxxii/3 (2012).
Vinogradoff, Sir Paul, 'A constitutional history of Hungary', *Law Quarterly Review* xxi/ October (1905).
Vorländer, Hans, 'Integration durch Verfassung? Die symbolische Bedeutung der Verfassung im politischen Integrationsprozess', in H. Vorländer (ed.), *Integration durch Verfassung* (Wiesbaden, 2002).
Vörös, Imre, 'A történeti alkotmány az Alkotmánybíróság gyakorlatában', *Közjogi Szemle* ix/4 (2016).
Wandruszka, Adam, *Leopold II* (Vienna and Munich, 1965).
Wandycz, Piotr S., *The Price of Freedom. A History of East Central Europe from the Middle Ages to the Present* (London and New York, 2001).
Wangermann, Ernst, *From Joseph II to the Jacobin Trials* (London, 1959).
West, Robin, 'Tom Paine's constitution', *Virginia Law Review* lxxxix (2003).
Whittington, Keith E., 'The status of unwritten constitutional conventions in the United States', *University of Illinois Law Review* 2013/5.
Windisch, Éva V., *Kovachich Márton György, a forráskutató* (Budapest, 1998).
Winters, Stanley and Joseph Held (eds), *Intellectual and Social Developments in the Habsburg Empire from Maria Theresa to World War One* (New York and London, 1975).
Wright, Herbert F. (ed.), *Constitutions of the States at War, 1914–1918* (Washington DC, 1919).
Zászkaliczky, Márton, 'Eszmetörténeti szempontok a történeti alkotmányosság közép- és kora újkori magyarországi történetéhez', *Közjogi Szemle* 2015/3.
Zétényi, Zsolt, *A történeti alkotmány. Magyarország ősi alkotmánya* (Budapest, 2010).
Zinner, Tibor, 'A legjelentősebb "bűnper"-ek 1956 ősze előtt', *Jogtörténeti Szemle* viii/3 (2006).
——— 'Minden bírósági ügy az osztályharc egyik epizódja', *Jogtörténeti Szemle* viii/3 (2006).
Zlinszky, János, *Az ügyvédség kialakulása Magyarországon és története Fejér megyében* (Székesfehérvár, 1976).

INDEX

abortion, 4
absolutism, 13–14, 48, 51, 55–6, 66, 68–9, 75, 83–4, 91, 103, 113, 297
Ackerman, Bruce, 137, 186
adultery, 257
Albert, King of Hungary, 31
Albrecht, Archduke, 147
Alden, Percy, 141
aliens, rights of, 336–7
Alliance of Free Democrats (SZDSZ), 4
Alliance of Young Democrats *See* Fidesz
American constitution, 221, 230
ancien régime, 65, 93, 106
Andrássy, Gyula (the Elder), 123, 127–9, 134, 301
Andrássy, Gyula (the Younger), 141–2, 144–5, 153, 165, 176, 181
Andrew II, King, 40, 75, 247, 253, 257, 259, 263
Anonymus, 72
Antall, József, 115, 229
Ányos, Pál, 88
antisemitism, 4, 21
apostasy, 81
Apponyi, Albert, 141–2, 144–5
Archbishop of Esztergom, 31, 33, 55, 194, 233, 251–2, 274
Archbishop of Kalocsa, 250–2

armalistae, 50
Arthur, King, 31
association, right of, 123, 128, 150, 188, 200, 303, 305–6, 309, 336–7, 339
asylum, right of, 328, 337
Ausgleich See Settlement of 1867
Austria, 9, 11, 16–18, 28, 49, 89, 93, 95, 97, 106–7, 125, 128, 130, 134, 136, 146, 150, 160–1, 263, 266, 274, 301, 307
Austrian constitutions, 28, 161
Austrian Netherlands, 71, 89
avicitas, 273

Baden, 101
bailiffs, 249
Balogh, Péter, 79–80, 91
Baltic States, 230
banderia, 71–2
Bánffy, Dezső, 146, 153
banks, 196, 208, 314
Baranya County, 180, 252
Barcsay, Ákos, 52
Barons, 8, 31–32, 252, 254–5, 257, 259, 267
Batthyány, József Archbishop, 55
Batthyány, Lajos, 97, 106, 108 –10
Bavaria, 49, 101

INDEX

Beccaria, Cesare, 64
Beér János, 198, 201
Beksics, Gusztáv, 125, 136–7
Béla IV, King, 253
Belgium, constitution of, 102
bene possessionati, 52–3, 56–7, 77, 80, 112
Beniczky, Ödön, 165
Beöthy, Imre, 58
Bethlen, István, 167
Bibó, István, 205
bishops, 51, 249–51, 252, 270, 274
Bismarck, Otto von, 127, 243
Bodin, Jean, 55
Bohemia, 7, 11, 32, 35, 49, 254, 263
Bolsheviks, 20, 154–6, 161, 167, 340
Borié, Egid von, 55
Bosnia, 253
bourgeoisie, 108, 112, 117, 139, 187, 201, 204, 304, 306, 332
Bratislava (Pozsony), 31, 90, 93, 102–3, 105–7
Brunswick, 101
Budapest, 23, 36, 131–4, 142–3, 200, 330
  including Buda and Pest, 17, 20, 23, 36, 47, 70–71, 79, 82, 90–1, 93, 95, 99, 102, 104–8, 112, 114, 122, 128, 132, 142–3, 151, 156, 261, 273–4, 276, 278, 291, 303, 308, 330
Budapesti Közlöny, 168
Bulgaria, 253
Burgenland, 181
burghers, 54, 117, 262
Byzantium, 10

Calvinism, 268, 271
capitalists, 304–5, 312–13
capital punishment, 82, 130, 210
cardinal laws, 5, 64, 66–7, 224
Carolina Resolutio, 50
Carpathian Basin, 6–7, 18, 83, 145, 342

Cartledge, Bryan, 155
Catholicism, 7, 55, 69, 80–1, 90, 152, 256, 262, 267, 269, 271
Central (also Eastern) Europe, 26, 136, 205
change of domicile, right of, 83
Charles Robert, King, 31
Charles III, King, 47, 50, 82
Charles IV, King, 19–21, 142, 154, 160–1, 163, 165–7, 169, 172–5, 178, 180
Charles VII, Emperor, 49
Christendom, 254
Cisleithania, 17, 134, 138 *See also* Austria
civil courts, 58, 155, 262, 270, 277, 324, 335–6
clergy, 8, 38, 49, 52, 152, 268
coinage, 35, 40, 248, 262
commissars, 155
commissioners, 39, 41, 104, 128
communism, 2, 4, 22–25, 187, 196–8, 229
communist manifesto, 113
communist regime in Hungary, 2, 4, 23–4, 115, 150, 195, 197, 199–200, 211, 215, 218–19, 228–9, 342
Concha, Győző, 153
conscience, freedom of, 200, 306, 327–8, 336
conservativism, 16, 124, 148–9, 164
Constant, Benjamin, 101
Constantinople, 10
contributio, 48, 50–4, 148, 300
co-operative societies, 313–14, 322, 333–334
coronation, 11–12, 17, 30–2, 41–2, 52, 58, 60, 73, 79, 82, 88, 123, 127, 142, 145, 233, 260, 261
corruption, 24, 146
Corvin, John, 32
Corvinus, Matthias, 31–2, 35, 41, 253

Council of Ministers, 198, 200, 276, 282, 315–17, 319–21, 330
Council of Ónod, 309
Council of the Palatine, 106–7
Counter-Reformation, 10, 48, 50
counties, Hungarian, 8, 12, 35, 37–8, 48–9, 51, 53, 58, 74, 79, 91, 108, 128, 135, 142, 151, 248–49, 263, 270, 321
craftsmen, 280
criminal law, 125, 133, 191, 195, 208, 210, 257, 262, 278, 335–6, 338, 342
Croatia, 7, 10, 15–16, 74, 94, 161, 247, 263, 271, 282
Csatskó, Imre, 129
Csemegi, Károly, 129
Cserhalmi, György, 114
customary law, 9–10, 12–15, 18, 29–30, 32–4, 37, 39, 41–2, 54, 65–6, 68–70, 74, 76, 79, 97–8, 112, 144, 146, 151–2, 170, 173, 223–5, 234–5, 254, 322
customs, 7, 11, 22, 24, 30, 52, 60, 66, 76, 84, 94, 150–1, 156, 164, 180, 191, 209, 217–18, 221–2, 226, 235, 253, 259, 263–4, 311
Czechoslovak constitutions, 28
Czechoslovakia, 19, 28, 154, 209
Czech provinces *See also* Bohemia, 49
Czindery, Pál, 59–60, 62

Dacso, Leonard, 252
Dalmatia, 7, 247, 253, 263, 271
De Tocqueville, Alexis, 101
Deák, Ferenc, 17, 18, 46, 49, 98, 113, 121, 123, 127, 133, 139, 146
Deák, István, 15, 95, 110
Debrecen, 58, 94, 143, 166, 179, 309
De Foix-Candale, Anne, 32
December Patent, 138
democracy, 2–3, 23–4, 64, 89, 96, 114, 128, 130, 132–7, 139, 154–5, 187, 193, 195–6, 199, 201–3, 206, 211, 229, 231, 310, 312, 325, 328–9, 332, 342–3
deputies, 35, 37–8, 49, 51–52, 54, 56–9, 74, 249, 323
despotism, 68, 149
desuetudo, 225, 235
Dezemberverfassung, 125, 138
Dicasteria, 263, 268
Dicey, A.V., 102
Dickson, Peter, 49
Diet of Croatia, 10
Diet of Transylvania, 34
dignity, right to, 123, 335, 342
diplomacy, 187, 286, 305, 317
discrimination, 98, 144, 152, 200, 310, 327, 338
divorce, 17, 81, 152, 262, 270
Doctrine of the Holy Crown, 144, 227–9, 231, 233, 239, 246
Domokos, Lajos, 58
Donauschwaben, 13 *See also Volksdeutsche*
dower, 249 *See also* inheritance
dualism, 36–37, 48, 50, 60, 67, 192, 194–5

Eckartsau, Declaration of, 165, 169, 173–4
Eckhart, Ferenc, 21, 69, 149
education, 21, 88, 126, 131, 143, 151, 200, 262, 273, 275, 306, 309, 320, 326–8, 335, 337, 339–0
employment, right of, 210, 337–8
England, 5, 8, 37, 64, 68, 101, 131, 135–6, 149–50 *See also* Great Britain
Enlightened Absolutism, 13, 51, 53, 55–6, 83
Enlightenment, 13–14, 54, 69, 123
ennoblement, right of, 256
environment, 335, 339
equality, 69, 78, 90, 97, 123, 133–4, 200, 281, 337–8

INDEX 359

estates, 8, 13, 41–2, 46–8, 50–60, 67–8, 76–7, 80, 87–8, 96, 248–50, 256–7, 259, 263–4, 273, 278
Esztergom, Archbishop of, 31, 33, 194, 233, 250, 251, 252
Eugene of Savoy, 50
European Union, 21, 25
Evans, R.J.W., 49, 55
excommunication, 40

Farkas, Mihály, 203
Farkas, Sándor Bölöni, 101
fascism, 2, 21, 219, 312
Federal Republic of Germany, 242
Ferdinand, 1, Holy Roman Emperor, 33–4
Ferdinand I of Austria, 33–4
Ferdinand II, 34, 60
Ferdinand I & V, 92, 106, 177, 273
Fejérváry, Géza, 148
Ferenczy, Árpád, 147, 149
Festetich, György, 55
feudalism, 16, 66, 69, 71, 79, 83–4, 87–8, 90, 96, 107, 109, 112, 139, 154, 165, 209, 273
Fidesz ('Hungarian Civic Alliance'), 1, 4, 115, 212, 231, 239
foreign trade, 90, 127, 143, 280, 314, 319
France, 14, 17, 20, 31, 48, 56, 58–9, 63–4, 78, 84, 91, 93, 101, 123, 149, 243
Francis I, 59, 261,
Francis II, 14, 84, 90, 91,
Francis Joseph, 16, 17, 19, 30, 104, 107, 113, 122, 123, 129, 138, 142, 143, 147, 148, 150, 152, 157, 177, 181, 301
Francis of Lorraine, 38
Frederick III, 32
Free-electors, 35, 163–4, 166–7, 169, 173–4
Freemasons, 79, 88, 90

French Constitution, 64–5, 102, 123
French Revolution, 14, 56, 58, 63, 64, 70–1, 88, 90–1, 98, 100
Friedrich, István, 161, 165, 168, 170, 180
Fundamental Law of Hungary, 1–5, 24, 115–16, 179, 212–16, 225, 227, 233, 239, 243, 341–3
fundamental laws, 54–5, 57, 96, 124, 138, 153

Galicia, 89, 247
Gambling, 262
Geiger, Imre, 203
gendarmerie, 133
gentry, 48, 50, 52
Gergely, András, 96, 101
German Confederation, 101, 127
German constitutions, 161, 225
German Federal Constitutional Court, 225
German language, 13, 53, 73, 105, 117, 129, 147, 262
Gerő, Ernő, 203
Gesamtstaat, 97
Golden Bull of 1222, 5, 8, 11, 24, 40–2, 45, 68, 75, 150, 229, 247
Gorove, István, 127
Governing (Liberal) Party, 127–8, 130, 134, 139, 148
Grand Trianon Palace, 122
gravamina, 37, 67–8
Great Britain, 20, 96, 101, 149, 220, 223, 225, 233, 245
Grősz, József, 203
Guizot, François, 101

Habsburg, House of, 2, 6, 10–14, 16–17, 19–20, 25, 32–4, 37, 41, 46–9, 51, 54, 68–9, 71, 74, 82–5, 90, 92–3, 95–7, 104–5, 110, 113, 117, 123, 136, 141–2, 144–5, 148–9, 154, 160–1, 163–7, 172–5, 177, 179, 273, 284

Habsburg, Ottó, 174
Hajnóczy, József, 78–9, 84, 88, 90–1
Hanebrink, Paul, 152
Hatvan, Diet of 1525, 36
Haugwitz, Count Friedrich Wilhelm, 49
Herder, Johann Gottfried, 73
hereditary monarchy, 7, 10, 31, 33–5, 47, 75, 79, 84, 163, 166, 169, 192, 261, 263
historical (or ancient) constitution, 2–6, 9, 11, 14, 17, 21–2, 24–5, 29, 42–3, 52, 54–60, 63, 65–71, 73–7, 80, 83–5, 87–8, 93, 96–9, 110–11, 141–2, 144–50, 152–4, 156, 160, 162–5, 167–9, 171–2, 177–80, 185–6, 188, 190–4, 209, 213–19, 222, 227–30, 233, 237–40, 242–4, 263, 271, 274, 277, 289, 307, 342–3
historical constitution, 2–3, 5–6, 14, 17, 20, 22, 24–5, 92–6, 98–9, 110, 141–2, 145, 147–8, 150, 152, 154, 156, 160, 162–3, 165, 169, 172, 177–8, 184–5, 188, 190–4, 204–5, 208–9, 211–20, 222, 225, 227–31, 236–40, 242–5, 342–3
historical constitutions, 25, 179–80, 216, 218, 220, 222, 226, 230
Holocaust, 186
Holy Alliance, 94
Holy Crown of Hungary, 7, 10, 24, 31, 34, 47, 70–2, 82, 144–5, 170–2, 214, 217, 228–9, 231, 233, 239, 243, 246, 256–7, 261, 273, 342
Holy Roman Empire, 7, 101, 263
homicide, 257
Horthy, Miklós, 20–1, 114, 161, 170, 173, 186
Horvát, Boldizsár, 129
Hungarian Academy of Sciences, 109, 129
Hungarian chancellery, 274, 276
Hungarian Communist Party, 4, 22–3, 114, 186, 195–8, 203–4, 231
Hungarian Constitution
1919, 20, 155, 159, 206, 304–6
1949, 3, 22, 184–6, 196–202, 204, 207, 209, 312–31, 342
1989, 23–24, 211–212, 217, 224, 231, 332–40
Hungarian Constitutional Court, 217, 224, 236
Hungarian Diet
before 1526, 9, 30, 32–3, 35–6, 39, 41, 252, 260
1526–1791, 11–14, 34, 37–9, 41, 46–59, 67–8, 70–83, 85, 88, 90–1, 145, 261–2, 264, 285
1792–1867, 15–16, 92–4, 100, 102–7, 109–12, 123, 145, 151, 163, 273, 276–279, 283–95, 297–9
Hungarian 'Forty-Eighter' Party, 134
Hungarian Home Guard (*Honvédség*), 126, 142, 147
Hungarian language, 14–15, 70–4, 78, 91, 147, 253, 264–5, 281, 291–2, 342
Hungarian law, 8–9, 13, 29, 80, 82, 98, 126, 135–6, 139, 142, 148, 175, 177, 195, 200, 228, 336
Hungarian Monarchist Party, 168, 170
Hungarian National Council, 19, 181, 302, 311
Hungarian nationalism, 11, 14–16, 19–20, 57, 69, 71–5, 83, 115, 144, 152–5, 199
Hungarian National Museum, 24, 90, 143
Hungarian nobility, 10–14, 41, 54, 56, 60, 64–5, 68–9, 73, 75, 88, 95–7, 101, 145, 226
Hungarian Parliament, 1, 16–17, 53, 124, 135, 212, 229, 302
Hungarian parliamentary court, 278

INDEX 361

Hungarian Responsible Ministry, 293–4
Hungarian Social Democratic Party, 154, 197
Hungarian Socialist Federal Republic of Councils, 2, 20, 155–6, 304–6
Hungarian Socialist Party, 1, 4, 231
Hungarian Soviet Republic, 161, 206
Hungarian State Television, 114
Hungarian Supreme Court, 282, 324
Huns, 72
Hunyadi, John, 32
hussars, 73, 86

Imperial War Council, Vienna, 79
inaugural diploma, 11, 42, 48, 58, 60, 80, 82, 84, 260–1
Irányi Dániel, 130, 134,
Irinyi József, 104–6
Ishmaelites, 250

Jacobin Conspiracy, 15, 58, 78, 88, 90, 91
Japan, 167, 225–6
Japanese constitution, 226
Japanese Constitutional Court, 226
Jászi, Oszkár, 154
Jelačić, Josip, 94
Jerusalem, 257
Jews, 2, 20–21, 40, 82, 108, 250, 262
Jókai Mór, 99, 118
Joseph I, 34, 41, 259
Joseph II, 11–14, 27, 41, 53–4, 58, 63–4, 68–9, 71–3, 77, 81, 83–4, 89–91, 123, 145, 261
judicial practice, 23, 25, 30, 48, 87, 96, 125–6, 130–2, 150, 155, 168, 179, 203, 217, 221–3, 226, 230, 234–5, 241, 243, 248–50, 256–7, 261, 271, 277, 295, 303–4, 318, 320–2, 324–5, 335–6, 338
judicial courts, 22, 30, 39, 58, 131, 142, 145, 155, 168, 189, 262, 264, 268, 270

judiciary, 22, 24, 64, 124, 130, 145–6, 150, 179, 190, 194, 200, 203, 215, 220–5, 240–1, 243, 248, 264, 273, 296, 324–5

Kádár, János, 203
Károlyi, Mihály, 20, 154, 155, 161, 180, 302
Kazinczy, Ferenc, 91
Kemény, Zsigmond, 109, 120
Kmety, Károly, 166
Koloman, King of Hungary, 250
Kontler, László, 143, 149, 206
Körner, Axel, 115
Koselleck, Reinhart, 98
Kossuth, Lajos, 15–17, 92, 94, 97–98, 100, 103–12, 115, 119–20, 123, 127–8, 134–5
Kovács, Béla, 195
Kovács, István, 175
Kun Béla, 20, 154

Ladislas V, 31–2
landlords, 7, 267, 272–3, 312
Lappic language, 72
Latin language, 8, 14, 67, 73–4, 87, 265
Latvia, 230, 236
Lawful Revolution, 15, 95, 108, 110, 113, 115
legal continuity, 17, 20–1, 23, 162–6, 172–3, 175–80
legal scholars, 4, 23, 98–9, 147–8, 153, 166, 174, 179, 184, 192, 195, 198, 213, 215–217, 220, 223, 226, 228, 231, 233, 241, 280
legitimists, 35, 163–5, 169, 174–5
Leibniz, Gottfried Wilhelm, 55
Leninism, 20, 155
Leopold I, 34, 41, 47
Leopold II, 11, 14, 53, 71, 73, 75, 78, 80–2, 84, 90–1, 261, 263
Leopold, Alexander, 82, 261

liberalism, 1–2, 16–17, 53, 122–130, 134, 136–7, 141, 148, 150–1, 204, 212, 231
libertas, 35, 69
liberties (civil), 22–3, 124–5, 128–9, 132–3, 138, 245
liberties (noble), 11, 13, 30, 40–2, 77, 138, 247, 254, 256–257, 259, 268
liberties (religious), 83, 268, 327–8
liberty, 11, 38, 56, 63, 97, 99, 115, 136, 220, 247, 249–250, 257, 271, 273, 277, 295, 313, 327–8, 333, 335–6, 342
liberty of the press, 105, 114, 273
Lieutenancy Council, 58, 269
Linz, Treaty of, 80–1
local councils, 106, 200, 280, 306, 321–3
Locke, John, 64
Lónyay, Menyhért, 134, 138
Louis I, 31, 40, 253
Louis II, 10, 32–3, 35, 41
Louis XIV of France, 48
Lutherans, 80, 90–91, 268, 271

Macartney, C.A., 6–7, 11, 15, 142, 146, 151
Machiavelli, Niccolo, 55
magistrates, 270
Magna Carta, 5, 24, 150
magnates, 8, 52, 69, 72, 78–9, 91, 252, 257, 263, 267, 277, 279, 284, 300
Magyar tribes, 6–7, 18
Marczali, Henrik, 54, 63–4, 74
Maria Theresa, 11, 38, 42, 47, 49, 52, 82–3, 262
marriage, laws on, 17, 81, 130, 134, 152, 262, 270–271, 327, 334
Martini, Carl Anton von, 75, 89
Martinovics, Ignác, 15, 58, 90–1
Marxism–Leninism, 113, 143, 198–9, 201–2
Matica slovenská, 153

Matica srpska, 153
Matthias Corvinus, 31–2, 34–5, 41, 253
Mauksch, Thomas, 266
Maximilian, Emperor, 32
Metternich, Klemens von, 97, 105
Mezey, Barna, 54
military, 13, 24, 35, 39, 48, 88, 94, 107, 109, 147, 201, 287, 304
millennial celebrations (1896), 18
Mindszenty, József, Cardinal, 194, 208
mining, 274, 305
mining towns, 82, 262, 270
minority languages, defence of, 73–4, 152–153, 306, 337, 342
Miru, György, 98
Mittermaier, Carl, 124
Mohács, Battle of, 10 33
Montesquieu, Charles-Louis de Secondat, 49, 52, 54, 64, 68, 70, 145, 195
Murphy, James B, 222
Muslims, 40

Nagy Imre, 115
Nagyatádi Szabó, István, 165
Napoleon, 15, 124
natio hungarica, 8, 26
National Casino, 109
newspapers, 128, 143
nobility, 7–16, 29–37, 40–2, 47–54, 56–7, 60, 63–5, 67–9, 71–80, 82–8, 90–1, 95–8, 100–1, 103, 108, 111–12, 142, 145, 149, 151, 226, 247–8, 250–2, 254–7, 259, 261–3, 266–7, 271–4
noblewomen, 14
nomenklatura, 24
North America, 14, 101, 124, 135
notaries, 280, 291–2

oaths, 7, 11, 21, 24, 41–2, 45, 48, 56–8, 66, 80, 82, 88, 145, 154,

INDEX

206, 226, 257, 259–61, 263, 270, 311, 329
officials, 8, 16, 21, 37, 40, 42, 53, 55–56, 58, 79, 82, 88, 91, 106–7, 128, 152–3, 155, 250, 252, 269, 271, 274–9, 290–1, 316–17, 325, 333
oligarchy, 65, 89, 203
Orbán, Viktor, 1, 212
Orthodox religion, 262
Ottoman Empire, 10, 12–13, 34–5, 47–48, 149, 259

pacts, 32, 67, 75, 89
pagans, 145
Paine, Thomas, 64
Palatine, 8, 32, 79, 82, 103–7, 248, 250, 252, 255, 261, 273–6, 278, 282
pamphlets, 69, 73, 78, 124
Papacy, 7, 233, 250
paper constitutions, 149
  See also written
parental rights, 327
parliament, 1–2, 11, 16–19, 21, 23–4, 37, 39, 53, 90, 92, 94, 96, 100–1, 104, 107, 115, 122, 124–5, 127, 129, 132, 134–5, 142–3, 145–6, 148, 151–4, 156, 161–5, 169–70, 173–7, 181, 183, 187, 189, 191, 193–5, 197–9, 207, 209, 211–12, 215, 229, 231, 273, 290, 302, 307–8, 315–19, 321–5, 329–30, 332, 338
Party of Christian National Union (KNEP), 164, 166, 169
Party of Independent Smallholders, 22, 187, 196
pastors *SeeSee also* priests, 280
Pászthory, Sándor, 55
patriotism, 11, 14, 55, 57, 72, 81, 84, 89, 147
Pauler, Tivadar, 146

peasantry, 13, 16, 51, 71, 77–79, 83, 85, 87, 90, 106, 128, 199, 257, 262, 266–7, 272–3, 280, 312–14
Peidl, Gyula, 161, 168
penalties, 130, 134, 267, 272, 278, 329
Pest *See* Budapest
Péter, Gábor, 203
Petőfi, Sándor, 99
plague, 48
plebiscite, 317
poets, 16, 88, 99, 105
Poland, 7, 12, 28, 32, 53, 79
police, 91, 119, 128–33, 139, 195, 203, 269
Polish constitutions, 28
Pozsgay, Imre, 115
Pragmatic Sanction, 11, 46–7, 97, 110–11, 173–4, 283–6, 288–90, 296–7
prefects, 79 *See also* officials
prelates, 8, 80, 151, 254–5, 257, 259
  See also bishops
Presidential Council, 196, 199, 315–20
press, 90, 105, 114, 123–4, 128, 132, 273, 281, 303, 305, 328, 336
  See also newspapers
priests, 269, 271 *See also* clergy
Prime Minister, 1, 3, 16, 21–2, 97, 106, 108, 115, 128–9, 142, 146, 148, 153, 161, 167, 168, 170–2, 180–1, 183, 189–90, 192, 194, 204, 212, 229–30, 275–6, 301, 311
Prince Eugene of Savoy, 50
Prince Primate of Hungary, 194, 263
privacy, right of, 123, 130, 200, 328, 336
Prohászka, Ottokár, 166
proletariat, 155, 199, 304–6
propaganda, 114–15, 306

property, 29, 40, 82, 134, 150–1, 188, 220, 257, 271, 273, 277, 309, 313–14, 322, 329, 334, 338
protestants, 10, 38, 47, 50, 69, 74, 78, 80–3, 91, 94, 262, 267–72
Prussia, 17, 49, 71, 82
public prosecutors, 200, 325–6

qualifications, 151, 269, 338
quarantine, 39
quartering, 287
queens, 11, 31, 38, 250

race, 137, 306, 337–8
railways, 143, 299, 314
Rajk, László, 203
Rakóczi, Ferenc, 34, 41, 47–8, 51, 61, 148
reconquest of Hungary, 12–13, 47
recruitment, 38, 262, 287
Red Terror, 20, 155
referendum, 23, 167, 194
regency, 21, 24, 161, 168–70, 173, 175, 180, 186, 190, 274, 276, 282
Regency Council, 276, 282
regicide, 130
Regnum Marianum, 81
regulations, 3, 6, 39, 46–7, 64, 124–5, 132, 150, 155, 171, 214, 222–6, 241, 268, 279–80, 298, 318, 320, 322–3, 343
Reichenbach, Treaty of, 82
religion, 17, 34, 38, 50, 69–70, 77–83, 123, 130, 134, 152, 165, 180–1, 188, 200, 243, 262, 264, 266–73, 275, 280–1, 306, 309, 320, 327, 336–8, 341
reparations, 305
republicanism, 34, 56–57, 64, 72, 80, 135, 168, 185, 190, 192–3, 204
Republic of Councils, 2, 20, 155, 180–1, 304–5
retainers, 36, 40, 249–51

revenues, 41–2, 257, 293, 299
revolution in 1918/1919, 20, 154–5, 160–1, 163, 167, 171, 178–80, 228, 305–6, 309, 312
revolution of 1848, 2, 15–17, 47, 93, 95, 99, 102–10, 112–13, 115, 119, 123, 144, 146–7, 150, 228, 274, 309
revolution of 1956, 115–16, 203, 342
right of resistance, 10–11, 30, 40–2, 47, 66, 226, 251, 257
right of revolt, 89
right of succession, 9, 11, 13, 30–5, 40, 46, 77, 79–80, 163–4, 174, 261, 263, 284
robbery, 248, 257, 280
Roma, 21
Romania, 7, 16, 19–20, 154, 156, 180
Roman law, 30
Roosevelt, Franklin D., 224
Rothenberg, Gunther, 147
Roundtable Talks, 23, 114
Rousseau, Jean-Jacques, 64, 69–70, 79
Royal Council, 32, 35–37, 91, 112, 274
royal court, 8–9, 16, 23–6, 35, 55, 58, 67, 72, 79–80, 83, 89–94, 97, 100, 102, 104–8, 112, 117, 155, 215, 217, 221, 224–6, 231–4, 236, 240–1, 245, 249–51, 270, 277–8, 282, 324, 335–6, 338
royal palace, 8, 122
Rubinek, Gyula, 165
Rupert, Rezső, 165
Russia, 16, 71, 94, 109, 120, 149, 239
Russian Tsar, 94, 109, 113, 120
Ruthenia, 21

sable tax, 250
saints, 259, 263, 270
Sajnovics, János, 72
Saxony, 101
schools, 55–6, 71, 143, 262, 267–271, 281, 326
science, 73, 78, 327, 335, 339

INDEX 365

Scythians, 72, 253
seals, 10, 38, 170, 250, 255
seers, 31
self-governance, 10, 16, 49, 128, 135, 142, 309, 334
Senate, 79–80
Septemviralis Court, 91, 270
Serbia, 10, 16, 19, 153–4, 180, 247, 253
serfdom, 82, 98, 104, 106, 108, 110
sergeants-at-arms, 280
servientes, 40, 248–50
servitude, 80, 254–5
Seton-Watson, R.W., 150
Settlement of 1867, *see also Ausgleich*, 17–18, 46, 48–9, 95, 98, 113–14, 121, 123–4, 126–8, 130–1, 134–7, 141, 143–4, 146–8, 151, 155, 160, 165–6, 173, 177–8, 180–1, 333
sexual identity, 4, 327, 338
sheriffs, 8, 151
Sigismund, King of Hungary, 31, 35
Silesia, 49
Simon of Kéza, 72
Simonyi-Semadam, Sándor, 171
slavery, 107 *See also* serfdom
Slovakia, 16, 21, 153–4
Slovak National Council, 154
Smallholder Party, 165–6, 169, 175
smallholders, 182 *See also* peasants
socialism, 19, 22–3, 144, 156, 197–202, 204, 304–5, 312–15, 325, 328, 332
Sólyom, László, 203, 233, 245
Sonnenfels, Joseph von, 55, 75, 89
sovereignty, claims of, 11, 69, 80–1, 83–4, 89, 199, 217, 227–228, 233, 307, 315, 332
Soviet Union, 2, 21–2, 114, 155, 186–7, 195–6, 200–2, 204, 230, 238, 312
stalinism, 2, 115, 184–5, 187, 196–7, 201–3, 209

stamps, 170, 172
statute books, 21, 25, 39–40, 98, 126, 178 *See also Corpus Juris Hungarici*
statute of limitations, 4, 342
statutory law, 9, 29, 34, 41, 97–8, 112, 144–5, 150–2
Stephen, Francis Viktor, Archduke and Palatine, 103, 104–6, 274
Stephen, King and Saint, 7, 9, 24, 47, 74, 81, 116, 233, 247–8, 341
Styria, 34
Sylvester II, Pope, 7
synods, 268
Szabad, György, 97, 119
Szakasits, Árpád, 196
Szálasi, Ferenc, 2, 21, 186,
Szapolyai, János, 11
Szatmár, Treaty of, 48, 51
Széchényi, Ferenc, 27, 78, 90
Szechényi, István, 27, 90, 104, 109
Szeged, 183
Szekfű, Gyula, 49, 61
Szűcs, Jenő, 205

Takáts, József, 54
tariffs (and tolls), 250, 257, 298–300
Tatra Mountains, 266 *See also* Slovakia
taxation, 8–9, 12–13, 37, 41, 48–54, 59, 78–9, 126, 131, 139, 147–8, 250, 257, 261, 267, 269, 273, 281, 288, 293, 298–9, 340
teachers, 82, 265, 280–281, 336, 339
Teleki, Pál, 180, 183
telephones, 143, 314
theoreticians, 55, 64, 102, 136, 142, 146, 153, 237, 245 *See also* legal scholars
thieves, 248 *See also* robbery
Tildy, Zoltán, 196, 206
Tisza, István, 153
Tisza River, 180
tithes, 79, 248–50, 273
totalitarianism, 22, 114–15, 149, 197, 203, 228, 238

towns, 7, 82, 143, 155–6, 262, 267, 270, 281, 313, 321
Townson, Robert, 266
tractatus diaetalis, 11, 13, 17, 37, 48, 59, 67, 80, 82, 94, 100, 123–124, 287, 289, 298
trades unions, 161, 328, 333
Transdanubia (and Pannonia), 38, 91
Transylvania, 7, 10, 17, 21, 33–4, 47–8, 252, 255, 273, 281
treasury, 269, 274, 276, 279
trials, 84, 91, 155, 203, 296, 303, 335
Trianon, Treaty of, 4, 19, 21, 114, 161, 167, 176
Tripartitum, 9–10, 29, 33, 39, 41–2, 68, 70, 145, 256
Turi, Béla, 165, 169, 175, 176
Turkey, 10, 71 *See also* Ottoman Empire
Turkic language, 40

Unger, Aryeh, 155
universities, 82, 143, 265
Ürményi, József, 55, 75–7, 82, 88–9, 91
USSR constitution, 155, 202, 204, 210

vassals, 35
Vasvári, Pál, 106
Vay, József, 58
Venice Commission, 3
vice-lieutenant, 59–60, 90–1, 262
vice-presidents, 199, 279, 317
vice-regent, 154
Vienna, 12, 16–18, 47, 49–50, 53, 60, 71–3, 78–9, 91–4, 102–7, 113, 119, 147–8, 266, 291, 301
Vienna, Treaty of, 80–1
Világos, battle of, 16
villages, 156, 248–249, 257, 267
violence, 16, 36, 60, 93, 132, 238, 254, 257, 271

Virgin Mary, 259, 263, 270
virilism, 134, 139
Voivode of Transylvania, 33, 252, 255
Volksdeutsche, 186
Voltaire, 64
voting, 1, 21, 23, 38, 51–2, 74, 79, 115, 127, 130, 151, 154, 163, 183, 187, 196, 239, 254, 277, 280–1, 286, 291–4, 296, 310–11, 316, 322, 329–330, 338
See also elections
Vyshinsky, A. J., 202

War of the Austrian Succession, 49
War of the Spanish Succession, 48
Warsaw Pact, 23
weaponry, 73, 147, 253
Wekerle, Sándor, 148
Werbőczy, István, 9–10, 29, 33, 35, 41–3, 68–9, 78–9, 145, 256
Westminster, palace of, 143
White Terror, 20
Wladislas I, 31, 32, 41
Wladislas II, 32, 33, 35, 41, 252, 254
Wolff, Christian, 55
women, 4, 6, 18, 21, 73, 154, 200, 249, 280, 303, 308, 327–8, 337
workers, 199, 201, 204, 304–6, 313–15, 322–3, 325–9, 333, 338
written constitution, 14–15, 179, 222, 224–5
Württemberg, 101

Yalta, 206
youth, 93, 99, 102, 108, 115, 335, 337, 343
Yugoslavia, 21

Zichy, Károly, 77, 82